Self-Destructive Behavior in Children And Adolescents

Self-Destructive Behavior in Children And Adolescents

Edited by

Carl F. Wells, Ph.D.
Irving R. Stuart, Ph.D.

VAN NOSTRAND REINHOLD COMPANY
NEW YORK CINCINNATI ATLANTA DALLAS SAN FRANCISCO
LONDON TORONTO MELBOURNE

Van Nostrand Reinhold Company Regional Offices:
New York Cincinnati Atlanta Dallas San Francisco

Van Nostrand Reinhold Company International Offices:
London Toronto Melbourne

Library of Congress Catalog Card Number: 80-25059
ISBN: 0-442-24741-9

Manufactured in the United States of America

Published by Van Nostrand Reinhold Company
135 West 50th Street, New York, N.Y. 10020

Published simultaneously in Canada by Van Nostrand Reinhold Ltd.

15 14 13 12 11 10 9 8 7 6 5 4 3 2 1

Library of Congress Cataloging in Publication Data
Main entry under title:

Self-destructive behavior in children and adolescents.

Includes index.
1. Self-destructive behavior in children. 2. Children
—Suicidal behavior. 3. Youth—Suicidal behavior.
I. Wells, Carl F. II. Stuart, Irving R. [DNLM:
1. Child behavior disorders. 2. Suicide—In adolescence.
3. Suicide—In infancy and childhood. 4. Suicide,
Attempted—In infancy and childhood. 5. Suicide,
Attempted—In adolescence. HV 6545 S3654]
RJ506.S39S44 618.92′8582 80-25059
ISBN 0-442-24741-9

Contributors

Anderson, David R., Ph.D
Assistant Professor of Psychiatry, Rush-Presbyterian-St. Luke's Medical Center, Chicago, Illinois

Angle, Carol R., M.D.
Department of Pediatrics, Creighton University, School of Medicine and Professor, Department of Pediatrics, University of Nebraska Medical Center, Omaha, Nebraska

Autry, Bess, ACSW
Division of Child and Adolescent Psychiatry, Department of Psychiatry, Duke University Medical Center, Durham, North Carolina

Curry, John C., Ph.D.
Division of Child and Adolescent Psychiatry, Department of Psychiatry, Duke University Medical Center, Durham, North Carolina

Fisher, Prudence, B.A.
Research Assistant, New York State Psychiatric Institute, Columbia College of Physicians and Surgeons

Fishman, H. Charles, M.D.
Staff Psychiatrist, Philadelphia Child Guidance Clinic

Gordon, Barbara, M.D.
Staff Psychiatrist, Department of Psychiatry, Long Island Jewish-Hillside Medical Center; Instructor, New York University School of Medicine

Hammond, David, M.D.
Instructor of Psychiatry, Cornell University Medical College

Kaplan, Stuart L., M.D.
Director, Child & Adolescent Psychiatry, Department of Psychiatry, Long Island Jewish-Hillside Medical Center; Assistant Professor, Psychiatry, State University of New York at Stony Brook

Keefe, Francis J., Ph.D.
Assistant Professor of Medical Psychology, Duke University Medical Center, Durham, North Carolina

Keith, Charles, M.D.
Division of Child and Adolescent Psychiatry, Department of Psychiatry, Duke University Medical Center, Durham, North Carolina

Khuri, Elizabeth T., M.D.
Assistant Professor of Public Health, Cornell University Medical College

McIntire, Matilda, M.D.
Professor of Pediatrics, Creighton University School of Medicine, Omaha, Nebraska

McNamee, Abigail S., Ed.D.
Assistant Professor and Coordinator, Early Childhood Graduate Program, Herbert H. Lehman College, City University of New York

McNamee, Joseph E., Ph.D.
Psychologist; Consultant Alfred Adler Mental Hygiene Clinic, New York, New York

Millman, Robert B., M.D.
Clinical Professor of Public Health, Clinical Associate Professor of Psychiatry, Cornell University Medical College

Neidengard, Ted, M.D.
Chief of Service, Cabrini Alcoholism Program, Cabrini Medical Center, New York, New York

Nilson, Patricia, Ph.D.
Staff Psychologist, Suffolk County Consultation, Service Center, Hauppauge, New York

Pfeffer, Cynthia R., M.D.
Assistant Professor of Psychiatry, Cornell University Medical College, and Chief, Child Psychiatry Inpatient Service, New York Hospital

Richman, Joseph, Ph.D.
Associate Professor, Department of Psychiatry, Albert Einstein College of Medicine, Bronx, New York

Rosman, Bernice L., Ph.D.
Director of Research, Philadelphia Child Guidance Clinic
Assistant Clinical Professor, Department of Psychiatry, University of Pennsylvania Medical School

Rousey, Clyde L., Ph.D.
Speech Pathologist, C.C.C., Topeka, Kansas

Rudd, Lucie, M.D.
Chief, Adolescent Service, The Roosevelt Hospital, Assistant Clinical Professor of Pediatrics Columbia University, College of Medicine

Russell, Donald Hayes, M.D.
Associate Clinical Professor, Harvard Medical School; Director, Massachusetts Court Clinics Program; Chief, Delinquency Section, Judge Baker Guidance Center

Shaffer, David, M.B., B.S., M.R.C.P., M.R.R., Psych. D.P.M.
Professor of Clinical Psychiatry and Pediatrics, Columbia University, New York and New York State Psychiatric Institute

Shenker, I. Ronald, M.D.
Chief, Adolescent Medicine, Department of Pediatrics, Long Island Jewish-Hillside Medical Center; Associate Professor, Pediatrics, State University of New York at Stony Brook

Ward, Eric M., Ph.D.
Assistant Professor, The Medical College of Wisconsin, Department of Neurology, Milwaukee, Wisconsin

Weinhold, Chantal
Research Assistant, Long Island Jewish-Hillside Medical Center, New Hyde Park, New York

Yalisove, Daniel, Ph.D.
Chief Psychologist, Cabrini Alcoholism Program, Cabrini Medical Center, New York, New York

Preface

Within the last decade increasing attention has been given to depression, suicide, and other self-destructive behaviors in children and adolescents. That children and adolescents are increasingly resorting to self-destructive acts, which had previously been considered typical only of adults, was the theme of a study, "Causes, Detection, and Treatment of Childhood Depression," published by the National Institute of Mental Health in 1978. It is estimated that self-destructive behavior exists in one out of five children. Many experts believe that childhood depression exceeds the rate for the middle-aged.

In a New York *Times* Magazine article of January 1978, the statistics of the Mortality Branch of the National Center for Health Statistics are cited as reporting that 1306 children between the ages of ten and fourteen took their own lives between 1968 and 1976. This represents an increase of 32%. Suicide has also become the third leading cause of death in the 15–24 year age group. With respect to suicide statistics it must be remembered that the actual figures presented are underestimated to some unknown degree because of the reluctance of families to state the true circumstances of the death.

In addition to overt acts which are clearly self-destructive, attention has recently been called to "indirect" self-destructive behaviors by Norman Farberow in his presidential address to the International Association for Suicide Prevention in 1977. He pointed out that there are unconscious suicidal tendencies that the individual seems unaware of, or at least denies, that these actions are intended to destroy or injure the self. He also notes that Emile Durkheim in his classic work on suicide published in 1897, emphasized that suicides were not unrelated to other forms of ordinary conduct. The difference was one of degree and a lesser chance of death. If such indirect self-destructive behaviors are taken into consideration in viewing depressed children, the extent of the problem increases enormously—contingent, of course, on the ability to establish agreement regarding what constitutes "indirect self-destructive behavior." This recent viewpoint has led many professionals to recognize certain behaviors such as eating disturbances, substance abuse, running away, promiscuity and prostitution, and repeated unwanted pregnancies as possible manifestations of serious self-destructive wishes in children and adolescents. As a consequence, quite different treatment approaches have often been used with these children.

One of the continuing controversies with regard to self-destructive behavior in children and adolescents has to do with the definition and conceptualization of depression. Some experts in the field question the existence of depression in children and take the position that the symptoms are transient and dissipate with time. On the other hand, the position of the majority of professionals working in this area is that depression during this developmental period is in fact a real condition. (The use of antidepressant medication by some pediatricians and child psychiatrists underscores their belief that the depression is real.) Further ambiguity is created by the use of the terms, "masked depression" or "depressive equivalents" which has led to many more symptoms being viewed as evidence for the existence of depression. Some authors consider some problem behaviors, such as delinquency, as an expression of an underlying depression, while others view it as a defense used by the child against feeling depressed.

While there is considerable disagreement regarding the existence of depression and the clinical picture prior to adolescence, there seems to be little doubt about its existence after puberty. The problem becomes one of distinguishing normal mood changes so typical of adolescent behavior from true depression.

We do not intend in the present volume to attack these problems concerning the nature of depression in children at different stages of development. Rather our goal is to focus upon overt behaviors which without any doubt are harmful to the individual child. If it is possible to make a meaningful distinction between symptoms of depression and self-destructive behaviors, then we might say that we are concerned with the consequences of the behaviors rather than with questions of conscious or unconscious intent of the actor—although it should be recognized that the clinician most often cannot ignore causal factors in the treatment of many types of such behavior. The authors contributing to this volume are concerned with recurrent and persistent self-destructive behaviors not with temporary responses to stress; the concern is with children who harm themselves seriously and repeatedly if there is no appropriate intervention.

As new forms of self-destructive behavior are recognized as such, new treatment approaches (such as behavior-modification techniques and conjoint family therapy) are being applied to these problems. We believed that it would be a useful contribution to draw together contemporary developments in this field in one volume which could be helpful to professionals working with troubled children and adolescents who harm themselves. Therefore, our major emphasis in the present volume is on the management and treatment of a variety of selected problems representative of self-destructive behavior as suggested by a group of experts in psychiatry, pediatrics, psychology, social work, and education who have devoted much of their thinking and clinical work to troubled children.

C.F.W
I.R.S.

Contents

Preface ix

1. Psychological Profiles of Runaway Children and Adolescents, *Patricia Nilson* 2
2. Diagnosis and Prediction of Sucidal Risk among Adolescents, *David R. Anderson,* 45
3. On Running Away, *Donald Hayes Russell,* 61
4. Suicide in Children and Young Adolescents, *David Shaffer* and *Prudence Fisher,* 75
5. The Distinctive Features of Children Who Theaten and Attempt Suicide, *Cynthia R. Pfeffer,* 106
6. Perspectives On Drug Use and Abuse, *Robert B. Millman, Elizabeth T. Khuri,* and *David Hammond,* 122
7. Juvenile Alcoholism and Alcohol Abuse, *Ted Neidengard* and *Daniel Yalisove,* 150
8. Depression in Anorexia Nervosa and Obesity, *Stuart L. Kaplan, I. Ronald Shenker, Barbara Gordon,* and *Chantal Weinhold,* 164
9. Stressful Life Experiences in the Early Educational Setting, *Abigail S. McNamee,* and *Joseph E. McNamee,* 180
10. Pregnancies and Abortions, *Lucie Rudd,* 208
11. The Taxonomy of Suicide and Self-Poisoning: a Pediatric Perspective, *Matilda S. McIntire* and *Carol R. Angle,* 224
12. Psychogenic Hearing Loss, *Clyde L. Rousey,* 251
13. Family Treatment of Suicidal Children and Adolescents, *Joseph Richman,* 274

14. A Therapeutic Approach to Self-Destructive Behavior In Adolescence: The Family as the Patient, *H. Charles Fishman* and *Bernice L. Rosman,* 292

15. Behavioral Approaches to the Management of Self-Destructive Children, *Francis J. Keefe* and *Eric M. Ward,* 309

16. Self-Destructive Forces in the Psychotherapy of Children: The Negative Therapeutic Reaction, *Charles Keith, John C. Curry,* and *Bess Autry,* 329

Index 347

Self-Destructive Behavior in Children And Adolescents

This is an informative report by Dr. Patricia Nilson, a practicing psychologist involved in the evaluation and formulation of treatment plans for those legally considered to be Juvenile Delinquents (JD) and/or Persons in Need of Supervision (PINS), and for those referred by social agencies. She discusses and evaluates the reported behavior, relating it to a variety of familial situations including deaths, divorces, and remarriages, as well as birth order, child abuse and neglect, suicide, sex role expectations, and minimal brain dysfunctioning accompanied by learning disabilities. Supporting the discussion and conclusions of the research with numerous quotes from actual case records, as well as examples of psychological test material, she vividly illustrates the relationship between the underlying depressive aspects with its self-destructive behavior.

1
Psychological Profiles of Runaway Children and Adolescents

Patricia Nilson, Ph.D.

INTRODUCTION

"The boy is all alone because he ran away, he's in a deserted house. The police found him and took him to the precinct. They sent him home. (He feels) sad. He ran away again, and went some place else."

"A gun, he shot himself—he or she—dying . . . she was probably put down. No one cared for her."

"He looks like he's sad, he can't play in the concert with all his friends (because) he ain't as good as them. He's thinking about the fun it could be to be there. He feels depressed. (In the end) he takes his violin and bangs it against the desk and sits and cries."

"Looks like she's choking her, let's see, a mother yelling at her daughter because she came in late from a party. The mother's mad, the daughter can't see why, she was only a few minutes late. (The daughter feels) just as mad. They're arguing. The daughter wishes the mother would leave her alone. (In the end) she just sends her up to her room."

"A stranded dog in an abandoned building. He can't get out. Don't know how he got in. It's all boarded up, the top part is on fire. The dog's trying to get out, he never makes it."

"Looks like she takes drugs. She took on overdose. Now she's sick. She stays in the hospital for a long time, comes out and quits drugs."

"This boy has problems with his parents, his parents threw him out, so he went to live with some other people. He felt very bad, because he realized he can't live without his parents, but when he went back, his parents didn't want him. He felt bad."

The stories quoted above are from the Thematic Apperception Test (TAT) stories of runaway youngsters who were referred by social agencies for psychological and psychiatric evaluation and formulation of treatment plans.

Every year an estimated one million children under the age of eighteen run away from home.[1, 2] Walker,[1] in a Department of Health, Education and Welfare publication, surveys the literature and indicates that there have been many attempts to discover the basic reasons for running away, with very little consensus except for general agreement that disturbed parent-child relationships are involved in the majority of cases. She indicates that some authors emphasize that some children run because of a healthy sense of adventure and desire to be independent. Others focus on intrapsychic problems or deficiencies in coping skills (with the implication that the child is at fault), and still others on environmental pressure (with the implication that the parents or society in general are at fault). The differences in viewpoint seem to be due both to differences in the author's orientation and to differences in the populations studied.

None of the children in this study could be considered to be "healthy adventurers." The children in this study were all referred by social agencies (judges, Probation Department, Social Services), and all were suffering severe problems, both in family interactions and within themselves. The "healthy adventurer" tends to run away only once[3] and is unlikely to come to the attention of public agencies. In fact, the referral process is such that runaway children usually do not become involved in the juvenile justice system until the situation is desperate. Golbin[4] in a comparison study of youth charged with juvenile delinquency (JD) and Person in Need of Supervision (PINS) petitions found that the PINS children came from more disturbed families and had more severe problems than the JD youngsters. A youngster who commits an act which would be considered a crime if committed by an adult (JD) is much more likely to be brought to the attention of public agencies than is the child who runs away from home or is truant from school. The latter two reasons are the most usual reasons for establishing PINS petitions. In actual practice, however, this distinction is not really clear cut since many runaways have also engaged in delinquent acts, and since plea bargaining is often used to reduce a JD to a PINS petition. Golbin indicates that in 1976, almost half (41.2%) of the children remanded to the Suffolk County Children's Shelter were PINS runaways.

Some authors feel that children run because they are deficient in coping skills and cannot handle the ordinary pressures of life. In a previous study,[5] it was hypothesized that the children referred to the agency were lacking in coping skills. A comparison was made of Interpersonal Problem-Solving skills of children confined to the Shelter with those of children in a public school of similar racial and economic composition and age. To our surprise, we found no significant differences in problem solving ability. Instead, a startling difference was found in terms of family structure. The shelter children suffered three times as many deaths of parents, and ten times as many divorces, remarriages, and placements of the children outside of the home, compared to the public school population. There was also a significant difference in their feelings about their ability to control their environment (Locus of Control), with the shelter children feeling more helpless and ineffective than the control group children. Thus these youths have to face overwhelming problems while equipped with only average problem-solving skills, and they quite naturally have feelings of being unable to cope with their fragmented and chaotic home environments. A recent study[6] comparing runaways with boarding school students also reports the finding that runaways are not deficient in coping skills. Thus the reasons for running away are not because of a deficiency in the child, per se, nor is family or social pressure alone a sufficient explanation, since some youngsters in the same situations do not run away. To fully understand the dynamics it is necessary to have an objective evaluation of the family situation and parental attitudes as well as an in-depth understanding of the youngster's inner feelings and reactions. This study will focus on family circumstances and the youngster's reactions to them, both for runaway children and for a control group of nonrunaway children who were referred by the same agencies.

DESCRIPTION OF SAMPLE

This chapter explores the psychological profiles of forty-six youngsters. They were selected from three sources: participation in a previous research project, referral to me privately, and successive referrals to the Suffolk County Consultation Services Center (CSC) from April to July of 1979. All of the referrals were made by county agencies (Social Services, Probation Department or judges). Referrals from the judges and Probation Department usually involved PINS petitions for running away, PINS petitions for other reasons (mostly truancy), and JD Petitions. Referrals from Social Services were more likely to be because of running away connected with child abuse or neglect. In some instances the original referral was for some reason other than running away, but during the course of the evaluation, it was found that the youngster had run away. Of these forty-six children, twenty-eight were considered to be runaways and eighteen had not run away as far as we could determine. In the runaway group, the ages varied from eight to seventeen with most being fourteen. There were fifteen boys and thirteen girls, twenty-two were white and six were nonwhite. Most were lower or lower middle class, and all were from Suffolk County, NY. In the nonrunaway group, the age range was from ten to fifteen with a mode of fifteen. Thirteen were white and five nonwhite. There were seventeen boys and one girl. There was no discernible reason for the predominance of boys in this group. Because of this extremely uneven distribution, both groups were further subdivided into boys versus girls, and comparisons were made on this basis, as well as runaway versus nonrunaway.

Runaway behavior in this sample varies from an eight-year-old schizophrenic boy who "wanders away from home for hours" and was frequently picked up by police and returned home, to teenagers who were gone for months at a time, some of whom traveled as far away as Florida and California. A few who had traveled far stole cars to aid their ventures. However, most of the youngsters in this group were thirteen to fifteen year olds, who would leave for a few days or weeks, and would usually go to stay at a friend's house either with or without the knowledge of the friend's parents. Sometimes the parents of the runaways would know where the youngster was, but make no move to have him or her return home. Some were told to leave home, and in several instances the parents refused to allow the child to return home and the youth was remanded to a detention home. One of the children in this group had run away only once, but the rest ran away repeatedly. One fifteen year old began running away from home at the age of eight, and had run from residential treatment centers a total of eighteen times. There was much overlapping of youngsters who had run away from home, from institutions and from foster homes, and there were no clear-cut divisions. There was a broad range of psychopathology, from childhood schizophrenia to adjustment reaction. The sample is heterogeneous, which may be a disadvantage in trying to isolate individual variables, but has the advantage of being generalizable to a larger population.

Evaluation Procedure

It is clear that a full evaluation of the situation must involve a thorough understanding of the family circumstances and the child's abilities, disabilities, and inner feelings. Our evaluations therefore include as much information as it is possible to gather, and involve interviews with parents as well as psychological evaluations of the children. In child abuse cases, the parents are frequently given psychological evaluations also. Emphasis is on understanding the problems and making practical recommendations for treatment, and not on placing blame on anyone.

The usual battery of psychological tests includes the Bender Gestalt Visual Motor Test, Benton Revised Visual Retention Test, Wechsler Intelligence Scale for Children—Revised (WISC-R), Wide Range Achievement Test (WRAT), Rorschach, Thematic Apperception Test (TAT), or Children's Apperception Test (CAT), and/or Despert Fables (for young children), Draw a Person (DAP), House-Tree-Person (HTP), Kinetic Family Drawing (KFD), and a Sentence Completion Test which has been compiled from several other such tests, with adaptations and additions selected for use with this population. Interpretations are not done "blindly," but whenever possible are based on full background information including family structure, school reports, probation department investigations and/or caseworker's report, and interview of both child and parents by a psychiatrist or social worker. Staffing conferences to formulate treatment plans usually include the psychologist(s), psychiatrist(s), social worker(s), and caseworker and/or probation officer.

A broad range of factors will be analyzed and discussed in this paper, with illustrations drawn from various portions of the test battery utilizing the children's actual responses. The drawings and other responses are used to illustrate various points, and individual responses are not analyzed in depth in this chapter. The experienced reader will undoubtedly think of many additional possible interpretations for the drawings and other responses. Listed below are the sentence completion responses of the runaway group to the sentence stem "If I ever thought about running away it would be because . . ."

"... I can't take my father."
"... my father wants to put me away."
"... of self-consciousness, about how I am about my parents."
"... of my mother."
"... I want to—get away, don't feel like going home."
"... they treat me mean and bad."
"... it will solve my problems."
"... I can't stand my parents."
"... Joe." (Mother's boyfriend who beats child—not his real name).
"... something happened in the house. I got blamed."
"... he (father) is hitting me."
"... I wanted to."
"... I feel my parents don't love me."
"... don't want to live."
"... scared (Q.) of my father hitting me."
"... that's dumb. Don't run away. I would get killed by robbers."
"... get in trouble, can't face the world."
"... they, (parents) get on my nerves (because of too many restrictions)."

Most of these responses, as well as the quotes from the TAT stories given at the beginning of this chapter, suggest that the family relationships are severely disturbed, particularly in regard to the relationships between the parental figures and the child. The unstable family structure and the complicated inter-relationships will be explored in more depth, both from a factual point of view and from the point of view of the youngster's feelings of being unloved and rejected. ("I feel my parents don't love me." "A stranded dog in a deserted building.") Some of the responses also suggest that the parents' rejection is quite obvious, and that sometimes the parents either covertly or overtly encourage the runaway episode, ("My father wants to put me away." "His parents threw him out.") There are suggestions of child abuse ("he is hitting me" . . . "scared of my father hitting me") and this is explored both factually and dynamically. Suicidal feelings are expressed ("don't want to live" . . . "he shot himself") and the extent and dynamics of these feelings and their relationship to running away are explored along with the extent and nature of psychopathology and the relationship with drug and alcohol abuse ("looks like . . . she took an overdose").

School problems often contribute to the youngster's sense of frustration and self-destructive reactions. The child's feelings about achievement can often be inferred from the story to TAT card one, e.g., "He ain't as good as them . . . bangs (his violin) against the desk and sits and cries." Feelings about school, vocation, and achievement are explored, in connection with findings regarding IQ scores and incidence of minimal brain dysfunction, and other school problems. In short, the *Results and Discussion* section will focus on the following areas:

- I Family Structure
  - (a) deaths, divorces, remarriages, etc. of parents, and the children's reactions.
  - (b) birth order effect
- II Child Abuse and Neglect
- III Severity of Pathology
- IV Suicide (attempts, gestures, feelings)
- V Self-Image and Sexual Role Expectations
- VI School Problems, Minimal Brain Dysfunctioning (MBD), and Learning Disabilities

RESULTS AND DISCUSSION

Family Structure

The family structure of both groups of youngsters was unstable and dysfunctional. In the runaway group of twenty-eight children only five

(18%) could be considered to have come from an "intact" family (both natural parents and child live together). (See Table 1.1.) In fourteen cases (50%) the parents were divorced or separated or one parent had deserted. Death of a parental figure occurred in five families (18%). (The mother died in two cases, stepfather in one, and both parents in two cases.) Two of the children (7%) were adopted and two (7%) removed from the home because of abuse and/or neglect. However, even in the "intact" homes there was still serious deprivation of emotional needs.

Family structure was not appreciably different in the nonrunaway group, with twelve out of eighteen (66%) coming from homes where the parents were separated or divorced. There were two adoptions (11%) and no parental deaths, leaving four (22%) "intact" families. There were two instances of death of a sibling.

These descriptive measures by themselves give some idea of the crushing life circumstances with which these youngsters are faced. A detailed look at the individual family histories and the child's reaction provides greater depth of understanding. The children's real names were changed to protect their identity, and some of the histories are slightly altered to preserve confidentiality.

Thirteen-year-old Adam was the first of two children born to a retarded mother. His father expressed no interest in him or his mother, and Adam has never seen his natural father. A year later a sister was born with a dif-

Table 1-1. Family Hiştory of Referred Children.

FAMILY EVENT	RUNAWAY GIRLS		RUNAWAY BOYS		RUNAWAY GROUP TOTAL		NONRUNAWAY GIRLS		NONRUNAWAY BOYS		NONRUNAWAY GROUP TOTAL	
	NO.	%	NO.	%	NO.	%	NO.	%	NO.	%	NO.	%
Mother died	1		1		2							
Father died		15	1	20	1	18						
Both died	1		1		2							
Parents divorced or separated	4	31	10	66	14	50	1	100	11	65	12	66
Child removed for abuse or neglect	0		2	13	2	7						
Child Adopted	2	15	0	0	2	7			2	12	2	11
Intact Family	5	18	0	0	5	18			4	23	4	22
Total	13		15		28		1		17		18	

ferent father. Adam has a vague memory of the stepfather, whom he thought was his real father, and who also disappeared from his life at a very early age. When he was five, his mother died. He and his sister then lived with the grandparents. When he was eight, his grandmother died, and a few months later the grandfather died. He then went to live with an aunt and her family, but frequently ran away. He would often run to the home of another aunt, who lived in the house were he had previously lived with his grandparents.

He has no feeling of having a real home. He feels that whatever home he had has crumbled around him. Adam's House-Tree-Person (HTP) drawing is presented in Figure 1-1. He indicates the person is a twenty-year-old man who lives alone. The tree is dead and the house is "bad-rocky (fall down)—bad bad." In the Kinetic Family Drawing (KFD) in which the children are asked to draw everybody in their family doing something, he draws a tiny house in the distance (with the aunt, uncle, cousins, and sister in the house) and shows himself "feeding the birds" (See Figure 1-2). The birds seem to have a far larger house than he does, and he seems to feel more at home with the birds than with the family.

Fourteen-year-old Bill refused to do the KFD. His HTP drawing is shown in Figure 1-3. The house looks as if it is being blown over. He says the *best* thing about the house is that "it's burning" and the worst that "it fell down." The tree is also "burning down with the house" and the owner is waiting for the firemen. Bill is the second of four full siblings whose natural mother severely neglected them and then deserted the family. Bill believes she is dead. The children remained with the father, who also had several children from his first marriage. The father married a third time, and this wife brought three children from her previous marriage, and they now have one child from the father's third marriage. Bill was abused in the home by the father and stepmother, and was placed in a foster home, and also in a residential treatment center. He is alleged to have set fires in the foster home, threatened a foster child with a knife, maltreated pets, and run away from the institution. His anger at the tremendous lack of nurturance and his feelings of instability at home are graphically presented in the fire themes. He is a very seriously disturbed child, whose wishes and fears are quite confused (the *best* thing about the house is that it's burning down). The tree seems to have an anthropomorphic look about it, as if the two branches on the sides were a person's arms, and the top his head. This emphasizes even more the feeling that he is burning down along with the house and illustrates the self-destructive aspects of his tumultous feelings.

Tremendous anger toward the abusing family is also expressed in fourteen-year-old Carl's HTP drawing (Figure 1-4), in which he indicates the man is going to chop down the tree (the family). Carl's parents are

Figure 1–1. Adam: House-Tree-Person. "He lives in the house. Twenty years old, nobody else. (Something good about the house is) way it looks outside, come in and eat. (Something bad about the house is) rocky, fall down, bad, bad." (The tree is) dead."

Figure 1-2. Adam: Kinetic Family Drawing. The person is "me, 13 years old, feeding my birds."

divorced, and he lived with his mother and stepfather for a while, then spent a year with his natural father (who is now married to this stepfather's first wife). Both father figures were abusive to him. In the last two years he has run away many times, has been in three different foster homes, and a short-term residential center for runaways.

Some of the runaway youngsters refused to draw themselves in the KFD. Figure 1-5 shows Ann's drawing of her family, which purposely does not include her. She comes from an "intact" family but sees her mother as totally absorbed in religion and her father preoccupied with yelling. She ran away from home because her father beats her, and she has nightmares about him raping her.

Figure 1-6 shows fourteen-year-old Betty's KFD. She is an abused child whose parents separated three years ago. She draws the foster family she is living with. She sees this family sharply separated into different boxes and far from each other. The father and nine-year-old son are seen as interacting, but the others are isolated. Even with such rigid separation she still does not feel enough of a part of the family to place herself in the picture.

Figure 1-7 was drawn by Dan, who ran away from a residential treatment facility a total of eighteen times. He continues to run from home, usually for a day or two at a time, which meets with complete indifference on the part of his mother. Dan's father left when he was an infant. His stepfather was alcoholic and abusive and left three years ago. The mother provides no supervision. Much of the roof of the house is missing, and I have found this fairly often in children of divorced parents. This may sug-

Figure 1–3. Bill: House-Tree-Person. ''Man, 28 years old (feels) sad, (doing) waiting for firemen. (Thinking) his house is on fire. (The best thing about the house is) he's buying a new house. (The worst thing is) he has no car.''
The tree is a ''pine tree. (The best thing about it is) growing pine. (The worst thing about it is) burning down with the house.''
House. ''(The best thing about it is) it's burning. (The worst thing is) it fell down.''

Figure 1–4. Carl: House-Tree-Person. ''Stick man's house. (The worst thing is) it's ugly. Tree. (The best thing is) it's nice. (The worst thing is) the guy is going to chop it down.''

Figure 1–5. Ann: Kinetic Family Drawing. Figures from left to right top row:
Mother (saying) "Praise God." (Working part-time. Very religious.) Brother playing baseball. Younger sister "she's the baby in the family, everybody loves her." Older brother "likes to drink beer. (Works with his father, gets along well with him). The figure on the bottom is the father saying "you son of a bitch." He is "angry all of the time."

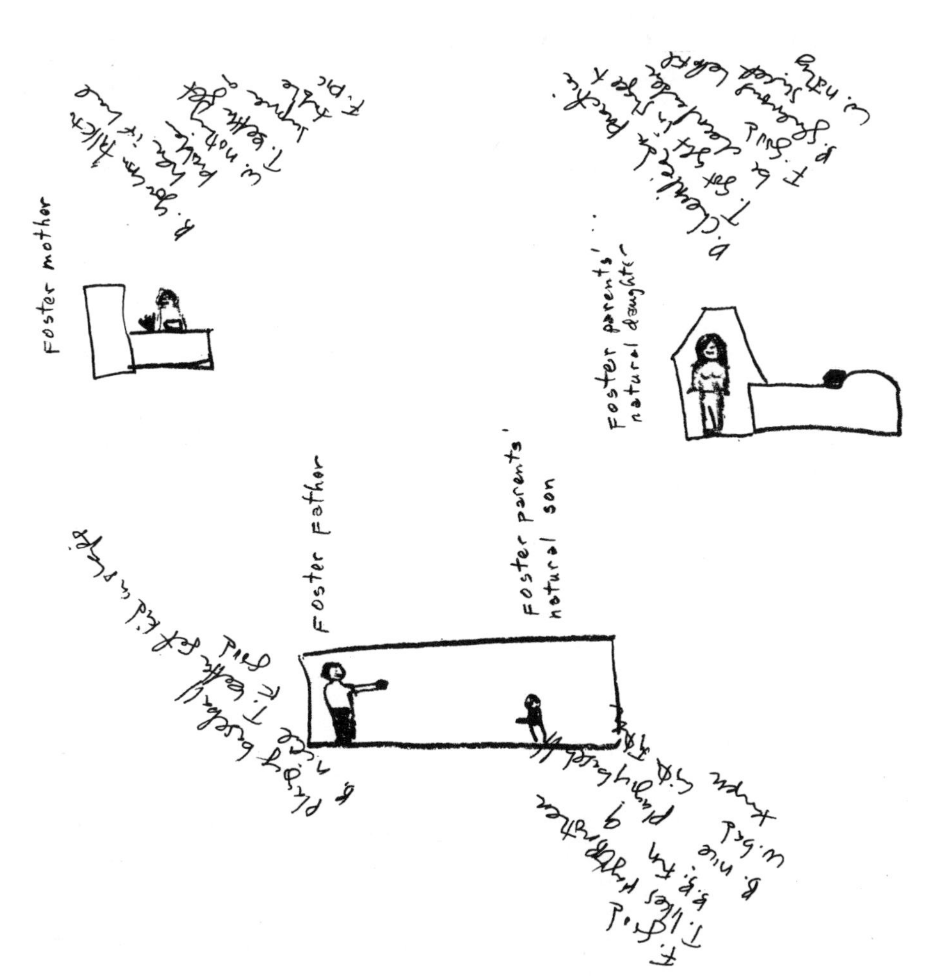

Figure 1-6. Betty: Kinetic Family Drawing. Figure on upper left is foster mother. (The best thing is) you can talk to her if you have a problem. (The worst thing is) nothing. She's saying "I better get supper on the table." The figure in the upper right is the foster parent's natural daughter. What she's doing is "cheerleader practice." (She thinking) I've got to get in shape and be a cheerleader. (She feels) good. (The best thing is) she's sweet. (The worst thing is) nothing." In the box at the bottom are on the left the foster father "playing baseball." (The best thing is) nice. (He's thinking) "better get the kid in shape." (He feels) good. The figure at the right is the foster parents natural son. (He feels) good. (He's thinking) he likes playing baseball with his father, he's 9 years old. (The best thing is) he's nice. (The worst thing is) bad temper.

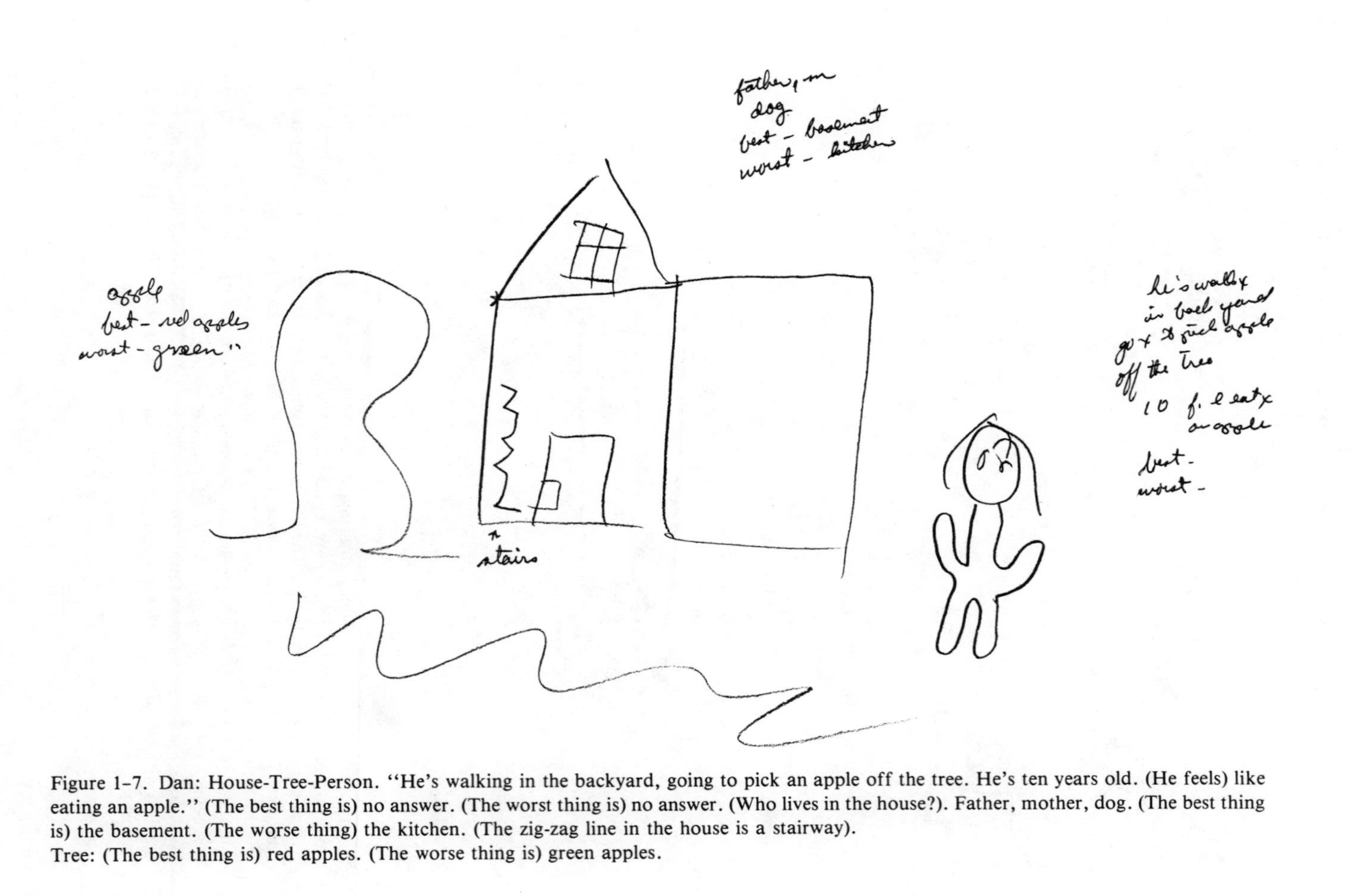

Figure 1–7. Dan: House-Tree-Person. "He's walking in the backyard, going to pick an apple off the tree. He's ten years old. (He feels) like eating an apple." (The best thing is) no answer. (The worst thing is) no answer. (Who lives in the house?). Father, mother, dog. (The best thing is) the basement. (The worse thing) the kitchen. (The zig-zag line in the house is a stairway).
Tree: (The best thing is) red apples. (The worse thing is) green apples.

gest the child's feeling that a major portion of the household is missing. Since such symbols are multiply determined, this probably also reflects his own feelings of inferiority intellectually and emotionally. Dan is a very disturbed youngster who appears on the brink of a psychotic episode. The appearance of the drawing and the transparency (an outside view of the house, which shows the inside stairs through the wall) suggest severe problems in reality testing.

Sometimes the youngster will present an idealized version of what he wishes the family to be like. Fifteen-year-old Earl's parents have been separated for nine years and the father lives in a different state. Nevertheless, he still cherishes the fantasy that they would get back together and have a happy family with lots of nurturance (all sitting down at a picnic). His KFD is shown in Figure 1-8. His referral to the 12-year-old sister as his "baby sister" is not by chance. The sister is profoundly retarded, has cerebral palsy, and requires twenty-four-hour-a-day care. The mother devoted herself to the task of caring for this child at the expense of the emotional needs of the other children. The mother finally had a "nervous breakdown" and placed the handicapped sister in an institution.

As noted in the beginning of this section, both the runaway and nonrunaway group have suffered from severe feelings of deprivation. The differences lie elsewhere. Ten-year-old Ed, who has never run away, was adopted at the age of six months. The adoptive father deserted the home. The adoptive mother seriously abused and neglected him, strapping him to the crib, etc. At the age of five he was placed in a foster home. He is now up for adoption a second time, and the foster parents do not want him. His HTP drawing (Figure 1-9) shows an elaborate house belonging to someone else. His own home is a shed drawn at the bottom of the page.

The decision to run away is not easy, and most youngsters suffer from severe conflict about it. Fourteen-year-old Betty responds to TAT card 13MF with this story: "His wife died and he's upset. She had cancer and just died. He feels terrible . . . He's feeling guilty because he should have stayed home and not gone to work when he heard his wife was sick . . ."

Although the age and sex of the hero in this story are different, this story, along with several others suggest that Betty fears that her running away may have disastrous consequences to the parents, and she feels very guilty about this. Some parents play on this, and blame the child for all of the parents' difficulties. Some youngsters express the feeling (frequently to TAT card 2) that the child should stay home and help the parents, rather than pursue his or her own career.

The child's desire to make it on his own may be at war with his dependency needs and inferiority feelings, ". . . he realized he couldn't survive without his parents. . ." Twelve-year-old Laurence, to card 7BM,

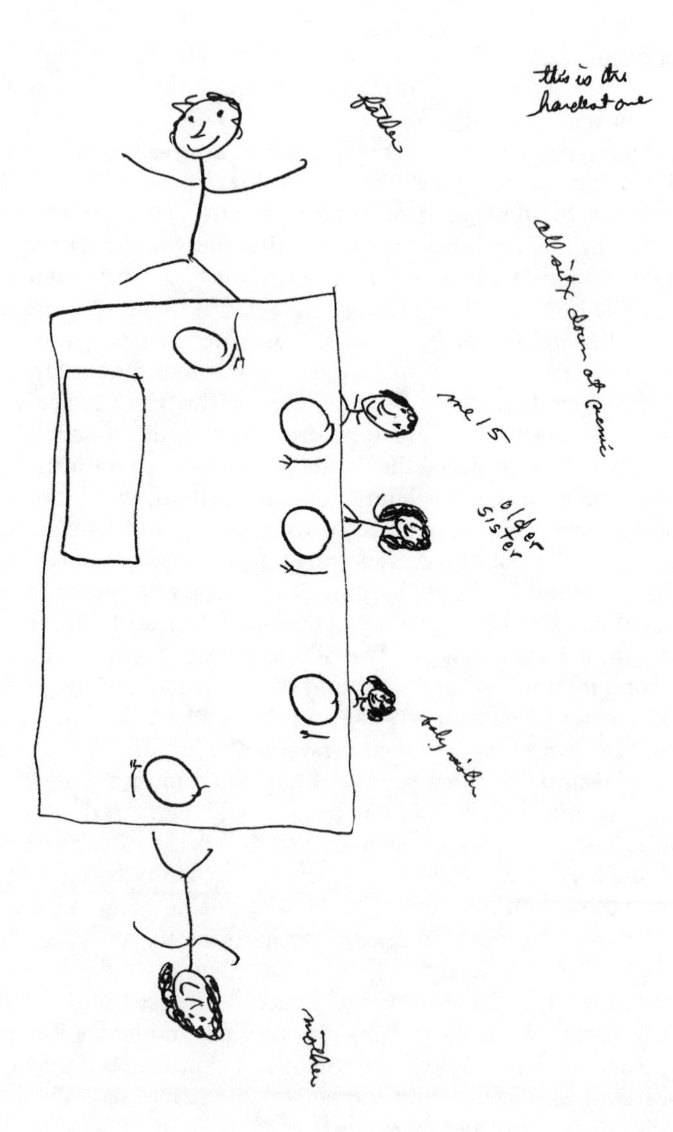

Figure 1-8. Earl: Kinetic Family Drawing. "This is the hardest one." Going from top to bottom the figures are father (at the end of the table) "me age 15, older sister, baby sister, mother (at other end of the table) all sitting down at a picnic."

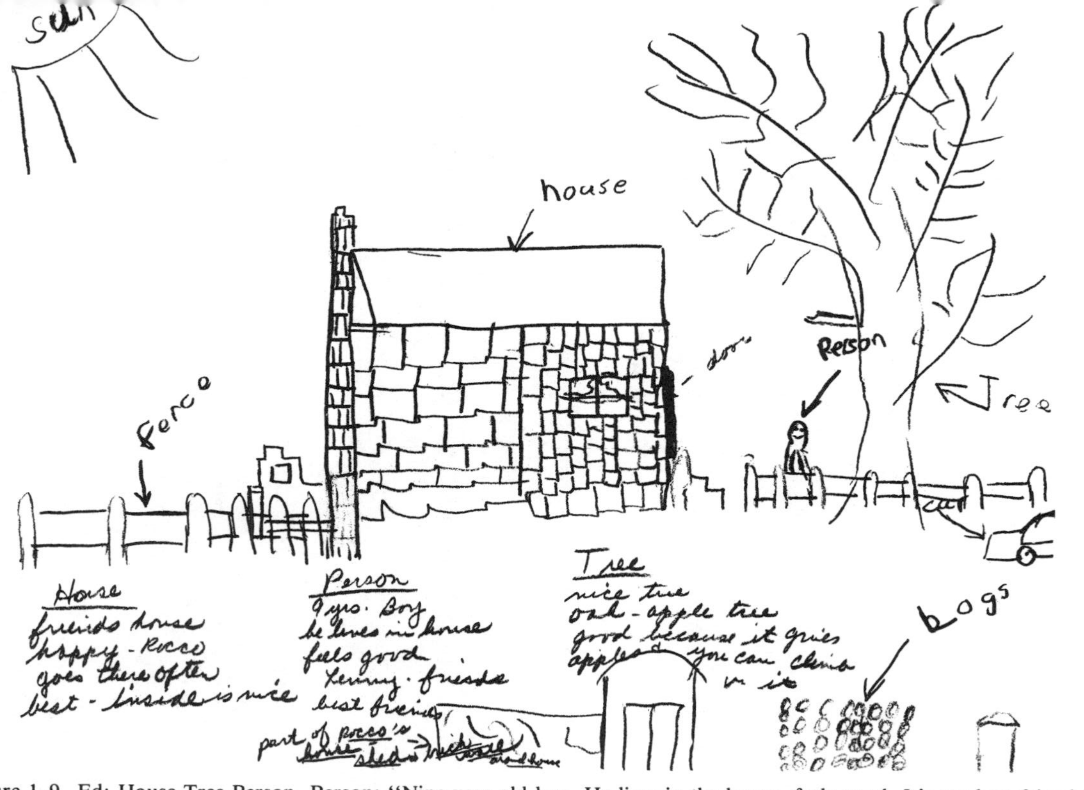

Figure 1–9. Ed: House-Tree-Person. Person: "Nine-year-old boy. He lives in the house, feels good. It's my best friend." House: "Friend's house, I go there often. (The best thing is) the inside is nice."
At bottom of the page is "part of Ed's house, a shed, brick wall."
Tree: "Nice tree, oak—apple tree. Good because it gives apples and you can climb in it."

expresses dreams of achievement, fear of failure, and guilt about opposing his parents and leaving home; ". . . he had to go to the Army. The father was afraid he might get killed. He went to the Army, got out in four years as a general. His father told him not to go back in the army, but he did and got killed."

Sometimes children who are placed in foster homes feel disloyal to the natural family if they allow themselves to become a real part of the foster family. Feelings of alienation in the foster family often show up in card 7GF, where the girl will sometimes see the mother figure as someone who is paid to care for them (a maid or governess) rather than as a real mother. Some of these youngsters run from the foster home, and may try to return to the natural family.

The possibility of birth order effect was considered. Galbreath[7] in a study of over five hundred youngsters, compared children charged with PINS petitions for running away with those on PINS petitions for truancy, and those charged with J.D. petitions. She found that runaways tended to be second in birth order, while truants and J.D.'s were third or fourth in the family.

In the present study (see Table 1-2), in the runaway group, nine children (32%) were first or only children, twelve (43%) were second children, and seven (25%) were third or more in birth order. The mean number of children in the family was 3.53.

In the nonrunaway group, four (22%) were first or only children, five (27%) second children, and nine (50%) were third, or more, in birth order. The mean number of children in the family was 4.0. Most of the children in this group were referred for truancy or juvenile delinquency. These differences are not statistically significant, although they are in the expected direction.

Studies on birth order[8] have suggested that first or only children tend to be more responsible and higher achievers than later children, so one might

Table 1-2. Birth Order in Referred Children.

CATEGOY	RUNAWAY GIRLS NO.	%	RUNAWAY BOYS NO.	%	RUNAWAY GROUP TOTAL NO.	%	NONRUNAWAY GIRLS NO.	%	NONRUNAWAY BOYS NO.	%	NONRUNAWAY GROUP TOTAL NO.	%
1st or only	4	31	5	33	9	32	0		4	23	4	22
2nd	5	38	7	47	12	43	0		5	29	5	27
3rd or more	4	31	3	20	7	25	1	100	8	47	9	50
Mean number of children in family	$\overline{X} = 3.97$		$\overline{X} = 2.86$		$\overline{X} = 3.53$				$\overline{X} = 3.88$		$\overline{X} = 4.0$	

expect first-borns in general to be less likely to run away. However, Shellow et al.[9] found that 51% of his sample of runaways were oldest children.

First-born or oldest girls in the family sometimes run away because of sexual abuse by the father figure and/or others, and those working with runaways should be aware of this possibility. However, sometimes the older girl will remain in this incestuous situation in order to protect her younger sisters, who might otherwise be subjected to similar treatment. Full understanding of birth order effects in runaways and nonrunaways is far from clear, and warrants further research.

Child Abuse and Neglect

As noted in the case histories cited above, many of the children come from seriously abusive homes (See Table 1-3). Of the twenty-eight runaways, eighteen (64%) were considered to have suffered abuse, compared to six (33%) of the nonrunaway group. Most of these families had come to the attention of Child Protective Services (CPS), and in the others, either the child or the case worker or probation officer indicated abuse.

This definition of abuse is rather hazy, but generally refers to serious beatings or sometimes to bizarre sorts of abuse, and/or sexual abuse. One teenager in this group was beaten into unconsciousness by his father, and remained in critical condition, in a coma, for three weeks. There may have been abuse in some of the other cases as well, but this was not known to us. It is quite frequent for abused children to protect the parents and not tell what has been happening at home. The parents are almost always reluctant to reveal any abuse and/or neglect, both because they don't want to appear

Table 1-3. Child Abuse or Neglect in Referred Children.

Abuse	Runaway Girls No.	Runaway Girls %	Runaway Boys No.	Runaway Boys %	Runaway Group Total No.	Runaway Group Total %	Nonrunaway Girls No.	Nonrunaway Girls %	Nonrunaway Boys No.	Nonrunaway Boys %	Nonrunaway Group Total No.	Nonrunaway Group Total %
Known to have been abused or neglected	9	69	9	60	18	64	0		6	35	6	33
Not known to have been abused or neglected	4	31	6	40	10	36	1	100	11	65	12	67
Total	13	100	15	100	28	100	1	100	17	100	18	100

to be "bad parents" and also because of the possibility of prosecution in the courts. Those who work with runaway youth in any setting should be alert to the possibilities of abuse, including incestuous sexual abuse. Although this sample is mostly lower class, many studies indicate that abuse also occurs frequently in middle-class homes, but is usually covered up and not reported.[10]

Thirteen-year-old Carol ran away from her home because of bizarre abuse by her father. He would force her to kneel or squat in one position for hours on end, would not allow her to communicate with her siblings, and would not let her eat meals with the rest of the family. The father and stepmother were interviewed and they admitted to the charges, but indicated that they felt their methods of discipline were completely appropriate. Prior to this, Carol had been severely neglected by her natural mother, and the children had to take over the household duties. In abusive and neglectful families, it has often been found that the mother herself was abused as a child, never receiving the nurturance she needed, and therefore was unable to provide this nurturance for her children.[10] This intergenerational aspect of child abuse is neatly illustrated in one story to card 7GF, "the girl is mad at her doll because she is mad at her mother." Thus this girl is likely to grow up and abuse her own children because of the abuse she herself has been subjected to. In abusive families there is frequently a role reversal, with the child (usually the oldest girl) taking over the mother role and trying to nurture her own mother as well as her siblings. In some instances the girl finds herself expected to assume the mother role in all aspects, and this may even extend to becoming involved in incestuous relations with the father.[11] Carol and one of her sisters were raped by their older half-brother (from the mother's first marriage) and may have been molested by the father as well. Her disturbed and distressed feelings are reflected in her psychological protocols. In the Rorschach, she had extreme difficulty with card VI, the "male sexuality card," and could give no response, even though she had been responding fairly easily to the cards prior to that. To card IV, the "father card" she responds it looks like a "bull with tusks." This suggests that she sees the father as being extremely aggressive, perhaps including sexually aggressive. In the TAT to card 6GF she gives the story: "The father sneaks up on her and scares her. After he scares her she says, 'what did you do that for?' 'Well, you're my daughter aren't you?' "

The implication of this last statement is that the father regards her as property, with which he is free to do anything he wishes. Unfortunately, this attitude is still widespread, and contributes to the severity and extent of child abuse. Carol's Draw-A-Person Test (DAP), (Figure 1–10), shows an

Figure 1-10. Carol: Draw A Person. Girl age 13 "unhappy because of a stain on her new dress, from eating in a restaurant. . . . Waiting for a ride, for her mother to pick her up. (She's thinking) what her mother is going to say to her about the dress. (The best thing is) nothing, everything on her is wrong, her hair. (The worst thing is) her looks."

unhappy girl, with a prominent dark spot in the genital area. This suggests that the sexual abuse has been extremely traumatic to her. However, the extent of the trauma suffered by these youngsters is not always as obvious as it is in Carol's case. When an older girl in a family runs away, the clinician should be alert to the possibility of incestuous abuse.

The effects of neglect and abuse are readily apparent in the responses of eight-year-old Fred. Fred is schizophrenic, and the underlying primary process material is close to the surface and pours out freely. Fred "wanders away for hours." In the Sentence Completion Test he states, if I had my own way—"I'd go anywhere I want to. Go to the mall, steal all the candy, sleep there." What bugs me is—"I'll be hungry and thirsty and I'll die." If I could change just one thing about my mother I would like her to—"like me, love."

In the Despert Fables Test, in which the examiner presents the beginning of stories and asks the child to make up the endings, he indicates "the daddy is mad because they left. Q. There was nothing in the house to eat and he was hungry and thirsty and tired like I am." In response to another story, which deals with a family not having enough food for everybody, he indicates the parents "leave all the kids in the forest, took them to the woods and ran away." Food themes also show up in the Rorschach. To card IX he gives the response "looks like a monster with the two things, they're pulling food . . . pushes it in and burns them all up in flames." To card VI "a big insect and a little butterfly going to pow it and pull it and ate it all up. . . . it *is* a monster, pulling it away and take to its babies." In the Sentence Completion Test one of his wishes for a "bow and arrow to kill some meat." In the Children's Apperception Test (CAT) to card one he states "birds. Eating porridge. The mother bird is dead and they have a statue of the mother. People give the birds some food . . . one day they had no food and died. The people cried." Most of these responses are quite bizarre, but clearly convey his feelings of deprivation and victimization, and at times the need to fight back aggressively to obtain whatever gratification he can. At times he identifies with the aggressor and himself becomes aggressive. Figure 1-11 shows his drawing for the Draw-A-Person (DAP) Test. He describes the person as being "very happy because he stoled, got out of jail and stole stuff." In the KFD (Figure 1-12) he identified himself as the "bad guy. I really like being the bad guy."

Severity of Pathology

Fred is a very disturbed child, but such severe pathology is not typical of runaways in general. The children in this sample would be expected to be rather disturbed by virtue of the selection process that is involved in the referrals. In the runaway group (See Table 1.4), 2 of the twenty-eight youngsters (7%) were definitely schizophrenic, and another six (21%) could be considered borderline or showing potential for developing serious pathology or the possibility of decompensating into an overt psychosis. Five (18%) had basically good reality testing, but showed signs of magical thinking and/or unrealistic ideas about death, and fourteen (50%) did not

Figure 1-11. Fred: Draw A Person. Fifteen-year-old boy "very happy because he stoled he got out of jail and stole stuff. He was couped up in there. The police are still looking for him. (His name is) Ben Cune. (The best thing is) everytime they look for him, he has took with him a file in his pocket or sock. They don't look there, he cuts the bars and bends and escapes. (The worst thing is) he kills seven men, because he wanted to escape. He killed seven police men."
"(He is holding) a bag with jewelry and dollar bills, he's escaping from jail, he stole a lot of stuff."

have any evidence of severe pathology. In the nonrunaway group, five (28%) were considered borderline, seven (39%) showed magical thinking or paranoid ideas, none were overtly schizophrenic, and six (33%) showed adequate reality testing.

Figure 1–12. Fred: Kinetic Family Drawing. From left to right: Brother age 5, "playing Army. Me age 8, playing I'm the bad guy, I really like being the bad guy. Mother—she just cleans up the house, she don't do anything. Father—fix cars."

Suicide

Magical thinking and unrealistic ideas about death are of particular concern when assessing possible suicide risk. Half (14) of the runaway group were known to have made suicide attempts or gestures of various kinds (See Table 1–5). Of course there may also have been other incidents which went

Table 1-4. Severity of Pathology in Referred Children.

CATEGORY	RUNAWAY GROUP NO.	%	NONRUNAWAY GROUP NO.	%
Schizophrenic	2	7	0	0
Borderline or incipient	6	21	5	28
Magical thinking or unrealistic ideas about death	5	18	7	39
No severe pathology	14	50	6	33
Not tested	1	4		
Total	28	100	18	100

unrecorded. Of these fourteen, four (14%) were considered to have made more than one suicide attempt, and three (10%) made one attempt.

An incident was considered to be an attempt if the youngster expressed his intention to die and acted in a way that could have resulted in death if

Table 1-5. Incidence of Suicide Attempts or Gestures in Referred Children.

CATEGORY	RUNAWAY GIRLS NO.	%	RUNAWAY BOYS NO.	%	RUNAWAY GROUP TOTAL NO.	%	NONRUNAWAY GIRLS NO.	%	NONRUNAWAY BOYS NO.	%	NONRUNAWAY GROUP TOTAL NO.	%
2 or more attempts	4	31			4	14						
1 attempt	1	8	2	13	3	10			1	6	1	6
1 "disguised"			2	13	2	7						
2 or more "gestures"	3	10			3	23			1	6	1	6
1 "gesture"			1	7	1	3						
1 "disguised" gesture			1	7	1	3						
Total attempts &/or gestures	8	62	6	40	14	49			2	12	2	11
Suicidal ideation or signs in testing	3	23	7	47	10	36	1		10	59	11	61
No signs	1	8	1	7	2	7			5	29	5	28
Not tested	1	8	1	7	2	7						
Rounded Total entire group	13	100	15	100	28	100	1		17	100	18	100

there had been no intervention. Two youngsters (7%) made a "disguised" attempt, which involved the same sort of action as an attempt, but with a denial of intention to die. These "disguised" incidents usually involved overdosing on liquor and/or drugs. Four children (26%) made one or more suicidal "gestures," (a stated intention to die, but an act that was unlikely to actually result in death.) Most of these gestures involved superficial cutting of the wrists, arms, or face. There was one "disguised gesture" (an act similar to the above, without a statement of intention to die).

Of the remaining youngsters in the runaway group, who had made no known attempts or gestures, ten showed suicidal ideation or signs in the psychological testing, and only two (7% of the entire group) showed no signs. Two were not tested.

Comparable figures for the nonrunaway group were in marked contrast, with only two of the eighteen (11%) having made an attempt or gesture, compared to 50% of the runaway group. Eleven (61%) of the nonrunaways showed suicidal signs or ideation in the psychological protocols, and five (28%) showed no signs. Thus the vast majority of both groups suffered from severe underlying depression, and suicidal feelings, but the runaway group had acted out these feelings much more frequently than the nonrunaway group. The comparison of suicide attempts and/or gestures for the runaway *vs.* nonrunaway group does reach statistical significance ($\chi^2 = 5.68$ $p < .02$ $df = 1$).

Since there might be important sex differences involved in the attempted suicide rates (girls usually more likely to make an attempt than boys, boys more likely to succeed) and since the nonrunaway group was almost all boys, the groups were subdivided by sex. In the runaway group, 62% of the girls and 40% of the boys had made attempts or gestures. The 40% rate of runaway boys is still much higher than the 12% rate for nonrunaway boys.

These figures dramatically illustrate the underlying depressive feelings and self-destructive tendencies of these runaway youngsters. It is my feeling that underlying motives for running away, for drug and alcohol abuse, and for suicidal behavior seem to have much in common. One of these motives is concerned with a deep longing for peace and for being with someone they feel or hope will be loving and nurturing to them. George, who did not live with his elderly, and seriously ill parents, but lived with a variety of relatives most of his life, expresses this longing on the Sentence Completion Test; The best time—"I had is when I'm with my Mamma." A mother—"is nice." The happiest time—"when I'm with my family." On his KFD (Figure 1-13) he draws the entire family, including a dead sister, as if they were all alive and well. However, the tiny ant-like figures suggest strong depressive feelings.

When youngsters run away, they are frequently seen to be searching for

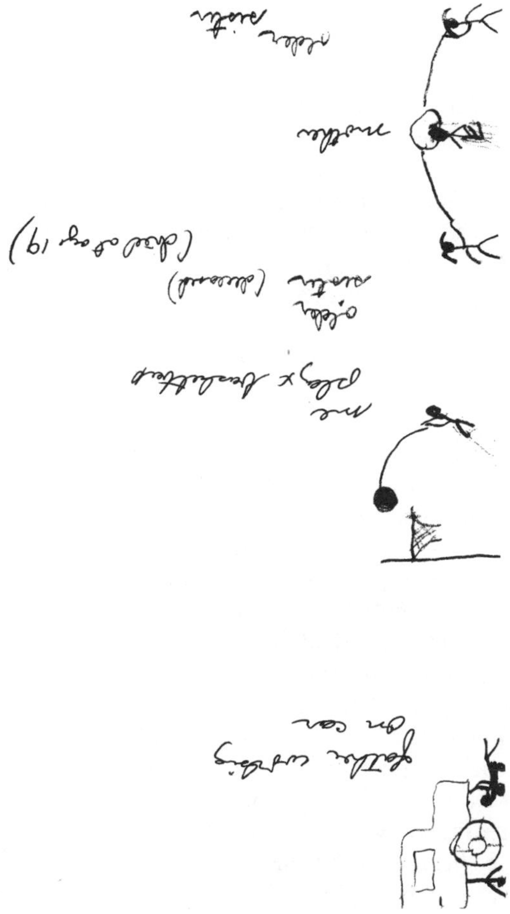

Figure 1-13. George: Kinetic Family Drawing. From left to right: Father working on car. Me playing basketball. Older sister (died at age nineteen), mother, older sister.''

loving parents, and many will go to a friend's home when they run, in the hopes that they will find nurturance from the friend's parents. Some youngsters may go back and forth between divorced parents' homes or to other relatives. When a loved parental figure has died, the youngster may see death as a way to be with this person. Doris, who was neglected and abused by her parents, remembered her great-grandfather who died when she was six or seven years old, with great affection. One of Doris' TAT stories is "He's in a graveyard saying prayers to a grave . . . praying whoever's there will come alive or he goes with the person."

Religious beliefs become important because the child may see death as peaceful, or may believe in reincarnation and expect to return to another life. Children under age ten may believe in the reversability of death, and not realize the permanence of suicidal acts[12]. Thus the maintenance of unrealistic ideas about death and the continuation of magical thinking is of particular concern in evaluating self-destructive potential. Many of the children in the samples give long, complicated TAT stories featuring characters similar to Frankenstein, Dracula, witches, monsters, etc. Card 15 of the Tat is particularly useful in "pulling" the child's beliefs about death.

The dynamics of self-destructive behavior usually involve the youngster's tremendous rage toward the unloving, dead, absent, or abusive parent, with strong death wishes toward this figure. When the parent figure then dies or becomes ill, the child may feel that his anger and thoughts caused this, and he is flooded with guilt feelings. He may then feel he must expiate the guilt by suicide, either directly or by experimenting with alcohol and/or liquor, or driving fast, or other self-destructive behavior.

Ellen dearly loved her grandmother, and related to the grandmother as her mother. She was accused of robbing the grandmother's neighbor, and the grandmother had a heart attack when she heard about it. Ellen attempted suicide shortly after this.

When the parent figure has been abusive and the child has been brought up in an atmosphere of violence, he may fear retaliation for his murderous wishes toward the abusive figure. Henry was an out-of-wedlock child who never knew his natural father and whose mother never showed affection for him. His stepfather, who was severely abusive toward him, died of a heart attack three years ago. His mother's current boyfriend continues the abuse. Henry denies any suicidal ideation, but he "OD'd" on Valium. He ran away many times, once stole a van and went to another state and was gone for weeks. In the TAT he gives these stories:

"His mother and father had an argument. The father was drunk. He (the boy) hid in his bedroom and cried. Then he went to his father's bedroom and found a gun and shot his father . . . He's crying because he loves his father and it's going to be on his conscience for the rest of his life. His father's spirit is standing behind his back ready to stick a knife in him."

"His wife died three years ago, and he tries to get her back. He cries. His wife rises and says, 'Get him!' and she attacks him and beats his head off."

Henry's first story mentions the parents being drunk, and parental abuse of alcohol does loom large in these children's lives. Although the histories are somewhat sketchy, alcoholism or alcohol abuse by the parents was known for ten (36%) in the runaway group, and four (22%) of the nonrunaways, (See Table 1-6).

Within the runaway group, known parental alcohol abuse was higher for the boys (seven cases—47%) than for girls (three cases—23%), but this trend was reversed in regard to the youngsters' own use. Ten girls (77%) and five boys (33%) admitted to drug and/or alcohol use. Very heavy use of drugs (every day and/or had overdosed) was admitted by six girls (46%) and three boys (20%). This seems to be related to the high suicide attempt rate among the runaway girls, who often chose overdosing as a method.

Table 1-6. Admitting Drug and Alcohol Abuse in Referred Children.

CATEGORY	RUNAWAY GIRLS		RUNAWAY BOYS		RUNAWAY GROUP TOTAL		NONRUNAWAY GIRLS		NONRUNAWAY BOYS		NONRUNAWAY GROUP TOTAL	
	NO.	%	NO.	%	NO.	%	NO.	%	NO.	%	NO.	%
Admitted to using everyday or had O.D.'d.	6	46	3	20	9	32			2	12	2	11
Admitted use of drugs and/ or alcohol or parents indicated	4	31	2	13	6	22	1		5	29	6	33
Total admitting drug and/or alcohol abuse	10	77	5	33	15	54			7	31	8	44
Does not admit drug and/or alcohol use	3	23	10	67	13	46			10	59	10	55
Rounded Total entire group	13	100	15	100	28	100	1		17	100	18	100
Alcohol problem in parents	3	23	7	47	10	36			4	23	4	22

It should be pointed out that these figures for drug abuse undoubtedly greatly underestimate the actual use, since the youngsters and their families are reluctant to admit such use in any circumstances, and especially in a court setting.

Drug use, suicide, and running away may all represent ways of trying to escape from a painful home environment and from their own dysphoric feelings as well. There is also an element of the feeling that the parents "will be sorry when I'm gone," although one boy felt his parents would be *glad* when he died. Running away and drug use are also frequently encouraged by the peer group, and many youngsters are greatly influenced by peer pressure. They are desperately seeking acceptance and affection, and when they don't find it at home, they look elsewhere.

Self-Image and Sexual Role Expectations

All of the youngsters in the sample have a very poor self-image. They frequently feel defective, torn apart, ugly, powerless, dumb, criminal, etc. Kaufman and Heims,[13] in a very interesting article, describe the body image of a group of delinquent children (including runaways) and indicate that they have feelings about themselves which are similar to those in this sample. The delinquent and runaway actions are seen as a defense against a deep-seated, underlying depression which is usually not apparent on the surface. In this sample, George (See Figure 1-13) draws tiny ant-like figures in his KFD. Jim (Figure 1-14) draws a small dirty-looking figure and indicates "the whole picture stinks." Parents may sometimes contribute to these feelings of lack of self-worth, and may covertly encourage running away and other forms of acting-out.[3]

Sometimes the parents will refuse to take the children back after a runaway episode. The parents frequently regard the child as some sort of criminal, or "bad seed," often from birth onward. Lee's parents described him as being "a thorn in my side." With boys, identification with the father may contribute to a poor self-image. The mother may tell the boy "your're just like your father." If she sees the father as a criminal (whether he is or not), the boy will frequently accept this evaluation of himself and begin to live up to it. Fred (Figures 1-11 and 1-12) identifies himself as a criminal. Adam sees himself as "born to steal and lie like my father."

When the father actually is abusive, violent, and/or criminal, the boy may come to identify with the aggressor, and adopt similar behavior himself. Henry's father and stepfather both abused him. His mother describes him as a "bad kid." His TAT stories were saturated with violence and expressed sadistic pleasure: ". . . They're killing this guy just because they feel it's fun." ". . . He likes raping girls." To TAT card 6BM, he

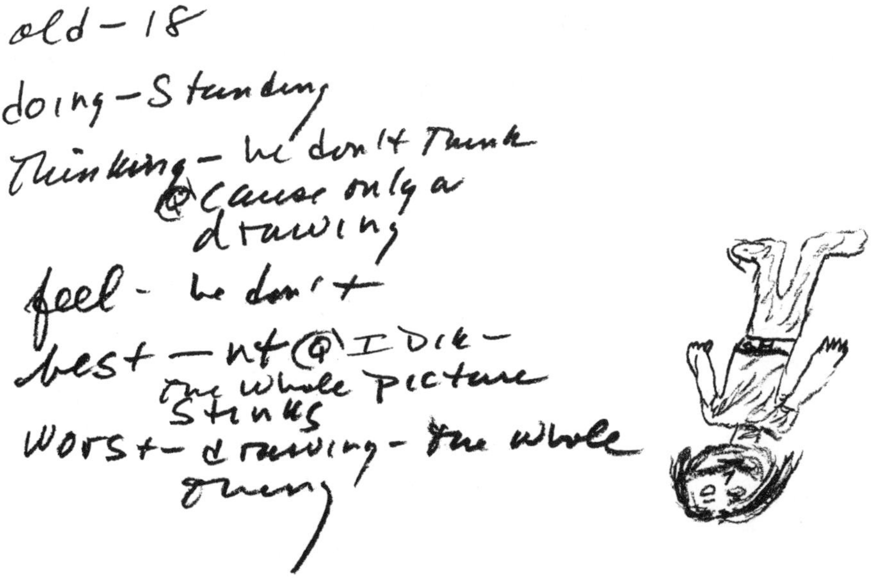

Figure 1-14. Jim: Draw A Person. Eighteen years old. "Standing." "(He is thinking) he don't think. Q. Cause it's only a drawing. (He feels) he don't. (The best thing is) nothing. Q. I don't know, the whole pictures stinks. (The worst thing) is the drawing. The whole thing."

gives this story: "He's a gangster and his mother . . . she's looking out of the window for the police. He's nervous, afraid of the cops, just robbed the National Bank. (His mother says) 'Look what I brought up—a criminal.' Feels bad for both of them. She helps him, he goes to Mexico on a motorcycle."

He sees his mother as condemning him but also helping him to get away with criminal behavior and encouraging him to run away.

Some boys choose a somewhat healthier way to try to compensate for feelings of inferiority, by building up muscles, or fantasizing themselves as a super hero. Kenneth (Figure 1-15) draws himself as Superman.

For the girls, the parents may covertly encourage sexual acting-out. They may call her a whore, be suspicious of her, etc. One of the girls in this sample, seen when she was thirteen years old, had already experienced a pregnancy and abortion. Sometimes these girls come to accept the parents' evaluation and regard themselves as prostitutes, which further lowers their self-esteem. It is also important to be aware of the high incidence of sexual abuse (more often of daughters by father figures), and the devasting effect this has on the girls' self-image.

Both girls and boys in both groups tended to see male-female relation-

II - That's me
WEARING Superman shirt

Figure 1-15. Kenneth: Draw A Person. "That's me, wearing a superman shirt."

ships in a very negative manner, with the man being very aggressive. TAT card 13MF has obvious sexual implications. In the runaway group, fifteen (75%) of the twenty who responded to this card indicated the woman had been killed. Six (30%) of these specified she was raped and killed. Four (20%) indicated she died of natural causes. One gave an unusual response involving prostitution.

In the nonrunaway group, sixteen responded. Six (37%) said he killed the girl (mostly because of jealousy) with only one of these mentioning rape. Two (12%) indicated she died of natural causes, one (6%) said he beat her up. One gave a vague sexual response, "What a wild thing they had." Five (31%) of this group denied the sexual implications of the picture and said the man was going to work, or was late to work.

Another aspect of self-image is revealed in the animal identifications. In the Sentence Completion Test, one sentence stem was "If I could be any animal I would most like to be is a ______________." In the runaway group, eight of the seventeen that responded (47%) gave a response of some sort of bird, mostly because "they can fly, they are free." Two (12%) gave a horse, one of these specifying "because it can run fast." Three (18%) said some kind of dog "because it gets taken care of." One (6%) a Koala bear and one a deer "because it's cute."

In the nonrunaway group, six of the eleven who responded (54%) gave a response of an aggressive animal (tiger, black panther, Doberman Pinscher, "so nobody will bother me," etc.). Three (27%) gave a dolphin or monkey "because they're smart," one (9%) dog, "it gets fed," and one a pigeon.

School Problems, Minimal Brain Dysfunction (MBD) and Learning Disabilities

The poor self-image of many of these youngsters is often exacerbated by severe school problems of one sort or another and many of the youngsters suffer from learning disabilities. However, they are not generally lacking in intellectual potential.

IQ scores (WISC–R) were available for twenty-two of the runaway children, and the mean full-scale IQ score was 95.9, which is well within the average range. Full-scale IQ scores varied from 65 to 120, with only two falling below the dull normal score of 80. The mean IQ score for the nonrunaway group was 91.8. In a previous study[5], IQ scores of children in the Shelter were not significantly different from those of children in a public school of similar socioeconomic and racial makeup.

In this sample, four of the runaways (14%) were known to be in classes for learning disabled youngsters, one (4%) in a class for educably retarded, one in a "slow" class and two (7%) in classes for emotionally disturbed children. None of them had much insight into their learning problems, and they felt themselves to be defective. It is of great concern that many of the youngsters had severe learning problems, and needed special help, but were just pushed along from one grade to the next without ever mastering the work at any level. The opposite also happens sometimes. The one youngster in the "slow" class was a fifteen-year-old girl with an IQ of 114, who was reading on grade level 12.8 (she was in 9th grade). Not surprisingly, she was bored with the class, and has not gone to school at all for the last year. There were five (18%) in the runaway group who had not attended school at all for months or years, seven (25%) who were excessively truant, and many others with severe school problems of one sort or another.

For some of these youngsters, the poor attendance occurred during the runaway episodes, although a few continued to attend school during this time. There has been some discussion in the literature as to which comes first, the school problems or the running away[1]. My feeling is that there is almost always an interaction between these two elements, and that it is neither possible nor helpful to try to decide which element is primary. Regardless of the origin of the problem, a complete therapeutic plan must encompass educational as well as other needs. The nonrunaway group also displayed severe school problems as would be expected, since ten of the eighteen (55%) were referred because the schools had taken out PINS petitions for truancy.

Many of the youngsters in both groups demonstrated perceptual motor problems in the psychologicals (See Table 1-7). Nine (35%) of the runaway group were definitely considered to be suffering from minimal brain dysfunction (MBD), and 44% of the nonrunaway group was considered to have MBD. For nine children (35%) of the runaway group, it was considered unlikely that there was MBD but it could not be ruled out. The corresponding figure for the nonrunaway group was 4 or 22%. Almost all of the youths in both samples demonstrated poor impulse control, both in their overt behavior and in the testing protocols. Typically, they are tightly defended,with extremely constricted Rorschach protocols and much use of denial and repression, with a tendency to sudden explosive acting out. One girl described herself as having "two personalities," one friendly and one violent. The poor impulse control may stem partly from minimal brain dysfunction in some youngsters, and is very likely exacerbated by the chaotic home life.

The children's feelings about these disabilities were expressed in many parts of the projective testing. Card 1 of the TAT is particularly helful in uncovering some of these feelings. Following are some of these stories:

Table 1-7. Incidence of Minimal Brain Dysfunction in Referred Children.

CATEGORY	RUNAWAY GIRLS		RUNAWAY BOYS		RUNAWAY GROUP TOTAL		NONRUNAWAY GIRLS		NONRUNAWAY BOYS		NONRUNAWAY GROUP TOTAL	
	NO.	%	NO.	%	NO.	%	NO.	%	NO.	%	NO.	%
MBD very likely	4	33	5	36	9	35	1		7	41	8	44
MBD unlikely but can't be ruled out	3	25	6	43	9	35			4	23	4	22
No indications of MBD	5	42	3	21	8	30			6	35	6	33
Not tested	1		1		2							
Rounded Total	13	100	15	100	28	100	1		17	100	18	100

"He always wanted to be a violin player but never did it right and started to give up . . . there's no one around to teach him. He feels terrible . . . he'll quit."

"The kids broke his violin, He's trying to fix it. He can't, he's sad."

"He does not like playing the violin. His mother wants him to, but he just sits and thinks how much he hates it. Finally, he says he's giving up the violin."

The latter story suggests a passive-aggressive struggle with the mother, and this appears to be a frequent problem with these youngsters and their school difficulties.

Another reason for school problems and truancy may involve conflicted feelings about separation and indivualization. It was interesting to note that a small subgroup of four boys (22%) of the nonrunaway group, some of whom were referred because the school took out a PINS petition for truancy, seemed to have what might be considered an opposite reaction from the runaways. Both groups felt unloved and rejected, but the runaways recognized these feelings and tried to run away, while those in the other subgroup appeared to have a reaction formation instead. Rather than feeling angry with the parent and wishing him or her dead, the reaction formation youngster represses these feelings, and then fears that harm may come to the parent. He may have trouble going to school because he feels he must be on guard to protect and watch over the parent. The youngsters who seem to have this difficulty had never attended school regularly and consistently, with school problems typically beginning in the kindergarten and first grade, and then becoming much worse in junior high school. Both this reaction and the runaway reaction are quite concerned with the issue of separation and individualization. Many of the runaway group are determined to "make it" on their own with a complete cut-off of relationship with the parents, while the school phobic group is afraid to separate even briefly.

SUMMARY OF FINDINGS

In a previous study, we found that a group of children comparable to our entire group did not differ from a "normal" control group of public school children in either intelligence or ability to cope with interpersonal problem situations. However, they did differ dramatically in family history, with these children having a far greater number of deaths, divorces, and separations of the parents, and placements of the child outside of the family. They also differed in their feelings about the amount of control they had over their own lives (greater External Locus of Control).

In the present gorup, when the runaways were compared to the nonrunaways, it was found again that both groups came from grossly disrupted families, with many deaths, divorces, separations, remarriages, adoptions, etc. Both groups had a very high incidence of Minimal Brain Dysfunction (MBD) and concomitant learning disabilities and problems in impulse control. The two groups did not differ greatly in intelligence. Both groups showed a wide range of pathology.

In the projective testing, both groups demonstrated extremely strong feelings of being deprived of the nurturance everyone needs. Although many of the youngsters appeared defiant, rebellious, cheerful, or brash on the surface, almost all had severe underlying feelings of depression which were basically due to these feelings of deprivation, of being unloved, unwanted, rejected, abused, etc. All had severe problems in self-image.

The runaway and nonrunawy groups did differ dramatically from each other in the amount and extent of known child abuse, and in suicidal behavior. Sixty-five percent of the runaway children were known to have been neglected and/or abused, compared to 33% of the nonrunaway group. Half of the runaway children were known to have made one or more suicide attempts or gestures. This was in marked contrast to the nonrunaway group, where only 11% had acted on their suicidal feelings. There were more girls (62%) than boys (49%) who made attempts, but when runaway boys were compared with nonrunaway boys, the rate was still far higher (49% compared to 12%). There appeared to be a higher rate of drug and alcohol abuse both in the parents and the children of the runaway group. There also seemed to be some birth order effect, with the runaways more often being second children, and the nonrunaways third or later children. Much more research is needed to clarify this issue.

Both groups had a generally poor self-image, but in their animal identification the runaway group tended to identify more with animals which are "free" and can fly or run fast, while the nonrunaway group tended to identify more with aggressive animals.

Thus, the general pattern suggests that both groups of children, with very good reason, feel severely deprived of love, rejected, unwanted, abused, homeless, abandoned, etc. For the most part both groups react to this with strong turbulent feelings of anger at the ungiving parent, and severe underlying depression. They all have a poor self-image, which becomes worse and worse. School problems compound the difficulty, lowering the self-image even more, and the parents frequently punish the child for this, which leads to further anger and deterioration of self-image and of parent/child interactions.

Most of those in the runaway group attempt to flee from both the actual physical and/or sexual abuse, and from their own feelings of agony by physically running away, escaping through drugs and/or alcohol, and by suicidal acts. They hope to find peace and love through these means, as well as attempting to punish the parents, but they frequently destroy themselves in their desperate search.

Those in the nonrunaway group start off with similar feelings of anger at the parents they perceive as unloving, but many try to repress and deny these feelings. A small subgroup of nonrunaways seemed to utilize a reaction formation, converting their anger toward the parents into a fear that the parents might come to harm, and they could not comfortably separate from them for even a brief period, with subsequent school phobia and extreme truancy throughout the school years. This appears to be the other end of the spectrum from the runaways who are often trying to establish independence.

It is important to consider whether these findings can be generalized from this particular sample to other populations of runaway youngsters. The one element which almost all studies agree on is that there are extremely severe problems in parent-child relationships. Some youngsters in other populations may run away because of a feeling of healthy adventurousness, but for the most of the others, I feel that the underlying dynamics of deprivation of affection, anger and depression may well be applicable to most runaways, regardless of what social class they belong to, and whether or not they have been involved with public agencies. The clinician should be alert to the possibility of physical and/or sexual abuse and suicidal feelings in runaways, regardless of social class.

IMPLICATIONS FOR THERAPY

There are many possible levels of intervention in trying to help runaway youngsters. Of course, the most basic need is for food and shelter and many communities are trying to provide "crash pads" either through group homes or through a system of emergency foster homes. Some of these programs provide limited counseling, but most do not go beyond this. The prognosis for runaway youngsters has been generally poor[14,15], and as we have seen in this study, the youngsters who are brought to the attention of public agencies are suffering from very severe problems, both intrapsychically and environmentally. Their treatment needs to begin with a thorough evaluation of the child and the family, which encompasses the unique abilities and disabilities of each youngster, the individual and family dynamics and a formulation of treatment plans that includes all elements. However, there is frequently great resistance to treatment on the part of both the youngster and the family, and there are tremendous gaps in the ability of the system to provide adequate treatment. In a follow-up study of children who had been in the Shelter[16] I found that when the youngsters were returned to the community, they received virtually no help. Only 20% of them received any therapy at all, and this was only a few sessions. Not one child who was returned to the community received adequate treatment. In sharp contrast, there was a high improvement rate among youngsters sent to residential treatment centers, although it is not entirely clear whether the improvement was maintained after returning home.

There is a strong social movement (deinstitutionalization) to keep children in the home community and out of institutions. This is certainly laudable in theory, but has not worked out in practice. Some authors feel that runaway youngsters should be completely removed from the juvenile justice system.[17] This again sounds good in theory, but poor in actual implementation. If there were no involvement with social agencies, there would be no therapeutic intervention of any kind for most of these youngsters.

Many authors feel that traditional psychoanalytically oriented therapy is of limited usefulness with these youngsters.[1] New and innovative types of therapy need to be developed to deal with the severe problems these youngster's face. Wallach and I[18] have developed a short-term group problem-solving therapy for a runaway and delinquent population, which makes extensive use of role playing. This was found to improve their interpersonal problem-solving skills, but much longer term individual therapy, preferably with parental involvement, is needed for completely effective intervention.

In individual therapy, the therapist needs a great deal of ingenuity and inventiveness to overcome the extreme resistance. Adam was totally resistant to therapy at first, refusing to discuss any of his feelings or problems, and refusing to play any of the therapeutic games available, or to engage in any activity. He finally indicated he liked to play checkers, so I developed a new way to use checkers to engage him in higher level therapy. A small charm from a dental supply house (such as a gun, glasses, animal, person, ball) was placed on each checker. When a checker was jumped, reinforcement was given for discussing the item, and further reinforcement for telling a story about it. This enabled me to use Gardner's mutual story-telling technique[19]. Eventually, Adam was able to talk directly about his problems.

However, even when out-patient treatment is provided, this is often insufficient in view of the overwhelming nature of the problems. It is often necessary to remove the youngster from the home and provide a program which works on many levels simultaneously. Edelstein[20] has developed a multidimensional therapeutic program for a residential treatment center which actively involves the parents as well as the adolescent, and deals with all aspects of the youngster's life. The facility (Wayside School for Girls) is organized with several small groups of six to eight girls in a dormitory, with two live-in counselors and a therapist (psychologist or social worker) for each group in a surrogate family arrangement. Each child is thoroughly evaluated both by traditional methods and by use of Edelstein's diagnostic and therapeutic "Everything is Possible" (EIP) game. This game is also used in family interaction with the girl's family and also in peer group interaction in the dormitory. The sessions are videotaped and replayed at subsequent sessions for further therapy with the child. The very high incidence of various sorts of school problems, learning disabilities, MBD, truancy, boredom, peer problems, behavior problems, etc., is handled by providing an individualized educational program for each girl. The whole setting provides a therapeutic milieu with total coordination among therapy, school, work, recreation, religion, peer relationships, and family interactions.

Unfortunately, there are very few such comprehensive programs available, and even these are, for the most part, unable to provide for the very seriously disturbed youngsters (psychotic or borderline). Society simply does not even begin to provide adequate help for the many thousands of runaway youngsters who are unable to break free from the self-destructive, repetitive intergenerational cycle of anger, depression, acting out, and increasingly disturbed family relationships. Child abuse, including incest, is often a hidden factor, and must be recognized. There is now a very strong social movement to "save money" by cutting back on what little help is available and offering totally inadequate services. Even from a purely economic point of view, it would be far better to spend money now for comprehensive and innovative treatment, rather than to spend it years later to maintain these same youngsters in jails and/or on welfare. We must be willing to expend more time, effort, ingenuity, and money if we are to help these desperate youngsters.

REFERENCES

1. Walker, Deborah Klein. *Runaway Youth: An Annotated Bibliography and Literature Overview.* Department of Health, Education, and Welfare., 1975.
2. Senior, B. E., and Henry, R. C. Answers as to why children run away. *American Journal of Correction* **39** (4):8, 42, 1977.
3. Meeks, J. E. Behavioral and antisocial disorders. *In:* J. D. Nosphpitz (ed.) *Basic Handbook of Child Psychiatry, Vol. II.* New York: Basic Books, 1979.
4. Golbin, G., Young, L., and Tolan, W. *An Analysis of the Juvenile Delinquent and Person in Need of Supervision Population in Suffolk County.* Suffolk County Department of Probation publication, 1977.
5. Nilson, P., and Wallach, J. *Comparison of Family Structure in Delinquent and Nondelinquent Adolescents.* Unpublished manuscript, Suffolk County Consultation Services Center, Hauppauge, New York, 1974.
6. Vandeloo, M. C. A study of coping behavior of runaway adolescents as related to situational stresses. *Dissertation Abstracts International.* Ann Arbor, Michigan Univ M-films, No. 77-24837, 129 pp. (From Walker.)
7. Gilbreath, M. E., Ovedovitz, A. C., Pelletier, J. E., and Claffie, B. A. *Secure Detention for Juveniles in Suffolk County, an Analysis of the Population of the Children's Shelter.* Criminal Justice Coordinating Council, Sept. 1976.
8. Forer, Lucille, and Still, Henry, *The Birth Order Factor.* New York: Pocket Books, 1977.
9. Shellow, Robert, Schamp, Juliana, R., Liebow, Elliot and Unger, Elizabeth, Suburban runaways of the 1960's. *Monographs of the Society for Research in Child Development.* 1967, **32** (3)—Serial No. 111.
10. Helfer, R. E., and Kempe, C. H. *The Battered Child,* Second Ed. University of Chicago Press, 1974.
11. Zilbach, J. J., Family development and familial factors in etiology. *In: Basic Handbook of Child Psychiatry.* Vol. 2, by Joseph D. Noshpitz (ed.) New York: Basic Books, 1979.
12. Toolin, James, M. Therapy of depressed and suicidal children. *American Journal of Psychotherapy.* **32** (2):243-251, 1978.
13. Kaufman, I., and Heims, L. The body image of the junvenile delinquent. *American Journal of Orthopsychiatry.* **28:** 146-159, 1958.
14. Olson, L. R. *A pilot follow-up report on suburban runaways of the 1960's.* (Unpublished paper). Adelphi, Md.: NIMH, 1976 10pp.
15. Puller, Ingrid, and Nissen, Gerhardt. Symptoms and prognosis of runaway children: Results of a follow-up study. Zur symtomatik und prognose des weglaufens—Ergebnisse einer katamnestichen untersuchung. *Zeitschrift für Kinder—und jugendpsychiatrie,* (Stuttgart). **4**(3):259-271, 1976.
16. Nilson, P. *De-institutionalization: Friend or foe? Treatment needs of youth in the Juvenile Justice System.* Paper presented at the Annual Meeting of the National Council of Community Mental Health Centers, Washington, D. C., February 24, 1979.
17. Murphy, Patrick T. *Our Kindly Parent—the State: The Juvenile Justice System and How it Works.* New York: Viking, 1974.

18. Wallach, J. and Nilson, P. *Problem solving groups for young adolescents.* Paper presented at the Annual Meeting of the National Council of Community Mental Health Centers, Washington, D.C., February 24, 1979.
19. Gardner, Richard A. *Therapeutic Communication With Children: The Mutual Storytelling Technique.* New York: Jason Arnsen, 1971.
20. Edelstein, Rivcka, *Modified family therapy in a residential treatment setting: A model and case illustration.* Paper presented at the Annual Meeting of the National Council of Community Mental Health Centers, Washington, D.C., February 24, 1979.

Dr. David R. Anderson focuses upon research directed towards identifying potential self-destructive behavior. With critical judgment, he examines and discusses the conclusions of major sociological, biographical, and psychological test attempts to predict such behavior. A significant proportion of his chapter is concerned with personality profiles derived from commonly used psychological tests. Considering all variables, he concludes that the potential adolescent suicide can be traced through a series of disruptive, meaningful, interpersonal social relations, accentuated by taking leave of the normal social environment of which the home and the school are essential elements. Suicide in adolescents is the culmination, he emphasizes, of a developmental process with identifiable stages.

2
Diagnosis and Prediction of Suicidal Risk Among Adolescents

David R. Anderson, Ph.D.

The first step in the effective prevention and treatment of suicidal behavior is the identification of those individuals likely to take their own lives and the prediction of immediate suicide risk. In the ideal situation, identification of a unitary suicidal personality type would lead to highly accurate predictions of suicidal behavior. Research endeavors designed to demonstrate the existence of such a personality type, however, have not met with great success,[25] leading investigators to agree that the act of suicide may be the common endpoint of several different pathways, and it may occur among a variety of personality types.[14]

In the past, predictive statements concerning suicidal behavior were often based upon demographic variables. While the use of such statistical information suggests large groups of individuals at higher risk for suicide, this approach leads to a high percentage of false positive predictions and in the absence of supporting clinical data, is of little help in the individual case. More recently, results of concentrated research efforts have suggested a number of common features among suicidal individuals ranging from sociological and social events to specific clinical states.[15] While it is unlikely that any clinician could claim to identify the potentially suicidal individual in every case, careful clinical assessment and attention to various combinations of biographical and psychological factors may well improve predictive capabilities.

This chapter will first focus on the research which suggests that various sociological and biographical events are common to many suicidal adolescents, and that knowledge of such events acquired through case histories and direct interviews may assist in identifying adolescents who are likely to take their own lives. Secondly, consideration will be given to research efforts involving the use of psychological tests and suicide assessment scales to predict suicidal behavior.

ADOLESCENT SUICIDE

Recent studies indicate that suicide is the third leading cause of death among adolescents in the United States.[22,23] The total number of completed suicides in 1975 among ten- to fourteen-year-olds was 170, or a rate of .8 per 100,000; among fifteen- to nineteen-year-olds there were 1594 suicides, or 7.6 per 100,000; and among twenty- to twenty-four-year-olds there were 3142 completed suicides, or 16.5 per 100,000. The 1975 rate for the fifteen to twenty-four age group, 11.8 per 100,000, was the highest ever recorded in the United States, and represented a rate more than double that documented in 1961 (131% increase).

In contrast to the number of adolescents who complete suicide, estimates suggest as many as eight to ten times as many attempt suicide, or an annual rate of 45.6 per 100,000.[42] It has also been estimated that 12% of all suicide attempts in the nation are made by adolescents, and 90% of those are made by adolescent girls.[9] Recent evidence suggests that the average age of suicide attempters has been dropping and that the commonly identified differential of two or three female attempters for every male attempter may be decreasing.[19,42]

Despite the dramatic statistical increase in adolescent suicide rates, it is generally agreed that estimates of both completed and attempted suicides are low. In many cases, suicides are intentionally covered up, the deaths being attributed to accidents or other causes, thereby shielding the parents from the shame and guilt feelings associated with self-inflicted deaths.[2] In other cases, suicides may be unintentionally misclassified as accidents, even though certain automobile accidents, pedestrian deaths, or falling from high places may represent suicidal tendencies. Holinger,[23] in discussing violent deaths among adolescents, states that even homicides, especially those which are victim precipitated, may represent suicidal tendencies.

IDENTIFICATION OF SUICIDAL ADOLESCENTS: DIAGNOSTIC INDICATORS

Concern over the dramatic increase in adolescent suicide rates in the United States as well as in other Western nations over the past two decades has been reflected in the number of publications devoted strictly to adolescent suicide.[17,21,24,42] This literature suggests numerous biographical and psychological factors which are frequently found among adolescents who have completed or attempted suicide. Attention to such factors, which often provide clear warning signs, may assist in the early identification of individuals at high risk for suicide and may ultimately lead to the prevention of many suicides.

One approach to the study and organization of suicidal indicators is based upon the idea that the act of suicide is the culmination of a developmental process which begins in childhood.[24,42] In general, this process involves three identifiable stages, the first of which is a long-standing history of problems from childhood to early adolescence, primarily involving social and family instability. These environmental problems may play a role in the development of essentially stable personality characteristics which are often related to chronic suicidal risk.[15,16] Within the context of a problematic history, the second identifiable stage commences with the onset of adolescence and involves an escalation of problems and acute behavioral changes. Finally, there is a stage immediately preceding the suicide attempt, often involving a total breakdown of interpersonal relationships,[24,42] or failure situations[15,16] which dramatically increase immediate suicidal risk. Thus, a longitudinal perspective of the suicidal adolescent would often reveal a sequence of events leading up to the suicidal act.

Based upon research on adolescent suicide attempters carried out at the Los Angeles County-University of Southern California Medical Center, Teicher[42] claims that the five years prior to the suicide attempt are frequently marked by personal, medical, social, and family difficulties. In 72% of the reported cases, one or both natural parents were absent from the home due to divorce, separation, or death. Separation from parental figures at critical periods of development has frequently been implicated as a major factor in predisposing an adolescent to suicide.[40] In one study, twenty-three of forty-five adolescent suicide attempters had lost one or both natural parents.[3] Another study revealed 65% of the attempters came from broken homes,[44] while Margolin and Teicher[30] identified early and chronic separation trauma, with fathers being absent from the family in eleven of thirteen cases.

Glaser[20] states that loss or abondonment of a parenting figure provokes grief, anger, and depression in the adolescent, and in the case of a parental death, they may express suicidal thoughts in the wish to join the parent. Guilt may be prevalent, especially when the relationship with the parent was poor and conscious or subconscious death wishes were present. Self-accusations, depression, and self-punishing behaviors are attempts to atone for the guilt. Dorpat, Jackson, and Ripley[13] stated that unresolved object loss in childhood results in an inability to sustain object losses in later life. This in turn leads to depressive reactions culminating in suicidal behavior. They commented further that parental death was more often a factor in completed adolescent suicides, while attempted suicides more frequently experienced losses through desertion or divorce.

In addition to separation from one or both parents, Teicher[42] summarizes a number of additional factors which were frequently found among adolescent suicide attempters. It was found, for example, that 84% of those with stepparents were contending with an unwanted stepparent, 58% had a parent who was married more than once, 62% had both parents or their only parent working, and 16% had problems with a parent due to parental alcoholism. The average number of serious, problem-making environmental changes experienced by the adolescent suicide attempter was 10.42, and included events such as parents getting remarried, hospitalizations, deaths, school changes, siblings leaving home, and being in juvenile hall. They had 53% more environmental changes than a control group, 15% more residential mobility, and were far more subject to unexpected and often multiple separations from meaningful social relationships earlier in life than were control subjects.

Tuckman and Connon[43] also described poor home conditions, disorganization and parental disharmony in the lives of adolescent suicide attempters, and Barter and his colleagues found that in those families where there wasn't a loss, there was the persistent threat of loss due to parental marital problems and frequent discussion of divorce.[3] Rosenkrantz[37] notes that such home situations do not provide the ego development, healthy identity crystalization, and intimacy necessary to resolve the adjustment problems of adolescence.

In some instances where the loss of a father occurs through separation or death, male suicide attempters are often cast into the role of "maternal husbands." While they cannot possibly fulfill this role, their dependency needs result in an identification with the mother's depressed state.[30] Frequently, the onset of suicide behavior occurred concurrently with serious suicidal preoccupations by the mother. Interestingly, Teicher[42] states that 40% of the suicide attempters in his study had parents, relatives, or close friends who attempted suicide, and 13% of the suicidal children in Shaffer's[41] study had first-degree relatives who made known suicide attempts. He points out that familiarity with suicide and modeling increase the risk of suicidal behavior.

Ambivalent parental attitudes toward the child may also be a factor in suicidal behaviors. Margolin and Teicher[30] found a large percentage of mothers of male adolescent suicide attempters who revealed that they had not wished for the pregnancy, and that they were depressed at the time of the infant's birth. In other cases, the mothers did not visit the adolescent suicide attempter while he was hospitalized. Sabbath[38] states that the adolescent is frequently viewed as a burden by these parents who may consciously or unconsciously wish that he did not exist. Such attitudes are conveyed both directly and indirectly to the adolescent who then may feel abandoned by his parents. He has become expendable, and the felt rejection sets off a suicide attempt. In one case familiar to the author, the parents conveyed mixed messages to their adolescent son who had made a previous suicidal gesture. While overtly expressing their concern and support, they left large quantities of medication in the kitchen cupboard, and a rifle with a large supply of ammunition "for hunting" in the boy's closet. Their ambivalent attitudes toward their son were quite striking!

Childhood experiences in environments which are nonsupportive, unpredictable, or overtly hostile may be related to the development of relatively stable personality characteristics which have been associated with high suicide risk. Shaffer[41] attempted to categorize personality characteristics of completed childhood suicides, and identified four separate types. Twenty-five percent of those cases which could be categorized were said to be "quiet, difficult to get through to, and uncommunicative"; another 25% had a chip on the shoulder, "felt people didn't like them and felt people were unduly critical of them;" 16% were "impulsive, had no self control, and were volatile and erratic"; and 16% were "perfectionistic, neat, tidy, methodical, self critical, had high standards, and were afraid of making mistakes." Parallel findings are reported in the literature on adult suicide attempters. Fawcett[15] and Fawcett and Susman[16] label these characteristics chronic prelethal features, and include such factors as a life-long inability to maintain warm, mutually interdependent relationships and an impaired capacity for interpersonal relating, the presence of paranoid symptomatology, a high frequency of loss of control, including episodes of rage and tantrumlike behaviors, and pathological perfectionism. Many of these features represent defenses against depression or depressive equivalents, and their breakdown or failure may greatly increase the risk of suicide.

In summary, suicidal risk appears to be greater for those adolescents who have experienced significant and repeated object losses, or who have grown up in an unstable or hostile environment which offers little support or opportunity to establish and maintain meaningful relationships. Clearly, not every adolescent who has experienced loss and instability will attempt suicide, however, constellations of long-standing problems and certain personality features may alert us to an individual who is insecure and less able to cope with the increased stresses encountered in adolescence.

Within the context of a long-standing history of problems, a second stage occurs in the process leading to a suicide attempt.[24,42] This stage involves an escalation of problems associated with the onset of adolescence and often includes acute behavioral changes. Many of the problems which occur at this time involve attempts by the parents to contend with a new, unfamiliar stage of development. The adolescent often feels misunderstood, punished inappropriately, and may try several adaptive techniques including rebellion, destructiveness, antisocial behavior, psychosomatic illness, and finally withdrawal as mechanisms to communicate with the parents.[42,45] The parents, however, may view these adaptive techniques as misbehavior and gradually the adaptive options narrow to a suicide attempt as an attention-getting device.[42]

In addition to behavior problems, the escalation stage may involve several other factors. Physical or mental illness within the family may contribute to the escalation of problems for the suicide attempter. Teicher[42] states that in 48% of the cases in his study, the adolescent, a parent or a sibling was treated for mental illness or a physical complaint within five years prior to the attempt. He points out that intrafamily illnesses and hospitalizations serve to disrupt seriously the usual composition and interaction of the family and add considerably to the problems encountered by the adolescent who may face the prospect of dropping out of school to care for the ill and manage the household, or the possibility of losing a parent through death.

Several authors [3,41,42] have found that many suicide attempters were not enrolled in school at the time of the attempt. Most often, adolescents were out of school for medical reasons, behavior problems or "lack of interest."[42] Shaffer[41] found that 40% of the cases in his sample were not at school the day before their death and in another study,[3] poor grades, truancy, and disciplinary problems were reported for thirty-five of the forty-five suicide attempters. In several cases, these problems had begun within one or two years of the attempt, and many adolescents had dropped out or were contemplating dropping out of school at the time of the attempt.

Related to truancy or expulsion from school, peer relations suffer and social ties begin to be cut off.[42] Many suicide attempters have few close friends and no one to turn to when they need to talk to someone about their problems. Very often the potential suicide attempter has such intense dependency needs that his peers are threatened and ultimately reject him.

As a breakdown in social contacts begins, the adolescent may also begin to demonstrate acute behavioral changes. Otto,[35] in a study of presuicidal behavior change among Swedish children and adolescents, found the most common change to be neurotic, depressive symptoms such as agitation, insomnia, psychosomatic disturbances, and anxiety. Frederick[18] lists some acute behavioral clues preceding suicidal behavior, including the giving away of a prized possession, stating that it isn't needed anymore, a tendency to be more morose than usual, and the presence of some depressive symptoms such as worry, insomnia, and anorexia. Fawcett[15] and Fawcett and Susman,[16] in discussing acute prelethal features, point out the importance of recognizing abrupt clinical change. In some cases increased activity or even euphoria in a depressed patient has been observed to precede suicide, while in other cases a sudden worsening of a clinical state may signal a serious suicide attempt. At this stage, direct inquiry into a patient's thoughts may reveal a suicidal plan, including the method of suicide. Additional behavioral indicators of acute suicidal risk may include the development of an attitude of hopelessness, help negation, and the failure of previously intact psychological defenses.[15,16]

The final stage in the process leading to the adolescent suicide attempt generally involves a trigger situation or event. Jacobs[24] and Teicher[42] have discussed the role of the teenage romance in this process. They state that by the end of the escalation period, the parents have been totally alienated, and the adolescent seeks out a teenage romance to re-establish the spontaneity, openness, and intimacy that was a perceived part of an earlier relationship with the parents. Considerable energy and time is expended on this relationship, to the total exclusion of casual friendships. Thus, when the romance fails, the adolescent is left with no one and feels totally abandoned and isolated. They found 36% of all suicide attempters were in the terminal stages of a serious romance and 22% of all girls attempting suicide were pregnant or believed themselves to be pregnant as a result of their romance. Pregnancy further alienates the adolescent from society, and with the isolation complete, death appears to be the only solution.

The situational precursor implicated in the teenage romance is that of loss of the only remaining meaningful relationship left to the adolescent. Several additional studies have documented the loss of a significant person as a precipitating cause in suicide attempts.[3,17,44] In one study,[3] 66% of the attempts followed a loss or threatened loss of an object relationship. Thirty-three percent of the attempts grew out of an argument with a parent, while several others took place following a break up or threatened break-up with a boyfriend or a girlfriend.

Situational precursors of suicide may also include physical illness, and failure situations. Fawcett and Susman[16] cite a number of studies which found that suicidal risk was considerably higher in the presence of poor physical health. In the circumstances of a malignant or incurable illness, critical suicidal periods appear to be during the diagnostic phase while there is considerable uncertainty regarding the prognosis, and when the patient first realizes the upheavals and suffering which may follow. Suicidal risk is also higher for patients who fear important facial or body disfigurement as a result of surgery. Other patients may become obsessed with a given set of symptoms, or the completely erroneous belief or delusion that a certain disease is present.

A failure situation may also trigger a suicide or suicide attempt in a depressed individual. Frequently, this occurs when a patient is discharged from a hospital setting and attempts to resume normal functioning. The normal demands of a job or school are perceived as overwhelming. Actual failure or anticipation of failure may reactivate feelings of hopelessness and ultimately lead to the suicide attempt.[15] It has been pointed out that among college students, suicide attempts may follow the failure of an academic course. Sartore[39] states that the act in such cases appears greatly disproportionate to the situation. On the surface, the act of suicide may indeed appear disproportionate as a response to a difficult environmental situation. Frequently, there are statements communicating surprise and disbelief that such a "normal-appearing" and "well-adjusted" adolescent would take his own life. There is often little basis for predicting an impending suicide since adolescents are not prone to share problems with adults, nor are common clinical signs of depression always present. The preceding material, however, suggests that the suicide attempt is the endpoint of a developmental process with identifiable stages. Even a minimal biographical sketch of an adolescent may reveal factors often associated with suicidal behavior: a long-standing history of problems with recurring losses, family instability, and few meaningful relationships; an escalation of problems with the onset of adolescence and acute behavioral changes; and finally, increasing isolation and withdrawal as a result of additional object losses, physical illness, or failure situations. Without question, a clinical assessment of adolescents ought to include a detailed developmental history as a first step, giving careful consideration to the foregoing factors. While not every suicidal act can be predicted or prevented, knowledge of such suicidal indicators may go a long way toward identification and prediction of those individuals likely to take their own lives.

PREDICTION OF SUICIDAL RISK USING PSYCHOLOGICAL TESTS AND MEASURES

Increasingly high suicide rates and the need to quickly identify persons who are serious suicide risks have promoted continued research interest in the use of psychological tests and measures to predict suicidal behavior. The research in this area is complicated by numerous methodological problems,[25,27,28] many of which are related to difficulties in obtaining psychological test data on sufficient numbers of persons who eventually complete suicide in order to validate test predictions. This problem often led researchers to substitute test data on suicide attempters for that on completed suicides, claiming that much could be learned about suicide by studying the suicide attempters. The results of many studies were therefore based upon combined data from completed suicides, suicide attempters, and even those who had threatened but not attempted suicide. This methodology can be criticized in that suicide attempters may be quite different from those who complete suicide. One recent study demonstrated that only those suicide attempters who were "highly intent" on killing themselves are similar to completed suicides on measures of hopelessness and depression.[29]

A second major methodological problem involves the temporal relationship between test administration and the suicidal act. Ideally, test data should be collected immediately prior to the suicidal act since major personality changes may occur in the days or hours preceding the event. Such data, however, are unlikely to be obtained and certainly not in numbers large enough to statistically validate test predictions. The alternative is to obtain test data on large numbers of high-risk individuals and then follow the sample to determine who commits suicide. Unfortunately this method can be quite expensive and considerable attrition of the sample may occur during the follow-up interval.

Difficulties in validating suicide predictions from psychological test data may also result from ethical considerations.[15] The goal of correctly predicting suicide in itself constitutes a clinical failure. Ethically, if we identify an individual at high risk, some intervention should be made on the individual's behalf. This intervention then "interferes" with the validation of test predictions. Fawcett,[15] in considering the ethical question, has stated that prospective studies of individual prediction may be very difficult, if not inhuman, to carry out.

Despite the numerous problems characteristic of this research area, investigators have continued to be enticed by the possibility that persons who take their own lives may indicate their intent on an ink-blot[25] or in responses to specially constructed suicide scales. Unfortunately, very little work has been carried out on the prediction of adolescent suicide using psychological tests, although several studies have combined late adolescent and adult subjects. While the results of these studies cannot necessarily be generalized to strictly adolescent populations, attention to the research problems and current state of knowledge in the literature suggests directions for future research on the prediction of adolescent suicide.

Lester[27] reviewed the early attempts to utilize psychological tests as an aid in the recognition of potential suicides, considering both standard psychological tests and measures designed especially to assess suicide risk. He concluded that of the standard psychological tests only the Rorschach and MMPI had potential as predictors of suicidal behavior.

The Rorschach as a Suicide Predictor

Neuringer[23] reviewed the literature on research using the Rorschach to identify and predict suicidal behavior. He classified studies using the Rorschach into four groups: investigations of determinants and ratios, single signs, multiple signs, and content. Only those studies using single and multiple signs seemed to yield reliable results, with the signs identified by Martin [32] being of particular value. Further research on Rorschach signs by Appelbaum and Holzman[1] demonstrated that the use of color and shading as a determinant of at least one response was more frequent in those who had attempted suicide than in comparison groups. While many of the early studies seemed to offer promising results, Lester[27] reports that replication studies were often inconsistent and the studies were characterized by methodological problems.

More recently, Blatt and Ritzler[6] reported that individuals who commit suicide give a greater number of transparency (e.g., "a light bulb") and cross-sectional (e.g., "x-ray") responses on the Rorschach than matched nonsuicidal controls. An attempted replication study,[25] however, found no differences between completed suicides and nonsuicidal control subjects in the number of transparency and cross-sectional responses. Neither were differences found between the groups in Barrier or Penetration categories, decay responses (reference to death, destruction, rotting flesh, a diseased body part, etc.), or color-shading responses, all of which had been previously suggested as useful suicide predictors. Finally, the results of a recent study suggest that when the number of transparency, translucency, and cross-sectional responses were totaled, a suicide group showed a significantly greater number of criterial responses than did a control group.[36] When transparency and cross-sectional responses were analyzed separately, however, there were no differences between the two groups. The authors conclude that the study represented a satisfactory crosss-validation of the findings of Blatt and Ritzler[6] and that a single sign on the Rorschach may be a useful predictor of suicide.

Results of current research appear to offer some support for the predictive value of single or multiple signs on the Rorschach. The evidence is not clear-cut, however, leading some authors to conclude that the value of the Rorschach for predicting suicide remains limited,[14,25] and that other techniques may be more diagnostically sensitive.[34]

The MMPI as a Suicide Predictor

In summarizing many of the early studies on the use of the MMPI as a suicide predictor, Lester[27] stated that there is no evidence for the utility of any single MMPI scale for the identification of attempted suicides. An alternative approach, however, using profile analysis was found to be somewhat more promising. Devries and Farberow[11] studied groups of patients who had threatened suicide prior to testing, who had attempted suicide before testing, and a nonsuicidal group. They also looked at a sample of MMPIs from patients who had completed suicide. Considering only the Pa, Sc, Pt, Ma, Pd, and D scales, they found that the groups could be distinguished from each other by means of the MMPI with greater accuracy than without the test. A later study,[12] however, showed that general trends for suicide patients were not identifiable, and a "suicidal" profile could not be demonstrated.

Marks and Haller[31] reported the results of large-scale study on emotionally disturbed adolescents in which an MMPI had been routinely administered. Significant MMPI differences for boys were found on scales 1 and 5; with suicide attempters scoring higher than nonattempters. For girls, MMPI profiles yielded significantly higher scores for attempters on scales 2 and 3, as compared to nonattempters. They concluded that suicidal adolescents have many unique characteristics, however, they also point out striking sex differences which suggest that the sexes should be studied separately.

Recent studies using the MMPI to predict suicidal behavior among psychiatric patients have yielded rather discouraging results. In one study,[8] multivariate procedures were used to determine whether suicidal and nonsuicidal psychiatric patients could be differentiated on the basis of MMPI profiles. A discriminant analysis for males showed that nearly all patients were correctly classified in the original analysis; however, when cross-validation was carried out, all suicidal male patients were misclassified. For females, cross-validation also weakened the degree of differentiation between suicidal and nonsuicidal patients. The authors question whether the degree of differentiation between suicidal and nonsuicidal patients found in several early studies would have similarly been obliterated if the results had been cross-validated.

In another study, Clopton and Baucom[7] presented MMPI profiles of twenty male psychiatric patients who commited suicide and MMPI profiles of twenty patients who did not attempt or complete suicide to six highly qualified psychologists with expertise in MMPI interpretation. The clinicians were asked to classify each MMPI profile as coming from a patient who did or did not later commit suicide. Results of the study indicated that the judges could not differentiate between the MMPI profiles of patients who commited suicide and the patients who did not commit suicide. Only 36% of the patients were correctly classified, a situation which becomes even more discouraging since the judges were not clinicians with routine training in MMPI interpretation, but rather individuals recognized for their expertise in the use of MMPI.

Despite some promising results in the earlier MMPI literature, several well-designed and appropriately cross-validated studies have recently found little evidence that standard MMPI scales or MMPI profile analysis can reliably predict suicide at useful levels. Clopton and Baucom[7] conclude that predictions of suicide risk made on the basis of MMPI profiles are unlikely to be accurate enough to justify using the MMPI in suicide risk assessment.

Suicide Assessment Scales

In contrast to the use of standard psychological tests in the prediction and identification of suicide risk, Lester[27] discussed more favorably the use of specially constructed scales consisting of items characteristic of suicidal individuals. Devries,[10] for example, constructed a scale of thirteen items which differentiated suicidal patients from nonsuicidal patients at the .05 level of significance or better. Lester[26] administered the thirteen-item questionnaire to undergraduate students and found that it successfully differentiated nonsuicidal, considered suicide, and attempted or threatened suicide groups.

Recent work in this area has focused on the construction of scales to assess suicidal intent. Beck, Kovacs, and Weissman[4] reported on the reliability and validity of a suicidal intent scale for suicide attempters, and most recently have extended their investigations to suicidal ideators who may have plans and wishes to commit suicide but have not made overt suicide attempts.[5] They have focused on the intensity, pervasiveness, and characteristics of the ideation and wish in order to assess current suicidal intention and potentially to predict later suicidal risk. In addition, they have constructed a scale (The Scale for Suicide Ideation), in order to quantify relevant facets of suicidal intent applicable to suicide ideators, and they are conducting long-term prospective studies that may eventually establish its usefulness as a clinical predictor of suicidal risk.

CONCLUSION

The identification of individual adolescents who are at risk to take their own lives remains a difficult task requiring attention to a wide-range of diagnostic indicators. Literature in the area suggests that knowledge of various sociological and biographical factors gained through case histories and direct clinical interviews may be most helpful in improving our predictive capabilities. The majority of research related to the prediction of suicide using psychological tests and suicide assessment scales has been carried out on adult populations and cannot necessarily be generalized to adolescents. In the decade since Lester's[27] review on the use of psychological tests in suicide prediction first appeared, little progress has been made in this area despite increasing clarification of research goals and methodologies. Lester's[27] statement that the use of standard psychological tests in the prediction and identification of suicidal risk has not been fruitful, and the level of prediction is too low to warrant individual application remains true at present. Alternatively, he pointed to the potential of suicide assessment scales consisting of items based on admissions data and possibly incorporating certain signs from test protocols. The challenge for those interested primarily in the diagnosis and prediction of suicidal risk among adolescents appears to be in the direction of validating existing suicide scales on adolescent populations, or developing new scales more pertinent to adolescents.

REFERENCES

1. Appelbaum, S. A., and Holzman, P. S. The color-shading response and suicide. *J. Proj. Techniques* **26:**155–161 (1962).
2. Bakwin, H. Suicide in children and adolescents. *J. Pediatr.* **50:**749–769 (1957).
3. Barter, J. T., Swaback, D. O., and Todd, D. Adolescent suicide attempts: A follow-up study of hospitalized patients. *Arch. Gen. Psychiatry* **19:**523–527 (1968).
4. Beck, A. T., Kovacs, M., and Weissman, A. Hopelessness and suicidal behavior: An overview. *J. Am. Med. Assn.* **234:**1146–1149 (1975).
5. Beck, A. T., Kovacs, M., and Weissman, A. Assessment of suicidal intention: The scale for suicide ideation. *J. Consult. Clin. Psychol.* **47:**343–352 (1979).
6. Blatt, S. J., and Ritzler, B. Suicide and the representation of transparency and cross-sections on the Rorschach. *J. Consult. Clin. Psychol.* **42:**280–287 (1974).
7. Clopton, J. R., and Baucom, D. H. MMPI ratings of suicide risk. *J. Pers. Assess.* **43:**293–296 (1979).
8. Clopton, J. R., Pallis, D. J., and Birtchnell, J. Minnesota Multiphasic Personality Inventory profile patterns of suicide attempters. *J. Consult. Clin. Psychol.* **47:**135–139 (1979).
9. Corder, B. F. A study of social and psychological characteristics of adolescent suicide attempters in an urban, disadvantaged area. *Adolescence* **9:**1–6 (1974).
10. Devries, A. G. A potential suicide personality inventory. *Psychol. Rep.* **18:**731–738 (1966).
11. Devries, A. G., and Farberow, N. L. A multivariate profile analysis of MMPIs of suicidal and nonsuicidal neuropsychiatric patients. *J. Proj. Techniques* **31:**81–84 (1967).
12. Devries, A. G., and Shneidman, E. S. Multiple MMPI profiles of suicidal persons. *Psychol. Rep.* **21:**401–405 (1967).
13. Dorpat, T. L., Jackson, J. K., and Ripley, H. S. Broken homes and attempted and completed suicides. *Arch. Gen. Psychiatry* **12:**213–216 (1965).

14. Farberow, N. L. Use of the Rorschach in predicting and understanding suicide. *J. Pers. Assess.* **38**:411–419 (1974).
15. Fawcett, J. A. Saving the suicidal patient—The state of the art. *In: Mood Disorders: The World's Major Public Health Problem,* F. J. Ayd and I. J. Taylor (eds.), Baltimore: Ayd Medical Publications, 1978.
16. Fawcett, J. A., and Susman, P. The clinical assessment of acute suicidal potential: A review. *Rush Presbyterian St. Luke's Med. Bull.* **14**:86–104 (1975).
17. Finch, S., and Poznanski, E. *Adolescent Suicide.* Springfield: Charles C. Thomas, 1971.
18. Frederick, C. J. The school guidance counselor as a preventive agent to self-destructive behavior. *In: Self-destructive Behavior: A National Crisis,* B. Q. Hafen and E. J. Faux (eds.), Minneapolis: Burgess, 1972.
19. Frederick, C. J. Current trends in suicidal behavior in the United States. *Am. J. Psychother.* **32**:172–200 (1978).
20. Glaser, K. The treatment of depressed and suicidal adolescents. *Am. J. Psychother.* **32**:252–269 (1978).
21. Haim, A. *Adolescent Suicide.* New York: International Universities Press, 1970.
22. Holinger, P. C. Adolescent suicide: an epidemiological study of recent trends. *Am.J. Psychiatry* **135**:754–756 (1978).
23. Holinger, P. C. Violent deaths among the young: Recent trends in suicide, homicide, and accidents. *Am. J. Psychiatry* **136**:1144–1147 (1979).
24. Jacobs, J. *Adolescent Suicide.* New York: Wiley-Interscience, 1971.
25. Kestenbaum, J. M., and Lynch, D. Rorschach suicide predictors: A cross-validational study. *J. Clin. Psychol.* **34**:754–758 (1978).
26. Lester, D. Suicide as an aggressive act: A replication with a control for neuroticism. *J. Gen. Psychol.* **79**:83–86 (1968).
27. Lester, D. Attempts to predict suicidal risk using psychological tests. *Psychol. Bull.* **74**:1–17 (1970).
28. Lester, D. *Why People Kill Themselves—A Summary of Research Findings on Suicidal Behavior.* Springfield, Charles C. Thomas, 1972.
29. Lester, D., Beck, A. T., and Mitchell, B. Extrapolation from attempted suicides to completed suicides: A test. *J. Abnorm. Psychol.* **88**:78–80 (1979).
30. Margolin, N., and Teicher, J. D. Thirteen adolescent male suicide attempts. *J. Am. Acad. Child Psychiatry* **7**: 296–315 (1968).
31. Marks, P. A., and Haller, D. L. Now I lay me down for keeps: A study of adolescent suicide attempts. *J. Clin. Psychol.* **33**:390–400 (1977).
32. Martin, H. A. A Rorschach study of suicide. *Dissertation Abstracts* **20**:3837 (1960).
33. Neuringer, C. The Rorschach test as a research device for the identification, prediction, and understanding of suicidal ideation and behavior. *J. Projective Techniques* **29**:71–82 (1965).
34. Neuringer, C. Suicide and the Rorschach: A rueful postcript. *J. Pers. Assess.* **38**:535–539 (1974).
35. Otto, U. Changes in the behavior of children and adolescents preceding suicidal attempts. *Acta. Psychiat. Scand.* **40**:386–400 (1964).
36. Rierdan, J., Lang, E., and Eddy, S. Suicide and transparency responses on the Rorschach: A replication. *J. Consult. Clin. Psychol.* **46**:1162–1163 (1978).
37. Rosenkrantz, A. L. A note on adolescent suicide: Incidence, dynamics, and some suggestions for treatment. *Adolescence* **13**: 209–214 (1978).
38. Sabbath, J. C. The suicidal adolescent—The expendable child. *J. Am. Acad. Child Psychiatry* **8**:272–289 (1969).

39. Sartore, R. L. Students and suicide: An interpersonal tragedy. *Theory into Practice* **15**:337–339 (1976).
40. Schneer, H. I., and Kay, P. The suicidal adolescent. *In: Adolescents* S. Lorand and H. Schneer (eds.). New York: Hoeber, 1962.
41. Shaffer, D. Suicide in childhood and early adolescence. *J. Child. Psychol. Psychiatry* **15**:275–291 (1974).
42. Teicher, J. D. Suicide and suicide attempts. *In: Basic Handbook of Child Psychiatry,* J. D. Noshpitz (ed.), Vol. 2. New York: Basic Books, 1979.
43. Tuckman, J., and Connon, H. E. Attempted suicide in adolescents. *Am. J. Psychiatry* **119**:228–232 (1962).
44. Wenz, F. V. Sociological correlates of alienation among adolescent suicide attempts. *Adolescence* **14**:19–30 (1979).
45. Zeligs, R. *Children's Experience with Death.* Springfield: Charles C. Thomas, 1974.

Dr. Russell reviews the current status of the nuclear family and associated extended components and uses them as a frame within which to discuss the psychodynamics of runaways. Chaotic and disrupted home situations are more often found in the histories of runaways than abusive parents. Parent-related problems are however cited most frequently by those research studies of the problem. Acting-out by running away is accompanied by a search for closer interpersonal relations. The behavior itself is self-destructive reflecting inner hostility and consequent anxieties. What he describes as ego-shattering parental relations and kinetic substitutes for murderous rage are all involved in this behavior. He suggests considerations important for therapists, including a valuable description of the dynamics operating in such runaway decisions, and points out that not all families can benefit by counseling because of the personality and interpersonal relations of the parents themselves.

3
On Running Away

Donald Hayes Russell, M.D.

> Still as they run, they look behind,
> They hear a voice in every wind,
> And snatch a fearful joy.
> Alas, regardless of their doom,
> The little victims play;
> No sense have they of ills to come,
> Nor care beyond today.

These lines, written in 1742 by Thomas Gray[1] seem to capture well the spirit of the runaway child in modern times. We are well acquainted with the immediacy of their escapes and escapades, their hateful, longing, backward glances, their seeking and eager acceptance of the seductions of their freedom, and their buoyant sense of release and entitlement which counters fear in all that then befalls them.

Beginning in the 1960s and continuing through the 1970s and into the 1980s running away is an ever-increasing action or reaction among youths. This to the extent that in 1975 10.1% of all boys and 8.7% of all girls reported running away from home at least once, according to the National Center for Health Statistics. It is seen as a phenomenon of epidemic[2] proportions involving adolescents of all levels of society. They run from miserable ghettos, from affluent estates, and from the suburbias of the American dream. Might this then be basically a cultural phenomenon, perhaps consequent to, or congruent with our mobile society, the demise of the extended family, the fragmenting of the nuclear family, the intense climate of civil rights for the oppressed, easy survival with govenmental supports, the decline of religious influences, and the changes of traditional moral standards? Already in the 1950s[3] youth was becoming a caste rather than merely an age group, which then developed through the 1960s its counter-culture with its own causes, heroes, sages, and credos, epitomized by the grand celebration at Woodstock and the settling-in at Haight-Ashbury. While the extreme free-style of that era abated it has continued to have many influences upon our society, particularly with our young people. The ideas of "doing one's thing," of not having to accept arbitrarily imposed standards, and the freedom to leave an environment considered as restrictive or oppressive for a more compatible one, seems now, to a greater or lesser extent, to be passports of youth. While there have always been runaway children, it would appear that never has the social climate been so conducive as in these recent years.

Three earlier periods of manifest mobility in the history of this country may be cited: the colonization of the eastern seaboard, the great western movement, and the migration from farms to cities in the early years of the Industrial Revolution. While such migrations involved whole families, offering shared opportunity for economic betterment, the atmosphere of progress was such that individual youths of economically or emotionally oppressive home situations could see running away as a path to bettering their lot in life. Even so, in those times a child was firmly considered as belonging to the family and a child on the loose was an anathema. Unless a runaway boy was especially bright and strong, able to hold himself and work as a man, he was most likely to be ostracized or victimized, and if he had to resort to even petty crimes for his support, punishments were indeed most severe. The much fewer number of girls who ran away from home were seen as particularly disgraced and degraded, were everywhere unacceptable, and could only descend to the demimonde.

In those earlier years the progression of maturing from childhood to adulthood was an implicit operational process within the family structure. Boy-father and girl-mother role modeling were inherent, with graduated chores, tasks, and responsibilities manifesting the interdependence necessary for family survival. Even if children were not loved, in the deeper sense, they were needed, valued, had their place, and their identity was well formulated. Pervasive in all of this was the rigid system of morality and discipline, the boundaries between right and wrong, between good and evil, were clearly set, there were no gray areas and few, if any choices, and sanctions were immediate. This system was supported and reinforced by the extended family, the smaller and larger community, and the churches. It was never a consideration that children were being exploited, or that the often severe punishments constituted "child abuse." Children were so bound in their families that running away was practically unthinkable, and even in adolescence there was usually more to be gained by staying than by leaving. Many adolescent needs were automatically met, appropriate status and responsibilities conferred, needs for personal autonomy recognized, outlets for self-expression and self-realization provided, and mechanisms for controls and sublimations of developmental conflicts well internalized.

A recognition of the emotional needs of adolescents as integral with the need to prepare them for and initiate them into the adult society is as old as civilization itself. Aboriginal cultures gave this great importance with their formalized puberty rights, similar traditions continued through the Greek and Hebrew cultures, and with abridgements in some societies of more recent times. Adolescence may be seen as a developmental phenomenon, the product of physiological, psychological, and physical factors and forces which results in the breaking of the emotional dependency on family ties in order that personal autonomy be attained, identity consolidated, and heterosexual adjustment be established. Because it is a time for rebelling, for consideration of self over others, for power struggles and contentiousness, or ebulliousness with much need for tension release, prowess, and excitement, the adolescent, more often than not, has a considerable impact upon the status quo of the family. As a demanding force from within, adolescence may find expression and attain its goals in a favorable milieu, or may be met by serious counter-forces in family and society.

While it seems little recognized, some parents may experience real depression with their child's growing up in adolescence, changing and withdrawing from them, as it signals the end of a pleasant era, as well as the fact that they are growing older and things will never be the same again. Such depression is often expressed only in anger, intolerance, and withdrawal of needed supports from the child. Similarly where parents, for some reasons of circumstance within themselves, have from early on harbored an ambivalent attitude towards a particular child, such may reinforce the adolescent's own ambivalence about trying to break away from them to the point of his setting up situations to force their complete rejection of the child. Parents whose own adolescence was difficult and traumatic but who have repressed it are apt to become exceedingly anxious, sometimes to an irrational degree as their child comes into adolescence. The parents' own fears and doubts may then be projected upon the child, disrupting completely the child-parent relationship and driving the child to make more than prophesy of the parent's overconcerns. These are all situations which come to our attention, where in intact, seemingly well-ordered and caring families an adolescent becomes increasingly alienated, intractible, and provocative with mounting hostile interactions and confrontations with parents culminating in running away from home.

Illness or death of a parent in early or midadolescence is often very upsetting, sometimes devastating to a child; as may be any marked change in family circumstances, family moves from the family's neighborhood, and of course separation and divorce. The death of one parent, important in itself, may virtually involve the loss of both parents because of the immobilizing grief and depression in the remaining one. It is surprising to see how frequently children are not helped to share in grieving but are left to suppress, sometimes to act out, attendant feelings of deprivation and anger. Adolescence in itself is such an unstable state that a reasonably stable setting is prerequisite for its appropriate exercise. Though there may be much rebeling, resenting, even demeaning of parents and their standards, conversely, adolescents need their parents, need them to be healthy and well organized. When a father becomes ill or unemployed a situation may be created that can cause panic in a youngster. The familiar town, neighborhood, and particularly the long-term friends and acquaintances provide a great deal of stability for the adolescent process. With moving the peer group is lost and family dependence intensified, causing considerable conflict in adolescents which may lead to running away back to familiar scenes and relationships.

While there still seems a Machiavellian lack of appreciation, by all parties concerned, including the Courts, of the complex influences of marital separation, divorce and child custody disputes upon the emotional well-being and development of younger children, the incidence of adolescent problems, runaways, emotional disturbance, delinquency, and suicides from such broken homes is undeniable. The prodrome of divorce is often of considerable duration, with the children being witness to, even party to, the intense marital discord fraught with recriminations and denigrating blame-setting, mental and sometimes physical abuse. In divorce itself the children are as pawns in the battle for custody and visitation rights, which continue unrelentingly the same hostile themes. Such gross and perseverating emotional conflicts between the significant figures of their lives may seriously affect their developing sense of human trust and self-worthiness.

Not uncommonly in fatherless homes a son may be cast in the role of the father-husband of the family in a kind of conscious-unconscious conspiracy between mother and son. While the "little man" may shine in this role for a time, he can hardly withstand the threats of sexualization inherent in unresolved oedipal issues which arise in early adolescence. Then, flight may be a son's only available defense, often running to, or in search of the needed father, or allying himself with irresponsible older delinquent youths, seeking masculine identification and support in the bad image of the only father he ever had. Daughters in the custody of fathers may be caught up in a conversely similar experience, running away into devastating sexualized relationships of a self-destructive nature. It is also to be considered that with the presence of only one parent, usually the mother, in the home, an inordinate emotional burden may be placed on that singular relationship, creating an excessive degree of dependency which is all the harder for children to free themselves from in adolescence.

After divorce and also with the death of a parent sometimes comes remarriage with the advent of a stepparent and perhaps stepbrothers or sisters. It is observed that the stories of numbers of runaway boys and girls claiming rejection and abuse at the hands of stepparents would substantiate the legends of wicked stepmothers and cruel stepfathers. Most stepparents do seek to invest themselves and are used by the children very much as "real" parents to meet their developmental needs; in the earlier years needs for affection, caring, dependency, and identification and in adolescence as objects to devalue and rebel against. In this latter, however, the stepparent may have to bear the extra burden of anger and hostility projected from the child's inner feelings about desertion by the "real" parent. Some mothers, for neurotic reasons, may seek to maintain an exclusive relationship with a particular child (as can happen within a first marriage as well as a second) disallowing, even sabatoging the stepparent's exercising of any constructive parental role. The child loses out in such a situation, and when in adolescence serious acting out occurs in an effort to break the one-sided dependence, it may well be the stepparent who is scapegoated.

Family disruptions which necessitate the placing of children away from their home produce many disorganizing emotional conflicts which can render their adjustment in any new living situation problematical and can predispose them to running away. Such children feel hurt, lost, and completely dispossessed. As they cannot sort out their anger from their compensatory hopes and fantasies for idealized family reunion, they in turn reject helping efforts, as they were rejected, and take flight on their fantasies. It is noted that returning a child home in adolescence, after a more or less satisfactory placement in earlier years, may bring explosion of the long-harbored fantasies with release of the suppressed hostility. Thus, confronted with not belonging anywhere a severe compulsive pattern of running from everywhere may establish itself.

Though adolescence of itself may provide the capabilities and motive forces for running away, some children are prone to running at much earlier ages. Prepubertal and younger children who manifest this behavior may categorically be considered as severely emotionally disturbed or suffering from extreme chronic neglect with the absence of basic care and supervision. The so-called "hyperactive" children constitute a significant percentage of the younger runaways, some being known to begin to take off as soon as they are able to walk. Much is written[4] about this condition which manifests itself in early infancy and is characterized by marked restlessness and destractibility, defective attention, mercurial emotional reactivity, tempestuousness, destructiveness, and consequent poor relatedness to others. Another, perhaps rarer and less clinically recognized group, are children who have shown a particular emotional disturbance since early infancy. They are variously diagnosed as "Primitive Emotional Disturbance," "Unsocialized Aggressive Reaction of Childhood," and "Untamed and Friendless: A Syndrome of Arrested Narcissism."[5] These children are characterized by their pervasive primary narcissism with its lack of objects, which exist for them only in terms of primitive ego needs for original omnipotence, and its inability to bind primitive reactive impulses by counter-cathexis. While not psychotic, they show only scanty defenses against both hostility and libidinous wishes, which appear consequently in speech and behavior with assaultiveness, fire-setting, sexual misbehavior, and running away being frequent concommitants. The triad of "firesetting, eneuresis and cruelty to animals"[6] which has frequently been quoted in the literature as prognostic of serious delinquency seems to apply more specifically to this group rather than to delinquency or firesetting in general.

As the tasks of adolescent development embody much that is contrary to their previous experience and existence, regression and remission in certain ego functions occur, allowing for a justifying sense of legitimacy in the expression of their drives for self-realization. However, in adolescence there is characteristically a resurgence and surfacing of any unresolved intrapsychic issues which may exist concerning remnants of developmental conflicts and unmet earlier emotional needs. These may be the consequences of early emotional deprivations and rejections with deficiencies in capacities of object relationships, of compromised identification processes with faulty defense mechanisms for managing aggression and passivity and an incomplete sense of self, and of unresolved oedipal issues. The externalization and projection of such emotional artifacts, often with great force and self-justification, can be most disruptive of child-family relationships, creating situations which may be escaped or perversely satisfied only in running away. As if in retribution, for rejection, they reject in turn; for deprivation, they feel entitled. The poor self-image which they feel has been inflicted upon them they embrace and exercise in illicit, often self-injurious behavior and activities.

Much has been written on the subject of runaways, and in reviewing the professional literature it becomes apparent that observations may reflect differences in view of their having been made in quite different circumstances and of rather different groups of children. Runaways are seen and studied in the offices of private clinicians, in child guidance clinics, social service agencies, protective service agencies, in voluntary runaway shelters, by juvenile police bureaus, by juvenile courts, probation and court clinics, in juvenile detention facilities and in juvenile institutions. Some are long-distance runners, some are gone for months, some only stay away overnight, some are perpetually running, and with some there are concommitant reported delinquencies while with others there are not. Jenkins[7] in his study of runaway behavior in the context of formal psychiatric diagnostic categories cites three pertinent groups: "runaway reaction," "unsocialized aggressive reaction," and "group delinquent reaction." The runaway reaction child is seen as emotionally immature, apathetic and seclusive, is unwanted and rejected at home and comes from a small family. The unsocialized aggressive child shows the most psychopathology of the three groups. The group delinquents showed more normal personality profiles, were socialized with an adaptive, aggressive, albeit predatory style. Wolk and Brandon[8] in investigating a solicited sample of adolescents from runaway houses in sururban Maryland found that: "(a) runaway adolescents report more punishment and less support from their parent; (b) runaway girls report the most and runaway boys the least degrees of parental control; (c) runaways hold a less favorable self-concept, specifically on the dimensions of anxiety, self-doubt, poor interpersonal relationships, and self-defensiveness; (d) runaways also manifest as an aspect of the self, a readiness for counselling." They further state: "Therefore, runaway adolescents, compared to non-runaways, manifest a self-concept that is more defensive, self-doubting and less trusting. It is a self-concept that also reflects a difficulty in maintaining interpersonal relationships and a preoccupation with and a pessimism for resolving personal problems." They interpret the runaway act "as an extreme form of response to what is perceived by the adolescent as a lack of validation of the struggle for autonomy," and further opine "that runaway boys may be responding to the absence of sufficient control, while runaway girls are repelled by too much control." Reilly[9] in his analysis of fifty girls charged in the Boston Juvenile Court with running away noted their associated self-destructive behavior and the prevalence of severe family disturbance which reflected in part the urban areas of their residences. In his series evidence indicated that there was marked anxiety around conflicts of the oedipal type, "in part because sexual impulses and control of anger were not adequately developed in these girls who, in general, had a poor self-image and low self-esteem. The basic relationship with neither parent was sufficiently strong to deal with the anxieties resulting from these conflicts." He stresses the self-destructive degraded position in which these girls place themselves, with their sexually promiscuous involvement with older boys and men with the high risk of pregnancy, venereal disease, and subsequent prostitution, as well as their record of drug involvement and overdoses, with or without suicidal intent. It is interesting to note that an earlier study of Robey,[10] of runaway girls in a Court Clinic serving middle-class suburban communities, also stressed anxieties and conflicts over oedipal issues as motivational and in their families the disturbances tended to be more covert, but were nonetheless present and operational.

Leventhal[11,12] in his study of a group of runaway children focused on the subject of control in general rather than on drive-conflicts. Having established the finding that "runaways perceived themselves as having relatively little control over external happenings (termed "outer uncontrol"), he then investigated the "inner control-uncontrol" and the relationship between control over inner events and control over outer events. Contrasted with a control group of nonrunaways, he found that runaways manifested "significantly more inner-uncontrol and gave more indications of discharge type behavior, of deficient regulatory mechanisms, and of a helpless self-image." It is noted that his sample, half police referred and half "noncorrectional," consisted of twenty-seven boys and fifteen girls, with a median age for boys of 12.7 years, and girls 14.8 years. Saunders, et al.,[13] believing the construct of impulsivity to be deserving of critical examination, particularly as it seems commonly applied to adolescence and delinquency, divided the entire population of a state training school into runners and nonrunners, subjecting both groups to a battery of impulsivity rating scales. They concluded that empirical evidence based on standard tests of impulsivity did not support the popular hypothesis that delinquents are more impulsive than are nondelinquents; or the notion that running away from reform school is an impulsive delinquent behavior, and that, in terms of correlations between standard measurements of impulsivity, the conception of impulsivity as a unitary character trait is not supported.

A one-year follow-up interview study of a selected group of runaways is reported by Howell, et al.[14] They culled forty-one runaways (eighteen girls, twenty-three boys) from the records of the 649 "visitors" to Project Place, the principal runaway haven in Boston during the year 1970. Their sample was restricted to "youngsters who had run away for more than three days from two-parent families that appeared stable, i.e., had not been described by the youngsters as troubled by parental quarreling, alcohol or drug abuse, or child abuse." The majority seemed to have come from middle-class families. It appeared "that the majority were troubled (before running away) by rather ordinary problems of growing up," and for only 10% was there any indication of a major behavior problem prior to the run. While the runaways of their sample varied in their verbal abilities, the authors questioned if runaways as a group are relatively inarticulate, unable to conceptualize their problems and work them out in words, and thus committed to action that may be self-destructive. In recounting their experiences of running and their situations at home a year later, 74% of the boys and 78% of the girls said that their lives were better now than before they had left; relationships with mothers (reported as less troubled to start with) were seen as improved by 80% of the youngsters; relationships with fathers were seen as improved by 54%, boys reporting significantly more than did girls. While 60% of the boys and 72% of the girls said that in retrospect the running away had been a positive experience, only 11% of the boys and 17% of the girls said that they would recommend running away to a troubled sibling or friend.

Stierlin[15] presents a classification of runaways with formulations of relevant "transactional modes" of family dynamics. He grouped runaways as: abortive, lonely schizoid, casual, and crisis. For family investigation the "crisis" group seemed most pertinent. He conceived "transactional modes" as "transitional and interpersonal processes reflecting salient contributions of the parents and of the children, and operating as the covert organizing transactional background to the more overt and specific child-parent interactions." Three "modes" are described: the "binding mode" by which families interact with their offspring in ways which seem designed to keep the children locked into the family; the "expelling mode," where there are enduring neglect and rejection of children who are seen as nuisances and hindrances to the parents; and the "delegating mode" in which there is a blending of binding and expelling elements, the children being allowed a certain autonomy for the purpose of acting upon covert parental goals or fantasies. Gray and Gray[16] report the treatment of juveniles, in a court clinic, based on General System Precursor Formulation Theory, by which specific acts are seen as system formations which have developed in response to specific system precursors both intrapsychic and interpersonal. Truants and runaway children are seen as "locked in," the lock-in by parents being the precursor to the act of "breaking out" or running away.

To protect children, particularly younger children and children who are only stubborn, wayward, truants, or runaways and have not committed actions that would be crimes for an adult, from the possible legal abuses of the juvenile court process, new juvenile protectional laws were enacted in many states during the 1970s. An example is the Massachusetts law for Children in Need of Care which came into effect in 1973. It defines a new legal category, "a child in need of care," and instructs the court not to prosecute such cases but to implement their referrals to appropriate agencies, facilities or progams in the community for prescribed care, protection and treatment. The juvenile court still has jurisdictional responsibility with legal sanctions and due process applying in the apprehension of the child upon petition, making the investigation and determination, and detaining the child if deemed necessary, but the finding and the disposition are social rather than legal.

From our series of some 3000 juveniles who had been referred from the courts for clinical evaluation during the period from 1973 to 1979 a random sample of one hundred runaways who were under investigation as "Children in Need of Care" was taken for study. In the total series 72% were boys with the mean age of 15.2, and 28% were girls with the mean age of 14.9. Their court charges ranged from Stubborn to Murder, covering the gamut of delinquent acts and behaviors. Breaking and Entering, Larceny and Using a Motor Vehicle without Authority were the most common, with a descending incidence of Property Destruction, Assault and Battery, Arson, Armed Robbery, and Rape. Most of them were also truant and many had run away at one time or another. While the referrals were from statewide courts, the great majority of the children lived in the congested sections of the larger cities and were from welfare or working-class families. Divorce or separation had occurred in 49.7% of the families, serious parental illness in 26.1%, severe parental alcoholism in 20.1%, and in 16% of the families a parent had died. Clinically, of the total series, 12% were diagnosed as seriously emotionally disturbed, while the bulk of the others were seen as immature and unsupported children who were reacting rather extremely in adolescence to varying degrees of social, cultural, and emotional deprivations.

The runaway sample did not significantly differ in many respects and parameters from the greater series of delinquents from which it was drawn. Notably, however, the boy-girl proportions were reversed, 56% were girls and 44% were boys, and the mean ages were younger, being 14.5 for girls and 14.4 for boys. Even more notable are the findings that in the runaway sample the number of chaotic, disturbed, and disruptive home situations were twice as frequnt in occurrence as were the numbers of abusive, alcoholic fathers and of mothers who were alcoholic. On the other hand, 9% of the runaways came from intact, "middle-class" families which showed no outward signs of strife. The runaways were also frequently truants, 28% of the girls, 27% of the boys; and 16% of boys and girls alike had had behavior problems at school. Ninety percent of the children gave specific parent-related reasons for their running away: 28% (14% of girls, 14% of boys) ran because they felt that both parents were united in oppressing them; 46% (32% of girls, 14% of boys) because of very serious conflicts with their mothers; and 15% (5% of girls and 10% of boys) because they felt unbearably dominated and degraded by their fathers. It is usually impossible to document where children go when they run; but according to this sample 52% (37% of girls and 15% of boys) stayed with "friends," 9% of the girls ran explicitly to stay with older boy friends, and

32% (5% of girls and 27% of boys) spent the time "on the street." While on their runs 40% (8% of girls and 32% of boys) were involved in some forms of delinquencies; and 28% of the girls and 6% of the boys admitted to sexual activities. However, sexual acting out did not seem to appear as a special issue with this sample. Thre were several homosexual boys who ran to "hustle" on the streets, a few "normal" boys who occasionally sold their sexual favors, a number of girls who involved themselves sexually with peers or older men for one reason or another, and two girls who in connection with serious drug abuse had become prostitutes.

On psychometric testing (WISC-R) 19% of the sample were of above average intelligence (IQ: 105-130) contrasting with 3.4% of the larger series, but also there were more "Borderline-Retarded" (IQ: 60-80), 23% against 14.1%. Clinically, as a group the children of the sample gave the picture of exaggerated adolescent traits, self-centeredness, immature ego structures with a deficient sense of effective relatedness to others or to society at present or for the future, impoverishment with denial of passive needs, entitlement and defective self-image. Formal psychiatric diagnoses applied to only 24% of the sample: Psychotic—1%; Borderline Psychotic—7%; Primitive Character Disorder—4%; and Hysterical Character Disorder—12%. As might be expected there seemed little uniformity in the projective psychological testing records, although depression was notable in half the cases as were poor self-image, early deprivations, ambivalent parental images, poor impulse control, regressive tendencies, emotional immaturity and identity conflicts in a third. Definite self-destructive signs were seen in 10%. The findings of this study suggest that with few notable exceptions, a greater percentage of children of the highest and the lowest IQ spectrum, and the increased incidence of chaotic homes, the sample does not differ appreciably from the larger delinquent series.

Perhaps some generalizations may be made about the complex phenomena which seem to lead to running away, and the variously constituted children who do, from diverse homes and environments:

1. Running away is easier today, and is seen as a socially acceptable, or at least commonplace form of protest in adolescence.
2. There seems a greater prevalence of oppressive home situations today, either in terms of serious neglect or abuse, or in terms of increased tendencies for the direct, or indirect, externalization of emotional conflicts within families.
3. There is a greater number of incomplete and inadequately structured families which are unable to provide the emotional supports necessary to accomplishing the tasks of adolescent development.
4. Most runaways do manifest signs of immature or incomplete ego

development, in relation to themselves, their parents, and society. Some few are emotionally disturbed.

5. There are many self-harming implications in running away, but running can also be seen as a protection, as a defense against ego-shattering parental relationships, or against the acting out of murderous rage.[17]

The following considerations are most pertinent to dealing with the problems of runaways. It is important that special havens and shelters continue to be provided, not only for their security and protection but also for them to be helped to begin looking at themselves and their life situation. Whenever feasible, and in any possible way, families should be investigated and parents involved. However, as Zastrow[18] reports of some of his efforts to counsel such parents: "talking about conflicts with one's spouse is more socially acceptable than talking about parent-child conflicts." Also, it is seen that in some instances parent-child counseling may be unconstructive, even regressive, and that individual therapy, or even peer group placement for the adolescent may be indicated. It is essential that the legal handling of runaways as espoused in Children in Need of Care legislation continues to be improved and implemented in order to protect children and to bring them earlier and younger to the services which they require. We must never lose sight of the fact that runaway children are the indicators of, and the victims of family stress, cultural unrest, and social change.

REFERENCES

1. Gray, T. "On a Distant Prospect of Eton College."
2. Justice, B., and Duncan, D. Running away: An epidemic problem of adolescence. *Adolescence* **XI:**43, Fall 1976.
3. Lewis, P. *The Fifties.* New York, Lippincott, 1979.
4. Safer, D., and Allen, R. *Hyperactive Children: Diagnosis and Management.* Baltimore, MD: University Park Press, 1976.
5. Russell, D., and Harper, G. Untamed and friendless: A syndrome of arrested narcissism. Boston: Judge Baker Guidance Center, 1975.
6. Michaels, J. *Disorders of Character.* Springfield, Ill.: Charles C. Thomas, 1955.
7. Jenkins, R. The runaway reaction. *Am. J. Psychiat.* **128:**2, August, 1971.
8. Wolk, S., and Brandon, J. The runaway adolescent's perceptions of parents and self. *Adolescence* **12:**46, Summer 1977.
9. Reilly, R. What makes adolescent girls flee from their homes? *Clinical Pediatrics,* December, 1978.
10. Robey, A. The runaway girl. *In: Family Dynamics and Female Sexual Delinquency,* O. Pollak, and A. Friedman, (ed.) Palo Alto, CA: Science and Behavior Books, 1969.
11. Leventhal, T. Control problems in runaway children. *Arch. Gen. Psychiat.* **9,** 1963.
12. Leventhal, T. Inner control deficiencies in runaway children. *Arch. Gen. Psychiat.* **11,** August 1964.

13. Saunders, J., Reppucci, N., and Sarata, B. An examination of impulsivity as a trait characterizing delinquent youth. *Am. J. Orthopsychiat.* **43**:5, October, 1973.
14. Howell, M., Emmons, B., and Frank D. Reminiscences of runaway adolescents. *Am. J. Orthopsychiat.* **43**:5 October, 1973.
15. Stierlin, H. A family perspective on adolescent runaways. *Arch. Gen. Psychiat.* **29**, July 1973.
16. Gray L., and Gray, W. System precursor/system formation approval in the treatment of "locked in" children. Malden Court Clinic, Malden, MA 02148 (to be published).
17. Russell, D. Ingredients of juvenile murder. *Int. J. Offender Ther. and Comp. Criminology,* **23**:1, 1979.
18. Zastrow, C., and Navarre, R. Help for runaways and their parents. *Social Casework,* February 1975.

The authors point out that the significance of childhood suicide, which is a relatively rare occurrence in all countries, lies in what it can tell us about factors which prevent suicide. Suicide rates from 1964 to 1977 have been relatively stable for the ten to fourteen-year-old age group in contrast to an increase in the fifteen to nineteen-year-old group. The fact that suicide in the younger age group is relatively rare holds up even after careful examination of possible sources of error which would make for under-representation. The methods used by children to commit suicide are broadly similar to those used by adults. Three different conceptual models of suicide are reviewed and detailed characteristics of children who commit suicide are then presented. The consistent theme of the chapter is that children are protected from the suicidal urges shown by adults. The question of which factors protect children and adolescents from suicide is reviewed.

4
Suicide in Children and Young Adolescents

David Shaffer, M.B., B.S., M.R.C.P., M.R.R. Psych.D.P.M.
Prudence Fisher, B.A.

INTRODUCTION

A child's suicide is always a shocking event. It will distress those who knew the child and very often it will capture headlines. Relatives and journalists will often depersonalize the death and seek an explanation for it in the changing nature of society or a deteriorating educational system. The publicity given to any one incident may lead many to conclude that childhood suicide is an overlooked and growing phenomenon.

This chapter sets out to examine these issues and specifically to investigate:

1. How *often* children commit suicide.
2. Whether the frequency of childhood suicide is *increasing*.
3. *How* children commit suicide.
4. The extent to which we can *rely* upon official statistics to answer questions about childhood suicide.
5. What *type of child* commits suicide.
6. Whether it is possible to generalize on *societal influences* on suicide.
7. Whether we can *anticipate* or *prevent* childhood suicide.

We will confine ourselves to a review of knowledge about completed or "successful" suicide, although studies of attempted suicide will be referred to where approprite. Most emphasis will be put on childhood suicide, which we define as a self-inflicted death occurring before a child's fifteenth birthday, and this will be contrasted with adolescent suicide, i.e., death between ages fifteen and nineteen. These are convenient groupings for they coincide with those used by both the World Health Organization and the National Center for Health Statistics.

SUICIDE RATES

In 1977, 158 boys and 30 girls aged between ten and fourteen committed suicide in the United States. Only two children under the age of ten committed suicide. In that same year there were 19 million live 10–14 year old children in the United States yielding an age specific mortality rate from suicide of 1 in 102,000 (or 0.98 per 100,000). The 188 deaths represented 2.8% of all deaths occurring in this age group. It should be noted that whereas the 19 million live children represented just under 9% of the total U.S. population the 188 child deaths represented fewer than 1% of all suicides. (See Figure 4–1)

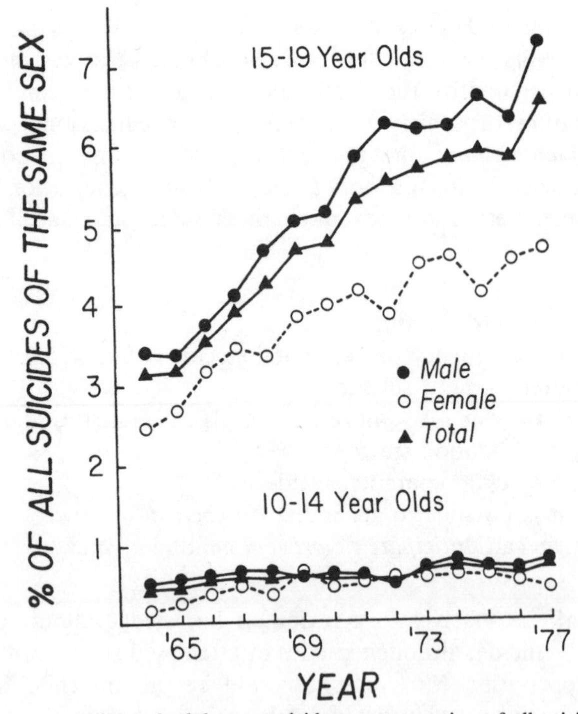

Figure 4–1. Child and adolescent suicide as a proportion of all suicides.

Statistics available for older adolescents (ages fifteen to nineteen) show that 1,521 boys and 350 adolescent girls committed suicide in the same year. The size of the population was 21 million so that the mortality rate was 1 per 11,280 live adolescents (or 8.87 per 100,000) i.e., nearly a tenfold increase over the younger age group. Suicide accounted for 8.7% of all deaths occuring in late adolescence. The 21 million live 15–19 year olds represented 10% of the population, although the 1,871 suicides represented only 6.52% of all suicides. (See Table 4–1)

These statistics reveal a *moderate* under-representation of suicide in the 15–19 year age group and a *very considerable* under-representation in 10–14 year olds. It follows from these findings that the significance of childhood suicide lies not in its importance as a public health problem—for the condition is a rare one—but rather in what it may tell us about factors which *protect* individuals from suicide. This protection seems to be a universal phenomenon for the proportion of suicides which occur in childhood is remarkedly similar in all countries from which sound data are available (See Table 4–2).

Even though completed suicide is rare in childhood and early adolescence, suicidal threats and attempts are not uncommon. Surveys of clinic populations in the United States and United Kingdom (Schneer and Kay, 1961; Mattsson, et al., 1969; Leese, 1969; Lukianowicz, 1968; and Marks and Haller, 1977) have been consistent in reporting that between 7 and 10% of all referrals to Child Psychiatric Clinics are for the investigation or treatment of threatened or attempted suicide. Suicidal children form an even larger proportion of referrals to child emergency or crisis clinics.

Table 4-1. Suicide by Age—1977.

AGE GROUP	TOTAL POPULATION N*	(%)	SUICIDE N	(%)
0–9	32417	(14.98)	2	(.01)
10–14	19203	(8.87)	188	(.66)
15–19	21105	(9.75)	1871	(6.52)
19+	143675	(66.39)	26620	(92.81)
Total	216400	(100.00)	28681	(100.00)

* in thousands

Source: Vital Statistics of the United States, 1977 Vol. *II, Mortality,* Part B (unpublished) U.S. Bureau of the Census *Current Population* Reports—Series P.25, No. 870.

Table 4-2. Proportion of all Suicides Committed by 5-14 Year Olds.

COUNTRY	YEAR	% OF TOTAL SUICIDE RATE
East Germany	1974	.8
West Germany	1976	.8
Switzerland	1977	.6
UNITED STATES	1976	.6
Finland	1975	.4
France	1976	.4
The Netherlands	1977	.4
Norway	1977	.4
Denmark	1977	.3
United Kingdom	1977	.2
Sweden	1977	.1

Source: World Health Statistics Annual, 1977.

SECULAR CHANGES

Changes in suicide rate over time provide potentially important data. However changes in rate could indicate either a change in some external influence of a change in reporting procedure. In turn, external influences do not necessarily take the form of a change in the precipitants of suicide. Rates may change as a result of increased or diminished opportunity or, where a method does not result in instant death, from an improvement in treatment techniques. An example of a fall in suicide rates consequent to diminished opportunity was noted after the introduction of nontoxic household gas to replace coal gas in certain cities in the United Kingdom. The effects of treatment availability can be seen in the high mortality rate from drug overdose in Bangalore in India. Sathyavathi (1975) noted that 53% of successful child suicides were alive at the time of discovery compared with only 6% in Shaffer's British series (1974).

Bearing in mind the difficulties in interpreting secular changes we find in reviewing suicide rates for children and adolescents over the period 1964 to 1977 (See Figure 4-2) that rates for the 10–14 year age group have been largely stable. This is in contrast to the sizeable increase in rate in the 15–19 year age group, among whom there has been an increase of 125% in males and 70% in females. The stability of the suicide rate in childhood is not confined to the recent past. Mulcock (1955) reviewed child suicide statistics in the United Kingdom for a 16-year period up until 1953 noting little change during that time.

Given the changes in environmental circumstances over the period covered by these reviews, the stability of rate for younger children suggests

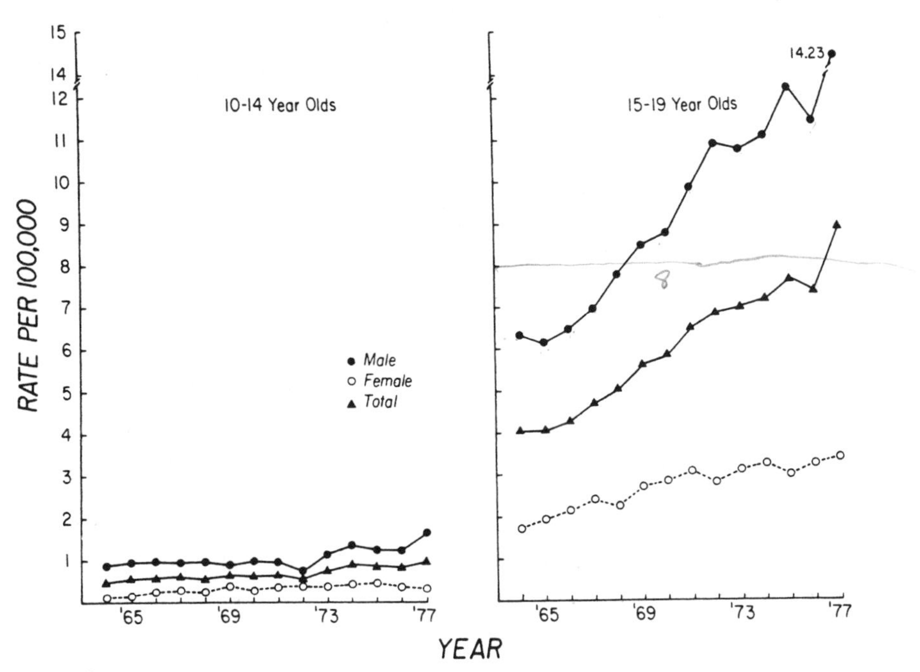

Figure 4–2. Changes in suicide rate for children and adolescents (1964–1977).

that there are strong protective factors and that these do not seem to be sensitive to the degree of environmental change that has been experienced during this time. This issue will be discussed at greater length in a subsequent section of this chapter.

DEMOGRAPHIC CHARACTERISTICS OF CHILD AND ADOLESCENT SUICIDES

The suicide rate for children and adolescents of differing age, sex and race during the year 1975 is provided in Figure 4–3. From this it will be seen that very few deaths occur before the age of thirteen, that suicide in childhood is more common at all ages in whites than nonwhites and that the ratio of males to females decreases with age. (See also Table 4–3)

Methods

The methods used by both children and adults to commit suicide vary with their acessibility. Thus, Sathyavathi (1975) reported that suicide by

Table 4-3. Child and Adolescent Suicide by Sex—1977

AGE GROUP	RATES OF SUICIDES—MALES:FEMALES
10–14 years	5.03
15–19 years	4.21
20–24 years	4.06
25–29 years	3.36

Source: Vital Statistics of the United States, 1977 Vol. *II, Mortality,* Part B (unpublished).

burning or drowning in household wells accounted for approximately 40% of deaths in children in the City of Bangalore from 1967 to 1973. These methods are extremely uncommon in North America and Western Europe. In the United Kingdom where access to firearms is restricted but where coal gas is used widely for cooking, gassing accounted for half of all child suicides over an 8-year period (Shaffer 1974). The most common methods currently used in the United States are listed in Table 4-4. Death by firearms is the most common method used with equal frequency by both sexes. This is followed by hanging, a method used predominantly by boys and then by death from drug overdose, a method used mainly by girls.

Table 4-4. Child and Adolescent Suicide in the U.S.A. 1973–1977. Methods Used—Ages 10–14

METHOD	MALE		FEMALE		TOTAL	
	N	%	N	%	N	%
Firearms and explosives	320	(47.62)	91	(48.67)	411	(47.85)
Hanging, strangulation, and suffocation	326	(48.51)	37	(19.79)	363	(42.26)
Poisoning by a solid or liquid substance	8	(1.19)	46	(24.60)	54	(6.29)
Poisoning by gases	7	(1.04)	2	(1.07)	9	(1.05)
Other	11	(1.64)	11	(5.89)	22	(2.56)
Total	672	(100)	187	(100)	859	(100)

Source: Mortality Statistics Branch, Division of Vital Statistics, National Center for Health Statistics, *Vital Statistics of the United States,* Volume *II, Mortality,* (published and unpublished data).

However even within the United States there are ethnically related differences. As an example, Hendin (1969) comparing methods used by different ethnic groups within New York City found that jumping from a high place accounted for a significantly greater proportion of deaths among blacks than whites.

Sex differences in method have been widely noted. Shaffer (1974) examined this question in his detailed study of a total population of child suicidees. Suicidal incidents were grouped into those with a high probability and those with a low probability of being lethal.

A method was considered to have a high probability of being lethal if its application was likely to result in instantaneous death or, if a slow-acting method was used, there was evidence of special precautions having been taken to ensure success. Methods were considered to have a low potential for being lethal when the method was both unlikely to result in rapid death *and* when the child had taken active steps to inform other people of his or her suicidal behavior. It was possible to dichotomize intent in this way in twenty-one out of the thirty cases studied. Fourteen boys but only one girl used a highly lethal method, a statistically significant difference. These findings suggest that sex differences in method reflect differences in intent rather than any sex specific dynamic related to the method. This is supported by the finding of a high female to male sex ratio in attempted suicide (Bergstrand & Otto, 1962) in contrast to a high male to female ratio in successful suicide.

RELIABILITY AND VALIDITY OF MORTALITY STATISTICS

We have used mortality statistics to show that successful suicide:

1. Is rare in prepubertal children.
2. Occurs more often in boys than girls, but that the sex ratio shows a trend to flatten out with increasing age.
3. Is performed in different ways by boys and girls.
4. Has shown little tendency to increase over the years in young children but has shown a marked tendency to increase in older adolescents, and
5. Occurs at different rates in different ethnic groups.

Bakwin (1957), Jacobziner (1965), Schrut (1964), Shaw and Shelkun (1965), Toolan (1975) and others have all suggested that the social stigma associated with suicide leads to its systematic misreporting and that this is particularly probable in the case of childhood suicide.

Misreporting may take the form of systematic *under-reporting* which might of course affect the conclusion that suicide in childhood is rare; or it might take the form of *idiosyncratic* or *biased reporting* which would limit the conclusions that could be drawn from changes in suicide rate.

The opportunities for variation in reporting practices are, of course, considerable. Nelson et al. (1978) have pointed out the marked differences in definition and reporting practices within eleven western states in the United States. One might think that differences in reporting procedures and definitions in suicide between nations would be even greater, and both Sainsbury and Barraclough (1968) and Lester (1972) have used this assumption to examine the impact of varying reporting procedures on suicide rates. National suicide rates were contrasted with the suicide rates of immigrants to the United States (Sainsbury and Barraclough, 1968) and Australia (Lester, 1972). In both surveys the rank ordering of rates within the immigrant country was similar to the rank ordering of rates of the country of birth, between nations. In another approach to this problem Sainsbury and Barraclough (1968) showed that the incidence of suicide within a particular coroner's district was unaffected by a change in the coroner. This might of course be due to the fact that the coroner or medical examiner is only the final common pathway to the certification of suicide and that various officials such as police and pathologists are the most important source of variance. This possibility was studied by Barraclough et al. (1976) who examined variation in suicide rates in different geographical areas in London presided over by the same coroner yet served by different police officers, pathologists etc. Records were examined for a period of time which covered a change in the subsidiary staff members but during which there was no change in the coroner. They noted that suicide rates between the geographical areas differed from each other but remained stable over time. One is left to conclude from studies of this kind that idiosyncratic or biased reporting is *not* an important source of error.

Under-reporting, on the other hand, is almost certainly a problem. Wilkins (1970) has studied this problem systematically using a sample frame of 1311 individuals (all ages) who had contacted a suicide prevention program in Chicago. Death certifications were reviewed nineteen months or more after the last individual had contacted the prevention center. Seventeen individuals were found to have died during that period, but only four of these deaths had been certified as due to suicide. Each case was reinvestigated intensively and Wilkins concluded that the true suicide rate was probably two to three times greater than that which had been officially recorded.

Since 1968, it has been possible for Medical Examiners to categorize unnatural death as "undetermined whether death is accidental or purposefully inflicted." Shaffer (1974) reviewed coroners records in the United Kingdom for all children aged nine to fourteen, where this category was applied. The number of such verdicts was small but it seemed likely that most of the cases were in fact suicidal in nature. However, even if *all* of these cases thus categorized were taken to be suicidal the rate of suicide in children remained extremely low and continued to be confined mainly to children aged twelver and over. Table 4-5 illustrates the frequency of various "undetermined" classifications in the United States together with unqualified suicide verdicts. Barraclough (1973) has suggested that this is likely to provide a more accurate representation of the "true" suicide rate. Using this procedure the suicide rate for ten- to fourteen year-olds in 1977 would be increased from .98 to 1.44, in fifteen- to nineteen- year-olds from 8.87 to 10.7 and in the population age twenty years and older from 18.52 to 21.23 per 100,000 live population. In other words suicides in 10–14 year olds would remain extremely uncommon for under-reporting is not disproportionately prevalent in the youngest age group.

Another possibility is that suicidal deaths in childhood are sometimes misclassified as accidents. Shaffer (1974) reviewed coroners' inquest dispositions on a cohort of children under the age of fifteen who were certified as having died from the same causes as children who were reported to have commited suicide in the same year. Most of the suicidal deaths were due to asphyxiation by domestic gas, mechanical suffocation (hanging), and firearm missiles. The survey revealed that most verdicts of accidental death from these causes occurred in the infant and toddler age groups and it is reasonable to assume that these were not suicidal. There were very few accidental deaths from these causes in the ten- to fourteen-year age group.

Winn and Halla (1966) noted that threats to jump in front of a car are among the most common suicidal utterances made by young children. Each year about 416, nine- to fourteen-year-old child pedestrians are killed in road traffic accidents in the United States. Although some of these may be suicidally motivated it is worth noting that we have come across no published case reports of suicidal death in a child resulting from this method. Given the consequences to the assailant driver, an automobile accident that results in death of a child is likely to be subject to considerable scrutiny in the judicial system. We therefore doubt if many cases of suicide are cloaked within the statistics of automobile accidents.

In summary, even if we assume that all "undetermined" verdicts and a proportion of accidental deaths from hanging, gassing, falling, and firearm injuries are suicidally motivated, suicide would remain an uncommon event in the nine- to fourteen-year-old age group.

Table 4-5. Suicide and Undetermined Verdicts 1973-1977.

METHOD	10–14 YEARS OLD						15–19 YEARS OLD					
	SUICIDE		UNDETERMINED		TOTAL		SUICIDE		UNDETERMINED		TOTAL	
	N	(%)	N	(%)	N	(%)	N	(%)	N	(%)	N	(%)
Firearms and explosives	411	(47.85)	136	(29.31)	547	(41.38)	4721	(59.48)	671	(36.75)	5392	(56.13)
Hanging, strangulation and suffocation	363	(42.26)	107	(23.06)	470	(35.55)	1292	(20.49)	88	(4.82)	1380	(14.36)
Poisoning by solid or liquid substance	54	(6.29)	32	(6.90)	86	(6.51)	793	(9.99)	418	(22.89)	1211	(12.61)
Poisoning by Gases	9	(1.09)	—	—	9	(.68)	512	(6.45)	1	(.05)	513	(5.34)
Other	22	(2.56)	188	(40.52)	210	(15.89)	463	(5.83)	648	(35.49)	1111	(11.56)
Total suicide & underdetermined	859	(100)	463	(100)	1322	(100)	7781	(100)	1826	(100)	9607	(100)
Total—Population			101,025.00						104,459,000			
Rates per 100,000	.85		.46		1.31		7.45		1.75		9.19	

Source: Unpublished Work Table Data, National Center for Health Statistics, Mortality Statistics Branch, and U.S. Bureau of the Census, *Current Population Reports,* Series P-25, No. 721.

THE CHARACTERISTICS OF SUCCESSFUL CHILD SUICIDES—METHODOLOGICAL AND CONCEPTUAL ISSUES

Official statistics—regardless of their reliability—cannot reveal many of those characteristics of childhood suicide that are of interest to the clinician. However, the literature includes a number of individual case reports of children who committed suicide after psychiatric evaluation or during treatment (e.g., Aleksandrowicz, 1975, Kallman, 1949) and also various detailed psychopathological studies of children who attempted suicide (e.g., Teicher and Jacobs, 1966).

The first type of study will be biased by reporting on only those children who have first been seen by a psychiatrist, and there is evidence that only a minority of successful suicides in childhood and adolescence are ever seen psychiatrically or medically before their death (Shaffer, 1974). The second group of studies—those on attempted suicide—must also be interpreted with caution given that there are known to be gross differences, as for example in male:female sex ratios, which distinguish those who attempt from those who commit suicide.

Robins et al. (1959) first pointed out that only a study of unselected, consecutive suicides could indicate: (a) The proportion who showed evidence of psychiatric disturbance before death; (b) the factors which might be helpful in predicting suicide; and (c) how often the presuicidal individual is perceived as a clinical problem (i.e., what proportion of such children have previously been referred to a clinic). Robins et al. (1959) and other researchers (e.g., Dorpat et al., 1965; Barraclough et al., 1969) have dealt with these problems by using the technique of "psychological postmortem" in which a detailed history of a suicide's previous behavior and treatment is obtained from survivors of a consecutive group of suicides shortly after the subject's death. However the infrequency of childhood suicide would make it difficult even in a large population center, to obtain detailed information of this type of any sizable unselected or consecutive sample of child suicides.

Another approach to the problem is to examine coroner's and any other records of a consecutive group of children in a defined population area. Relatively few studies of this sort have been conducted in childhood. Jan-Tausch (1964) reported on fourteen, seven- to fourteen-year-olds and twenty-seven, fifteen- to nineteen-year-olds who were known to the New Jersey Educational Administration as having committed suicide during 1960 to 1963. The report does not describe the ascertainment procedure and does not present findings separately for the older and the younger groups.

Amir (1973) has reported on all known nine- to eighteen-year-olds who either attempted or committed suicide over a three-year period in Israel. Police and probation records are reported on but attempted and completed suicides are not differentiated except for their demographic characteristics.

Sathyavathi (1975) abstracted information from the coroner's files of forty-five children under the age of fifteen who committed suicide in the City of Bangalore during a seven-year period. The data available in this study mainly concern precipitating events, methods used, and the occupational status of the children.

The most comprehensive record examination is that carried out by Shaffer (1974) who studied a wide range of records of all children (n = 31) on whom a coroner's verdict of suicide has been passed, over an eight-year period in England and Wales. The data examined included inquest depositions, educational and medical records, and where available, the psychiatric and social welfare records of the dead children and the medical and psychiatric records of the deceased children's parents and siblings. This study was facilitated by the existence, in Great Britain, of extensive standardized medical records available through a central source. Findings from all of these studies will be referred to below.

Before considering findings from these studies it may be worthwhile for the reader to consider three quite different conceptual models of suicide: (1) That suicide occurs in the context of a psychiatric illness; (2) That suicide arises as a result of internal or subconscious conflicts and that these will vary in nature and intensity at different ages; (3) That suicide is an intended and logical behavior understandable in the context of an individual's life situation or position in society.

There is strong support for the first of these models from at least two psychological postmortem studies that have been carried out in adults. The first of these by Robins et al. (1959) investigated 134 consecutive suicides by extensive interviewing of the relatives of the deceased suicides and a study of pre-existing records. Robins concluded that 94% had some form of psychiatric illness at the time of their death. In a study which used a similar method, but which differed by the inclusion of a control group, Barraclough et al. (1974) studied 100 consecutive suicides in Great Britain. The control group was drawn from a general practice registry and was matched for age, sex, and marital status. The investigators concluded that all but a few of the suicides had shown signs of psychiatric disorder before their death, the most common diagnosis having been depression. Depression was defined as requiring a change from the individual's usual psychological state, the presence of vegetative symptoms, depressive ideation, and anhedonia.

These studies present convincing evidence that suicide—at least in adults—occurs most commonly in the context of a discrete psychiatric illness. Although depression was the most common type of disorder identified; it is by no means the only one; Robins found that 23%, and Barraclough that 15%, of their groups had been chronic alcoholics.

The second model does not utilize diagnostic concepts but rather refers to purported dynamics such as the internalization of anger, suicide as a manipulative attempt to gain love or inflict punishment, or the need to identify with or join a deceased love object. More detailed exposition of such theories can be found in Freud (1917) and Abraham (1927) or in reviews by Zilboorg (1936) and Toolan (1962). The clinical observations which led to the dynamic theories of depression and suicidal ideation may well be valid. However the reversibility of such phenomena as self-denigratory thought and morbid preoccupation with deceased loved ones through modern antidepressant treatment, suggests that they are a consequence, rather than a cause, of affective disturbance. Further, by definition this model will be the most difficult one to investigate by systematic research. Psychological insights are most likely to be available from individuals who committed suicide during the course of psychiatric treatment and the problem of how representative this group is, has been discussed above. There are of course other problems in the reliable documentation and interpretation of intrapsychic dynamics.

The third conceptual model owes its origins to Durkheim (1897). This emphasizes social isolation, or lack of social integration and suggets that suicide is a rational and intentional act. In this respect it resembles the notion that suicide is an "only solution" allowing a subject to escape from an intolerable situation (Zilboorg, 1936). Recent findings (e.g., Brown and Harris, 1978) indicate that depression, at least in adults, is indeed more common in those with an impoverished social network and might seem to support the social integration theories of suicide. However the position of social isolation, within a causal chain can be questioned. Does depression lead to social isolation or vice versa?

DETAILED CHARACTERISTICS OF CHILDREN WHO COMMIT SUICIDE

Circumstances of Death

Notes. A suicide note may provide the most direct indication of the reason for committing suicide. However only Shaffer's study has looked at this issue. Just under half of his sample left a note. The children who left notes did not differ in age, I.Q., habitual personality description, or the method that they used to commit suicide from those who did not.

In a third of these cases the child stated that he/she was committing suicide because of being in trouble. A further one-third referred to a feeling of depression. The notes were analyzed for "direction of hostility" using the method described by Tuckman et al. (1962). One third of the notes showed "outwardly directed" hostility, e.g., "I hate" or "I killed myself because of" and only two showed inwardly directed hostility, e.g., "At least where I'm going I won't be able to do any more harm."

Precipitating Circumstances. The precipitating circumstances in Shaffer's study are described in Table 4-6. The most frequent precipitant was a "disciplinary crisis" which accounted for just over a third of all cases. In half of these the disciplinary crisis consisted of the child having been told by a school official that their parents would be informed by letter of truanting or some other antisocial behavior about which the parents had not previously been aware. In the remaining cases the child was anticipating punishment at school or court action. Sathyavathi (1975) similarly noted that 72% of his sample of children in India committed suicide shortly after getting into trouble. Studies of adolescents by Maris (1969), Breed (1970), and Connell (1965) all suggest that suicidal ideation is particularly prevalent amongst young people who have recently been arrested.

Shaffer found that few instances of childhood suicide took place after an argument or disagreement with another member of the child's immediate family. Two suicides were precipitated by fantasy models, one taking place after the child had read of the suicide of a public figure and reference was made to this event in the suicide note. A similar phenomenon was noted in the United States when suicide rates increased after the suicidal death of Marilyn Monroe, (Shneidman, 1980) it be that events of this type have an effect of reducing social constraints on suicidal behavior.

No fewer than seven of the thirty children in Shaffer's series died within two weeks of their birthdate. This was nearly three times as often as might

Table 4-6. Precipitating Circumstances.

	BOY	GIRL	TOTAL
Disciplinary crisis	8	3	11 (36%)
Fight with peers other than close friend of opposite sex	3	1	4 (13.33%)
Dispute with close friend of opposite sex	1	2	3 (10%)
Dispute with parent	1	2	3 (10%)
Being dropped from a school team	2	0	2 (7%)
Fantasy "model"	1	0	2 (7%)
Interaction with psychotic parent	2	0	2 (9%)
No precipitant disclosed	3	0	3 (10%)

be expected by chance. It is only possible to speculate on the explanation for this finding. Birthdays are a time when special recognition is given to an individual and it may be that anticipation or experience of an unfulfilling birthdate could serve as a precipitant.

Social Isolation. A number of suicidologists have commented on the importance of social isolation at the time of an individual's choosing to commit suicide. The Suicide Prevention Movement is based on the premise that providing social support and breaking social isolation at this crucial moment reduces the propensity to commit suicide. Jan-Tausch noted that none of the children in the New Jersey series were fully engaged in extracurricular activities and that just over a half engaged in no extracurricular activities at all. No control data are given and so the significance of this observation is not clear. In Shaffer's series approximately 40% of the subjects were not at school on the day *before* their death. A third of the children were on vacation, a third were chronic school refusers and the others were truants. It may well be that the primary psychiatric disturbance led to a child being away from school in these last two groups but that the consequences of being out of the school environment rendered the child more isolated and thus more vulnerable to the suicidal act.

Demographic Characteristics

a. Age. National and international statistics are usually presented in five-year blocks. However, a more detailed examination of the age distribution within the ten- to fourteen-year-old age grouping for a sample year (See Figure 4–3) shows that very few children under the age of twelve commit suicide. (See also Shaffer, 1974; Jan-Tausch, 1964; and Amir, 1977).

b. Sex. In North America and in Great Britain boys outnumber girls as successful suicides by a ratio of approximately two to one. However Amir (1977) reports an even sex distribution between males and females in Israel and Sathyavathi reports a female predominance in India. These findings suggest that the male-female ratio is determined by cultural rather than by fundamental psychopathological factors. However the sample described by Sathyavathi in India in which the female predominance was of the order of three to one included many children and young adolescents who announced their suicidal behavior, and showed other characteristics that more closely typify suicide attempters than completers. It may well be that the discrepant male-female ratio in the Indian sample can be accounted for by less adequate access to resuscitation procedures and the consequent inclusion of a disproportionate number of suicide attempts that "went wrong."

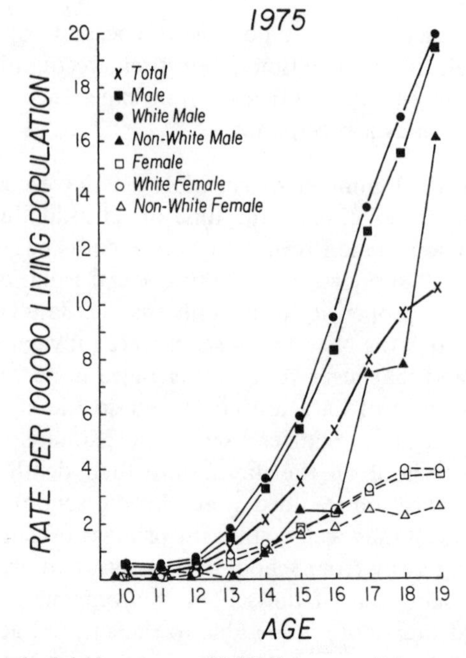

Figure 4-3. Suicide rate per 100,000 living population, ages 10-19.

The relationship between sex of suicidee and psychiatric diagnosis was examined by Shaffer (1974). No significant difference in the form of psychopathology was found to discriminate between victims of different sex. (See Table 4-7)

The question of sex differences in diagnosis has been examined in children who have attempted suicide. In a multicentered study Marks and Haller (1977) screened 830 white twelve- to eighteen-year-olds of normal intelligence who were attending a number of different psychiatric clinics and who had been examined in a standardized fashion. Thirty-one boys and sixty-seven girls (8% of the sample) had been referred to a clinic because of

Table 4-7. Number of Children in Whom Psychiatric Symptoms were Reported.

	BOY	GIRL	TOTAL
Antisocial only	3 (14%)	2 (22%)	5 (17%)
Mixed antisocial, emotional/affective	14 (47%)	3 (33%)	17 (57%)
Emotional, affective		4 (45%)	4 (13%)
None	4 (19%)		4 (13%)

suicidal behavior. Comparisons were drawn between male and female attempted suicidees. The boys showed more perfectionistic anxious and suspicious behavior, the females more conduct disorders. The prevalence of depressive symptoms was similar for each sex.

Intelligence

Jan-Tausch (1964) obtained both I.Q. and reading level data on the forty-one children in the New Jersey sample. Fifteen had a superior I.Q. but only three were reading at a superior level. By contrast only two had an I.Q. in the retarded range although seventeen of the total sample were reading retarded. These findings suggest a disproportionate number of children with specific learning difficulties within the suicidal group.

Shaffer (1974) was able to obtain I.Q. estimates on all but two of the children in his series. These indicated that nearly half of the children had a very superior I.Q. Approximately one in five of the children scored in the retarded range. There was thus a bimodal distribution with a disproportionate representation of retarded and very intelligent children.

Physical Development

Most children over the age of twelve are undergoing the biological changes of puberty (Tanner, 1962). The fact that so few children commit suicide before this age suggests that the onset of puberty coincides with the loss of an important protective factor.

Shaffer was able to obtain measurements of height taken at the post mortem examination of a number of children in his series. One-third of the subjects were over the 75th percentile for their height. The children who had committed suicide were therefore precocious both intellectually and physically.

Emotional and Behavior Characteristics

Shaffer attempted to group the personality characteristics of the deceased children in his series by noting descriptions of the child that appeared within the child's psychiatric and probation records and which were given during an interview with the child's class teacher. Using these limited techniques it was possible to categorize children into four main groups. These are dipicted in Table 4–8. There was a certain amount of overlap between the first (paranoid) group and all others. However no children described in the terms used to define Group 2 were also described in the terms used to define Groups 3 and 4.

Table 4-8. Personality Description.

1. "Chip on the shoulder—felt people didn't like him—felt people were unduly critical of him"	9 cases
2. "Impulsive—no self-control—volatile—erratic"	6 cases
3. "Quiet—difficult to get through to—uncommunicative"	9 cases
4. "Perfectionist—high standards—neat—tidy, methodical—self-critical—afraid of making mistakes"	6 cases
5. "Insufficient information" or none of the above	6 cases

In addition to these descriptions of characteristic behaviors Shaffer screened records for evidence of antisocial or emotional symptoms. (See Table 4-9) Antisocial symptoms were present twenty-two of thirty children, emotional or affective symptoms in twenty-one, and a combination of both of these in seventeen of the children. The high prevalence of antisocial behaviors is striking. A number of surveys (e.g. Rutter et al., 1970, Edenbroch and Achenbach 1978; Gould, 1980) have noted that children with conduct disorders are frequently unhappy or miserable. However it is not clear whether the conduct disturbance is a manifestation of an underlying depression or whether antisocial behavior leads to circumstances which induce depression.

Previous Accidents

Menninger (1938); Schechter (1957); Toolan (1962); Yacoubian and Lourie (1969) among others have suggested that repeated accidents are on a continuum of self-destructive behavior with suicide. Indeed this is an

Table 4-9. Symptoms Shown by Children Who Committed Suicide.

ANTISOCIAL	BOY	GIRL	TOTAL
Bullying and fighting	7	2	9
Stealing	6	3	9
Truancy	7	2	9
Running away	3	0	3
EMOTIONAL AFFECTIVE			
Depressed mood or tearfulness	7	6	13
Hypochondriasis	2	2	4
Excessive fears	4	0	4
School refusal	4	0	4
Ideas of reference or self-denigration	2	2	4
Morbid preoccupations	4	0	4
Boredom	2	0	2

assumption reflected in the title of this volume. However other work on accident proneness (See Mannheimer and Mellinger, 1967; Sobel, 1970) suggests that temperamental factors and the competence and mental state of the child's caretakers are more significant factors in determining accident proneness.

Because of the interest in this issue Shaffer (1974) systematically searched the general practice and hospital records of each child in his series to determine the cumulative prevalence of accidents. Only one child out of the thirty children had ever been involved in an accident severe enough to have needed medical treatment. These findings of course are not conclusive because no control group was similarly examined and medical and hospital records may not have taken into account minor but repeated accidents that did not require medical intervention. However Shaffer's findings in completed suicides are supported by those of Remschmidt and Schwartz (1978) who found previous "self-mutilating" behavior and accidents to have been uncommon in their study of 157 adolescents with a history of nonfatal suicidal behavior.

Home and Family Circumstances.

None of the systematic studies report a particularly high proportion of children living in an anomalous situation. In Shaffer's series 94% of the children were living at home with one or both natural parents at the time of their death. In Jan-Tausch's series 90% of the children were living at home and in Sathyavathi's series 80% were living at home. In the Indian group a substantial number of those not living with their parents were serving as indentured servants at the time of their death.

In Shaffer's series 23% of the children lived in a single-parent family. This was similar to the rate found in other psychiatrically disturbed child populations in Great Britain at the time of the investigation. (Rutter, et al., 1970).

Several studies (Caplan and Douglas, 1969; Greer, et al., 1966; and Brown, et al., 1977) have suggested that the death of a parent in childhood increases the risk to an individual of developing a later depressive illness or showing suicidal behavior. This is a research field with many methodological complexities in which adequate control for year of birth of the patient's parents and social class is important (See Dennehy, 1966; and Gregory, 1966). In their studies of parental loss among groups of child and adolescent suicide attemptors in which such factors were not taken into account, neither Mattsson et al. (1969) nor Stanley and Barter (1970) could find any significant differences in the prevalence of orphanhood between suicidal and control patients. In Shaffer's study 10% of the children had been orphaned (three children). Because of the small number in the sample it is not possible to know whether this number was in excess of that which might be expected. However it was interesting to note that parental death in two of the three orphaned children took place after a separation or divorce. It may be that it is particularly stressful to a child to lose a parent of an unhappy marriage.

The data of family breakup in Shaffer's study give no indication of the quality of the intact marriages. An interesting finding was that at the time that the follow-up was conducted (one to four years after the children's deaths) no fewer than one quarter of the previously intact families had broken up after the child's suicide. This may reflect stress resulting from the child's death or it may indicate that the threat of separation or divorce was present at the time of the child's death. This would fit in with the findings of Margolin and Teicher (1968) who studied a small number of suicidal adolescent boys and found that the threat of desertion of the boy's mother through divorce or separation was an important precipitating factor in their suicidal adolescent group.

Family History of Mental Illness

Jan-Tausch noted that 10% of his sample had parents who had been "psychotic," however, the source and criteria for this diagnosis are not provided.

In Shaffer's study 55% of the dead children had a first-degree relative who had had treatment for psychiatric disturbance *before* the child's death. In four of these cases treatment was for suicidal behavior. Eight of the children's fathers and one of their mothers were described as heavy drinkers. These findings are compatible with either a learning or genetic hypothesis. Kreitman et al. (1970) studied several groups of psychiatric patients with and without a history of suicidal behavior. They noted an excess of suicidal behavior among the close contacts and/or relatives of the suicidal patients. Kreitman suggested that suicidal behavior had assumed value as a mode of communication within this "subculture." On the other hand there is evidence (Buchsbaum et al., 1976 and 1977) that suicidal behavior occurs more often in families of college students who have low platelet MAO levels. And it may be that the high rates of affective disorder in the families of the suicidal children were attributable to genetic rather than environmental influences.

ENVIRONMENTAL DETERMINANTS OF SUICIDAL BEHAVIOR

The increase in the rate of adolescent suicide over the past decade has been widely attributed to changes in the social environment. Environmental factors could operate either by enhancing a predisposition to suicidal behavior or by weakening suicide inhibiting factors or in both ways.

An increase in predisposition could be brought about by the experience of life stresses which could, for example, act to increase the prevalence of depression and with it suicide. An increase in suicide behavior within a subculture could then have a multiplier effect through modeling, or through reducing inhibitory constraints against suicide. There are reports of epidemics of successful suicide in children in Eastern Europe in the nineteenth and early part of the twentieth centuries (Bakwin 1957; Miner, 1922).

One way in which this question can be studied is through an examination of cross-cultural differences *within* a community. Amir (1973) has conceptualized that cultural factors may influence suicide rates in three different ways: (a) by producing differential stress; (b) by differential acceptance or rejection of suicide as an acceptable behavior; and (c) by providing alternative opportunities for adaptations and adjustment to stress. Douglas (1967) has cautioned that the differential acceptance or rejection of suicide as an acceptable behavior may in turn influence suicide reporting practices.

As can be seen from Figure 4–3 the rate of suicides within the United States varies between the races with black adolescents having a lower rate than whites.

On the face of it this would seem to rule out a "stress" hypothesis for it is clear that by almost all measures, black adolescents can be shown to suffer more stress than their white peers. This would, in turn, suggest that black adolescents enjoy some protective factor from suicide. Two hypotheses suggest themselves. The first is the traditional dynamic notion of a reciprocal relationship between inwardly and outwardly directed aggression. Black adolescents have higher rates of delinquency and aggressive behavior, i.e., outwardly directed aggression, and therefore they might be expected to show a lower rate of suicidal behavior. However Shaffer (1974) has shown that suicidal behavior in children and young adolescents is related *directly* rather than *reciprocally* to delinquency. Similarly Breed (1970) found that 50% of black suicide attempters, had recently been in trouble with the law compared with only 10% of white suicides. These findings would make one question the hypothesis that blacks are protected from suicide by their aggressive behavior.

The second hypothesis is that in spite of their having to endure an excess of external stress, cultural factors or convention make suicide a less acceptable or "necessary" behavior. For example, Bush (1976) has suggested that blacks have more effective social support systems than whites. Bohannon (1961) reports that suicide rates in Africa are particularly low (although one needs to question both the validity of reporting procedures in underdeveloped nations as well as the generalizability of cultural factors from Africans to North American blacks). Amir (1973) has noted that the ratio of suicides of European-born to African-born Jewish immigrants in Israel

Table 4-10. 15-19 Year Olds (1970).

STATE	% OF NONWHITE POPULATION THAT IS BLACK	NO. OF SUICIDES ALL RACES	NONWHITE % OF POP.	NONWHITE % OF SUICIDE
MICHIGAN	95.80	59	12.52	13.56
PENNSYLVANIA	97.11	60	9.64	6.67
MARYLAND	97.35	13	20.84	23.08
ALABAMA	99.43	10	31.64	10
GEORGIA	99.28	21	30.51	14.29
MISSISSIPPI	99.10	9	43.33	33.33
S. CAROLINA	99.29	9	36.31	—

Source: U.S. Bureau of the Census, *1970 Census of the Population. Characteristics of the Population,* Vols. *2,12,22,24,26,40,43* and *Vital Statistics of the United States, 1970,* Vol. *II,* Part B.

2.5 to 1. Other sociologists such as Gibbs and Martin (1964) suggested that status integration may be enhanced by discrimination and by narrowed employment opportunities and that this in turn would reduce the likelihood of suicide.

If we assume that a measure of protection from suicidal behaviors is provided in a black subculture then this is likely to be more marked in those reared in a traditonal setting and it might be expected to break down with deculturation. We have examined this possibility by contrasting black and white adolescent suicide rates in four Deep South states with those in three northern and eastern industrial states (See Table 4-10). These data demonstrate that the protection from suicide enjoyed by blacks is confined to those living in the south. Rates in the North are closely comparable for both races, and given the differential stress levels this observation lends support to the notion of deculturation or loss of protection rather than increase of stress. It should be noted that a factor that cannot be excluded in any analysis of this sort is selective migration of genetically predisposed families from a rural (southern) to an urban (northern) setting.

WHAT PROTECTS YOUNG CHILDREN FROM SUICIDE?

The repeated theme in this chapter has been that children and adolescents are protected from the suicidal urges shown by their elders. This could be explained in a number of different ways. Thus, it could be that affective illness is the most common cause of suicide and that, although depression undoubtedly occurs in children (Puig-Antich et al., 1977), its prevalence within the child population is probably considerably lower than among adults. A second possibility is that integration within the framework of a family protects children from suicidal behavior through the reduction of isolation and the extension of social and emotional support. Alternatively, it could be that a degree of conceptual maturity is required before a child can be victim to such notions as despair or hopelessness and that this maturity develops *pari passu* with the enhancement of formal operations.

There is evidence to support all of these explanations. Thus, the reported prevalence of depressive disorder in childhood (See Rutter et al., 1970) is a good deal less than that which is reported in the adult population (Essen-Moller, 1965; Brown et al., 1975). Similarly responses to mourning in prepubertal children are less likely to be marked by persistent sadness than they are in adolescence (See Rutter, 1966).

The second possibility, i.e., that the family protects the child from suicide through a reduction in isolation and the provision of social support has parallels in the correlates of adult suicide. Single male adults living alone have higher suicide rates than their married counterparts. The importance of social isolation at the point of deciding about the suicidal act has already been discussed.

The notion that conceptual or cognitive immaturities might explain the unusualness of suicide in childhood has attracted a good deal of interest. Schilder and Wechsler (1934) suggested that distortions in the younger child's concept of death were in some way related to suicide in children. A number of studies concerning the development of concepts of death and dying in childhood (Schilder and Wechsler 1934; Freud and Burlingham, 1944; Nagy, 1965; McIntyre and Angle, 1970) have found that many children believe death to be reversible as late as age thirteen. Koocher (1973) is the only researcher who has linked children's concepts of death to epochal changes in Piagetan stages of cognition. In that study it was noted that no children who had attained the stage of concrete or formal operations believed in the reversibility of dying but that preoperational thought was found in children as old as eleven.

Most authors have interpreted finding the persistence of immature notions of death as in some way explaining a predisposition to suicide. Schilder and Wechsler based their findings on children who had been admitted to Bellevue Hospital after making a suicide threat. Most authors put forward the reasonable notion that belief in the reversibility of death will act to reduce constraints on suicidal behavior. However, what needs to be explained is not some factor which predisposes children to suicidal behavior but rather the reverse. Given that beliefs in the reversibility of death are common and that suicide is uncommon in childhood it cannot follow that one finding explains the other!

However, other cognitive abilities develop during adolescence including the ability to show foresight and planning, a greater awareness of the self as seen by others and a greater preoccupation with abstract notions. Each of these new skills may penetrate the protection afforded to the child. Shaffer found that many of the children in his study who succeeded in their suicidal purpose had shown secretive planning and deliberate behavior. Thus, the children who gassed themselves, succeeded when they had access to an empty house and when they had taken special measures such as pretending to go to school so as not to arouse suspicion, carefully sealing windows and positioning themselves to ensure a lethal build of coal gas within the time available to them. Other methods, such as hanging, required a certain technical sophistication and careful selection of an appropriate and private site. Few of the deaths were obviously impulsive and evidence of prior planning was present in most. Amongst the deaths not requiring forward planning it was noted that two out of the three children who shot themselves were intoxicated at the time. Three of the four children who took a drug overdose had informed others before they lost consciousness and so their seriousness of intent must be questioned. It seems likely therefore, that this capacity to plan ahead is important in achieving suicidal purpose and it may be that this aspect of cognitive development is not common until later childhood.

THE PREDICTION OF SUICIDE

Because successful suicide in childhood occurs so rarely, attempts to elaborate a predictive guide are likely to be overwhelmed by the weight of false positive judgments (Rosen, 1954). Nevertheless certain features lend themselves to prediction from the literature.

Previous Suicidal Behavior

Only Shaffer has reported on previous suicidal behavior. However, as that study relied solely upon written records and post hoc interviews with teachers and physicians and *not* on interviews with relatives it is likely to have underestimated the prevalence of this behavior.

The findings were that 46% of the children had previously discussed, threatened, or attempted suicide. Children who killed themselves after a disciplinary crisis were *less* likely to have attempted or threatened suicide previously. Given the reportedly high incidence of attempted suicide in children and adolescents (Mattsson et al., 1969; Leese, 1969; Lukianowicz, 1968) it is not clear how much significance can be placed on these suicidal behaviors although clinical prudence dictates that suicidal behavior be taken seriously if only as a "cry for help."

Previous Psychiatric Illness

In their study of adults, Guze and Robins (1970) estimated that approximately 15% of depressives would go on to die by suicide. Pokorny (1964) studying recently institutionalized psychiatrically disturbed adults noted that the risk of suicide was greatest during the period immediately following release from an institution. Barraclough et al. (1974) noted that a combination of depressive disorder and alcoholism increased the probability of later suicide in adults. However it is not clear that any of these findings can be generalized to childhood and no comparable studies of successful suicide have been carried out with the exception of an inadequate prospective study by Paulson, Stone and Sposto (1978). These authors studied thirty-four, four- to 12-year-old depressed and suicidal children, identified from a frame of 662 child psychiatric in- and out-patients. At the time of a three-to seven-year follow-up at which only 13 of the 34 children had been located, none had committed suicide. The small numbers and incomplete follow-up make this a difficult study from which to generalize.

In both Shaffer's and Jan-Tausch's studies antisocial behavior was a prominent abnormality in the children who had committed suicide. Barter et al., (1968) contrasted adolescents who made a second or repeated attempt at suicide with those who made an initial attempt only. Those most likely to show a recurrence of suicidal behavior were those *not* living with their families, those who had experienced an earlier parental loss and those with few social resources. Stanley and Barter (1970) noted that a return to school discriminated between suicide attempt repeaters and those who made only a single attempt.

Acute precipitations. The most commonly occurring situation before suicide in each study has been one in which the child was facing some disciplinary crisis. Shaffer and Jan-Tausch noted that many suicides took place after a period of absence from school and this has been noted in the studies of attempted suicide as well (Stanley and Barter, 1970; Teicher and Jacobs, 1966). In their study Stanley and Barter noted that the best predictor of a good outcome after a suicide attempt was a return to school accompanied by a normal pattern of attendance.

SUMMARY

Suicide before puberty and in early adolescence is uncommon and the incidence has changed little over the past decade. Suicide in older adolescence, although less common than in adulthood, has been subject to a striking increase in rate over the past decade. Estimates suggest that the incidence of suicide in children might be unreported by a twofold factor. However even if this is taken into account the actual rate of child and adolescent suicides remains low.

When children do commit suicide, they do so in a broadly similar way to adults. In the United States both sexes most commonly use firearms and males will frequently hang themselves.

A comparison of black and white suicide rates suggests that social and family stresses do not in themselves account for an increase in the suicide rate of older adolescents. By analogy this is more likely to have resulted from an erosion in some protective factor.

Suicide in childhood is of interest because of the insight that it may provide into factors which protect the individual from suicide. Such factors could include the support received by the child from the family network, an age-related lack of predisposition to affective disorder, and cognitive immaturity.

A review of studies of risk factors for suicide could be taken to include: age over twelve, male sex, high or low intelligence, previous or present suicidal behavior, impetuous and /or antisocial behavior and social isolation, a family history of depression, alcoholism, or suicidal behavior, physical precocity, and exposure to a disciplinary crisis. However as we do not know how often the whole or any part of this combination of characteristics occurs in children who *do not* go on to commit suicide it is not possible to state what degree of risk is represented.

REFERENCES

Abraham, K. (1927). Notes on the psychoanalytic investigation and treatment of manic depressive insanity and allied conditions. *In: Selected Papers.* London: Hogarth Press.

Aleksandrowicz, M. K. (1975). The biological strangers: An attempted suicide of a seven-and-a-half-year-old-girl. *Bulletin of the Menninger Clinic,* **39**(2):163–176.

Amir, A. (1973). Suicide among minors in Israel. *Israel Annals of Psychiatry and Related Disciplines,* **11**(3):219–269.

Bakwin, H. (1957). Suicide in children and adolescents. *J. Pediatr.,* **50**:749–769.

Barraclough, B. M. (1972). Are the Scottish and English suicide rates really different? *Brit. J. Psychiat.,* **120**:267–273.

Barraclough, B. M. (1973). Differences between national suicide rates. *British J. of Psychiatry,* **122**:95–96.

Barraclough, B. M. (1973). Suicide rate. *Brit. Med. J.:* 329 (letter).

Barraclough, B., Bunch, J., Nelson, B., Sainsbury, P. (1974). A hundred cases of suicide: Clinical aspects. *Brit. J. Psychiat.,* **125**:355–373.

Barraclough, B., Holding, T., and Fayers, P. (1976). Influence of coroners' officers and pathologists on suicide verdicts. *Brit. J. Psychiat.* **128**:471–474.

Barraclough, B. M., Nelson, B., Bunch, J., and Sainsbury, P. (1969). The diagnostic Classification and Psychiatric Treatment of 100 Suicides. Proceedings of the Fifth International Conference for Suicide Prevention, London.

Barter, J., Swaback, D., and Todd, D. (1968). Adolescent suicide attempts; A follow-up study of hospitalized patients. *Arch. Gen. Psychiat.,* **19:**523–527.

Bergstrand, C. G. and Otto, U. (1962). Suicidal attempts in adolescence and childhood. *Acta Paediatrica,* **51:**17–26.

Bohannon, P. (1960). Patterns of murder and suicide. *In: African Homicide and Suicide.* P. Bohannon (ed.). Princeton, N.J.: Princeton University Press 230–266.

Breed, W. (1970). The Negro and fatalistic suicide. *Pacific Sociological Review,* **13:**156–162.

Brown, G. W., Bhrolchain, M. N., and Harris T. O. (1975). Social class and psychiatric disturbance among women in an urban population. *Sociology,* **9:**225–254.

Brown, G. W., and Harris, T. (1978). *Social Origins of Depression. A Study of Psychiatric Disorder in Women.* London: Tavistock.

Brown, G. W., Harris, T. O., and Copeland, J. R. (1977). Depression and loss. *Brit. J. of Psychiat.,* **130:**1–18.

Buchsbaum, M. S., Coursey, R. D., and Murphy, D. L. (1976). The biochemical high-risk paradigm: Behavioral and familial correlates of low platelet monoamine oxidase activity. *Science,* **194:**339–341. No. 4262.

Buchsbaum, M. S., Haier, R. J., and Murphy D. L. (1977). Suicide attempts, platelet monoamine oxidase and the average evoked response. *Acta psychiat. Scand.* **56:**69–79.

Bush, J. A. (1976). Suicide and blacks: A conceptual framework. *Suicide and Life-Threatening Behavior.* **6**(4):216–222.

Caplan, M. G., and Douglas V. I. (1969). Incidence of parental loss in children with depressed mood. *J. Child Psychol. Psychiat.,* **10:**225–232.

Connell, P. H. (1965). Suicidal attempts in childhood and adolescence *In: Modern Perspectives in Child Psychiatry.* J. G. Howells, (ed.) Boyd Publishers Edinburgh and London: 403.

Dennehy, C. M. (1966) Childhood bereavement and psychiatric illness. *Brit. J. Psychiat.,* **112:**1049–1069.

Dorpat, T. L., Jackson, J. K., and Ripley, H. S. (1965). Broken homes and attempted and completed suicide. *Arch. Gen. Psychiat.,* **12:**213–216.

Douglas J. D. (1967). *The Social Meanings of Suicide.* Princeton, N. J.: Princeton University Press.

Durkheim E., (1897). *Suicide: A study in Sociology.* New York: Free Press, 1951.

Edenbroch, C. S., and Achenbach, T. M. (1978). Child Behavior Profile Patterns of Children Referred for Clinical Services. Paper presented at the American Psychological Association, Toronto.

Essen-Moller, E. (1965). Individual traits and morbidity in a Swedish rural population. *Acta Psychiatrica et Neurologica Scandinavica, Suppl. 100.*

Freud, A., and Burlingham D. (1944). *Infants Without Families.* New York: International University Press.

Freud, S., (1917). *Mourning and Melancholia.* Standard Edition, **14:**243–358, 1957.

Gibbs, J. P., and Martin, W. T. (1964). *Status Integration and Suicide.* Eugene, Oregon: University of Oregon Press.

Gould, M. S. (1980). A Typology of Adolescent Behavior Profiles: An Empirical Approach to Classification. Unpublished Doctoral Dissertation, Columbia University.

Greer, S., Gunn, J. C., and Koller, K. M. (1966). Aetiological factors in attempted suicide. *Brit. Med. J.* **2:**1352–1355.

Gregory, I. (1966). Retrospective data concerning childhood loss of parents—II. Category of parental loss by decade of birth: Diagnosis and MMPI. *Arch. Gen. Psychiat.,* **15:**362–367.

Guze, S. B., and Robins, E. (1970). Suicide and primary affective disorders. *Brit. J. Psychiat.,* **117:**437–438.

Hendin, H. (1969). Black suicide. *Arch. Gen. Psychiat.* **21**:407–422.

Jacobziner, H. (1965). Attempted suicide in adolescence. *J. Amer. Med. Assn.,* **191**:7–11.

Jan-Tausch, J. (1964). *Suicide of Children 1960–63. New Jersey Public Schools.* Division of Curriculum and Instruction—Office of Special Education Services, Department of Education 225 West State Street, Trenton, New Jersey.

Kallam, F. J., et al. (1949). Suicide in twins and only children. *Am. J. Hum. Genet.* **1**:113–126.

Koocher, G. P. (1973). Childhood, death and cognitive development. *Developmental Psychology,* **9**(3): 369–375.

Kreitman, N., Smith, P., and Tan E.-S. (1970). Attempted suicide as language: An empirical [illegible]y. *Brit. J. Psychiat.,* **116**:465–473.

L[illegible]e, S. M. (1969). Suicide behavior in twenty adolescents. *Brit. J. Psychiat.,* **115**:479–480.

[illegible]ster, D. (1972). Migration and suicide (letter). *The Med. J. of Australia.* **1**–59th Yr. (18):941–942.

Lukianowicz, N. (1968). Attempted suicide in children. *Acta Psychiatrica Scandinavica,* **44**:FASC(4):415–435.

McIntire, M. S. and Angle, C. R. The taxonomy of suicide as seen in poison control center. Pediatr. Clin. N.A. **17**:697–706 (1970).

McIntire, M. S., Angle, C. R., and Struempler, L. J. (1972). The concept of death in midwestern children and youth. *Amer. J. Dis. Child.,* **123**: 527–532.

Manheimer, D. I., and Mellinger, G. D. (1967). Personality characteristics of the child accident repeater. *Child Development,* **35**(2): 491–513.

Margolin, N. L., and Teicher, J. D., (1968). Thirteen adolescent male suicide attempts dynamic considerations. *J. Am. Acad. Child Psychiat.* **7**(2):296–315.

Maris, R. W. (1969). *Social Forces in Urban Suicide.* Homewood, Ill.: Dorsey Press.

Marks, P. A., and Haller, D. L. (1977). Now I lay me down for keeps: A study of adolescent suicide attempts. *J. Clin. Psychol.* **33**(2): 390–400.

Mattsson, A., Seese, L. R., and Hawkins, J. W. (1969). Suicidal behavior as a child psychiatric emergency clinical characteristics and follow-up results. *Arch. Gen. Psychiat.,* **20**:100–109.

Menninger, K. (1938). *Man Against Himself.* New York: Harcourt, Brace & World.

Miner, J. R. (1922). Suicide and its relations to climatic and other facts. *Am. J. Hygiene. Monograph Series.*

Mulcock, D. (1955). Juvenile suicide: A study of suicide and attempted suicide over a 16-Year period. *The Medical Officer.* 155–160.

Nagy, M. L. (1965). The child's view of death. *In: The Meaning of Death,* H. Feifel (ed.). New York: McGraw-Hill.

National Center for Health Statistics. *Vital Statistics of the United States 1964–1977 Inclusive,* Vol. *II,* Parts A & B, U.S. Department of H.E.W.—Mortality Statistics Branch (published and unpublished data).

Nelson, F. L., Farberow, N., and McKinnon, D. R. (1978). The certification of suicide in eleven western states: An inquiry into the validity of reported suicide rates. *Suicide and Life-Threaten Behavior* **8**(2):75–88.

Paulson, M. J., Stone, D., and Sposto, R. (1978). Suicide potential and behavior in children ages 4 to 12. *Suicide and Life-Threatening Behavior.* **8**(4):225–242.

Pokorny, A. D. (1964). Suicide rates in various psychiatric disorders. *J. Nerv. Ment. Dis.,* **139**:399–405.

Puig-Antich, J., Blau, S., Marx, N., Greenhill, L., and Chambers, W. (1978). Prepubertal major depressive disorder—A pilot study. *J. Am. Acad. Child Psychiat.,* **17**:695–707.

Remschmidt, H., Schwab, T. (1978). Suizidversuche im Kindes- und Jugendalter. *Acta paedopsychiat.,* **43:**197–208.

Robins, E., Murphy, G. E., Wilkinson, R. H., Jr., Gassner, S., and Kayes, J. (1959). Some clinical considerations in the prevention of suicide based on a study of 134 successful suicides. *Amer. J. Publ. Hlth.,* **49:**888–899.

Rosen, A., (1954). Detection of suicidal patients. An example of some limitations in the prediction of infrequent events. *J. Consult. Psychol.,* **18:**397–403.

Rutter, M., (1966). *Children of Sick Parents: An Environmental and Psychiatric study.* Institute of Psychiatry, Maudsley Monographs No. 16. London: Oxford University Press.

Rutter, M., Tizard, J., and Whitmore, K. (1970). *Education, Health and Behavior.* London: Longmans.

Sainsbury, P., and Barraclough, B. (1968). Differences between suicide rates. *Nature* **220:**1252.

Sathyavathi, K. (1975). Suicide among children in Bangalore. *Indian J. of Pediatrics,* **42**(329): 149–157.

Schechter, E. B. (1957). The recognition and treatment of suicide in children. *In: Clues to Suicide,* E. B. Shneidman and N. L. Farberow (eds.). New York: McGraw Hill, 31.

Schilder, P. and Wechsler, D. (1934). The attitudes of children toward death. *J. genet. psychol.* **45:**406–451.

Schneer, H. I., and Kay, P., (1961). The suicidal adolescent. *In: Adolescents.* S. Lorand and H. Schneer (eds.). New York: Paul Hoeber, 180–201.

Schrut, A. (1964). Suicidal Adolescents and Children. *J. Am. Med. Assn.* **188:**1103–1107.

Shaffer, D. (1974). Suicide in childhood and early adolescence. *J. Child Psychol. Psychiat.* **15:**275–291.

Shaw, C. R., and Schelkun, R. F. (1965). Suicidal behavior in children. *Psychiatry,* **28:** 157–168.

Shneidman, E. (1980). Personal communication.

Sobel, R. (1970). The psychiatric implication of accidental poisoning in childhood. *Pediatric Clinics of North America,* **17**(3):653–685.

Stanley, E. J., and Barter, J. T. (1970). Adolescent suicidal behavior. *American J. Orthopsychiat.,* **40**(1):87–93.

Tanner, J. M. (1962). *Growth at Adolescence.* Oxford, England: Blackwell Scientific Publications.

Teicher, J. D. and Jacobs, J. (1966). Adolescents who attempt suicide: Preliminary findings. *Am. J. of Psychiat.,* **122:**1248–1257.

Toolan, J. M. (1962). Suicide and suicidal attempts in children and adolescents. *Am. J. of Psychiat.,* **118:**719–724.

Toolan, J. M. (1975). Suicide in children and adolescents. *Am. J. Psychother.,* **29**(3):339–344.

Tuckman J., Kleiner R. J., and Lavell M., (1962). Emotional content of suicide notes. *Amer. J. Psychiat.* **116:**59–63.

U.S. Bureau of the Census, *Current Population Reports* Series P–25, No. 519 "Estimates of the Population of the United States, by Age, Sex, and Race: April 1, 1960 to July 1, 1973," U.S. Government Printing Office, Washington, D.C., 1974.

U.S. Bureau of the Census, *Current Population Reports,* Series P–25, No. 721, "Estimates of the Population of the United States, by Age, Sex and Race: 1970–1977," U.S. Government Printing Office, Washington, D.C., 1978.

U.S. Bureau of the Census, *Current Population Reports,* Series P–25, No. 870, "Estimates of the Population of the United States, by Age, Race, and Sex: 1976–1979," U.S. Government Printing Office, Washington, D.C., 1980.

U.S. Bureau of Census, *1970 Census of Population: Characteristics of the Population,* Vols. *2, 12, 22, 24, 26, 40, 43*. U.S. Government Printing Office, Washington, D.C., 1973.

World Health Organization (1977). *World Health Statistics Annual.*

Wilkins, J. L. (1970). Producing suicides. *American Behavioral Scientist,* **14**(2):185–201.

Winn D., and Halla R. (1966). Observations of children who threaten to kill themselves. *Canadian Psychiat. Assoc. J. 11: Suppl.:* 283–294.

Yacoubian, J. H., and Lourie, R. S. (1969). Suicide and attempted suicide in children and adolescents. *Clinical Proceedings of Children's Hospital,* **XXV**(11).

Zilboorg, G. (1936). Consideration on suicide with particular reference to that of the young. *Am. J. Orthopsychiatry,* **7**: 15–35.

Zilboorg, G. (1936). Suicide among primitive and civilized races. *Amer. J. Psychiat.,* **92:**1346–1369.

The author, utilizing her years of experience with potentially suicidal children, differentiates with supporting illustrations from case histories, how the assessment of childhood suicidal risk differs from that of adolescent self-destructive threats. Dr. Pfeffer discusses the incidence, presentation and factors associated with the risk of childhood suicidal behavior. She emphasizes the need to develop facility to spot early signs of impending suicidal action for young children, providing examples from her own experiences. A family oriented approach is supported as the most promising in prevention and treatment.

5
The Distinctive Features of Children Who Threaten and Attempt Suicide

Cynthia R. Pfeffer, M.D.

The desperation of some children is most poignantly conveyed by suicidal children. This chapter is based on a review of the literature and experience in evaluating and treating suicidal latency age children who are between the ages of six and twelve years. It will discuss the incidence, presentation, and factors associated with risk of childhood suicidal behavior.

Children may be considered suicidal when their thoughts and/or their actions could lead to serious self-injury or death. The following case vividly depicts some of the features of suicidal phenomena of latency age children.

Sammy, a slightly built ten-year-old boy, was brought to the hospital by his mother after he attempted to jump out a fourth floor window. The event was preceded by episodes in which he held his head under water in a bath tub and a pillowcase over his head. He stated that "no one loved me," and "everyone says I'm ugly." He believed that he would "go to hell if he died."

Sammy's difficulties increased six months before hospitalization. At that time his play became noticeably wilder and he became more difficult to manage. Fighting intensified with his eight-year-old brother, Jonathan. In addition, Sammy peeled paint off the walls and disarranged the furniture, especially whenever his mother slept.

A significant issue in Sammy's depression was that he had always believed that his mother's current husband was also his father. The intense rivalry between Sammy and his brother led to Jonathan teasing Sammy that, "I have a daddy and you don't." Finally, his mother, concerned about the increasing confusion that Sammy felt, revealed that her husband was not Sammy's natural father. Subsequently, Sammy became more destructive at home, ran away several times, and continually asked his mother to search for his father.

Several weeks later, during the week before Sammy's eighteen-year-old brother Eric, whom Sammy admired, entered the Army, his stepfather refused to take Sammy with Jonathan and his mother to buy new clothes. The stepfather stated that, "I would only take my own child." Sammy was left at home with his older brother Eric. Sammy ran away and four hours later was found by police wandering the streets. He told the police that his mother did not care for him, that she was an alcoholic and that she beat him.

Sammy's distress intensified after Eric left for the service. This loss was overwhelming for both Sammy and his mother. They considered Eric to be "the man of the house" and his departure left the family feeling abandoned and helpless. Sammy broke furniture in the house, became wild, banged his head on the floor and told his mother that he would tell people what she had done to him. On one occasion his mother, attempting to calm him, gave him a sleeping pill and allowed him to sleep with her. The next morning, Sammy was quiet but later his sister found him trying to drown himself in the bath tub. After he was dragged from the tub, he tried to jump out a window but was restrained by his mother. As a result, Sammy was taken to the hospital and admitted.

Previous history revealed that the extreme family disorganization and Sammy's distress were evident by the time that Sammy had entered school. At that time, Sammy soiled his pants and urinated behind beds. His mother responded to this by hitting him with a belt. Eventually the soiling and urinating abated. When Sammy was six years old, his mother took him to the hospital for treatment of injuries sustained as the result of her beating him with a wire. She complained about his lack of self-control, fighting with other children, and "his dislike of punishment." His mother was evaluated and told that she was "very disturbed." She was psychiatrically hospitalized for seven months. During that time, Sammy and his younger brother were placed in foster care. Eventually they returned home to their mother.

Sammy had never seen his natural father who left the family during Sammy's mother's pregnancy. His mother was an anxious and disorganized woman who was afraid that her family would vanish and that she would be left alone. In addition, she felt exasperated by the problems inherent in raising them. Sammy's suicide attempts were barometric signals of extreme chronic family chaos.

This case illustrates that serious self-directed life-threatening behavior occurs in latency age children and that such behavior is the end point of the interaction of a variety of complicated variables. Dysfunction within the family, school, and intrapsychically were extreme in this case. Hospitalization was indicated to protect Sammy from harm while comprehensive evaluation and immediate intervention could occur (Pfeffer, 1978).

INCIDENCE AND TECHNIQUES OF CHILDHOOD SUICIDAL BEHAVIOR

Until recently, childhood suicidal behavior has been a relatively neglected area of systematic research and clinical concern. Several issues contributed to the lack of professional clinical involvement. First, completed suicide among children was considered to be rare (Shaffer, 1974). In addition, it was believed that because of a lack of physical prowess children could not effect a fatal self-injury (Gould, 1965). Since theoretical constructs presume that children younger than age eight to ten years old do not realize that death is final, it was thought that by definition, children could not be considered suicidal. These misconceptions, in part, have influenced the United States classification and data collecting system of suicidal behavior for children. As a result, in the United States, vital statistics do not catalog suicide as a cause of death in children under ten years of age.

The underestimation of suicide rates in children may be related to death reported as accidental. It is commonly known that accidents are the leading cause of death among young children. However, there may be a subgroup of children whose deaths, although reported as accidental, were actually suicides (Connell, 1972). In addition, various, social, legal, and religious restraints may limit the accurate reporting and postmortem assessment of the cause of the death. For example, one study specifically pointed out the lack of precision in reporting serious injury or death of children and adolescents. This study included a review of records of sixty patients, ages six to eighteen years old, who were treated in poison control centers in Nebraska. The hospital diagnoses of the cases documented 42% accidents and 58% suicidal behavior. In contrast, the investigators concluded that 4% of the cases were accidents, 70% of the cases were suicidal gestures, 2% of the cases were suicide attempts, 22% of the cases were intoxications, and 2% of the cases were homicides (McIntire and Angle, 1973).

During the last two decades the rate of completed suicide for youngsters, ages ten to fourteen years old, dramatically increased from 0.4 per 100,000 in 1955 to 1.2 per 100,000 in 1975 (Frederick, 1978). However, comparison with younger children is not possible since no data exists for children under ten years of age. Nevertheless, a study carried out in England and Wales, where medical, coroner, and social service records are available, concluded that completed suicide in children under twelve years old is rare (Shaffer, 1974). However, an important finding of the study was that there was a relatively high frequency of suicidal threats and attempts. Therefore clinicians should focus on children who attempt and threaten suicide which may be the most appropriate means of preventing future completed suicide.

Suicidal latency-age children utilize a wide variety of self-destructive techniques that are similar to those of adults. Such methods as hanging, stabbing, jumping from heights, overdosing, drowning, running into traffic, and burning have been reported (Ackerly, 1967; Lukianowicz, 1968; Paulson et al., 1978; Pfeffer et al., 1979a). Jumping from heights seems to be the most characteristic technique of latency age children (Pfeffer, 1979b). Unlike adult cases, there are no reports of children, ages six to twelve years old, using firearms.

Vivid, detailed descriptions of the suicidal impulses and episodes of children have been reported. Aleksandrowicz (1975) reported on a seven-and-a-half-year-old girl who opened the window in her room on the first floor and jumped out at night. Luckily, a sheet hanging on a clothesline beneath deflected the impact of the fall. The child was even more fortunate in landing in some bushes—she sustained fractures of the pelvis. After this event, the child worried that her parents would be angry at her.

Bender and Schilder (1937) described eighteen suicidal children under thirteen years of age. One example is an eight-year-old boy, Frank, who was preoccupied with death, dreamed of death, and thought of the death of members of his family. He wanted to kill himself because other children wanted to hit him. He said, "I have to die and grow up in heaven. I would have to stick a knife in my belly" (page 49). He often cut himself and tore at his clothes. Lukianowicz (1968) described the cases of ten children under thirteen years old who contemplated or acted out suicidal impulses. Among this group of children, Howard, age nine years, stated that he "often thought of killing himself, either by throwing himself under a lorrie or by jumping into the sea and drowning" (page 423). An explicit wish to die and a plan to carry it out is common among suicidal latency age children.

Ackerly (1967) discussed the suicidal threats and attempts of thirty-one latency age children. An example was of George, six years old, who repeatedly attempted to strangle himself. "He was afraid that the world was going to be destroyed in a war and he would rather die by his own hand than be in this war. He did not want a tank to come and crush him and since his mother told him that there was going to be another war, he would rather die by killing himself than by being killed by the war. He said he was unhappy because his mother did not want him and that he had no father after their divorce. On previous occasions he had turned on the gas jets and had once set his snowsuit on fire" (page 251).

It is obvious that such serious self-endangering behaviors definitely occur in latency age children and that there is a distinct determination to harm or kill themselves. Furthermore, the occurrence of such behavior seems to have become more frequent. In the 1960s, the incidence of suicidal behavior among children seen in child guidance clinics was reported to be 7 to 10% (Lukianowicz, 1968). More recently, it has been noted in a study of a municipal hospital's child psychiatric hospital referrals that 33% of over one hundred of the children evaluated annually displayed suicidal tendencies (Lomonaco and Pfeffer, 1974). Furthermore in the same municipal hospital, a study of fifty-eight psychiatrically hospitalized latency age children showed 72% of the children manifesting suicidal ideas, threats or attempts (Pfeffer et al., 1979a). Finally, a survey of thirty-nine children evaluated in the same municipal hospital child psychiatric outpatient clinic showed that 33% of the children distinctively had suicidal impulses (Pfeffer, et al., 1979b). It was concluded from these studies that suicidal behavior was one of the most common symptoms among severely disturbed children (Pfeffer et al., 1979a).

In consideration of demographic factors, it is clear that suicidal actions occur more frequently with advancing age and at the time of puberty (Garfinkel and Golombek, 1974). In contrast, there have been insufficient studies of large enough populations of suicidal latency age children to be able to characterize any racial ethnic distinctions that may exist. Similarly, because there have been insufficiently large populations of suicidal latency age children studied, differences in sex factors are also not clear. There are indications that boys show more frequent suicidal behavior than girls during the latency age phase of development (Mattsson et al. 1969; Pfeffer et al., 1979a). This may be in keeping with the greater frequency of boys evaluated for psychiatric disturbances than girls during the latency age phase of development. In adolescent and adult populations, men seem to use more violent suicidal techniques such as hanging, shooting, and stabbing, and women utilize more passive modes such as ingestion, but no conclusive distinctions are apparent in suicidal techniques for latency age boys and girls.

FACTORS THAT PROMOTE SUICIDAL RISK OF CHILDREN

Suicidal behavior of children is a very complex symptom that is influenced by the interactive effects of environmental, developmental, and intrapsychic factors. An evaluation of the degree of suicidal risk of children must include a systematic assessment of these variables. The relative significance of each factor may differ with the individual child. Nevertheless, the primary immediate concern ought to be the guarantee of the safety of the child and then an intensive evaluation of the underlying problem and intervention should be carried out. As a result, the strengths derived from the child's external support systems, such as family, peers, and school professionals, and his own ego assets, need to be defined and utilized to guarantee that harm does not occur.

In a study of fifty-eight psychiatrically hospitalized latency age children, the factors that were significantly correlated with risk of childhood suicidal behavior were depression, worthlessness, helplessness, preoccupations with death, concepts of death as temporary and pleasant, and depression and suicidal behavior of the parents (Pfeffer et al., 1979a). Other factors such as extreme family disruption, separations, abusive home atmosphere, learning disabilities of the child, and multiple deficits of ego functioning were associated with serious psychopathology which could include suicidal acting-out. Therefore, the significant factors to evaluate include the family background, affective state of the child, the child's beliefs about death, and the ego functioning of the child, and the interaction of these factors as they affect the child's fantasy life. These issues require further clarification by means of additional case reports and systematic research.

The following factors are most relevant to risk for childhood suicidal behavior. The factors should always be considered when evaluating a child for potential suicidal risk.

External Influences—Family Background

Most significant to the proneness for childhood suicidal behavior is the environment in which the child grows up. It may have a dramatic effect because it may contain specific factors leading to suicide proneness for the child. Loss of a parent by separation, divorce, or death, as well as psychic loss of the parent resulting from intense marital discord and violence, may increase the child's sense of helplessness and vulnerability (Gould, 1965; Mattsson, et al., 1969). Often the suicidal behavior of a child may not be the only problem within the family but rather it may be a signal of an entire family's problems (French and Steward, 1975). One form of communication pattern within the family leading to suicidal behavior of the child was described as the "expendable child concept" (Sabbath, 1966). This concept presumed that the parent had conscious and/or unconscious beliefs that the child is bad. The child sensing this felt rejected and wished to die. Another problematic interaction may be the mismatch between a parent's character style and a child's temperamental state. Aleksandrowicz (1979) vividly depicted the chronic plight of a mother and her seven-and-a-half-year-old daughter, who attempted suicide by jumping out her bedroom window at night. The child was upset by the long-standing family problems and was overwhelmed by guilt due to her ambivalent relationship with her mother. Her mother was chronically withdrawn, depressed, and resented her daughter's exuberance. It was surmised that the actual precipitant of the suicidal act was the culmination of the long-standing tension between the mother and her daughter, which made them "biological strangers."

There are almost no studies that have attempted to describe the characteristics of the parents of suicidal children. Pfeffer et al., 1979a based their findings on the clinical observations of the parents of fifty-eight psychiatrically hospitalized latency age children in which 72% of the children had suicidal ideas, had made threats, or had made actual attempts. The most significant finding was that the parents of suicidal children were severely depressed and had a higher incidence of suicidal behavior, ranging from suicidal ideas to completed suicides, than a population of parents of the nonsuicidal hospitalized children. The parents of the suicidal children felt overwhelmed by the extreme family disorganization and were unable to appreciate and respond appropriately to the developmental needs of their child. The parents projected onto their child their own wishes to be nurtured by the child. Such role reversal between parent and child was a common occurrence. The children were embued with omnipotent powers by their parents, and often the parents could not differentiate themselves from their offspring. One parent noted that her son "was just like me." Another mother refused to send her ten-year-old daughter to school when the mother was sick. This mother demanded that her daughter tend to her needs during the illness. Often these parents projected their rage resulting from helplessness onto their children who were viewed as demons, bad, and to blame for the family problems. Finally many parents openly threatened that if the child did not obey, the parent would leave or commit suicide. Such manipulation by the parents terrorized their children who often responded with similar manipulations. Therefore, it was noted that in the hospitalized population of suicidal children, that such children often identify with their parents' style of coping. As a result one form of response was acting out of suicidal impulses. The significant implication of these observations is that an important issue for suicide prevention of children is to evaluate and to treat the offspring of parents who have marked suicidal tendencies.

Childhood Depression

Until recently the affect states of children that were associated with suicidal behavior were not clear. For example, Despert (1952) believed that suicidal children were angry, impulsive, and prone to serious acting-out behavior. She noted that the suicidal children she studied showed no evidence of depression. Some theorists believed that depression in latency age children does not exist. They based their remarks upon the notion that since the mature psychic structural organization had not yet been established during the latency age phase of development, that depressive responses similar to those of adult life were not possible (Rochlin, 1965). Controversy is generated by the theoretical model put forth by Sandler and Joffe (1965). They believed that depression is a basic affect like anxiety and that it can result from a state of ego helplessness and a loss of ego well-being. Using such an ego psychological framework, they believe that childhood depression exists as a clinical entity. Finally, until recently, these issues were clouded by the lack of definitive clinical criteria for diagnosing and observing depression in children.

At present, studies to discover whether depression in young children exists and to define its characteristics have utilized adult clinical criteria of diagnosing depression such as dysphoric mood, poor appetite, weight loss, sleep difficulty, loss of energy, psychomotor agitation or retardation, loss of interest or pleasure, excessive guilt, poor concentration, and thoughts of death or suicide. It is becoming evident that latency age children often show these signs of depression (Puig-Antich, et al., 1978). Therefore, it behooves clinicians to specifically inquire about the clinical signs of depression when evaluating potentially suicidal children.

In a study of fifty-eight psychiatrically hospitalized latency age children, it was found that specific correlates for high risk for suicidal behavior were sadness, withdrawal, wishes to die, hopelessness, and worthlessness (Pfeffer et al., 1979a). However, suicidal behavior in children is a symptom which is not only related to the clinical diagnosis of depression but also found in association with a variety of other psychiatric diagnoses ranging from acute situational reactions, behavior disorders, organic brain syndrome, and psychotic reactions. In addition, depressive affect may also be associated with a wide variety of clinical diagnoses.

The following cases will illustrate that suicidal behavior of children can occur in those who have different diagnoses.

CASE I—ARTHUR. Severe behavior disorder with borderline personality organization. Arthur, age ten years, was hospitalized immediately after he injured another child with a bottle in a fight and threatened to jump out the fourth floor window at school. By threatening to jump out the window, Arthur explained that he merely intended to capture his teacher's attention and that he would not really jump because he could hurt himself. However, he had made other such threats, as he noted, "only with my mother." Arthur's mother had reported that he had been a problem for a long time. She described him as "spoiled, demanding, disobedient, and prone to temper tantrums when frustrated." He was a danger to himself because he often walked on railroad tracks or rode his bicycle in the middle of a busy street.

Arthur's mother dated the onset of his problems to his entry into the first grade. His kindergarten teacher commented that, "He does lovely work in a small group but at other times he has no control over his actions. He is a very angry child who constantly picks on his peers." As he got older, it was observed in school that when he did not get his way, he was disruptive either by breaking things or by fighting with other children.

Arthur was the youngest of four children. He lived with his mother, siblings, and his mother's boyfriend. His mother was an intelligent woman who appeared to be self-depreciating. She was easily overwhelmed with depression and anxiety, and was unable to approach others who might be helpful. She described feeling "impotent as I watched my family falling apart." This was emphasized when Arthur's mother recalled that during her first years of marriage the family was relatively comfortable. However, everything changed when Arthur's father became involved with drugs which resulted in multiple prison sentences, debt, and the giving up of a stable family life. Arthur's father repeatedly promised to reform. Although there were periods of transient improvement, Arthur's mother maintained her faith that change would occur. However, when Arthur was two years old his parents separated, and then divorced. Arthur's mother responded with relief and began to work. Nevertheless, Arthur's father maintained contact with the family despite the divorce. Arthur's mother met her current boyfriend a few years before Arthur was hospitalized. The man was an intensely jealous person who was prone to violence when Arthur's father visited.

In the hospital, Arthur was noted to be a very verbal child with appropriate reality testing. Typically, he appeared agitated and preoccupied with his need for constant attention. He related by clinging, demanding, and whining and when gratified he was calm and affectionate. When prohibited from doing something he wanted, he was easily aroused to yelling, cursing, and throwing objects and fighting with peers. His tendency to react with intense fear to memories of old traumatic experiences were marked. At these times his thinking became disorganized, confused, and depressed; thoughts of harming himself were very frequent.

CASE II—LAWRENCE: Psychosis. Eight-year-old Lawrence had a history of suicide threats for two years prior to his hospitalization. On the day of admission, he had a fight with another child in school. When it was stopped by his teacher, Lawrence rushed to the window sill screaming "I am going to jump out the window." He was restrained by his teacher who arranged for an emergency hospital evaluation.

Previous suicidal threats consisted of Lawrence standing at windows of his fourth-floor apartment while influenced by command hallucinations telling him that he must die. He believed the voices were those of the devil. In addition, Lawrence was upset by visual hallucinations of the devil chasing him, by poor reality testing, and by a delusion that he was powerful and could influence others. Lawrence claimed not to be afraid to fall from windows because "God will protect me." Lawrence had a chronic history of sleep difficulties, nightmares, and frequent episodes of crying at night.

Since beginning school, Lawrence was repeatedly truant, disobedient, and had poor academic performance. He rarely associated with classmates. When engaged in group activities, he demanded that he be the leader and that others must abide by his rules. He was mistrustful and believed that others did not like him and that they called him names.

Lawrence's mother had a tumultuous childhood beset by parental arguments and abuse. She began to associate with gay women during her adolescence. She met Lawrence's father at age fifteen and as a result was bisexual until her marriage when she was eighteen and decided to "go straight." However, within three years the parents separated and Lawrence's mother reverted to homosexuality. Lawrence was born when his mother was nineteen years old and his sister was born when she was twenty years old. Lawrence's mother had a history of three suicide attempts in which she cut her wrist and ingested pills. Other psychiatric history included persecutory hallucinations and a psychiatric hospitalization for six months.

Home life was unstructured and confusing. Lawrence's mother frequently stayed away from home for extended periods. His grandmother assumed caretaker responsibilities for the children. Lawrence's mother remained with other women and indulged in smoking marijuana and taking other drugs. Furthermore, Lawrence had not seen his father since infancy. He believed that the family was so disruptive because his father deserted him.

Lawrence's behavior was characterized by dependency, a need for undivided attention, and immaturity. His attention span was limited and his eye contact minimal. His thoughts were bizarre and included fears that he would be assaulted by demons. He was preoccupied with sexuality and on several occasions he attempted sexual relations with a girl in the hospital unit. However, while hospitalized, he felt less anxious and reported a decreased frequency of visual and auditory hallucinations.

Concepts of Death in Children

Theoretical and direct observational investigations of children have pointed out that it is not until eight to ten years of age that most children understand that death is final (Nagy, 1965; Piaget, 1923). However, the child's beliefs about death must be further studied especially with regard to a significance for suicidal behavior. It has been demonstrated in a study of severely disturbed psychiatrically hospitalized latency age children that suicidal children are intensely preoccupied with thoughts of their own death and the deaths of emotionally important people. Furthermore, these suicidal children have distinct concepts that death is reversible and that death provides a temporary state of pleasantness (Pfeffer et al., 1979a). Similarly, Orbach (1977) noted in two case reports of suicidal latency age children that the children unconsciously equated death with gratification of wishes from an all-giving and passive mother. Such death concepts may increase risk of suicidal actions.

One implication for the treatment of potentially suicidal children is to focus on the ego functioning of the child. Specifically treatment should attempt to help the child develop a conscious realization that death is final and that it will not provide the hoped for wishes of the child. Such an awareness may strengthen the child's ego functioning, especially his reality testing, and his ability to delay impulsive discharge.

Ego Functioning of Suicidal Children

There has been little comprehensive systematic study of such ego functioning as cognitive ability, impulse control, reality testing, and object relations of suicidal children. However, a variety of case reports have shed light on some of these issues. Suicidal behavior has been noted in populations of children who are mentally retarded, of average intelligence, and of superior intelligence (Lawler, et al. 1963; Pfeffer et al., 1979a). In addition, children with and without learning disabilities are susceptible to suicidal behavior. The most important issue relating to school seems to be the degree of the child's worry about poor achievement rather than actual scholastic performance. Low self-esteem generated by peer comparisons and fear that their parents will scorn and punish them add to the distress about school performance. Such children feel deprived of full acceptance of their peers and parents and feel unable to compete with their age group.

Hypotheses about ego functioning have centered on the decompensation of the ego and reorganization of ego defenses which then leads to acting out of suicidal impulses (Sandler and Joffe, 1965; Schechter, 1957). Ackerly (1967), basing his hypotheses on case reports, believed that threatened suicide of children resulted from the interplay of aggressive drive and narcissistic frustration and disappointment. He believed that children who attempted suicide were overcome by a major break with reality, a massive disruption of adaptive mechanisms and a withdrawal from the world. In these cases, he believed that a psychotic state existed. He believed that children who threatened suicide and those who actually attempted suicide are a distinct group rather than on a continuum of suicidal behavior.

In contrast, Pfeffer et al. (1979a) did not find distinctions in the ego functioning of suicidal and nonsuicidal children who were hospitalized on a psychiatric ward. Also, no differences in ego functioning were noted for children who threatened or attempted suicide. These investigators believe that suicidal behavior existed as a continuum which included suicidal ideas, threats, and attempts. They remarked that both the suicidal and nonsuicidal children displayed a variety of affects which included pleasure, empathy, anxiety, and intense anger. The object relations of these children were characterized by states in which the children clung to empathic adults in the hope that their needs would be met. However, when frustrated the children precipitously became enraged and uncontrollable. Often suicidal ideas were verbalized in an attempt to control the environment. At times, the children believed that they had omnipotent magical powers and that by their wishes alone they could make something happen. When this did not occur their disappointment was intense and feelings of hopelessness and vulnerability ensued. The children became involved in intense reactions with their therapists, which repeated the types of interactions that they had with their parents. The children often imparted parental roles to their therapist and when this was understood in therapy, the resolution of conflicts became more probable.

Randy, age eleven years, illustrates these issues. He was hospitalized after he lay down in the middle of a busy street hoping that a car would run over him. Work with his therapist was tumultous. He demanded that his desires be met and when disappointed he threatened to kill himself. Once he told his therapist that he thought that the hospital staff doesn't believe him or like him. He wanted his therapist to reprimand the staff. When his therapist attempted to inquire further about these ideas, Randy threatened to kill himself, especially if he were not allowed to leave the hospital. When his therapist told him that he was not going to be allowed to hurt himself and he was not going to leave the hospital, Randy smiled and admitted that he did not want to leave. Instead, he wanted someone to take him seriously. As a result of his confrontation, Randy was able to speak about his threats to leave home in an effort to get his mother to take him seriously. However, he admitted that he never wanted to leave home.

Fantasies Associated With Suicidal Behavior

In evaluating a suicidal child, one begins to understand the conflicts, dynamic motivations, wishes and fears promoting such acting out behavior. In almost all circumstances, there is a wish to avoid or leave an upsetting situation which may result from an abusive traumatic, and unhappy home life, or the intrapsychic stresses resulting from intense affects or psychotic disorganization. A child may wish to gain control of the situation in which he feels enraged, helpless, and vulnerable. Suicidal behavior may be the end point of a child's manipulative attempts. The fantasy that "see what you have done to me, you will be sorry when I am dead," is consonant with a child's manipulation. Intense loneliness, fears, and oppression may stimulate thoughts of achieving a happier feeling by rejoining a lost love object. Thoughts of absent or dead relatives or friends may increase the child's wishes to die. Intense guilt feelings produced by sexual or aggressive impulses generate the attempts at self-punishment by a self-destructive means. All of these fantasies are similar to those that are apparent in the conflicts of suicidal adolescents and adults.

Several of these fantasies are often present in the same child and may become apparent in the initial phases of evaluation or after therapeutic work has commenced. This was sensitively described in a case of an analysis of a fifteen-and-a-half-year-old girl (Kernberg, 1974). In that case it was noted that many suicidal fantasies existed because the treatment explored various levels of suicidal tendencies which were apparent at different stages of regression during the treatment sessions. It was also noted that the suicidal fantasies changed as the resolution of conflicts occurred. Similarly, in the treatment of latency-age children, interventions are geared to defining suicidal fantasies and promoting a deterrent ability to acting out of such impulses. With children, it is hoped that in treatment the child will channel impulses into play, verbalization, and sublimation (Pfeffer, 1979a).

DETERRENT INFLUENCES ON SUICIDAL BEHAVIOR OF CHILDREN

One of the most difficult tasks for a clinician is to assess whether the danger from a child's suicidal tendencies requires immediate measures to afford protection from harm, or whether the child may be able to remain in his/her home surroundings while the underlying problems are explored. When imminent harm appears most likely, psychiatric hospitalization may be the most effective acute intervention (Pfeffer, 1978).

Knowledge of contributing risk factors are essential to assess. In addition, the influences that may prevent subsequent suicidal actions must be defined. Most important is the assessment of the external support system of the family, friends, school teachers, as well as the diagnosis of the child's state of impulse control, reality testing, and object relations.

Childhood suicidal behavior must always be considered a family problem. Therefore, an immediate therapeutic alliance with the parents is essential. Their recognition, rather than a denial of the seriousness of their child's behavior, must become immediately apparent so that they may be helpful in the therapeutic task. Their ability to show insight into the need for family reorientation and change is an essential ingredient for a positive therapeutic outcome.

The most significant ego functioning of the child to assess is his ability to tolerate some frustration and delay action so that a therapeutic process can develop. Adequate reality testing is necessary to ensure that intrusions of impulses and frightening thoughts do not interfere with the child's ability to maintain an immediate stability. Finally, the ability of the child to show that he can form a therapeutic alliance with the therapist, to whom trust and hope can be imparted, may indicate that initial safety can be guaranteed.

CONCLUSION

Suicidal behavior of latency age children has been, until recently, a relatively neglected area of child psychopathology. It is apparent that suicidal ideas, threats, and attempts among children are common. While many of the characteristics of childhood suicidal behavior are similar to those of adolescent and adult suicidal behavior, the assessment of childhood suicidal risk is different and at times more difficult. Studies of adolescent suicidal behavior have clearly demonstrated that previous suicidal attempts or threats are a precursor to completed suicide. As a result, it is essential to develop facility to spot early signs of impending suicidal action for young children. In addition, more systematic research into the manifestations, etiology, and treatment of childhood depression and suicidal behavior are needed. Additional studies using a family-oriented approach may aid prevention of childhood suicide proneness as well as the treatment of suicidal children.

REFERENCES

1. Ackerly, W. C. (1967). Latency age children who threaten or attempt to kill themselves. *J. Am. Acad. Child Psychiat.,* **6**:242–261.
2. Aleksandrowicz, M. K. (1975). The biological strangers: an attempted suicide of a 7½-year-old-girl. *Bulletin Menninger Clinic,* **39**:163–176.
3. Bender, L. and Schilder, P. (1937). Suicidal preoccupations and attempts in childhood. *Am. J. of Orthopsych.* **7**:225–234.
4. Connell, H. M. (1972). Attempted suicide in school children. *Med. J. of Australia,* **1**:686–690.
5. Despert, F. L. (1952). Suicide and depression in children. *Nervous Child,* **9**:378–389.
6. Frederick, C. J. (1978). Current trends in suicidal behavior in the United States. *Am. J. Psycotherapy,* **321**:172–200.

7. French, A. P., and Steward, M. S. (1975). Family dynamics, childhood depression, and attempted suicide in a 7-year-old boy. *Suicide and Life Threatening Behavior,* **5**(1):29–37.
8. Garfinkel, B. D., and Golombek, H. (1974). Suicide and depression in childhood and adolescence. *Canadian Med. Ass. J.,* **110**:1278–1281.
9. Gould, R. E. (1965). Suicide problems in children and adolescents. *Am. J. of Psychotherapy,* **19**:228–246.
10. Kernberg, P. (1974). The analysis of a 15½-year-old girl with suicidal tendencies. *In: The Analyst and the Adolescent at Work.* M. Harley (ed.) New York: Quadrangle New York Book Co., pp. 232–268.
11. Lawler, R. H., Nakielny, W., and Wright, N. A. (1963). Suicidal attempts in children. *Canadian Med. Assoc. J.,* **89**:751–754.
12. Lomonaco, S., and Pfeffer, C. R. (1974). Suicidal and self-destructive behavior of latency age children. Read at Annual Meeting of the American Academy of Child Psychiatry, San Francisco, California.
13. Lukianowicz, N. (1968). Attempted suicide in children. *Acta Psychiatrica Scandinavica,* **44**:415–435.
14. Mattsson, A., Seese, L. R., and Hawkins, J. W. (1969). Suicidal behavior as a child psychiatry emergency. *Archives of J. Psychiatry,* **20**:100–109.
15. McIntire, M. S., and Angle, C. R. (1973). Psychological biopsy in self-poisoning of children and adolescents. *Am. J. Diseases of Children,* **126**:42–46.
16. Nagy, M. (1965). The child's theories concerning death. *J. of Genetic Psychology,* **73**:3–27.
17. Orbach, I (1977). Unique characteristics in children's suicidal behavior. *Proceedings Ninth International Congress in Suicide Prevention and Crisis Intervention,* 382–388.
18. Paulson, M. J., Stone, D., and Sposto, R. (1978). Suicide potential and behavior in children ages 4 to 12. *Suicide and Life Threatening Behavior,* **8**:225–242.
19. Pfeffer, C. R. (1978). Hospital treatment of suicidal latency age children. *Suicide and Life Threatening Behavior,* **8**:150–160.
20. Pfeffer, C. R. (1979a). A model for acute psychiatric inpatient treatment of latency-age children. *Hospital and Community Psychiatry,* **30**:547–551.
21. Pfeffer, C. R. (1979b). Clinical observations of play of suicidal latency age children. *Suicide and Life Threatening Behavior* (In Press).
22. Pfeffer, C. R., Conte, H. R., Plutchik, R., and Jerrett, I. (1979a). Suicidal behavior in latency age children: An empirical study *J. Am. Acad. of Child Psychiatry* **18**:679–692.
23. Pfeffer, C. R., Conte, H. R., Plutchik, R., and Jerrett, I. (1980). Suicidal behavior in latency age children: An empirical study II: An outpatient population. *J. Am. Acad. Child Psychiat.* **19**:703–710.
24. Piaget, J. (1923). Language and thought of the child. London: O. Routledge, I. Kegan.
25. Puig-Antich, J., Blau, S., Marx, N., Greenhill, L., and Chambers, W. (1978). Prepubertal major depression disorder: a pilot study. *J. Am. Acad. Child Psychiat.,* **17**:695–707.
26. Rochlin, G. N. (1965). *Griefs and Discontents: The Forces of Change.* Boston: Little Brown.
27. Sabbath, J. C. (1966). The suicidal adolescent—the expendable child. *J. Am. Acad. Child Psychiat.* **5**:272–289.
28. Sandler, J., and Joffee, W. G. (1965). Notes on childhood depression. *International J. of Psychoanalysis,* **46**:88–96.
29. Schechter, M. D. (1957). The recognition and treatment of suicide in children. *In: Clues to Suicide.* E. S. Schneidman and N. L. Farberow, (eds.) New York: McGraw-Hill, pp. 131–142.
30. Shaffer, D. (1974). Suicide in childhood and early adolescents. *J. Child Psychology and Psychiatry and Allied Disciplines,* **15**:275–291.

Psychoactive drug taking has become an integral part of coming of age in America. These behaviors are complexly determined by the interaction of social, psychobiological, and pharmacological factors. Most young people do not experience serious disability as a result of their drug taking; it is experimental or intermittent. At the same time, the behaviors are so prevalent that drug abuse has become a leading cause of disability and death in the youthful populations. The provision of appropriate treatment requires personnel and programs which are prepared to handle the multiple problems of adolescence in addition to drugs. In distinction to most other diseases in young people, drug abusers are often unwilling to seek treatment and may frustrate the efforts of treatment personnel. Then too, the negative attitudes and perspectives of therapists and health professionals may represent a significant obstacle to the provision of effective treatments. Drug-taking behaviors in some young people must be seen as chronic illnesses marked by remissions and exacerbations. Long-term, comprehensive treatment programs are therefore necessary for these people. Whereas increased initiatives in prevention and early treatment are indicated, it should be appreciated that much remains to be learned about the determinants of drug-abuse behaviors and the development of effective preventive measures.

6
Perspectives on Drug Use and Abuse

Robert B. Millman, M.D.
Elizabeth T. Khuri, M.D.
David Hammond, M.D.

INTRODUCTION

Most psychoactive drug use and abuse begins in the adolescent years (Abelson et al., 1977; Johnston et al., 1979). It is also during these early years that the impact of drug taking is most profound. To understand these complex behaviors, the psychological and social setting in which the drugs are used must be appreciated, as must the pharmacology and patterns of abuse of the particular psychoactive substances.

There is a higher risk for incurring the negative consequences of drug abuse during the adolescent years than at any other time of life. These include the direct sequelae of the drug use, such as overdose and physical disability, as well as deterioration in school and work performance, violent behavior, including suicide and homicide, and accidents of various kinds. In fact, the leading causes of death in young people may be ascribed to drug and alcohol use, either directly or indirectly (Blum and Richards, 1979; Hein et al., 1979). These are needless deaths foreclosing enormous possibilities for growth and change.

At the same time, recognition of the human cost of the misuse of these agents should not lead us to exaggerate the dangers. In some areas over 80% of high-school-age children have used one or more drugs for nonmedical purposes (Abelson et al., 1977; Johnston et al., 1979). Most of them do not get into trouble and the drug use may be considered "appropriate" for their age and location. In many of these young people the drug use may not be self-destructive in any sense of the term. There is frequently no sharp line that distinguishes appropriate use from abuse of any drug. Abuse may therefore be defined as the use of any substance in a manner that deviates from the accepted medical, social, or legal patterns within a given society (Millman, 1978; Oakley, 1972; Zinberg et al., 1975).

Since ancient times, people have used substances that induce alterations in mood, perception, and behavior, for medical, religious, or recreational purposes. No single factor is the basis of all drug-taking experience and no person's drug taking has a single etiology. Initially, psychoactive drugs may be taken merely to feel differently. Little children will spin around in place or hold their breath until they get dizzy; the smell of gasoline or glue is felt to be pleasurable for similar reasons. Drugs are taken to reduce tension and anxiety, to decrease fatigue and boredom, to facilitate social interaction, to change activity levels, to improve mood, to heighten sensation and awareness, to satisfy curiosity, and for many other reasons (Weil, 1972; Oakley, 1972). Many young people experiment with drugs that are considered dangerous from a medical or legal point of view and do not repeat the experience. Others use them intermittently in a controlled fashion and do not harm themselves. Still others persist in drug-abuse behavior patterns that lead to physical or psychosocial deterioration (Millman, 1978).

Psychological dependence or *habituation* occurs when an adolescent requires a particular drug or its comcomitant in order to function at what he/she perceives to be a satisfactory level. This varies in intensity and may culminate in a compulsive drug-abuse pattern where the supply and use of a particular drug become primary concerns of living. Certain drug classes have a further capacity to produce *physical dependence*. This is an altered physiological state induced by the repeated administration of a drug that requires the continued administration of the drug to prevent the appearance of a syndrome characteristic for each drug, the *withdrawal* or *abstinence* syndrome. The term *addiction* has been overused in the literature and by the media to refer to both behavioral and pharmacologic events. As used herein, it refers to a pattern of compulsive drug use that includes both physical dependence and an overwhelming involvement with the supply and use of a drug. Neither a compulsive user of marijuana nor a diabetic on insulin—nor a well-adjusted patient in methadone maintenance treatment—is an addict in this sense of the term. *Tolerance* refers to the need to increase the dose of a drug to elicit the same psychoactive or physiological effects (Jaffe, 1975; Millman, 1974).

The most important drugs that are subject to abuse may be grouped into six major classes according to their pharmacology: (1) opiates; (2) central nervous system depressants including hypnotics and tranquilizers. Alcohol shares many of the characteristics of this class and will be considered in a separate chapter; (3) central nervous system stimulants including the amphetamine group and cocaine; (4) cannabis; (5) psychedelics; and (6) miscellaneous inhalants. The epidemiology, patterns of abuse, and determinants of abuse of these substances will be considered prior to formulating general treatment principles. It is beyond the scope of this chapter to consider the various classes of drugs in any detail. This information may be obtained from the relevant sources listed in the bibliography. Brief mention will be made of some of the salient characteristics of these diverse substances to provide more precise focus for diagnostic or treatment efforts.

EPIDEMIOLOGY

It is difficult to accurately assess the incidence and prevalence of psychoactive drug abuse given the illicit or otherwise stigmatized nature of the phenomena, the rapidity of change, and the great cultural and geographical variation of these patterns (Hunt, 1979; Project DAWN V, 1977). Surveys of adolescents are often done in schools. Students who do not attend school regularly, often for drug-related reasons, will not be represented (Schnoll, 1979; A Survey, 1975). Then too, the responses of those who do reply may be biased by the fact that the surveys are school sponsored. An additional technical problem is that the age range of adolescents surveyed varies considerably in different studies (Blos, 1962; Schnoll, 1979). Some surveys exaggerate the prevalence or severity of the problem in order to demonstrate or dramatize the need for public funding and expansion of research and treatment programs. Others do not adequately distinguish between the intermittent, controlled use of drugs and more compulsive abuse syndromes. Despite these critical limitations of the data, it is nevertheless possible to outline some of the broad trends in adolescent substance abuse.

During the last twenty years, there has been an explosive increase in the use and abuse of all drugs. This was associated with the development of a media-popularized counterculture that rejected traditional values and sought to find meaning and truth in pharmacologically altered states of consciousness. A diverse and constantly changing series of social, religious and metaphysical beliefs provided a foundation for this search and served as a focus for group identification and pride. Marijuana use began to increase during the period 1962–67, particularly in males and those living in metropolitan areas. Use of other drugs remained at low levels during this period. During the period 1967–77, an explosive increase in the use of marijuana occurred in the young, associated with a significant, though less profound, increase in use of other drugs including heroin and other opiates, cocaine, amphetamines, and psychedelics. By 1977, more than one-fourth of all youth between the ages of twelve and seventeen reported having used marijuana at least once, as did more than one-half of young adults eighteen to twenty-five years old. Current users included 4% of twelve-year-olds, 15% of fourteen-year-olds, and 31% of young adults from eighteen to twenty-one years old. Use of stronger drugs increased to approximately 5 to 10% of samples studied. About one-third of the youth and one-fifth of the young adults who have ever had one of the stronger drugs may be considered current users. Current use of inhalants is rare (Abelson et al., 1977; Johnston et al., 1979, O'Donnell et al., 1976).

During the years between 1974 and 1978, surveys indicate a slight leveling off of the current use of psychedelics, opiates, amphetamines, and depressants. During this period, the use of phencyclidine (PCP) increased to approximately 6% of some populations (Abelson et al., 1977; Johnston et al., 1979). More recent reports indicate that there may also be a leveling off of phencyclidine use and adverse effects. It is possible that the decline in PCP use occurred incident to the barrage of media and street intelligence attesting to the dangers of this drug (Zinberg, 1975). Markedly increased heroin use is also being reported as measured by applications for treatment programs, overdoses, and arrests. This may be a function of increased heroin availability and purity, presumably coming from Iran and Southwest Asia. Cocaine use is also increasing, particularly among the middle-class and affluent.

Several general observations may be useful. Illicit drug use is strongly related to age and, in general, may be expected to wane as users reach maturity. Though current use rates are higher for young adults from eighteen to twenty-five years than for younger people, it appears as if drug use is moving downward to the younger age groups, where it may be more dangerous. During the past twenty years, drug use has spread from urban minority groups to middle-class whites and more rural areas. Then too, the initial preponderance of drug use in males versus females has decreased significantly (Abelson et al., 1977; Blum et al., 1979; Johnston et al., 1979).

Drug use in the young may be conceptualized as moving from an epidemic situation where use increased precipitously and involved naive youngsters across all social and psychological lines, to an endemic situation where use has become an integral part of the rites of passage in America. The various drugs are well known and patterns of abuse and adverse consequences have become part of popular culture. Where previously, a significant proportion of the drug use led to adverse consequences, as with alcohol, it is likely that the preponderance of current adolescent drug use is more sophisticated and controlled and will often not result in severe disability. It is the socially, psychologically, or even physically disabled youngsters who are most at risk of becoming compulsive users and suffering serious sequelae (Millman and Khuri, 1973; Zinberg, 1975).

ABUSE PATTERNS

Initial drug experiences are determined by social and cultural factors including the availability of particular psychoactive substances, peer pressure, media emphasis, and legal sanctions (Blum and Richards, 1979; Jessor, 1975; Wechsler, 1976). Subsequent patterns become more dependent on psychobiologic and pharmacologic factors (Meyer and Mirin, 1979; Oakley, 1972. The youthful are most often introduced or "turned on" to the various drugs by a close friend (Blum and Richards, 1979; Hughes and Crawford, 1972). The role of the adult "profiteer" preying on unsuspecting children in this process is minimal. Initial intentions may be to share an exciting or pleasurable experience or diffuse some of the shame or guilt associated with drug taking. The drug use may then become a focus for group interaction and identity (Becker, 1967; Jessor, 1975). Most young people believe that they are able to control their drug taking so that it will not be personally destructive despite the admonitions of parents, school authorities, and media regarding the dangers of drug use and despite the fact that they are often personally familiar with victims of these behaviors. In most cases they are right; the drug use is less destructive to them than they have been led to believe (Millman, 1978; Zinberg et al., 1975).

Young people typically experiment with psychoactive drugs at age thirteen to fourteen with nicotine, beer, wine, and occasionally hard liquor. They drink in association with friends at social functions or often with parents and other family members. During this period or somewhat later, the use of marijuana may begin. Some adolescents go on to try depressants, stimulants, and psychedelics, particularly LSD and phencyclidine; opiates and cocaine are often the last drugs in this decidedly nonlinear, complex progression. In some sociocultural contexts, opiate experimentation may begin early, just after the initial alcohol exposures (Hamburg et al., 1975; Kandel et al., 1976).

Most adolescents stop at particular points in this sequence, depending on a wide variety of factors. Others will use only one drug or group of drugs during a period. More often a variety of drugs will be used, depending on the availability of the drugs, the situation, and the needs of the user. This so-called *polydrug-abuse* pattern varies in severity from the intermittent use of carefully selected drugs on special occasions, to the disorganized, dangerous multiple drug-abuse patterns of severely disturbed youngsters. On certain occasions, a group of reasonably well-adjusted teen-agers will take marijuana, methaqualone, and cocaine in preparation for a concert. At the same time, they disdain the compulsive abuser of depressants or heroin who is unable to function socially or in school (Johnston et al., 1979; Millman, 1978). Significantly, as young people give up on the more exotic drugs further along in the sequence, they often return to the drugs they had used earlier, such as marijuana or alcohol (Hamburg et al., 1975).

The progression from intermittent, experimental use to compulsive abuse may in part be a function of social learning. The future drug abuser learns about the drug and the patterns of abuse from friends. This process of anticipatory socialization includes education about the pleasures of altered states of consciousness and a drug-dominated society. The drug administration is then associated with psychoactive and physiological effects that he learns to identify as pleasurable. The experience is then repeated (Becker, 1967). Withdrawal symptoms may then supervene, resulting in a compulsive abuse syndrome (Jaffe, 1975; Meyer and Mirin, 1979; Millman, 1974). It is likely that personality patterns significantly influence this sequence (Jaffe, 1975; Zinberg, 1975).

The question of whether marijuana use leads to so-called "harder" drug use is controversial (Goode, 1974). Though much of the enlightened literature denounces this belief as retrospective falsification, it merits further consideration. If one took no psychoactive drugs, including alcohol, nicotine, and coffee, obviously there could be no progression to other drugs (Blum and Richards, 1979; Hamburg et al., 1975). The experience of altering or controlling consciousness or mood with a psychoactive substance often provides the impetus for users to attempt other manipulations. Whereas the cannabis use may have been benign, the subsequent experimentation with heroin or depressants may facilitate the development of severe drug problems in some youngsters. It is clear, however, that the psychological and social predisposition of individual adolescents is more important in the development of these problems than whether he or she has ever used marijuana or nicotine (Millman, 1978).

DETERMINANTS OF DRUG-ABUSE BEHAVIOR

The literature is replete with discussions of the determinants of drug-abuse behavior; these include sociological, parental, psychobiological, genetic, and pharmacological factors (Bihari, 1976; Blum and Richards, 1979; Fenichel, 1945; Kamali and Steer, 1976). It should be noted that an association between these characteristics and the abuse of psychoactive substances does not necessarily represent a causal relationship. In fact, none of these characteristics and no testing of any kind has been shown to be predictive for the development of drug-abuse behavior nor which people will use which drug (Dole, 1972; Zinberg et al., 1975). It is also important to emphasize that these oft-quoted determinants are frequently associated with drug use of any kind or severity. Few attempts have been made to characterize the transition from experimentation to compulsive use.

Psychobiological Factors

Personality influences the choice of drugs as well as the patterns of abuse. In part, personality can determine the psychoactive effects that the drugs will elicit in a given setting. Considerable controversy exists as to whether drug abuse implies individual psychopathology that antedates drug use or whether specific patterns of abuse can correlate with certain personality types (Dole, 1972; Zinberg, 1975). It is likely that the intermittent use of psychoactive drugs is not necessarily an indication of underlying psychopathology. At the same time, compulsive drug use is frequently associated with serious psychopathology (Khantzian et al., 1974). Studies confirm that psychopathology varies considerably in drug-abusing populations, as do the psychological factors that may play an etiologic role in drug abuse (Steer and Schut, 1979). There is no consistent evidence supporting the existence of a defined ''addictive personality'' type or characteristic psychodynamic constellation in all compulsive drug users. Though in many cases premorbid personality disturbance can be clearly linked to compulsive drug use, in other cases such linkage is difficult to establish and observed psychopathology may be a result of drug use itself as well as a reaction of the individual to life in a society that condemns a drug-dependent life (Zinberg et. al., 1975).

The development and maintenance of compulsive drug-abuse patterns is often based on conditioned learning. The feelings of dysphoria that the drug-taking behavior allays or situations attendant to drug taking become, in time, a conditioned stimulus to the experience of drug taking. This can occur both in the presence and in the absence of physical dependence. Long-abstinent addicts often experience drug-craving and withdrawal syndromes when they return to the site of former drug use. The effects of individual drugs must also be understood as a learning response. Marijuana and alcohol will elicit different and sometimes contrasting responses depending on expectations and group pressure, particularly in the young. In some cultures, marijuana is used as a work stimulant or appetite depressant, in marked contrast to its well-publicized effects on American adolescents, of decreasing motivation and stimulating appetite (Meyer and Mirin, 1979).

Compulsive drug taking in some adolescents can be understood as an attempt at self-treatment of painful affects of shame, rage, loneliness, and depression (Khantzian et al., 1974). A so-called masked depression may be etiologic in some cases of drug use. The boredom, restlessness, apathy in school, wanderlust, philosophizing, sexual promiscuity, and frantic seeking of new activities may represent depressive states in young people (Gallemore and Wilson, 1972; Carlson and Cantwell, 1980). Others may be seeking to satisfy or control unacceptable drives, including sexual and security needs, as well as primitive, sadistic, and aggressive wishes. It has been suggested that for some young people there may be an impairment in drive defenses such that these feelings are experienced as overwhelming. Primitive defenses, including denial, splitting, and externalization, are also used against these overwhelming affects (Wurmser, 1974). Pathological extremes of narcissism and dependency may be identified. Many individuals who use drugs seem to have an inability to identify and articulate their emotions; they experience these as somatic complaints for which drugs offer special relief. Superego pathology based on faulty ego ideal formation, disordered value systems, or punitive and overly demanding superegos, may exist (Wurmser, 1974; Zinberg, 1975).

Drug taking has been related to pre-Oepidal pathology based on unresolved issues relating to attachment and separation from the mother. Drugs may serve as a loved object of symbiotic attachment for the user. One sees children who are unable to pursue their needs for admiration and for love. They seem unable to build a system of activity, interests, and relationships that serve as a buffer against powerful feelings of depression and boredom. Drugs become part of an intense narcissistic withdrawal (Kernberg, 1975). Some users have personality disorders; others show evidence of psychotic states (Kaufman, 1974; Steer and Schut, 1979). Borderline and psychotic adolescents may use drugs, particularly heroin, to cope with powerful paranoid and angry feelings. Amphetamines may provide compulsive users with feelings of power and confidence and relieve them from deep feelings of depression. Alcohol use has been related to the denial of feelings of vulnerability and loneliness. It allows the expression of long-suppressed anger (Milkman and Frosch, 1973; Wurmser, 1974).

Many severely disturbed young people will use only opiates or depressants and will not use marijuana, hallucinogens, or stimulants since these drugs further weaken their hold on reality and enhance anxious or paranoid feelings. At the same time, there are psychologically disabled people who preferentially abuse these drugs. It is possible that the intense psychoactive effects, however unpleasant, may insulate them from their own thoughts or feelings or perhaps facilitate attempts to rationalize their "craziness." There is also preliminary evidence that the pharmacologic actions of the various drugs may be important in the development of psychopathology. It is not difficult to accept the possibility that chronic use of euphoriants, such as the opiates or benzodiazepines, may result in chronic depressive or anxiety states. This is particularly provocative in light of the recent work on endogenous morphinelike substances or the discovery of naturally occurring high-affinity binding sites for benzodiazepines (e.g., Librium and Valium) in the brain (Millman, 1979).

While the choice of drugs can reflect personality characteristics, so do the patterns of abuse. A depressed and obsessive character may use heroin compulsively in a structured and organized fashion. Borderline psychotic youngsters may use a variety of drugs in a disorganized, chaotic manner such that they suffer frequent adverse reactions and overdoses. Some of these young people take great pride in calling themselves ''garbage heads'' who will take anything in any quantity, regardless of the dangers. They may have little else to be proud of (Zinberg, 1975). In Erickson's (1963) terms, they may depend on a ''negative identity'' for a measure of self-esteem and self-definition.

When drugs are withdrawn from severely disturbed individuals, deterioration of psychosocial functioning may result. It is not unusual for a seemingly well-compensated young heroin addict to become psychotic when detoxified or stabilized on methadone. In other cases, seemingly severe psychopathology will improve as drugs are withdrawn.

Sociological Factors

Adolescence is a time when the individual separates from his family, to be confronted with his own powerlessness in an alien, adult world. Experimentation is an integral part of the young person's search for an adult identity as he progresses from the dependence of childhood to the independence of maturity. Despite the importance of testing and experimentation, the rules of behavior for the adolescent are those of the adult; enthusiasm, curiosity, and spontaneity are often distrusted and initiative frequently mistaken for aggressiveness. Few adolescents believe that they will measure up to the demands of society; they lack an adult identity and often feel powerless. They are told that this is a critical period of preparation, but they have a realistic and profound dread of the future.

Societal institutions with which the adolescent comes into contact, including the family and the educational system, may be unresponsive or even hostile. Families often lack consistency in the setting and enforcing of limits. Gratification of material needs may be coupled with unrealistic demands for educational success. Adolescents may be made to feel that they cannot measure up, have severe psychological problems, and are morally inadequate. Peer affiliation and acceptance are crucial for the adolescent's growing sense of self. They need to compare what they believe they are to what they appear to be in the eyes of others, though many of them do not have experience or confidence to develop productive relationships.

Poverty and minority-group status compound the problems of being young and further reduce the enjoyment, uniqueness, sense of dignity, and power of the ''straight'' world. Families are often in disarray and successful role models in adult legitimate society are often unknown or distant. Many of these young people, particularly those who live in inner-city ghettos, develop an enormous and sophisticated range of survival skills on the street. They may be intelligent and highly perceptive judges of people and situations, yet they are unprepared for the educational system and find classes boring, irrelevant, or demeaning (Preble and Casey, 1969; Robins and Murphy, 1967; Hein et al., 1979; Blum and Richards, 1979). A sense of hopelessness, inevitable failure, or anger may result from these conditions (Blos, 1962; Millman, 1974).

Other frequently cited determinants include inadequate parental control and support, more delinquency, and less religiosity (Burkett, 1977; Hamburg et al., 1975; Kamali and Steer, 1976; O'Donnell et al., 1976).

The self-administration of psychoactive substances remains one of the few pleasurable options for many young people; it may be a predictable, reliable way to punctuate an otherwise unrewarding existence. The drug abuser obtains peer acceptance, a sense of control, and a pharmacological effect that enhances self-esteem and relieves tension and anxiety (Wider and Kaplan, 1969; Wurmser, 1974).

Sexual experiences in adolescent populations are frequently unsatisfactory or worse, due to lack of experience and feelings of inadequacy and anxiety. Many young people find that low doses of sedatives, opiates, or alcohol increase desire, relieve inhibitions, and improve performance. Males frequently report that they are unable to sustain an erection unless they are "stoned." The great vogue that Quāāludes have had in recent years relates to this phenomenon. The necessity to increase the dose of the various drugs, with the advent of tolerance, results in decreased ability, and recurrence of the depressed and anxious feelings. It should be emphasized that compulsive use of most drugs is associated with decreased sexual interest and performance.

Given these pressures, it is not surprising that many adolescents are unable to focus on long-range goals, that they seek immediate gratification, or that they are unable to appreciate the consequences of dangerous behaviors (Blos, 1962; Erikson, 1963; Millman, 1974).

GENERAL TREATMENT CONSIDERATIONS

The development of an appropriate treatment plan depends upon the accurate characterization of the adolescent, including his personality characteristics, psychopathology, social and family milieu, as well as the pattern and extent of drug abuse. Immediate dangers must be assessed rapidly. Whereas treatments may be provided by personnel of diverse training and background, to be effective these must be prepared to handle the multiple problems of adolescence in addition to drugs.

Youthful drug abusers often do not come into contact with treatment personnel until their behavior has progressed to the point that it is recognized by family, school, or legal authorities or they suffer adverse effects of the drug taking (Institute of Medicine, 1978). They often perceive their drug taking as enjoyable, safe, and controlled. It may well be, though often extreme denial is evident in their inability to appreciate the implications of this drug use (Litt and Cohen, 1974). They are also reluctant to seek help from conventional authorities. They are loath to reveal themselves to people with whom they believe they have no rapport. They believe they will not be respected or understood. The therapist, physician, teacher, and parent, though apparently well-meaning, are considered to be alien and even hostile presences (Bernstein and Shkuda, 1974; Lecker et al., 1973). At the same time, there are data suggesting that provision of early treatments to drug abusers before they have lost precious time or their compulsive drug-taking patterns have become chronic, will ensure better results.

The negative attitudes and conceptualizations of treatment personnel may also present serious obstacles to effective treatment. Treatment personnel often consider these youngsters weak, lacking in will-power, or even criminal (Chappel and Schnoll, 1977). Despite the obvious serious disability that may be present, the sense that "they did it to themselves" is often the foundation for inadequate therapeutic efforts. Disability that results from a disease is considered to be a significantly different situation. Interestingly, the behavior of patients with nondrug-abuse related phobic or compulsive disorders are considered to be part of disease processes. The idea that various determinants may cause a "disability of the will" is often difficult to accept (Sterne and Pittman, 1965; Gert and Duggan, 1979).

These patients commonly do not show consistent progress whatever the form of treatment employed, often being unable to cease drug use or resuming its use after detoxification and varying periods of abstinence. This is frustrating to the well-intentioned therapist or treatment team. The problem may be a conceptual one; therapists regard drug-taking behaviors as an acute illness and liable to complete cure. Since the nature of most of the etiologic psychosocial factors are chronic and the nature of the neurochemical impact of compulsive drug use may be more protracted than previously imagined, perhaps these behaviors should be viewed as chronic illnesses, with remissions and exacerbations, and more like diabetes or schizophrenia than pneumonia (Dole, 1972).

It is often difficult to engage adolescent drug abusers in regularly scheduled, formal therapy or counseling sessions. As distinct from most other patients, drug abusers frequently know more about the behavior and disability incident of drug taking than do their physicians. Then too, the chronic use of most drugs may be associated with a subculture that rejects conventional values and orientation. These difficulties are compounded if the therapist assumes the traditional stance of neutrality and reserve. It is often necessary, particularly at the outset of treatment, to schedule short, informal sessions with the therapist discussing practical issues of survival. Discussions of music, sports, or clothing may be valuable in establishing a therapeutic alliance. Drug use must of course be discussed, though the therapist should exercise care that he/she does not assume a critical parental role of exhortation and threats. Most of these kids have heard it all before; they will benefit most from a dignified, supportive relationship with an accepting, interested, knowledgeable adult. Optimally, they will come to appreciate their worth and potential in this relationship (Millman, 1978).

Adolescent patients will often minimize, or exaggerate, the extent of their drug use or in other ways distort historical data so as to create a desired effect. Direct confrontation of these failures to tell the truth, particularly in the early stages of treatment, may lead to increased resistance and power struggles. If, on the other hand, the therapist accepts the information without reservation, he/she may undermine the sense of trust and respect that is the basis of the therapeutic alliance. This may intensify the patient's already significant guilt feelings. If possible, the therapist must act as an ally such that the responsibility for behavior and improvement rests on the patient. It may sometimes be necessary to listen carefully, but neutrally, and gloss over questionable issues at different stages. Confirmed problems and behaviors may be preferentially considered with a view to returning to the possible inaccuracies at a later treatment stage. Confrontation and coercion are last resorts necessitated by compelling circumstances. Many adolescents will test limits and attempt to provoke punitive rejection. Strong action may be indicated by the threat of immediate danger to the welfare of the patient or others. There is no point in continuing interviews when the patient is obviously under the influence of drugs. This should be communicated to the adolescent in a gentle though firm manner. Every attempt should be made to keep these patients in treatment; these behaviors are an integral part of the disease. On occasion, when the drug-taking or antisocial behavior is disruptive to a group situation or has not improved over a period of time, it may be necessary to transfer a patient to another, perhaps more structured setting, or discharge him/her.

When appropriate, patients should be treated within the family group. On other occasions it is often more useful to see the youngster separately and allow him/her to feel that the therapist is his/her advocate and worthy of trust. Families must sometimes be advised to protect themselves from the abuses of a drug-using adolescent who steals to support his/her habit or engages in other antisocial acts. It is sometimes necessary to suggest that a family turn a drug user out so that he/she will be forced to seek treatment (Kaufman and Kaufman, 1979).

In the treatment of impoverished youngsters from the inner city or the rural poor, where the determinants of the drug taking are primarily sociologic, the emphasis should be on providing realistic, attractive alternatives to drug abuse. Introducing some of these deprived adolescents to pleasurable options such as sporting or cultural events and hobbies, may be beneficial. Group or milieu therapy is particularly useful for this group, particularly when supervised by therapists who have shared similar cultural experiences. The focus should be on common problems, methods of coping, the development of trusting relationships with each other, and sexual problems (Blum and Richards, 1979; Millman and Khuri, 1973).

After withdrawal from a drug or control of its use is accomplished, underlying psychopathology may be better identified. Treatment of the psychopathology will obviously depend on the individual patient, though several points should be emphasized. These people have been unable to get satisfaction from any phase of their lives with the exception of the drug-induced altered consciousness or the attendant life-style. Drugs have substituted for defenses, relationships, and other experiences. They generally feel disappointed in themselves and feel helpless, guilty, and inadequate in the face of the problems of living. Treatment personnel must be sensitive to this profound lack of self-esteem as well as to the various modes of denial they employ. Patients should be taught to identify the extremes of emotion, particularly anxiety and depression, that they have been unable to recognize. The overwhelming guilt that many of these youngsters feel should be recognized and to some degree assuaged (Lecker et al., 1973; Mechanic, 1979).

Most youthful drug abusers should be treated without medication, particularly those agents that are liable to abuse. Since many compulsive drug takers are self-medicating in order to function, it may sometimes be necessary to carefully, and in a highly controlled manner, administer psychotropic drugs. Antipsychotics, antidepressants, lithium, and on rare occasions, minor tranquilizers may be indicated (Khantzian et al., 1974).

Individual therapists are often unable to provide the intensive and comprehensive care necessary for many of these troubled youngsters. They may need to be seen daily and require legal, vocational, educational, medical, and psychological services. A variety of programs of differing and often undocumented effectiveness have been developed to treat drug-abusing adolescents. These include therapeutic communities, where the youngsters remain in a closed setting for prolonged periods, and programs based on a day-hospital model. School-based and community group-based programs have also proven useful. In general, the use of age-oriented comprehensive-treatment programs focused on the adolescent population appears to be the most effective and efficient means of providing care and preventive services to troubled youngsters. Many of these programs are run by graduates of the programs or by nonprofessional former drug users. Role models for responsible behavior are provided by staff and the sense of isolation that many of these young people feel may be reduced through the programs. A major problem with some of these has been an undue emphasis on confrontation and breaking down of unhealthy behavior patterns. Young people are often unwilling to enter these facilities; they don't want to leave family and friends to enter a repressive or unpleasant milieu. A related problem is that many of these programs are unprepared to handle adolescents with significant psychopathology. The professional component of these programs should probably be enhanced to serve this population (Lecker et al., 1973; Millman, 1978).

A model that provides the diverse treatment capability necessary for youthful drug abusers combines a coordinated inpatient and outpatient therapeutic community (or milieu therapy) structure with extensive medical and psychiatric backup. Clients may be admitted to the system at any point, depending on their needs, and move through it at different rates. They may enter at an inpatient phase, progress to an intensive day-care center phase and then to a more limited outpatient phase as they have less need of program services and support and develop stronger ties to the larger society. If relapse occurs, more supportive care is available. It is possible that the elements of this program should be kept reasonably separate, so that more naive, intact patients not be exposed to more "street-wise" patients.

Some of the adolescents who are referred to treatment programs, psychiatric facilities, or therapists are not in need of intensive treatment. While their drug use may be frightening or incomprehensible to their parents or other authorities, it may be reasonably normal within their social set and not be dangerous. There is a real danger of precipitous action or overtreatment here. They are intensely concerned about their abilities, potential, and even sanity, and inappropriate intervention may confirm their worst fears. Treatment attempts may represent a more disruptive influence than the sequelae of their drug use (Schnoll, 1979). After a thorough evaluation has determined that the youngster is in no serious danger and is developing reasonably well, it may be useful to reassure him/her as to his/her sanity and his prospects for the future. A few informal sessions with provision for follow-up care may be appropriate treatment (Millman, 1979).

PREVENTION

Since the causes of drug abuse are complex and varied, approaches to prevention should not be oversimplified. High-pressure educational campaigns aimed at the community or the schools, which have focused and sometimes exaggerated the dangers of drug use, have not proved to be particularly effective. Knowledge may sometimes increase, though behavior may not be influenced. Young people with some drug experience dismiss these efforts as scare tactics, and inexperienced adolescents may even be prompted to begin experimenting. A related phenomenon is the vogue for inviting well-rehabilitated ex-addicts to address students or community audiences on the dangers of drugs. They often speak so well and convey such magnetism that frightened and insecure adolescents are encouraged to continue these behaviors so they can be as "cool" as the speaker.

School-based programs are critical for prevention, case finding, evaluation, and early treatment efforts. Teachers may be the first to recognize a drug-abuse problem because of decreasing performance in school or frequent absences. In general, there is an educational component that teaches about the dangers of drugs. These are sometimes run according to a peer-group format administered by counselors with some training in drug and alcohol abuse. Some of these well-organized, carefully planned programs that require participation and discussion on the part of the young, have shown promise.

Innovative, well-packaged programs that emphasize the acquisition of skills which enable the youngster to live well and productively, are being tested. Handling stress and anxiety, relating to peers and authority figures, sex education, and developing effective work habits are among the commonly covered topics. Some of these programs have a built-in evaluation component with behavior assessment at intervals, after the program is administered.

The provision of reasonable, rewarding educational, vocational, and recreational alternatives to those at risk should probably be of prime concern. There is no need to belabor the obvious role of the family in drug-abuse prevention in the young. Families must appreciate the impact of their own behaviors, particularly with respect to drug and alcohol use, on their children (Jacobson and Zinberg, 1975; Millman and Khuri, 1973).

The effectiveness of stringent legal sanctions is controversial. The users of these drugs, though they are often dealers as well, are victims and should not be subjected to the criminal justice system prematurely. Programs that seek to direct so-called "juvenile offenders" into treatment systems have met with limited success. If the treatment programs could remain independent of the referring criminal justice system, a difficult and delicate task, effectiveness might be enhanced.

DRUGS OF ABUSE—BRIEFLY CONSIDERED

Central Nervous System Depressants

The central nervous system depressants are the most widely abused drugs in this country. This broad category of agents includes alcohol, hypnotics including barbiturates and methaqualone, and the minor tranquilizers including diazepam and chlordiazepoxide hydrochloride. Though chemically very different, these agents act as general suppressants of central nervous system functioning and in most ways are pharmacologically similar.

Most adolescent use of the depressants is intermittent and social; the drugs are used to release inhibitions, ameliorate anxiety, and generate a sense of well-being. The "high" that depressant users describe may be compared with the sense of peace or numbness that occurs just prior to sleep in normal individuals. There may be a feeling of freedom or aggressiveness that sometimes leads to antisocial or violent behavior. At low doses, enhanced sexual pleasue and ability are often experienced, but high doses impair sexual performance. Some youngsters become compulsive abusers, often in a polydrug-abuse pattern, where they seem to be seeking an obtundation that is close to unconsciousness in an attempt to cope with anxiety or fear (Kamali and Steer, 1976).

Pharmacology and Adverse Effects. Central nervous system effects vary from mild sedation to coma depending on the drug, the dose, the route of administration, individual sensitivity, and tolerance. Tolerance develops rapidly to all depressants, though in distinction to the opiates, the lethal dose does not increase significantly despite tolerance. Cross-tolerance occurs between all depressants. Depressant overdoses may occur as a result of sublethal combinations of drugs such as alcohol and methaqualone.

Physical dependence, as indicated by withdrawal signs and symptoms, develops to all the general depressants and is similar to the symptoms of the alcohol withdrawal syndrome. It varies in severity, but in contrast to the opiate abstinence syndrome, it may be life-threatening. Early symptoms include anxiety, insomnia, and tremors. Withdrawal from high doses of depressants may be marked by seizures early, and subsequently a delirium characterized by disorientation to time and place, auditory and visual hallucinations, and sensorial clouding. High fevers, rapid heart rate, agitation, and cardiovascular collapse may occur incidently to the delirium. The time course of the withdrawal syndrome is quite variable depending on the particular drug; with short-acting drugs, seizures occur within the first three days, and the syndrome clears by about the eighth day; with long-acting drugs, seizures may not occur until the seventh or eighth day (Jaffe, 1975; Smith et al., 1979).

Treatment. Mild depressant intoxication requires only supportive reassurance. If severe overdose is suspected, emergency hospitalization is indicated. If physical dependence is suspected, close observation or hospitalization is mandatory. Detoxification may be accomplished through the use of a suitable general depressant, diazepam and chlordiazepoxide hydrochloride have proven to be the most effective and safe drugs for treatment of the withdrawal syndrome.

Compulsive abusers of depressants, alone or in combination with other drugs, are often quite difficult to treat. The incidence of severe psychopathology is high in this group; they are frequently withdrawn, depressed, and may be suicidal. The course is generally marked by frequent relapses and antisocial or intoxicated behavior while in treatment. It is necessary to secure long-term hospitalization or residence in a therapeutic community for many of these young people, since they are unable to function in society without strong supports. Psychotherapy may be useful to motivate people to withdraw from the drugs or after the withdrawal has been accomplished (Smith et al., 1979).

OPIATES (NARCOTIC ANALGESICS)

The opiates have been used widely throughout human history for medical, religious, and recreational purposes. Drugs of this class remain the most important analgesics in use today. Herion is the most frequently abused opiate in the United States, though all other opiates, particularly morphine, codeine, and dilaudid, are also subject to abuse. Demerol, percodan, and Methadone are synthetic substances sumilar to the opiates.

Initially, the drug is taken by insufflation ("snorting"), but as tolerance develops, and more drug is needed to get the euphoric effects, the more efficient and more dangerous subcutaneous ("skin-popping") or intravenous ("mainlining") is used. For some adolescents the use of heroin becomes the central focus of life. The adolescent identifies with the "junkie" subculture, which emphasizes street skills and disregards all dignity and most scruples in the search for money for drugs. When heroin is not available, many use methadone or depressants as replacements. Adolescent opiate abusers are a heterogeneous group. The incidence of psychopathology is related to how deviant addiction is in the particular adolescent's social group. Thus, many inner-city adolescents exhibit surprisingly little psychopathology. Middle-class adolescents are more likely to demonstrate severe personality or cognitive disorders (Steer and Schut, 1979).

Pharmacology and Adverse Effects

Tolerance to any opiate develops rapidly, and the lethal dose increases proportionately. The acute abstinence syndrome ("kicking," "cold turkey'') is quite characteristic and begins approximately four to eight hours after the last heroin dose, and persists for three to five days. Symptoms include drug craving, irritability, anxiety, restlessness, depression, running eyes and nose, yawning, perspiration, dilated pupils, sneezing, coughing, nausea, vomiting, diarrhea, abdominal cramps, and ''bone'' pains. While severe medical sequelae such as convulsions or shock are rare, the expectations that some addicts have that their withdrawal symptoms may be life threatening must be taken seriously because addicts do act on their fears. Methadone withdrawal has a longer time course due to its longer half-life. After withdrawal from any opioid drug, many addicts experience a prolonged abstinence syndrome, characterized by drug craving and often severe depression. As some psychotic patients use opiates as self-medication, psychoses sometimes appear in detoxifying patients.

Adverse reactions are related to the illegality of use, i.e., the administration of unknown quantities of unknown substances in unsterile procedures. Three-quarters of the deaths are due to *acute heroin reactions,* marked by cyanosis, pulmonary edema, and coma. The etiology of these reactions is not fully understood, but true pharmacologic overdoses and allergic phenomena have been implicated. Other adverse effects involve infectious processes of all bodily systems, particularly skin, liver, and heart (Cherubin, 1968; Dole, 1972; Meyer and Mirin, 1979).

Treatment

Treatment must include a detoxification phase followed by long-term treatment. Detoxification may be accomplished in specialized centers or by utilizing decreasing doses of methadone on either an inpatient or outpatient basis (Millman et al., 1978; Cohen and Stimmel, 1978). Clonidine, an antihypertensive drug with no narcotic properties, is presently under investigation as a detoxification agent. Psychotherapy may be useful to motivate a youngster to undergo detoxification. Long-term treatment may require an inpatient phase in a therapeutic community or hospital. Outpatient treatment may be accomplished in a variety of programs though optimally, educational, legal, vocational, and psychological services should be available. Frequent contacts over a prolonged period will be necessary.

CENTRAL NERVOUS SYSTEM STIMULANTS

The most frequently abused drugs in this category include the amphetamines and cocaine, an alkaloid of the cocoa plant which grows in the Andes. Other stimulants that are frequently abused include methylphenidate hydrochloride (Ritalin), phenmetrazine hydrochloride (Preludin), and diethylpropion hydrochloride (Tepanil).

Stimulant use by hard-driving students, athletes, and musicians who want to increase their efficacy or productivity is common. Most often, the drugs are taken orally, used intermittently, and produce virtually no dependence. Rarely, individuals find they must continue to take the drugs in ever-increasing doses in order to perform satisfactorily. A different pattern of abuse occurs in polydrug-abusing adolescents, when the stimulants are used for their mood-elevating properties. Methamphetamine is the preferred agent and is most often "sniffed" or injected intramuscularly or intravenously. The "rush" that occurs after sniffing or injection is described as a feeling of great well-being, physical power, and intelligence. The drugs may be used compulsively in runs of days or weeks, followed by a period of prolonged sleep and depression ("crashing"). Depressants are often used to ensure sleep and concurrent dependence on both drug classes occurs.

Cocaine use has increased explosively in recent years, particularly in middle-class youth. Patterns of use and psychoactive effects are similar to those of the amphetamines, though cocaine is much shorter acting. In some societies it has become a symbol of affluence and sophistication and it is used as luxurious punctuation for a variety of occasions (Grinspoon and Bakalar, 1976; Petersen, 1977).

Pharmacology and Adverse Effects

Marked tolerance develops to amphetamine effects; tolerance to cocaine is controversial, but may develop on a considerably lower scale. Abrupt cessation of stimulant use does not result in a major withdrawal syndrome. Some workers believe that the depression, apathy, and prolonged sleep may be considered an abstinence syndrome and evidence of physical dependence.

The intravenous use of these drugs involves the same complications of nonsterile conditions previously discussed in the section on opiates. Nasal irritation or, rarely, perforation of the nasal septum is a complication of sniffing cocaine. Severe overdose reactions or death from these drugs is rare, though convulsions and strokes have been reported.

The most frequent adverse effects are irritability, paranoid ideation, and stereotyped, compulsive behavior. Sophisticated users are often aware of these reactions and will not act on paranoid ideas or delusions. When this insight is lost, antisocial or irrational behavior may result. Continued use may lead to an amphetamine or cocaine psychosis indistinguishable from acute functional psychotic reactions. The premorbid personality structure of the adolescent may determine the ease with which these ego disruptions occur and how long they will last. Psychotic breaks have been precipitated in some individuals after only one small dose of amphetamine. In general, the psychotic reactions appear while the youngster is under the influence of the drug and most often abate within a few days after drug use ceases. Prolonged psychotic episodes have been reported and probably relate to the pre-existing personality structure (Petersen, 1977; Grinspoon and Bakalar, 1976).

Treatment

Compulsive users of stimulants should be helped or, if necessary, pressured to terminate their use as quickly as possible. It may be necessary to hospitalize some adolescents or, if possible, confine them in a safe, supportive environment to attempt to reduce some of the anxiety attendant on the withdrawal process and prevent relapse to drug use. Short-term hospitalization and appropriate psychotropic medication are indicated for the treatment of severe paranoid ideation or overt psychotic episodes. Compulsive or polydrug abusers will require long-term supportive care as described in previous sections (Smith et al., 1979).

CANNABIS

Cannabis in its various forms has become an integral part of coming of age in this country. Both marijuana and hashish are derived from the hemp plant *Cannabis sativa,* which contains varying amounts of major psychoactive compound, delta-9-tetrahydrocannabinol. Where previously, most cannabis was imported from other countries, particularly Jamaica, Colombia, and Mexico, recently, highly potent forms have been cultivated in this country.

Many young people use the drug intermittently or regularly, but in a controlled or ritualistic fashion. A few adolescents develop a compulsive use pattern, where the acquisition and use of marijuana become the primary focus of living. These are often severely disturbed people who function poorly socially and in school. The drug use in these cases may represent an attempt at self-medication or a flight from reality (Burkett, 1977).

Pharmacology and Adverse Effects

Effects begin within minutes after inhalation, peak within one hour, and are dissipated, for the most part within three hours. There is some evidence to suggest that metabolites may persist for long periods of time, and that some psychoactive effects also persist. Acute physiologic effects include an increased heart rate, dryness of the mouth and throat, fine tremors of the fingers, congestion of the vasculature of the eyes, and altered sleep patterns.

Psychoactive effects depend on the dose, the route of administration, the personality of the user, his prior experience with the drug, his personal expectations, and the social setting in which the drug is used. An altered and often enhanced perception of visual, auditory, tactile, and gustatory stimuli is described by users. Mood changes are frequently reported as a sense of relaxed well-being, though anxiety and depression may also be precipitated. Motor performance, particularly of complex tasks, is improved as is reaction time. Short-term memory is impaired and time seems to pass slowly. Some tolerance develops to the psychoactive and physiologic effects of the drug, such that inexperienced users demonstrate greater decrements in performance and increased physical effects as compared with chronic users. There is no evidence for the development of physical dependence (Halikas et al., 1978).

There is controversy as to whether cannabis leads to adverse physical effects; to date, these have been of little clinical significance and no deaths have been reported. Some workers suggest that adverse effects on the immunological, respiratory, and genital systems may occur with chronic use.

Adverse effects are primarily psychologic in nature, infrequent, and similar to those seen with psychedelic drugs. Acute panic reactions, depersonalization, transient paranoid ideation, and depression are the most frequently seen complications of cannabis use and usually abate in several hours. Prolonged psychotic reactions have been precipitated by marijuana, though it is probable that these occurred in psychologically predisposed individuals. Flashback phenomena similar to those occurring incident to psychedelic use occur rarely (Halikas et al., 1978).

An "amotivational syndrome" has been reported, in which chronic marijuana users become apathetic and are unable to pursue useful goals. This is controversial, though it is likely that in predisposed young people marijuana does contribute to an impairment of goal-directed activity and ambition (Rubin and Comitas, 1975). Some of these youngsters may insulate themselves from the anxieties and tasks essential for the progression from childhood to maturity.

Treatment

Treatment of the frequently seen acute reactions is firm, supportive reassurance. The adolescent should be continually reminded that he is feeling this way because of the drug he took and that the effects will wane ("talking down"). Treatment of compulsive users is covered under General Treatment Considerations.

PSYCHEDELICS

During the late 1960s and early 1970s, the most frequently abused drugs in this class were lysergic acid diethylamide (LSD), psilocybin, and mescaline. Use was primarily by middle-class youth who were seeking a mystical, enriching experience. Use has apparently declined since then, perhaps related to a general disillusionment with the possibility that these drugs provide long-term answers to life's problems. Use of LSD and other psychedelics has generally been intermittent, varying from one "trip" weekly to one monthly or yearly. Rarely, some adolescents take these drugs more often, such that they remain intoxicated for prolonged periods. These people often have severe psychopathology and the drug use becomes part of a delusional system.

Pharmacology and Adverse Effects

Psychoactive effects of the psychedelics vary markedly depending on the personality and expectations of the user, the setting, and the dose. They produce bizarre alterations in perception, thought, feeling, and behavior. True hallucinations with loss of insight rarely occur, though some apparently susceptible people have them repeatedly. Tolerance to the psychedelics develops rapidly, such that repeated daily doses become ineffective in three to four days. Physical dependence does not occur (Cohen, 1971; Wesson and Smith, 1978).

Acute physical toxicity is rare at doses that produce marked psychological effects, and no toxic deaths have been reported. Increased chromosome breakage and an increased incidence of spontaneous abortion have been reported (Dishotsky et al., 1971). The acute panic reaction ("bad trip") is the most frequent complication of psychedelic use. Infrequently, prolonged psychotic reactions have been precipitated that are indistinguishable from the functional psychoses. As with marijuana, these may occur in psychologically predisposed young people. A "flashback" is the recurrence of some aspect of a previous "trip" when the individual is not presently intoxicated. In general, these episodes are mild, though severe episodes marked by psychotic behavior have been reported. It is not clear whether the psychedelics can precipitate prolonged psychotic reactions in reasonably healthy people (Wesson and Smith, 1978).

Treatment

Treatment of the acute panic reactions requires a warm, supportive environment and someone in constant attendance. The consensual reality should be gently though repeatedly affirmed. In particularly agitated patients, benzodiazepine medication may be indicated. Treatment of prolonged psychotic episodes is similar to treatment of functional psychoses (Wesson and Smith, 1978).

Phencyclidine

Phencyclidine ("angel dust") is an anaesthetic agent that is abused for its psychedelic effects. Use increased explosively over the past few years, and it received a remarkable amount of attention in the media, in schools, and in treatment programs. It is generally used in addition to a wide variety of other drugs as part of a polydrug-abuse syndrome. Psychoactive effects differ somewhat from the other psychedelics in that in addition to the perceptual distortions, there is a striking disorientation and numbness. The drug is also distinct from other psychedelics in that at high doses hypertension, hyperactive reflexes, seizures, and coma occur, and a number of deaths have been reported (Pittel, 1979).

An enormous number of acute and prolonged psychotic episodes have been attributed to phencyclidine abuse; these are sometimes marked by impulsive or violent behavior. It is likely that at least a portion of these are functional psychotic episodes erroneously attributed to the drug. It is as if it is more acceptable to families, friends, and the patients themselves to consider a psychotic episode as due to a toxic chemical rather than to a constitutional predisposition. Additional documentation of the role of phencyclidine in these reactions is necessary. Treatment of these psychotic episodes is generally similar to those occurring incident to the use of other psychedelics. In addition, it has been suggested that stimuli be kept to a minimum. More rapid clearance of phencyclidine from the body will occur if the urine is acidified (Luisada and Brown, 1976).

INHALANTS

Amyl nitrite, organic solvents, and nitrous oxide are abused by adolescents in various social groups. Use is intermittent and characterized by an instantaneous feeling ("rush") of flushing, dizziness, hilarity, and rapid heartbeat. Adverse physical effects are rare. Evaluation and treatment will depend on the role of the particular drug in the life of the youngster (Jaffe, 1975).

BIBLIOGRAPHY

A Survey of Substance Use Among Junior and Senior High School Students in New York State. Report No. 1: Prevalence of Drug and Alcohol Use, Winter 1974/75. New York, New York State Office of Drug Abuse Services, 1975.

Abelson, H. I., Fishburne, P. M., and Cisin, I. National Survey on Drug Abuse: 1977. National Institute on Drug Abuse, U.S. Dept of Health, Education and Welfare, Washington, D.C.

Becker, H. S. History, culture and subjective experience: An exploration of the social basis of drug-induced experiences. *J. Health Soc. Behav.* **8**:163–176 (September) 1967.

Bernstein, B., and Shkuda, A. N. The Young Drug User: Attitudes and Obstacles to Treatment. Center for New York City Affairs, New School for Social Research, New York, (June) 1974.

Bihari, B. Drug dependency: some etiological considerations. *Am. J. Drug and Alcohol Abuse* **3** (March) 1976.

Blos, P. *On Adolescence*. Glencoe, Illinois: The Free Press, 1962.

Blum, R., and Richards, L. Youthful drug use. *In:* R. I. Dupont, A. Goldstein, and J. O'Donnell, (eds.). *Handbook on Drug Abuse.* U.S. Dept of HEW *and* Office of Drug Abuse Policy, Executive Office of the President, National Institute on Drug Abuse, 1979, pp. 257-267.

Brecher, E. M. Editors of Consumer Reports. Licit and Illicit Drugs: the Consumers Union Report on narcotics, stimulants, depressants, inhalants, hallucinogens, and marijuana, including caffeine, nicotine, and alcohol. Mount Vernon, New York, Consumers Union, 1972.

Burkett, S. R.: Religion, parental influence and adolescent alcohol and marijuana use. *J. of Drug Issues* **7**:263-273, 1977.

Carlson, G. A., and Cantwell, D. P. Unmasking masked depression in children and adolescents. *Am. J. of Psychiatry* **137**(4):445-449, (April) 1980.

Chappel, J. N., and Schnoll, S. H. Physician attitudes: Effect on the treatment of chemically dependent patients. *J.A.M.A.* **237**:2318,2319, 1977.

Cherubin, C. E. A review of the medical complications of narcotic addiction. *International J. of the Addictions* **3**:167, 1968.

Cohen, A. Y.: The journey beyond trips. *J. Psychedelic Drugs* **3**:16-21, (February) 1971.

Cohen, M., and Stimmel, B. The use of methadone in narcotic dependency. *In* A. Schecter (ed.). *Treatment Aspects of Drug Dependence.* West Palm Beach, Florida: CRC Press, 1978, pp. 1-31.

Dishotsky, N. I., Loughman, W. D., Mogar, R. E., and Lipscomb, W. R. LSD and genetic damage. *Science* **172**:431, 1971.

Dole, V. P. Narcotic addiction, physical dependence and relapse. *N. Engl. J. Med.* **206**:988, 1972.

DuPont, R. L., and Greene, M. H. The dynamics of a heroin addiction epidemic. *Science* **181**:716-722, (August) 1973.

Erikson, E. *Childhood and Society,* Second ed. New York: W. W. Norton, 1963.

Fenichel, O. *The Psychoanalytic Theory of Neurosis.* New York: W. W. Norton, 1945.

Gallemore, J. L., and Wilson, W. P. Adolescent maladjustment or affective disorder? *Amer. J. Psychiatry* **129**:608-612, (November) 1972.

Gert, B., and Duggan, T. J. Free will as the ability to will. *Nous* **13**:197-217, 1979.

Goode, E. Marijuana use and the progression to dangerous drugs. *In:* L. L. Miller (ed.): *Effects on Human Behavior.* New York: Academic Press, 1974, pp. 303-338.

Grinspoon, L., and Bakalar, J. B. *Cocaine: A Drug and Its Social Evolution.* New York: Basic Books, 1976.

Halikas, J. A., Shapiro, T. M., and Weller, R. A. Marijuana: a critical review of sociological, medical and psychiatric questions. *In* A. Schecter (ed.): *Treatment Aspects of Drug Dependence.* West Palm Beach, Florida: CRC Press, 1978, pp 161-183.

Hamburg, B. A., Kraemer, H. C., and Jahnke, W. A. Hierarchy of drug use in adolescence: Behavioral and attitudinal correlates of substantial drug use. *Amer. J. Psychiatry* **132**:1155-1167, (November) 1975.

Hein, K., Cohen, M. I., and Litt, J. F. Illicit drug use among urban adolescents: a decade in retrospect. *Amer. J. of Diseases of Children* **133**:38-40, 1979.

Hughes, P. H., and Crawford, G. A. A contagious disease model for researching and intervening in heroin epidemics. *Arch. Gen. Psychiatry* **27**:149-155 (August) 1972.

Hunt, L. G. Incidence and prevalence of drug use and abuse. *In:* R. I. DuPont, A. Goldstein, and J. O'Donnell (eds): *Handbook on Drug Abuse.* National Institute on Drug Abuse, U.S. Department of HEW and Office of Drug Abuse Policy, 1979, pp 395–403.

Hunt, L. G., and Zinberg, N. E. *Heroin Use: A New Look.* Washington, DC, Drug Abuse Council, Inc., (September) 1976.

Institute of Medicine, A Conference Summary. *Adolescent Behavior and Health.* Washington, DC, National Academy of Sciences (October) 1978.

Jacobson, R., and Zinberg, N. E. *Social Basis of Drug Abuse Prevention.* Washington, DC, Drug Abuse Council, Inc, 1975.

Jaffe, J. H. Drug addiction and drug abuse. *In:* L.S. Goodman and A. Gilman (eds.): *The Pharmacological Basis of Therapeutics.* 1975, pp 284–324.

Jessor, R. Predicting time of onset of marijuana use: a developmental study of high school youth. *In:* D. J. Lettieri (ed.). *Predicting Adolescent Drug Abuse: A Review of Issues, Methods and Correlates.* Research Issues 11, Rockville, Maryland, National Institute on Drug Abuse, 1975.

Johnston, L. D., Bachman, J. G., and O'Malley, P. M. *1979 Highlights: Drugs and the Nation's High School Students, Five-Year National Trends.* U.S. Dept of HEW; Public Health Service: Alcohol, Drug Abuse and Mental Health Administration, 1979.

Kamali, K., and Steer, R. A. Polydrug use by high school students: Involvement and correlates. *Internat. J. of the Addictions* **11**:337–343, 1976.

Kandel, D., Single, E., and Kessler, R. C. The epidemiology of drug use among New York State high school students: Distribution, trends, and change in rates of use. *Amer. J. Public Health* **66**:43–53 (January) 1976.

Kaufman, E. The psychodynamics of opiate dependence: A new look. *Amer. J. of Drug and Alcohol Abuse* **1**:349–370 (March) 1974.

Kaufman, E., and Kaufman, P. N. *Family Therapy of Drug and Alcohol Abuse.* New York: Gardner Press, Inc, 1979.

Kernberg, O. F. *Borderline Conditions and Pathological Narcissism.* New York: Jason Aronson, 1975.

Khantzian, E. J. Opiate addiction: A critique to theory and some implications for treatment. *Amer. J. of Psychotherapy* **28**:59–70 (January) 1974.

Khantzian, E. J., Mack, J. E., and Schatzberg, A. F. Heroin use as an attempt to cope: Clinical observations. *Amer. J. Psychiatry* **131**:160–164 (February) 1974.

Lecker, S., Hendricks, L., and Turanski, J. New dimensions in adolescent psychotherapy: A therapeutic system approach. *Pediatric Clinics of North America* **20**:883–900 (November) 1973.

Litt, I. F., and Cohen, M. I. The drug-using adolescent as a pediatric patient. *J. Pediatr.* **77**:195–202 (August) 1970.

Litt, I. F., and Cohen, M. I. Prisons, adolescents, and the right to quality medical care: The time is now. *Am. J. Public Health* **64**:894–897 (September) 1974.

Luisada, P. V., and Brown, B. I. Clinical management of phencyclidine psychosis. *Clin. Toxicol.* **9**:539–545, 1976.

Mechanic, D. Development of psychological distress among young adults. *Arch. Gen. Psychiatry* **36**:1233–1239 (October) 1979.

Meyer, R. E., and Mirin, S. M. *The Heroin Stimulus: Implications for a Theory of Addiction.* New York and London: Plenum Medical Book Co, 1979.

Milkman, H., and Frosch, W. A. On the preferential abuse of heroin and amphetamine. *J. Nervous and Mental Disease* **156**:242–248 (April) 1973.

Millman, R. B. Drug abuse in adolescence: Current issues. *In:* E. Senay, and V. Shorty (eds.): *Developments in the Field of Drug Abuse,* Proceedings of the First National Drug Abuse

Conference, 1974. New York, National Association for the Prevention of Addiction to Narcotics, 1974.

Millman, R. B. Drug abuse, addiction and intoxication. *In:* P. B. Beeson, and W. McDermott (eds.). *Textbook of Medicine,* 15th ed. Philadelphia, W. B. Saunders, 1979, pp 692–714.

Millman, R. B. Drug and alcohol abuse. *In:* B. B. Wollman, J. Egan, and A. C. Ross (eds.). *Handbook of Mental Disorders in Childhood and Adolescence.* Englewood Cliffs, N.J. Prentice-Hall, 1978, pp 238-267.

Millman, R. B., and Khuri, E. T. Drug abuse and the need for alternatives. *In:* J. Schoolar (ed.). *Current Issues in Adolescent Psychiatry.* New York: Brunner/Mazel, 1973, pp 148–157.

Millman, R. B., Khuri, E. T., and Nyswander, M. E. Therapeutic detoxification of adolescent heroin addicts. *In:* B. Kissin, J. Lowinson, and R. B. Millman (eds.): *Recent Developments in Chemotherapy of Narcotic Addiction.* New York: Annals of the New York Academy of Sciences **311,** 1978, pp 153–164.

Oakley, S. R. *Drugs, Society and Human Behavior.* St Louis. C. V. Mosby, 1972.

O'Donnell, J. A., Voss, H. L., Clayton, R. R., et al.: Young Men and Drugs—A Nationwide Survey. NIDA Research Monograph 5. Rockville, Maryland, National Institute on Drug Abuse, 1976.

Petersen, R. C. Cocaine: An overview. *In:* R. C. Petersen, R. C. Stillman, (eds.). *Cocaine.* U.S. Government Printing Office, Washington, DC, 1977.

Pittel, S. M. The enigma of PCP. *In* R. I. DuPont, A. Goldstein, and J. O'Donnell, (eds.): *Handbook on Drug Abuse.* National Institute on Drug Abuse, U.S. Department of HEW and Office of Drug Abuse Policy, 1979, pp 249–254.

Preble, E., and Casey, J. J. Jr. Taking care of business—the heroin user's life on the street. *Internat. J. of the Addictions* **4**:1–24 (March) 1969.

Project DAWN V. Phase Five Report of the Drug Abuse Warning Network, May 1976–April 1977. DHEW Publ. No. (ADM) 78–618, IMS America, Ltd, 1977.

Robins, L. N., and Murphy, G. E. Drug use in a normal population of young Negro men. *Am. J. Public Health* **57**:1580–1596, 1967.

Rubin, V., and Comitas, L. *Ganja in Jamaica.* The Hague and Paris: Mouton and Co, 1975.

Schnoll, S. H. Alcohol and other substance abuse in adolescents. *In* E. L. Gottheil, A. Thomas, K. McLellan, A. Druley, and A. I. Alterman (eds.): *Addiction Research and Treatment: Converging Trends.* New York, Pergamon Press, 1979, PP 40–45.

Simonds, J. F., and Kashani, J. Drug abuse and criminal behavior in delinquent boys committed to a training school. *Am. J. Psychiatry* **136**:1444–1448 (November) 1979.

Smith, D. E., Wesson, D. R., and Buxton, M. E., et al. (eds.). *Amphetamine Use, Misuse, and Abuse.* Proceedings of the National Amphetamine Conference, 1978. Boston: G. K. Hall & Co, 1979.

Steer, R. A., and Schut, J. Types of psychopathology displayed by heroin addicts. *Am. J. Psychiatry* **136**:1463–1465 (November) 1979.

Sterne, M. W., and Pittman, D. J. The concept of motivation: A source of institutional and professional blockage in the treatment of alcoholics. *Quart. J. Studies Alcohol* **26**:41–57, 1965.

Tennant, F. S., Detels, R., and Clark, V. Some childhood antecedents of drug and alcohol abuse. *Am. J. of Epidemiology* **102**:377–385.

Wechsler, H. Alcohol intoxication and drug use among teen-agers. *Q. J. Studies Alcohol* **37**:1672–1679 (November) 1976.

Weil, A.: *The Natural Mind.* Boston: Houghton Mifflin, 1972.

Wesson, D. R., and Smith, D. E. Psychedelics. *In:* A. Schecter, (ed.). *Treatment Aspects of Drug Dependence.* West Palm Beach, Florida: CRC Press, 1978, pp 147–160.

Wider, H., and Kaplan, E. H. Drug use in adolescents. *Psychoanal. Study Child* **24**:399–431, 1969.

Wurmser, L. Psychoanalytic considerations of the etiology of compulsive drug use. *J. Amer. Psychoanal. Assoc.* **22**:820–843 (October) 1974.

Zinberg, N. E. Addiction and ego function. *In:* R. S. Eissler, A. Freud, M. Kris, and A. J. Solnit, (eds.) *The Psychoanalytic Study of the Child*. New Haven, Yale University Press, 1975.

Zinberg, N. E., Jacobson, R. C., and Harding, W. M. Social sanctions and rituals as a basis for drug abuse prevention. *Amer. J. Drugs and Alcohol Abuse* **2**:165–182, 1975.

The authors deal with the question of which adolescents should be treated for alcoholism and differentiate between adolescent alcoholism and adolescent alcohol abuse. For alcoholism, they describe the treatment approach taking into consideration criteria for detoxification in the hospital setting and the important process of preparation for aftercare treatment of the adolescent alcoholic on an outpatient basis. The authors point out several factors related to treatment of alcohol abuse, such as the likelihood that these adolescents also abuse other substances, and that different personality types abuse alcohol. They use case studies effectively to elucidate differences in personality types and the implications for treatment.

7 Juvenile Alcoholism and Alcohol Abuse

Ted Neidengard, M.D.
Daniel Yalisove, Ph.D.

Drinking patterns in adolescence range from abstinence to alcoholism. Within this range there are light, moderate, and heavy drinkers, many of whom drink safely. There are those who drink only occasionally but who have catastrophic reactions when they do. There are many factors which affect the drinking behavior of the adolescent: (1) The cultural attitudes toward drinking in their community; (2) familial drinking practices and attitudes; (3) situational pressures; (4) ego development; and (5) personality dynamics. To this could be added the adolescent's physiological response to alcohol. Some adolescents have a lower tolerance for alcohol, which will affect their drinking behavior. When one deals with any behavior pattern of adolescence, it is difficult to distinguish between the normal variations and the pathologic. It is no different with drinking behavior.

Typically, the average adolescent has had his first drink by age thirteen.[5] The average amount of alcohol ingested increases with age through high school.[19] Schuckit,[19] summarizing several studies, indicates that the typical teenage drinker uses low or moderate amounts of alcohol once a week to once a month. Since 1940, the number of adolescent drinkers has increased steadily. It is estimated that between 80 and 90% of adolescents are drinkers.[19] Smart[23] reports that there has been a large increase in the number of adolescents in Ontario entering treatment facilities for treatment of alcohol problems. However, the total number was small. It cannot be assumed that there is an increase in drinking problems in adolescence, since the increase in adolescents seeking treatment may simply be related to public awareness of an already existing problem. The normal patterns of drinking cited above must be taken as the standard to which to compare any adolescent referred for treatment. The drinking patterns of adolescents reflect the nature of the adult drinking society in which they live. For the most part, adolescents are learning how to drink as they will as adults. And, for the most part, this process will not lead to alcohol problems.

TREATMENT EVALUATION

Alcoholism

The question arises, who should be treated for alcoholism? The answer should include those adolescents who have lost control over drinking. In this category there is physiologic addiction, in that sudden discontinuation of alcohol use would result in physiologic withdrawal including symptoms of delirium tremors, shakes, anxiety, restlessness, agitation, nausea, vomiting, diarrhea, paranoid ideation, delusional thought, hallucinations, and in some instances convulsions.[22]

Alcohol Abuse

Another category includes adolescents who abuse alcohol to a point where general function is interfered with. There is school absenteeism or a decrease in school performance, family life is disrupted because of behavior at home, such as late hours. Social life may be affected in that the individual is rejected by certain members of social groups and accepted into others, e.g., those that drink. Goals which should be developing in this age group, such as career choice and plans, goals for marriage and family, are avoided in favor of ones that center around a chaotic social life and drinking.

Another category is pathologic intoxication in which alcohol even in small amounts causes unusual behavior. Behavior may be boisterous, violent, or bizarre. This condition may be protracted.[27]

In certain adolescents an affective component may be prominent. The individual may find much relief in alcohol from symptoms of anxiety and/or depression. Alcohol is primarily used for this goal.

In other adolescents only certain areas may be disrupted. An individual may perform well at school, even to the point of being outstanding. Home life may be adequate in that he or she may behave well at home, perform chores effectively and please parents with academic performance. Social situations may be disrupted when an individual becomes intoxicated on a date, behaves inappropriately, becomes unconscious or sick, resulting in rejection.

In addition, many adolescents are involved in serious incidents as a result of alcohol intoxication. Some feel this may be a greater problem than alcoholism.[5] This group will not be discussed here except to mention that an educational approach may suffice to correct the adolescent's lack of awareness of the effects of alcohol on judgment, perception and behavior.

The percentage of adolescents who are truly alcoholic is small. For example Schuckit et al.,[20] in evaluating 227 adolescents referred specifically for alcohol problems, found only 14% to be alcoholic. The largest proportion of adolescents referred are those who use alcohol in such a manner at to cause them serious difficulties coincidentally. This is commonly called alcohol abuse.

TREATMENT OF ADOLESCENT ALCOHOLISM AND ALCOHOL ABUSE

There are two factors that are relatively independent which must be evaluated in treating the adolescent problem-drinker.

1. The extent of use of alcohol and its effect on the adolescent.
2. Personality organization of the adolescent and the situational factors that may be affecting him/her.

When the symptoms of alcoholism are apparent, regardless of personality organization, they must be treated first. If there is an alcohol abuse problem, personality factors and environmental factors must be considered in association with the alcohol problem.

TREATMENT OF ADOLESCENT ALCOHOLISM

Detoxification

In the situation where there is loss of control over drinking, detoxification in the hospital setting should be considered. Sudden discontinuation of alcohol may result in development of delirium tremors and other physiologic withdrawal symptoms as mentioned above. Individuals in this category should be hospitalized for alcohol detoxification. Other individuals include those who would not necessarily undergo marked withdrawal symptoms, but those who cannot obtain abstinence and discontinue alcohol intake on their own because of continuing compulsion to drink. Hospitalization for alcohol detoxification should include complete physical history and examination including neurologic examination and appropriate laboratory studies, attention being given to the strong possibility of liver dysfunction associated with the drinking. Withdrawal regimen should begin immediately after physical assessment and include adequate sedation with medication such as benzodiazepine, chlordiazepoxide (Librium), or barbituate such as phenobarbitol. These should be adequate hydration and nutrition, usually administered orally, unless nausea, vomiting, and diarrhea interfere. Vitamins such as thiamine and folic acid may be indicated.

In reference to convulsions, the seizure threshold is lowered with alcohol. Some individuals convulse only when undergoing alcohol withdrawal, others have seizure disorders and are undergoing regular medication such as diphenylhydantoin (Dilantin) and barbituate such as phenobarbitol. Alcoholic individuals often discontinue medication when drinking and therefore are under increased risk of seizure when withdrawing. Treatment includes magnesium sulfate intramuscularly and resumption of usual anticonvulsant medication.

Treatment of withdrawal is usually accomplished in five to seven days. Sedative medication is gradually reduced and the individual is completely sedative free, except for specific medical indications, two days prior to discharge.[22]

Detoxification ideally takes place in an area set aside specifically for this purpose. In this situation therapy and education groups can be set up for orientation to alcoholism treatment, specifically to ongoing treatment on an outpatient basis after discharge. Alcoholics Anonymous groups and sessions can also be held with orientation to ongoing alcohol abstinence. After the detoxification period the adolescent should be admitted to continuing outpatient treatment as soon as possible. He or she should be seen regularly once or twice weekly in indiviudal and/or group therapy sessions.

Aftercare Treatment of Adolescent Alcoholism: Outpatient Treatment

Another therapeutic modality available to the adolescent is the use of disulfiram (Antabuse). Disulfiram has long been used in the treatment of chronic alcoholism with great success in many situations. Disulfiram is taken orally on a daily basis. If taken correctly, an individual becomes ill shortly after the ingestion of alcoholic beverages, even in small amounts. The alcohol/disulfiram reaction may begin minutes after intake of alcohol and includes flushing, anxiety, sweating, throbbing headache, and palpitation. Severity depends on the amount of alcohol taken and individual reaction to the combination. This very unpleasant reaction may last up to several hours and should be treated medically. Reports of morbidity and mortality do exist.

In the adolescent person the use of disulfiram has been reserved for those individuals who have had a fair trial of outpatient treatment and/or Alcoholics Anonymous and have not been able to maintain alcohol abstinence without it.

Disulfiram should not be administered without an individual's knowledge. It should not be prescribed to individuals who cannot understand its use. It should not be prescribed without thorough understanding of it by both the physician and patient. Informed consent is suggested.

After ten to fourteen days, an individual may again resume alcohol use without ill effect.

Disulfiram has been useful in the past in acting as a deterrent for drinking cycles initiated by impulsive urges; for example when an individual is invited for a celebration drink, or a crisis situation arises, or disappointment suddenly occurs.

Disulfiram has had limited success when used as a sole treatment modality for alcoholism. It may be invaluable, however, when used in overall treatment programs of the adolescent. When it is going to be used, it can be easily started on an outpatient basis after physical evaluation. If hospital detoxification is performed it is most easily started at this time. In the case of the adolescent it is not usually recommended at the time of first detoxification because adequate trial has not been given to test the ability of the adolescent to maintain self alcohol abstinence.[12]

Another beneficial modality helpful to the adolescent alcoholic is Alcoholics Anonymous (A.A.). Alcoholics Anonymous is a fellowship of indivials who have a problem with alcohol. The orientation is toward complete alcohol abstinence and reorientation of lifestyle around that goal.[1]

It has been helpful to many individuals over many years in their problems with alcohol. It can be very helpful to the adolescent who desires to stop drinking. The individual in ongoing treatment should be encouraged to attend and to utilize the sessions and what he/she can gain from them to his/her own self-benefit. Attempts should be made to direct him/her to meetings attended by other young people so indentification may be more easily developed. A.A. members tend to be older, but typically are accepting of adolescents.

Organizations which are not affiliated with Alcoholics Anonymous but have parallel goals are Al-Anon, Al-Ateen, and Al-Atot. Al-Anon is an organization for individuals who have significant others such as parents or spouses who are alcoholic. Al-Ateen is an organization for teenagers who have significant others who are alcoholic. Al-Atot is an organization for children who have significant others who are alcoholic.

The orientation of these organizations is toward helping and for the benefit of the significant other of the alcoholic person. It has long been recognized that alcoholism is a family disease and that family members of the alcoholic suffer. As a general rule, the family members of the alcoholic adolescent are encouraged to attend these meetings. It is usually of benefit to the alcoholic person as well as the significant others. When the alcoholic orients his/her life toward helping him/herself, the significant others avoid facilitating the drinking pattern in the alcoholic.

Since the family is almost certainly involved in the dynamics of the disorder, these organizations and attendance of their meetings can be helpful and can be an important therapeutic goal.

Since the chances are significant that some of the other family members are alcoholic or alcohol abusers, it can be helpful to the adolescent alcoholic to attend these meetings to gain support and perspective.

Once some degree of alcohol abstinence is achieved, underlying personality dynamics can be explored with psychotherapy either in individual or group therapy sessions.

TREATMENT OF ADOLESCENT ALCOHOL ABUSE

Before detailing the treatment of adolescent alcohol abusers, several considerations must be discussed. First, those adolescents who drink excessively are likely to abuse other drugs.[26,27] When treating an adolescent for alcohol abuse, it is essential to determine the pattern of other drug abuse.

Secondly, different personality types of adolescents abuse alcohol. The largest proportion and most often cited group are the delinquent adolescents. McKay,[17] in a study of correctional school admission, reported that 50 of 500 adolescents were addicted to alcohol and half were judged alcohol abusers. Blacker et al.[2] found that delinquents drank excessively two to three times more often than typical adolescents. The excessive drinking of the delinquents is probably a reflection of their generally antisocial attitude and must be treated in that context.

Some adolescents who are abusing alcohol are suffering from an affective disturbance, which is often depression. In one study of alcohol abusers, 5% of the abusers were categorized as suffering from an affective disturbance.[23] A third group of adolescents abusing alcohol are reacting primarily to a situation which they can't manage, such as the death of a parent or a chaotic family situation. A very small percentage of abusing alcoholics are drinking to alleviate the symptoms of psychosis. In these cases the psychosis must be considered first before treating the alcohol problem.

Factors Associated with Alcohol Abuse Cited in the Literature

Lourie,[15] in reporting on twenty cases from ages five to fourteen referred to Bellevue for habitual intoxication in the years 1936–41, found the following reasons: (1) As a means of escape from intolerable intrinsic or extrinsic conditions; (2) through identification with or aggression against alcoholic adults; (3) as a part of a pattern of delinquency; (4) associated with latent or overt homosexuality; (5) associated with psychosis.

In a study of adolescent alcohol abusers, McKay[16] reports on the characteristics of seventeen boys and three girls, thirteen to eighteen years of age. The boys all had alcoholic fathers who left the house before the boy reached adolescence, with one exception. Open hatred for the father and ambivalent feelings toward the mother were expressed. In the girls, alcoholism was common among the parents. The girls tended to express betrayal and a sense of being deserted by the alcoholic parent. Personality characteristics of the adolescents were: hostility, impulsiveness, depression, and sexual confusion. They displayed irritability, feelings of worthlessness, and fear of the future. They often had insomnia and had made suicide attempts. They felt they did not belong in the family, and drinking in groups, which was their pattern, served to alleviate some of these feelings.

Studies by Blane and Chafetz[3] and Zucker[28] indicate male adolescent alcohol abusers are likely to present a facade of independence and masculinity, denying the underlying fears of dependency and homosexuality.

The first task of the therapist is to determine which kind of adolescent he is treating. Often the extent of alcohol and other drug use cannot be accurately determined at the beginning of treatment because the adolescent does not trust the therapist and because of the presence of denial, which is common among all drug abusers.

CASE STUDIES

In order to elucidate the differences between these types, the following case studies are provided:

These adolescents were seen by one of the authors at the Cabrini Alcoholism Program clinic. Each was seen in individual therapy for a period of two months to one year on a once-a-week basis. The family was involved in the process through initial family interview and phone communication.

Maria is a seventeen-year-old Hispanic girl who came to the clinic because intoxication was leaving her in a vulnerable position. She either lost valuable possessions or they were easily taken from her when she was intoxicated. When she came to the clinic she became high as least two to three times a week. She took other drugs, especially marijuana in combination with alcohol. She readily agreed that she needed to stop drinking. She willingly attended several A.A. meetings and took Antabuse. Maria comes from a family with an active alcoholic father and a mother who is rooted in traditional Puerto Rican values. Also living at home is an older sister with whom Maria is always fighting. The neighborhood the family resides in is a dangerous ghetto area in Brooklyn, New York. Until Maria began to drink heavily, her school performance had been excellent. However, when she came to the clinic, she was failing several subjects. Once she stopped drinking, her school performance increased dramatically. However, she continued to have intractable arguments with her mother. Maria had a pattern of staying out late, until three and four o'clock in the morning, during the week without informing her mother. She also had a pattern of getting involved in dangerous situations such as walking alone at night in a dangerous neighborhood. Her mother would object to this and there would be a resulting conflict. Maria's friends were delinquents, though she was not delinquent herself. An acquaintance of hers had been murdered by a rival gang. Many of her male friends were involved in thefts and robbery. These friends as models made it difficult for her to accept a more controlled and responsible behavior pattern. Maria also had a strong belief in voodoo magic associated with the Puerto Rican culture. She benefited from treatment by getting acquainted with A.A., which she liked, maintaining a period of abstinence, and relating positively to an adult figure who seemed genuinely interested in her.

Jane is a seventeen-year-old self-proclaimed alcoholic. Her pattern of drug abuse was in conjunction with a female companion: they drank heavily and smoked marijuana together. She was often truant from school. She became despondent about her withdrawal from life and contacted A.A. She immediately became active, making several male friends. She has basically remained abstinent, though she had a few episodes of smoking marijuana. She came for therapy because she felt unable to cope with her family situation. Her father is an active alcoholic who comes and goes as he pleases from the house. Her mother is a severely phobic woman, who cannot set limits on the father. There is a younger brother who is infantalized by the mother. Jane has severe sexual identity problems, which she hoped to resolve by having intercourse with her A.A. boyfriend. However, she is fearful of penetraton, in part because of a rape at the age of twelve. Severe phobic behavior dates from this time. She slept in the same room with her brother, which contributed to her sexual anxieties, until the therapy began. She was fearful about talking about homosexual fantasies which she had. In therapy, though very conflicted, she formed a positive relationship with the therapist. Sessions focused on her relationship with A.A. and male A.A. members, as well as the traumatic rape and chaotic family situation. Her performance improved at school, she became successful in part-time employment, and less phobic.

John is a good-looking sixteen-year-old boy who abused alcohol and pills regularly. He was brought by a distraught mother who hoped to avoid detention for John for a conviction of assaulting a boy with a baseball bat. What gradually emerged in the course of treatment was a pattern of delinquent behavior dating back to an early age. This included carrying a loaded shotgun for two years, shooting boys with arrows, pushing drugs, and many assaultive acts. He expressed no remorse for any of his acts, showed little regard for his own safety, and remained essentially uninvolved in the brief therapy. His family included a mother very much older than he, she was 50 when he came for treatment, and a father who was on disability for heart disease. The father's attitude was a sore spot for John. The father was "a little king," who could order everyone about, and who would do nothing for himself. One older brother died in an alcohol-related traffic accident. No limits were ever placed on John. Mother always turned a blind eye to his delinquencies. Father didn't care. At the time of treatment, he was involved in an affair with an older woman, who had four children of her own. Therapy had to be discontinued when he continued to commit delinquent acts and his mother refused to enforce any prohibitions.

George is a sixteen-year-old high-school drop-out. He came to the clinic because of a conviction for stealing beer from the store beneath the apartment in which he lived. His pattern of drinking is basically one of drinking as much as he can whenever he drinks until he passes out. He often becomes belligerent when intoxicated. He agreed that he should stop drinking, but once therapy began and he drank again, he denied any need to stop. He did not report any pleasure in drinking, or a wish to express anger when drinking. George comes from an intact family; both mother and father work. As a result, George, for most of his life, has been unsupervised. He had very few limits enforced upon him. His childhood was largely uneventful and he caused his parents no problems. The problems seemed to begin when he had a sudden growth spurt at fourteen, which had him towering above everyone in the family. He began to miss school and get involved in fights. In sessions, he has a very cautious attitude, a great problem verbalizing, and reported no real interests in his life at all. He would like to make money. He had no hobbies, no girlfriend. His male companions are high-school drop-outs like himself. His only goal was to join the Navy when he turned seventeen.

If one were to categorize these adolescents in terms of the personality types outlined above, Jane would be considered to be suffering primarily from an affective disturbance. Maria, though having adequate object relations, had impulse control problems. She had some aspects of affective disturbance and immature ego development. John was clearly delinquent, having severely impaired ego development. George displays many characteristics of immature ego development, yet his problems dated from a specific occurrence. This suggests an important distinction between John and George. John has a life-long history of problems while George does not. This suggests that John's problems were more deeply rooted, while George's were more circumscribed and easier to treat.

Each of these types suggests a different approach to treatment. Those with immature egos need to develop verbalization and symbolization skills. The affective disorders can profit from the traditional psychotherapeutic stance. The delinquents need to focus primarily on the dynamics of their delinquency. As may be surmised by the brief case studies, the therapy achieved limited goals in terms of modifying drinking behavior and personality change. Such limited achievement is typical for the treatment of adolescent disorders. The adolescent's ego can be overwhelmed by factors that indeed must be eventually resolved. The adolescent stops treatment at the point where he can get along and will probably return to therapy at a later point or resolve some of the issues later on in his life.

One other aspect of treatment should be mentioned before detailing the spcific approaches. Krystal and Raskin[14] have introduced the term "affect tolerance" in discussing the adult drug-dependent person. They feel the drug-dependent person has a very limited range of affective experience and the expression of any strong affect or even feeling it, hence tolerating it, is extremely frightening to the person. Hence drugs, including alcohol come to be used to anaesthetize feelings or regulate them artificially. The same pattern is evident in the adolescent alcoholic and alcohol abuser. Thus, an important aspect of treatment with these adolescents is the encouragement to tolerate affects and express them. If feelings are acknowledged and expressed, the adolescent will not have to resort to drinking to relieve his discomfort.

One must also be sensitive to the issue of denial. It is common for all drug abusers to minimize the effect and extent of their drug involvement. One must keep this in mind when treating the adolescent. Confrontation at some point is appropriate. However, one must realize that too strong confrontation will simply alienate the child further. Unless the child is clearly alcoholic, any confrontation should be postponed until the adolescent trusts the therapist enough to bear this strain in the relationship.

Treatment Modalities

Individual[15] and group[16] therapy treatments have both been advocated in treating adolescents with drinking problems. For the most detailed reporting of a case study of an adolescent in treatment for alcohol abuse, see Falstein[8] who takes a psychodynamic point of view. Though family treatment has not been reported on, it would appear to be a promising approach for intact families. No matter what treatment is selected, initial contact with families is essential to ensure cooperation. Hopefully the family can become a positive force in the treatment through education, and the hostility directed toward the adolescent can be reduced. At the same time, the parents must be counseled not to become (or remain) enablers, i.e., in some manner encouraging the adolescent to continue drinking. The issue of control in adolescent treatment is a problematical one. But if the parents simply throw up their hands and let the adolescent do whatever he/she wants, he/she gets the message he/she can drink as much as he/she wants (or do anything else, too). The family should also be told in a general way what the treatment is to be, its approximate length, and the issues of confidentiality explained. What the adolescent tells the therapist must be held confidential to maintain the trust of the adolescent. Family members can give useful information about drinking patterns and important clues to trauma and problems which the adolescent may be unable or reluctant to verbalize. If the child is under eighteen, parental consent should be obtained before treatment can be initiated.

Treatment of Delinquents Referred for Alcohol Abuse

As indicated earlier, heavy drinking is associated with delinquency in adolescence. The distinction must be made whether the alcohol use is severe enough to warrant treatment. Sometimes, delinquent adolescents are referred simply because they had alcohol on their breath when apprehended in a delinquent act. This may or may not be reflective of alcohol abuse. If this determination can be made, the delinquent pattern must be treated primarily. Approaches to treating delinquency include dealing with negativism, negative identity, rebelliousness, and lack of inner controls. Referral should be made to an appropriate treatment facility.

The delinquent who has a pattern of abuse must first see his/her drinking problem as something that needs to change. It may be an expression of a generally negative attitude toward society. It may be just one aspect of a large variety of self-destructive behaviors. The adolescent must develop a sense of self-worth, future goals, and gratifications which are not antisocial or self-destructve. Group therapy has been recommended by Fischer[10] to facilitate these processes in adolescents abusing alcohol. The adolescents can identify with each other and share experiences. Thus the therapist, who is likely to be viewed suspiciously, can maintain a low profile or be more supportive.

The Nondelinquent Alcohol Abuser

In these adolescents, one generally has the cooperation of the adolescent. To deal with the alcohol problem, either a trial period of abstinence should be suggested or a monitoring approach should be taken. Those adolescents suffering from an affective disturbance can be treated with traditional techniques to deal with conflicts creating the problems. Those adolescents responding to a situational disturbance need guidance along with the family to deal with the specific events or situations causing the problems. Those adolescents with immature ego development need an approach to help establish inner controls along the lines suggested by Blos,[4] to develop verbalization and symbolization. Those adolescents who are psychotic need concurrent treatment with a child psychiatrist.

There are no data which report on the success rate of treating adolescent alcohol abusers. However, there are a number of studies which indicate alcoholics under twenty-five respond to treatment at least as well as older alcoholics.[25,10]

Relationship Between Early Drinking Problems and Alcoholism in Later Life

Do early drinking problems result in alcoholism in later years?

There is one study which gives some preliminary indication in answer to this question. Fillmore[9] did a twenty-year follow-up study of college students surveyed for current alcohol use. College students ranging from sixteen to twenty-five were followed up twenty years later. Forty-four percent were reported to be problem drinkers in college while only 19% were twenty years later. Furthermore, only half the group who reported having one while in college, shows a drinking problem in their thirties and forties. Segal,[21] reporting on data from Moscow hospitalization of alcoholics, found that alcoholic symptoms appeared later for those who began drinking earlier and that abuse of alcohol had only a small effect on the rapidity with which the more basic symptoms of alcoholism appeared. These data of course must be taken with caution. But at this point, one cannot say that early alcohol abuse problems necessarily lead to alcoholism in later life.

BIBLIOGRAPHY

1. *Alcoholics Anonymous,* New York: Alcoholics Anonymous Publishing, Inc., 1955.
2. Blacker, E., Demone, H. W., Jr., and Freeman, H. E. Drinking behavior of delinquent boys. *Q. J. S. A.* **26:**223–237 (1965).
3. Blane, H. T., and Chafetz, M. E. Dependency conflict and sex-role identity in drinking delinquents. *Q. J. S. A.* **32:**1025–1039 (1971).
4. Blos, P., Adolescent concretization: A contribution to the theory of delinquency. *In: Adolescent Passage,* P. Blos (ed.) pp. 278–303. New York: International Universities Press, 1979.

5. Chafetz, M. E., and Blane, H. T. High school drinking practices and problems. *Psychiatric Opinion* March pp. 17-19 (1979).
6. Coyle, B., and Fischer, J. A young problem drinker's program as a means of establishing and maintaining treatment contact. *In: Alcoholism and Drug Dependence,* J. S. Madden, R. Walker, and W. H. Kenyon (eds.), pp. 227-238 New York: Plenum Press, 1977.
7. Detre, Thomas P., M.D., and Jarecki, Henry G., M.D. *Modern Psychiatric Treatment,* p. 291. Philadelphia and Toronto: J.B. Lippincott Co., 1971.
8. Falstein, E. I. Juvenile alcoholism: A psychodynamic case study of addiction. *Am. J. of Ortho Psych.* **23**:530-551 (1953).
9. Fillmore, K. M. Drinking and problem drinking in early adulthood and middle age: An exploratory 12-year follow-up study. *Q. J. S. A.* **35**:819-840 (1974).
10. Fischer, J. Psychotherapy of adolescent alcohol abusers, *In: Practical Approaches to Alcoholism Psychotherapy,* S. Zimberg, J. Wallace, and S. Blume (eds.), pp. 219-235. New York: Plenum Press, 1978.
11. Gitlow, S. E. Alcoholism: A disease. *In: Alcoholism Progress, Research and Treatment,* P. G. Bowne, and R. Fox (eds.) pp. 1-9, New York: Academic Press, 1973.
12. Goodman, Louis S., and Gilman, Alfred (eds.). *The Pharmacologic Bases of Therapeutics,* Fifth Ed. pp. 148-149. New York: Macmillan Publishing Co., Inc.
13. Gwinner, P. D. V. The Young Alcoholic—Approaches to Treatment, *In: Alcoholism and Drug Dependence,* J. S. Madden, R. Walker, and W. H. Kenyon (eds.), pp. 263-270. New York: Plenum Press, 1977.
14. Krystal, S., and Raskin, A. *Drug Dependence: Aspects of Ego Functions.* Detroit: Wayne State University Press, 1970.
15. Lourie, R. S. Alcoholism in children. *Am. J. of Ortho Psych.* **13**:322-338 (1943).
16. MacKay, J. R. Clinical observations of adolescent problem drinkers. *Q. J. S. A.* **22**:124-134 (1961).
17. MacKay, J. R. Problem drinking among juvenile delinquents. *Crime and Delinquency* **9**:29-38 (1963).
18. McCord, W., and McCord, J. A longitudinal study of the personality of alcoholics. *In: Society, Culture and Drinking Patterns,* Ch. 24, D. S. Pittman, and C. R. Snyder (eds.) pp. 413-430 New York: John Wiley, 1962.
19. Schuckit, M. A. Alcohol and youth. *Advances in Alcoholism,* **1**(13) (1979).
20. Schuckit, M. A., Morrissey, E. R., Lewis, N. J., and Buck, W. T. Adolescent problem drinkers, *In: Currents in Alcoholism,* Vol. II, Frank A. Seixus (ed.). New York: Grune and Stratton, 1977.
21. Segal, B. M. The effect of the age factor on alcoholism, *In: Currents in Alcoholism,* Vol. II, pp. 377-393, Frank A. Seixus (ed.). New York: Grune and Stratton, 1977.
22. Shader, Richard I., M.D. *Manual of Psychiatric Therapeutics, practical Psychopharmacology and Psychiatry,* First Ed., Fifth printing, pp. 211-235, Boston: Little, Brown and Co., 1977.
23. Smart, R. G. *The New Drinkers: Teenage Use and Abuse of Alcohol,* Toronto: Addiction Research Foundation of Ontario, 1976.
24. Smart, R. G., Young alcoholics in treatment: Their characteristics and recovery rates at follow-up alcoholism. *Clinical and Experimental Research,* Vol. 3, pp. 19-23, 1979.
25. Unger, R. H. The treatment of adolescent alcoholism. *Social Casework* **59**:27-35 (1978).
26. Wechsler, H. Alcohol intoxification and drug use among teenagers. *J. S. A.* **37**:1672-1677 (1976).
27. Wechsler, H., and Thum, D. Teenage drinking, drug use and social correlates. *Q. J. S. A.* **34**:1220-1227 (1973).
28. Zucker, R. A. Sex-role identity patterns and drinking behavior of adolescents. *Q. J. S. A.* **29**:868-884 (1968).

The authors review recent literature reporting investigations concerned with the relationship between depression and the eating disorders of anorexia nervosa and obesity. They point out that research in this area has been hampered until recently by the belief that depression did not exist in children. After reviewing relevant studies, the authors conclude that the evidence strongly suggests that depressive illness does strike children. Several follow-up studies indicate that depression is significantly associated with anorexia nervosa in adolescents. It is further noted that in addition to depression being found in the morbidly obese, even fluctuations within the normal range of weight in adolescents are significantly related to depressive symptomatolgy. What seems to be an important determinant of depressive feelings in adolescents is how they perceive their bodies, rather than actual weight.

8
Depression in Anorexia Nervosa and Obesity

Stuart L. Kaplan, M.D.
I. Ronald Shenker, M.D.
Barbara Gordon, M.D.
Chantal Weinhold

Clinically there is a significant association between self-destructive or suicidal behavior and depression (Pokorny, 1964; Robins et al., 1959; Sainsbury, 1968). Suicidal ideation is included as one symptom among many in all depression inventories, and serves as one of the criteria among others for the diagnosis of the depressive illness in structured research interview schedules. Both anorexia nervosa and obesity have self-destructive consequences regardless of the conscious motivations of patients with these syndromes.

Obesity entails a substantial amount of social disapprobation and in older adults is associated with substantial morbidity because of the number of other illnesses to which obesity predisposes. The self-starvation of anorexia, which occasionally proceeds to the point where it is life threatening, is obviously self-destructive. Since depression and self-destructive behavior have a significant association, and anorexia nervosa and obesity are self-destructive, investigators have sought a relationship between depression and both obesity and anorexia nervosa. This chapter reviews recent literature investigating the relationship between depression and these two illnesses.

DEPRESSION IN CHILDHOOD

Orality as a libidinal stage has played a significant role in the development of psychoanalytic theories of depression as well as those relating to obesity and anorexia nervosa (Mendelson, 1974). These theoretical considerations have provided a framework for the work of contemporary investigators. Yet, until recently, there has been a relative lack of rigorous investigation of the relationship between depression and obesity or anorexia nervosa.

In childhood and adolescence the initiation of such an investigation would have been hampered further by the psychoanalytic conviction that depressive illness in children and adolescents cannot exist. This deductive conclusion rested upon the premise that the psychological complexity of the development of the mind necessary to develop a depressive illness was not found in children and adolescents, (Mendelson, 1974). Depression in childhood might serve as a defense against more painful affects. (Sandler and Jaffe, 1965) or other psychological problems of childhood might serve as "depressive equivalents" (Rie, 1966). But the existence of depression as an illness as it is found in adults with guilt, early morning awakening, appetite loss, anhedonia, diurnal variations of mood, etc., was thought to be rare if it could exist at all.

Mendelson (1974) argues convincingly that the question of whether or not depressive illness exists in childhood is not a theoretical question but an empirical one. It can only be answered by thoughtful, clinical examination of children and adolescents. At the time of Mendelson's classic review, he cited only a handful of studies and anecdotes from his own clinical experience to support the contention that children and adolescents can have a primary depressive illness identical with that of adults. The definitive demonstration of its existence has awaited the development of specific criteria for the diagnosis of depression. The Research Diagnostic Criteria (Spitzer et al., 1975), and the DSM III have provided diagnostic criteria such that patients who fulfill them would be regarded as depressed by both clinicians and investigators. Puig-Antich et al., (1978) Carlson and Cantwell, (1980) have demonstrated the existence of these adult forms of depression in children.

Carlson and Cantwell (1980) examined 102 children, ages seven to seventeen and their parents in a child psychiatric clinic with a one-hour semistructured interview of the child in which questions were specifically asked to elicit symptoms of depression listed in the Research Diagnostic Criteria for depression. The questions inquired about mood, self-esteem, psychomotor behavior, ability to have fun, appetite, fatigue, and suicidal ideation. Nonverbal items such as appearance of depression, spontaneity, activity in relationship to the examiner were also coded. Data from the parents was obtained in a semistructured interview with specific inquiries into mood disturbances in the child, and family history of psychiatric illness.

In addition, all children were administed the Child Depression Inventory (CDI). The Child Depression Inventory, developed by Kovacs and Beck (1977) is based on Beck's Adult Depression Inventory. The CDI is a twenty-one-item questionnaire which inquires into various aspects of depression and each item has four possible responses from 0–3. The larger the number, the more severe the depressive symptomatology. Ninety-three of the 102 children had an axis 1 DSM III clinical diagnosis. Of these 93 children, 28 children had an affective disorder according to DSM III criteria. Twelve children had a primary affective disorder. Those children with a primary affective disorder or secondary affective disorder had mean CDI scores significantly greater than those with other disorders without depression.

Cantwell concludes that it is possible to make a diagnosis of depressive illness in children using criteria identical to those used in adults. Also, he observes that unless the symptoms of depression are specifically inquired about from children and parents the diagnosis of depression can be missed. He noted that many of the children who meet criteria for depressive diagnosis also meet the criteria for the diagnosis of other disorders particularly, hyperactivity, conduct disorders, and anorexia nervosa. It is these problems rather than depression which usually leads to the child's referral for treatment and thus the clinician can overlook concomitant depression.

Puig-Antich et al. (1978) report thirteen children who met all of the Research Diagnostic Criteria for a major depressive disorder. Three of the thirteen met the criteria for an endogenous subtype (at least six of the following: diurnal variation of mood, quality of mood different from grief, early morning awakening, psychomotor retardation, lack of reactivity to environment changes, inappropriate guilt, poor appetite, weight loss, loss of pleasure). Three met the criteria for psychotic subtype of depression due to mood-related auditory hallucinations. Separation anxiety was present in all cases and the five boys in the study over ten years of age all presented with severe conduct disorders. History of frequent separations and severe family dysfunction were present in most of the cases. Eight of the thirteen children were treated with imipramine and six of the eight treated responded within three to four weeks with a dramatic improvement of their depression.

These two studies, as well as others (Weinberg et al., 1973; Kuhn and Kuhn, 1972), support the contention that depressive illness, as it is found in adults does exist in children. Having established this we can begin to consider the possibility of a relationship between depression in children and adolescents and obesity and anorexia nervosa.

OVERVIEW OF ANOREXIA NERVOSA

The primary symptom is the persistent refusal to eat. Despite severe weight loss, most of the patients complain that they are still overweight and engage in a variety of activities to ensure they maintain their cachectic state. These activities include vomiting, excessive use of cathartics with miniscule fluid intake and constant exercise. Many of the symptoms of anorexia such as loss of sexual interest, preoccupation with food and cooking, slow pulse rate, edema, low blood pressure, hypothermia, low basal metabolic rate, may be related to starvation. (Bemis, 1978). Amenorrhea found in 100% of postpubertal anorectic girls was believed to be related to the starvation state. However, it has been widely reported that menstruation ceases prior to weight loss in anorexia nervosa.

The syndrome of anorexia nervosa is much more common in girls; only 10 to 15% of anorexia patients are boys. (Bruch, 1973). The incidence of anorexia nervosa seems to be increasing dramatically. Variations in criteria for the illness makes comparisons difficult but review of hospital records suggests a significant increase. (Bemis, 1978)

The prevalence of the illness has been estimated between .24 (Theander, 1970) and 1.6 (Kendell et al., 1973) annual incidents per 100,000 population. An integral part of the illness is the patient's distorted body image. They perceive themselves to be overweight despite marked emaciation. Classically, the illness begins with a slightly overweight adolescent girl who decides to go on a diet as a result of a passing critical remark on her appearance. She continues to diet past the point where she has reduced to a desirable weight. These girls have been described as highly conscientious, obsessive-compulsive, shy, and introverted.

Fatality from the illness based on follow-up studies has ranged from 3–4% (Beck and Brochner-Mortenson, 1954) to 21% (Halmi et al. 1975). In follow-up studies, approximately half the patients do well controlling their weight; 25–50% of the patients experience a recurrence of symptoms (Moldofsky and Garfinkel, 1974). Thus, despite the recent development of a number of new treatment strategies for dealing with the illness, it continues to pose a formidable challenge to the mental health professional.

Depression and Anorexia Nervosa

Feighner et al.'s (1972) criteria for the diagnosis of anorexia nervosa are among the more widely utilized criteria and are listed in Table 8–1. Strict adherence to the Feighner criteria for the diagnosis of anorexia nervosa, ensures uniformity of diagnosis between clinical centers, provides a basis for the assessment of diverse treatment strategies and is a necessary condition for the investigation of psychosocial and physiological variables which might be related to the disease. The utilization of these criteria by clinicians and investigators assists in resolving the issue of whether or not a report of the study of anorexia is a study of this syndrome or another syndrome which has several features in common with anorexia such as a schizophrenic patient with food refusal. However, the Feighner criteria can lead to definitional clinical ambiguities and percipitous closure on the relationship between anorexia nervosa and depression.

For our purposes it is important to note that the Feighner criteria specifically excludes from the domain of anorexia nervosa those patients who have a diagnosable depressive disorder. This definitional exclusion of diagnosable depressive disorder from anorexia nervosa potentially could obfuscate the study of the relationship between anorexia nervosa and depression. The possibility that anorexia is closely related to depression and in some cases might represent a depressive equivalent or a concurrent illness, is an open possibility and one that should not be excluded on a definitional basis.

Feighner expected the criteria to be modified on the basis of further clinical land research experience. To enable clinicians and investigators to classify those patients who clinically seem to have anorexia nervosa but who do not meet the Feighner criteria, anorexia nervosa is divided into two groups: (1) Primary anorexia nervosa are those patients who meet the Feighner criteria; and (2) atypical anorexia nervosa are those patients who have a number of features of anorexia nervosa but who do not meet the

Table 8-1. Feighner Criteria For the Diagnosis of Anorexia Nervosa.

For a diagnosis of anorexia nervosa, A through E are required.

A. Age of onset prior to 25.
B. Anorexia with accompanying weight loss of at least 25% of original body weight.
C. A distorted, implacable attitude towards eating, food, or weight that overrides hunger, admonitions, reassurance and threats, e.g.:
   1. Denial of illness with a failure to recognize nutritional needs.
   2. Apparent enjoyment in losing weight with overt manifestations that food refusal is a pleasurable indulgence.
   3. A desired body image of extreme thinness with overt evidence that it is rewarding to the patient to achieve and maintain this state.
   4. Unusual hoarding or handling of food.
D. No known medical illness that could account for the anorexia and weight loss.
E. No other known psychiatric disorder, with particular reference to primary affective disorders, schizophrenia, obsessive compulsive and phobic neurosis. (The assumption is made that even though it may appear phobic or obsessional, food refusal alone is not sufficient to qualify for obsessive-compulsive or phobic disease.)
F. At least two of the following manifestations:
   1. Ammenorrhea
   2. Lanugo
   3. Bradycardia (persistent resulting pulse of 60 or less)
   4. Periods of overactivity
   5. Episodes of bulimia
   6. Vomiting (may be self-induced).

Feighner criteria. Anderson (1977) in a consideration of the classification and diagnosis of atypical anorexia nervosa notes that the illness may neet all of the Feighner criteria except that it has an onset after age twenty-five and does not have weight loss greater than 25% of body weight. According to Anderson these syndromes are quantitatively atypical. Qualitatively atypical syndromes are those with the Feigner criteria for age and amount of weight loss, but with simple neglect to eat without a morbid fear of gaining weight, or the fear of fat but comfort with weight gain as long as it is muscle tissue rather than adipose tissue. The concept of atypical anorexia nervosa provides a conceptual framework for classifying, studying and treating these illnesses.

Cantwell et al. (1977) reported a follow-up study of twenty-six patients diagnosed as primary anorectics by the Feighner criteria. Both parents and patients were interviewed and the data was analyzed separately. The mean number of years from discharge to the follow-up study was 4.9. Psychiatric diagnoses at the time of the follow-up were also based on Feighner criteria. Twenty-six parents were interviewed and eighteen patients were interviewed. Considering the parents' reports, twelve of the patients at follow-up were diagnosed as having an Affective Disorder; nine were definite and three were probable. Eight of the eighteen patients interviewed led to a diagnosis of Affective Disorder: seven were definite and one was probable. Among the symptoms of depression present at the follow-up were patient reports of dysphoric mood 56%, sleep difficulty 22%, loss of energy 33%, loss of concentration 70%, crying 28%, feelings of guilt 17%, feelings of worthlessness 28% and suicidal ideation 17%. Parents reported in their children dysphoric mood in 67% and also a high incidence of affective disorder in first-degree relatives. Two fathers, fifteen mothers, and six siblings were given a diagnosis of Affective Disorder. Alcohol abuse was present in many family members. Cantwell notes that in this sample there seems to be a strong relationship between affective disorder and anorexia nervosa.

The symptoms and diagnoses at the time of follow-up were not limited to affective disorders in Cantwell's study. Forty-four percent of the patients reported fears. The identical percentage reported a variety of obsessions.

Although only one patient had the full anorexic syndrome at the time of the follow-up study, five patients were overweight, and two thought they were overweight when their parents did not. Other follow-up studies have found that depressive symptamatology often accompanies anorexia nervosa. (See Table 8-2.)

Schildkraut's catecholamine hypothesis (Schildkraut et al., 1973) of depression has been an important stimulus for the study of the biochemical aspects of depression. Schildkraut on the basis of evidence available to him

Table 8-2. Follow-up Studies in Which Depression was Significantly Associated with Anorexia Nervosa.

INVESTIGATOR	INSTRUMENT USED TO MEASURE DEPRESSION	ACUTE ILLNESS			FOLLOW-UP			
		NUMBER OF CASES	% DEPRESSIVE SYMPTOMATOLOGY		DURATION	NUMBER OF CASES	% DEPRESSIVE SYMPTOMATOLOGY	
			PATIENT REPORT	PARENT REPORT			PATIENT REPORT	PARENT REPORT
Cantwell et al. (1977)	Feighner Criteria		61%	30%	$\overline{X}$ = 4.9 yrs.	26	56%	67%
Morgan & Russel (1975)	Clinical Symptoms of Depression	41	42%		4 yrs.	41	45%	
Warren (1968)	Clinical Symptoms of Depression	20	85%		5 yrs. 5 mos.	11	45%	
Theander (1970)	Clinical Symptoms of Depression	94	25%		$\overline{X}$ = 14 yrs.	82	28%	

at the time, proposed that depressed patients had low CNS catecholamines and that the efficacy of antidepressant medications depended upon their ability to raise CNS catecholamines. Most biochemical assays of catecholamines measure peripheral catecholes rather than central nervous system catecholamines. One metabolite, 3-methoxy-4-hydroxy-phenylglycol (MHPG), reflects the metabolism of CNS catecholamines. It has been reported that many depressed patients do have a lower MHPG than nondepressed patients.

Believing that many patients with anorexia nervosa are depressed, Halmi et al. (1978) studied MHPG and other norepinephrine metabolites in patients with anorexia nervosa. Patients were treated with cyroheptadine, an appetite stimulant medication, or a placebo. Twenty-four hour urine collections were gathered three days after admission to the unit and the urine collection was repeated during their last days on the ward. An MMPI was given at both of these times. Also, patients completed the Hopkins Symptom Check List (HSCL) twice during the pretreatment week and each five days thereafter. Nurses rated the patients during pretreatment and the last week of treatment on the HSCL. A control group of ten girls aged eleven through eighteen years and five adult women received assessments identical to the anorexia experimental population. The urinary MHPG level was lower in the experimentals than in the controls at the pretreatment data collection and at the treatment data collection points. In the experimental population, increases in urinary MHPG concentration correlated with a decrease in depression on the nurses' ratings of the HSCL (-.37) and on the MMPI depression scores (-.37). Peripheral metabolites of catecholamines did not correlate with changes in MHPG level.

Halmi notes that her patients were carefully selected to include only those with primary anorexia nervosa and patients with other psychiatric diagnoses including depression were excluded from her patient population. Patients were selected on an "as you come basis." She concludes that there does seem to be a significant relationship between MHPG and depressive symptomatology in patients with anorexia nervosa.

Another important source of information about the relationship between depression and anorexia nervosa are published reports of the treatment of anorexia nervosa patients with antidepressant medications. Moore (1977) treated a twenty-year-old college student with persistent gorging and vomiting, who lost over 30% of body weight. She vomited following gorging to have the satisfaction of eating and, at the same time, to lose weight. She was given a trial of diphenylhydantoin 100 mg TID for two months because of the possibility that her bulimia might be related to central nervous system dysfunction. The trial was unsuccessful and was followed by a three-month trial of imipramine, 150 mg per day to no effect. Amitriptyline at 150 mg per day produced almost immediate relief of her depressive symptomatology, her vomiting abated significantly, and her binge eating totally disappeared. After four months of treatment, she had achieved normal weight and her Amitriptyline was tapered over a two-week period. The day after complete cessation of Amitriptyline, she immediately resumed her bulimia and vomiting. She continued to vomit and gorge for the next two weeks. The Amitriptyline was restarted and within two days she lost her preoccupation with food, weight loss, and bulimia and vomiting ceased.

Moore notes that Coppen et al. (1976, 1973) have found decreased tryptophan levels in both patients with anorexia and patients with depression. In treated depressives, the tryptophan levels returned to normal but remained low in anorectics who returned to normal weight. The failure of tryptophan to return to normal levels, as well as the failure of some anorectics who returned to normal weight to resume menstruation, suggests that the underlying neurophysiological difficulties of the disease persist despite the return to normal weight by these patients.

Moore explains the failure of imipramine in his patient and the success of Amitriptyline by noting that Amitriptyline is a much more potent agent for raising 5-hydroxytryptamine (a serotonin precursor) than is imipramine. Thus, Amitriptyline may have acted in this patient by raising her serotonin levels.

Also, Amitriptyline was used by Needleman (1977) in the treatment of five women between the ages of eleven and seventeen years, and one sixteen-year-old man all of whom had greater than 20% weight loss with a severe aversion to food. All of the patients had feelings of sadness and motor retardation. The females in the study had amenorrhea. The duration of the patients' illness was between three and thirteen months. They were treated on a general pediatric ward with supportive milieu and ad lib visiting but did not receive any concurrent psychotherapy or any other program to force them into gaining weight.

All six patients were treated with Amitriptyline, 75 mgs to 150 mgs per day and all began to gain weight between the six and twelfth day of treatment. Immediately prior to their increase in weight there was dramatic improvement in their depressive demeanor. Patients continued to improve on this regimen.

DEPRESSION AND OBESITY IN CHILDREN AND ADOLESCENTS

Obesity is a serious pediatric problem in the United States. The overweight infant often becomes the overweight child, and the overweight child and adolescent becomes the obese adult (Heald and Hollander, 1965;

Abraham et al. 1960). Between 5 and 26% of all children are estimated to suffer from some degree of juvenile obesity (Charney et al., 1976). Obesity of juvenile onset appears to be most refractory to weight loss and is far more likely to be caused by psychological maladjustment than adult onset obesity (Stunkard, 1975; Heald and Khan, 1973). There are multiple medical and psychological problems associated with obesity. Medical problems as a result of obesity include depressed growth hormone, hyperinsuliemia, carbohydrate intolerance, cardiovascular disease, and elevated blood pressure (Knittle et al., 1975; Abraham et al. 1971).

Our society places a great emphasis on slimness that even kindergarten children were demonstrated to show a greater dislike for obese children than those with other physical handicaps (Richardson et al., 1961). The rate of college acceptance for obese adolescents was lower than their normal weight counterparts with the same grade point average (Canning and Mayer, 1966).

In a very recent review of the literature on the relationship between depression and obesity in adults, Halmi et al. (1980) note that in mild to moderate obesity five controlled studies failed to reveal significant differences in the emotional status of normal weight adults compared to mild and moderately obese adults. Also, she reviewed the literature on the morbidly obese (greater than 100% overweight) and found considerable variation in the prevalence of affective disorder in this population. In her own study, Halmi et al. found that 28.7% of 80 morbidly obese patients had an affective disorder based on DSM III criteria. She compared this prevalence of depression in the morbidly obese to an epidemiologic study of Weissman and Meyers who found 24.5% prevalence of depression utilizing Research Diagnostic Criteria in the normal population. Thus, the literature on depression and obesity in adults has failed to demonstrate consistent significant differences in the prevalence of depression in the morbidly obese and moderately obese compared to the nonobese.

There have been no studies of the prevalence of obesity and depression in obese prepubertal children because until recently valid criteria for diagnosing depression were not available for children.

There have been two controlled studies of the prevalence of depression with obesity in adolescence. Werkman and Greenberg (1967) administered an MMPI to eighty-eight obese adolescent girls and forty-four normal weight controls. Although there was no significant difference between the two groups on the D Scale of the MMPI, Werkman and Greenberg felt that clinically there were more depressive trends in the obese adolescents than the normal weight controls. In a study of ten obese adolescents and ten normal weight adolescents, Hammer et al. (1972) found more depression in the obese population with the Bell Adjustment Inventory.

Stunkard's classic work on body image disturbances in the obese provides us with an important contribution to our understanding of the psychological significance of obesity in childhood and adolescence. While disturbances in body image are not identical to depressive disorders in the obese, they are strongly associated with neurosis in obese adults. Also, body image disturbances in the obese suggest low self-esteem and thus seem related to at least that symptom of a depressive disorder.

Stunkard and Mendelson (1967) noted in hour-long interviews with seventy-four obese persons and psychotherapy with another twenty that many felt their body was repulsive. Those obese persons with poor body image are self-conscious, neurotic, and constantly preoccupied with what they believe to be the loathsome appearance of their body. Transient periods of depression often accentuate their self-loathing, but their intense dissatisfaction with their body is a constant preoccupation. It is impervious to successful dieting or to other good fortune in their lives. Adult onset obesity in these subjects was not associated with a disturbed body image; only a history of obesity during adolescence was strongly associated with it in adults.

In another study, Stunkard (Stunkard and Burt, 1967) interviewed forty girls between the ages of eleven and thirteen; twenty were obese and twenty were normal weight. Developing body image disturbances were found in four obese girls and three nonobese girls. Any unusual physical characteristic such as glasses, pigtails, or obesity which had become the subject of ridicule by peers and parents became a source of shame in these seven girls. Of the four obese girls only two were ashamed of their obesity and the other two obese girls were concerned with other matters such as braces. The intense self-disgust found in adults was not found in these seven girls. Thus, body image disturbance is not associated with childhood obesity.

In another study Stunkard and Burt interviewed ten adults who were obese at age twelve, had lost weight during adolescence and had maintained their weight loss into adulthood. Only three of these ten subjects had initiated their dieting in adolescence as a result of intense peer or parental criticism. These three were the only subjects to have a body image disturbance at the time of their interview twenty years after their adolescence. They remained excessively concerned about their weight and dieted constantly. Thus, criticism of the subject's obesity during adolescence tends to lead to a body image disturbance that persists into adulthood.

Stunkard (1975) in a review of adverse reactions to dieting regimens believes that obese adults with childhood and adolescent onset obesity are those who are vulnerable to the development of serious depressions and suicide attempts that are found in obese adults who subject themselves to strict dieting.

Kaplan et al. (1980) have studied the relationship between health habits and depression in a group of ostensibly normal adolescents selected on an availability basis. Eighty students (twenty-eight males and fifty-two females with an age range of fourteen to eighteen years), from the tenth and eleventh grades in an urban high school with a diverse socioeconomic population were administered the Beck Depression Inventory and Health Behavior Questionnaire which inquired about nutrition, exercise, smoking, drinking, and drug use. Items on the Health Behavior Questionnaire were weighted based on the face validity of the items. Those items which seemed most injurious to health received higher scores than behaviors which were not as injurious. The individual scores on the HBQ and the BDI significantly correlated ($r = .43$ $p < .01$).

Each subject reported his/her weight, height, and age and if he/she considered him/herself the correct weight, overweight, or underweight. The reported weights were compared with a standard table adjusted for sex, height and age. Weight was considered correct within plus or minus 5% of the ideal table weight; those who were greater than 5% table weight were classified as "overweight" and those who were less than 5% of the table's desirable weight were classified as "underweight." Of the distribution of weight by sex: 19 girls > 5% underweight; 5 boys > 5% underweight; 11 girls > 5% overweight; 7 boys > 5% overweight. Only two subjects, both males, were greater than 20% of their ideal weight. Five subjects refused to supply data about their weight and the remaining thirty-three subjects were within plus or minus 5% of the table's desirable weight.

Boys who were more than 5% underweight were more depressed than boys within plus or minus 5% of their desirable weight ($X_2 = 6.19$, $df = 1$, $p < .02$) as were boys who were greater than 5% of their desirable weight, ($X_2 = 6.43$, $df = 1$, $p < .02$). Furthermore, those boys who believed that they were underweight or overweight, irrespective of their actual weight, were more depressed than those boys who believed that they were at a desirable weight ($X_2 = 6.60$, $df = 1$, $p < .02$).

In another analysis, BDI scores were correlated with the number of pounds each subject varied from his desirable weight. The depression scores for girls who considered themselves overweight had a significant negative relationship with the number of pounds these girls differed from ideal weight ($r = -.428$, $df = 23$, $p < .05$). The closer the weight of a girl who perceived herself as overweight was to her ideal weight, the more depressed she was.

Girls who were more than 5% under their desirable weight had depression scores related to the number of pounds they differed from their desirable weight ($r = .428$, $df = 17$, $p < .05$). Neither the HBQ nor the BDI were related to the demographic variables of age, sex, and race.

Obesity is usually defined as body weight greater than 20% of desirable weight. This was a study of normal weight adolescents and the study suggests that fluctuations within the normal range of weight in adolescents are significantly related to depressive symptomatology.

The paucity of studies of depression in child and adolescent obesity precludes any conclusions about this topic. Instead, some issues and future directions for futher research are suggested.

If a greater prevalence of depression were to be found in obese children and adolescents, what inference could be made from such a finding? No causal relationship between depression and obesity could be established. We would not know if the patients were depressed because they were obese, or obese because they were depressed. or, the obesity and depression might simply be concurrent but unrelated. Perhaps separating populations of obese and depressed children and adolescents from their nondepressed obese peers to study further the former in comparison to the latter would be useful. Family histories of depression in both groups, as well as the depressed group's response to antidepressant medicaton might enhance our understanding of the relationship between depression and obesity in children and adolescents.

REFERENCES

Abraham, S., Collins, G., and Nordsieck, M. (1960). Relationship of excess weight in children and adults. *Public Health Report* **75**:263.

Abraham, S., Collins, G., and Nordsieck, M. (1971). Relationship of childhood weight status to morbidity in adults. *Public Health Report* **86**:273.

Anderson, A. E. (1977). Atypical anorexia nervosa. *In: Anorexia Nervosa,* R. A. Vigersky (ed.). New York: Raven Press.

Beck, J. C., and Brochner-Mortenson, K. (1954). Observations on the prognosis in anorexia nervosa. *Acta Medica Scandinavia* **149**:409–430.

Bemis, K. M. (1978). Current approaches to the etiology and treatment of anorexia nervosa. *Psychological Bulletin* **85**:593–617.

Brantly, H. T., and Clifford, E. (1979). Cognitive, self-concept, and body image measures of normal, cleft palate, and obese adolescents. *Cleft Palate Journal* **16**:177–182.

Bruch, H. (1973). *Eating Disorders: Obesity, Anorexia Nervosa, and the Person Within.* New York: Basic Books.

Canning, H., and Mayer, J. (1966). Obesity its possible effect on college acceptance. *New England J. Medicine* **275**:1172–1174.

Cantwell, D. P., Sturzenburger, S., Burroughs, J., Solkin, B., and Green, J. K. (1977). Anorexia nervosa an affective disorder? *Archives of General Psychiatry,* **34**:1087–1093.

Carlson, G. A., and Cantwell, D. P. (1980). Unmasking masked depression in children and adolescents. *American J. of Psychiatry* **137**:445–449.

Charney, E., Goodman, H. C., and McBride, M. (1976). Childhood antecedents of adult obesity. *New England J. Medicine* July.

Coppen, A., Eccleston, E. G., and Peet, M. (1973). Total and free tryptophan concentration in the plasma of depressive patients. *Lancet* **2**:60–63.

Coppen, A., Gutta, R. K., Eccleston, E. G., et al. (1976). Plasma tryptophan in anorexia nervosa. *Lancet* **2**:961.

Feighner, J., Robins, E., Guze, S., et al. (1972). Diagnostic criteria for use in psychiatric research. *Archives of General Psychiatry* **26**:57–63.

Halmi, K., Brodland, G., and Rigas, C. (1975). A follow-up study of 79 patients with anorexia nervosa: An evaluation of prognostic factors and diagnostic criteria. In: *Life History Research in Psychopathology 4,* R. D. Wirt, G. Winokus, and M. Roff (eds.) Minneapolis: University of Minnesota Press.

Halmi, K., Dekirmenjian, H., Davis, J., Casper, R., and Goldberg, S. (1978). Catecholamine metabolism in anorexia nervosa. *Archives of General Psychiatry* **35**:458–460.

Halmi, K., Long, M., Stunkard, A., and Mason, E. (1980). Psychiatric diagnosis of morbidly obese gastric bypass patients. *American J. of Psychiatry* **137**:470–472.

Hammer, S. L., Campbell, M., Campbell, V. A., Moores, N., Sareen, C., Goreis, F., and Lucas, B. (1972). An interdisciplinary study of adolescent obesity. *J. of Pediatrics* **80**:373–383.

Heald, F. P., and Kahn, M. A. (1973). Teenage obesity. *Pediatric Clinic of North America* **20**:4 Nov.

Heald, F. P., and Hollander, R. J. (1965). The relationship between obesity in early adolescence and early growth. *J. of Pediatrics* **67**:35.

Kaplan, S. L., Nussbaum, M., Skomorowsky, P., Shenker, I. R., and Ramsey, P. (1980). Health habits and depression in adolescence. *J. of Youth and Adol.* **9**(4) (In press)

Kendell, R. E., Hall, D. J., Hailey, A., and Babigian, H. M. (1973). The epidemiology of anorexia nervosa. *Psychological Medicine* **3**:200–203.

Knittle, J., and Ginsberg-Fellner, F. (1975) Can obesity be prevented? In *Childhood Obesity.* P. J. Collipp (ed.) Acron, Mass.: Publishing Sciences Group.

Kovacs, M., and Beck, A. T. (1977). An empirical-clinical approach toward a definition of childhood depression. *In: Depression in Childhood: Diagnosis, Treatment and Conceptual Models.* J. G. Schutterbrandt and A. Baskin, (eds.) New York: Raven Press.

Kuhn, V., and Kuhn, R. (1972). Drug therapy for depression in children. Indications and methods. In: *Depressive States in Childhood and Adolescence.* A. L. Annell (ed.) Stockholm: Almquist and Wiksell, 455–459.

Leon, G. R., Bemis, K. M., Meland, M., and Nussbaum, D. (1978). Aspects of body image perception in obese and normal weight youngsters. *J. of Abnormal Child Psychology* **6**:361–371.

Mendelson, M. (1974) *Psychoanalytic Concepts of Depression.* Second Ed. New York: Spectrum Publications, Inc.

Moldofsky, H., and Garfinkel, P. (1974). Problems of treatment of anorexia nervosa. *Canadian Psychiatric Assn. J.* **19**:169–175.

Moore, D. C. (1977). Amitriptyline therapy in anorexia nervosa. *American J. of Psychiatry* **134**:1303–1304.

Needleman, H. L., and Waber, D. (1977). The use of amitriptyline in anorexia nervosa. In: *Anorexia Nervosa,* R. A. Vigersky (ed.) New York: Raven Press.

Pokorny, A. D. (1964). Suicide rates in various psychiatric disorders. *J. of Nervous and Mental Diseases* **139**:499–506.

Puig-Antich, J., Blau, S., Marx, N., Greenhill, L., and Chambers, W. (1978). Prepubertal major depressive disorder: A pilot study. *J. of the American Academy of Child Psychiatry* **17**:695–707.

Richardson, S. A., Goodman, N., Hasdorf, A. H., et al. (1961). Cultural conformity in reaction to physical disabilities. *American Social Review* **26**:241.

Rie, H. E. (1966). Depression in childhood: A survey of some pertinent contributions. *J. of the American Academy of Child Psychiatry* **5**:653–685.

Robins, E., et al. (1959). The communication of suicidal intent: A study of 134 consecutive cases of successful (completed) suicide. *American J. of Psychiatry* **115**:724–733.

Sainsbury, P. (1968) Suicide and depression. In: *Recent Developments in Affective Disorders,* A. Coppen and A. Walk (eds.) Special Publication No. 2. London: Royal Medico-Psychological Assn.

Sandler, J., and Jaffe, W. G. (1965). Notes on childhood depression. *International J. of Psychoanalysis* **46**:88–96.

Schildkraut, J. J., Keeler, B. A., Papousek, M., et al. (1973). MHPG excretion in depressive disorders: Relation to clinical subtypes and desynchronized sleep. *Science* **181**:762–764.

Spitzer, R. L., Endicott, J., and Robins, E. (1975). *Research Diagnostic Criteria.* New York: Biometrics Research, N.Y.S. Psychiatric Institute.

Stunkard, A. (1975). The case of obesity. *Psychosomatic Medicine* V May-June.

Stunkard, A., and Burt, V. (1967). Obesity and the body image: II Age at onset of disturbances in the body image. *American J. of Psychiatry* **123**:1443–1447.

Stunkard, A., and Mendelson, M. (1967). Obesity and body image: I Characteristics of disturbances in the body image of some obese persons. *American J. of Psychiatry* **123**:1296–1300.

Stunkard, A., and Rush, J. (1974). Dieting and depression reexamined. *Annals of Internal Medicine* **81**:526–533.

Theander, S. (1970). Anorexia nervosa: A psychiatric investigation of 99 female patients. *Acta Psychiatrica Scandinavica* Suppl. 214.

Weinberg, W. A., Rutman, J., Sullivan, L., Penick, E. C., and Dietz, S. G. (1973). Depression in children referred to an educational diagnostic center: Diagnosis and treatment. *J. of Pediatrics* **83**:1065–1072.

Werkman, S. L., and Greenberg, E. S. (1967). Personality and interest patterns in obese adolescent girls. *Psychosomatic Medicine* **29**:72–80.

This chapter focuses on the components of a stressful life experience for a child within its early educational experiences. There is a description of numerous environmental and emotional variables affecting the developing child and the anticipated coping mechanisms employed. Detailing the behaviors to be anticipated when children are under stress in a classroom environment, Drs. Abigail and Joseph McNamee provide a number of suggested techniques for recognizing and dealing with such behaviors. The teacher is seen as a mediating agent between the child and the stressful life experience.

9
Stressful Life Experiences in the Early Childhood Educational Setting

Abigail S. McNamee, Ed.D.
Joseph E. McNamee, Ph.D.

Based on a longitudinal study of vulnerability, coping, and growth, wherein the subject children were followed from infancy through adolescence, Lois Murphy and Alice Moriarty (1976, p. 202) make the following statement:*

> Along the continuum of vulnerability, children may be distributed in different numbers: few if any are so robust, so completely lacking in small as well as moderate or major handicaps as to be totally free from some zone of vulnerability. Most children have a checkerboard of strengths and weakenesses, or an 'Achilles heel,' or a cluster of tendencies that interact in such a way as to produce one or another pattern of vulnerability as well as strength.

Young children bring their neuro-bio-psychological make-up (internal environment) with them to the variety of life experiences (external environment) which they encounter. Through the interaction of the internal and external environments children develop a perception of who they are (internal environment) in relation to their vulnerabilities and strengths, and a perception of what the world (external environment) is like. These perceptions of self and world affect their ability to cope.

* Reprinted with permission.

Rollo May writes in *The Meaning of Anxiety* (1950, 1977; p. 113) that anxiety is how the individual relates to, accepts, and interprets stress. ''Anxiety is how we handle stress.'' The ability of children to handle a stresful life experience successfully is evidenced in their moving into and through the anxiety confronted and moving on to other new and challenging life experiences. The inability of children to handle a stressful life experience successfully ''can deprive a child of essential learning experiences.'' (Wolff, 1969, p. xiii) In fact, as Josselyn (1955, p. 234) indicates, the child in school may be unable to learn because current functioning is commensurate with potential mental ability, is influenced by problems extraneous to school, is the result of a situation in the classroom environment. ''It is not safe to assume the child will 'outgrow' his problem. It is wiser to know what if anything can be done to assure and to facilitate that process of outgrowing.'' (p. 366) It is crucial that school personnel in

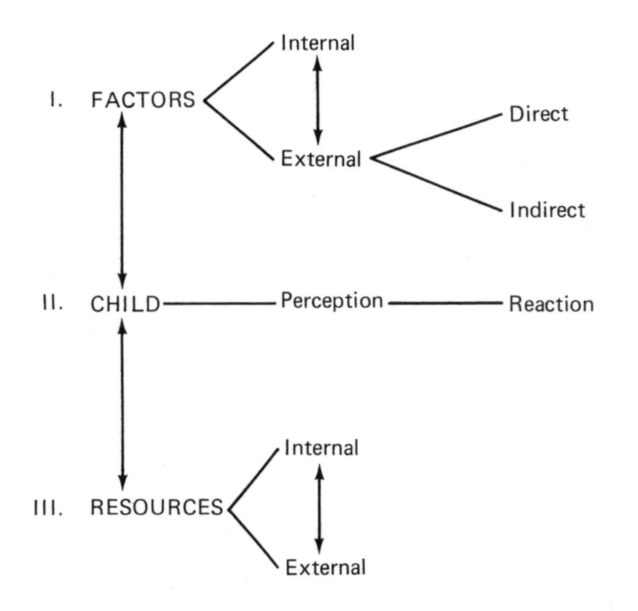

Figure 9–1. A stressful life experience.

the early childhood educational setting increase their awareness of the wide variety of stressful life experiences likely to be encountered by young children as well as strategies for helping them to cope.

This chapter will focus on the components of a stressful life experience for a child: 1. An interplay of internal and external factors which can contribute to a stressful life experience; 2. The child's perception of and reaction to a stressful life experience; 3. The resources available to help the child cope with a stressful life experience.

AN INTERPLAY OF INTERNAL AND EXTERNAL FACTORS WHICH CAN CONTRIBUTE TO A STRESSFUL LIFE EXPERIENCE

Internal Factors

Internal factors are those which come from inside the child and are, therefore, neuro-bio-psychological in nature. There are four categories on internal factors which can contribute to a stressful life experience:

1. *Congenital Organicity*
   a. Information processing dysfunction
      (1) Intelligence
      (2) Learning dysfunctions
         (a) perception (visual, auditory, kinesthetic, tactile)
         (b) memory (sequenced retention and recall)
         (c) cognition (integration and coordination of perception and memory functions)
         (d) hyper- or hyposensitivity to visual, auditory, kinesthetic, and/or tactile stimuli
      (3) Sensory-motor dysfunction
         (a) Coordination (fine motor, gross motor, etc.)
         (b) Sensory-motor integration (eye-hand, eye-ear-hand, etc.)
         (c) Balance
   b. Ethnicity
   c. Physical appearance
2. *Trauma or Disease and Their Sequela* (cerebral palsy, infantile paralysis, etc.)
3. *Age-appropriate Developmental Perceptions*
   a. Fears (Wolman, 1978, pp. 40–76)
      (1) Infancy (0–1 year): strangers, separation, animals, etc.
      (2) Toddlerhood (1–3 years): separation, animals, annihilation, going to sleep, engines, etc.

(3) Preschool (3–6 years): strangers, separation, snakes, large dogs, abandonment, dark rooms, sexuality, death, one's own hostility, etc.

(4) Middle Childhood (6–11 years): paternal health, family finances, interaction with family and neighbors, paternal criticism and rejection, sleeping away from home, getting lost, physical danger, etc.

b. Wishes

(1) One's own omnipotence.

(2) Harm to or displacement of parents/siblings.

4. *Mistaken, unhelpful, and self-defeating perceptions of self and/or others*

a. Perceiving self as bad, helpless, worthless, hopeless, ugly, clumsy, lazy, scatterbrained, dumb, etc.

b. Perceiving the world as self-centered, hostile, dangerous, unmanageable, overwhelming, out of control, fraught with the threat of loss, etc.

Internal factors are predisposing factors and, as such, are necessary, but often insufficient, to cause a stressful life experience in the absence of interplay between the child and the external environment. Consider two examples of how a child is affected by the interplay between internal factors and external environment:

• A child is intellectually retarded. She compares herself with others who are not so impaired and feels badly about herself. Her teacher, unable to respond to her as a special individual, directs several caustic comments to her. Her parents, feeling threatened by having a "dumb" child, try to rid themselves of their feelings of inadequacy and insecurity by rejecting her or, at least, her "dumbness." Perhaps they try to beat the "dumbness" out of her. Her peers, threatened by the dullness they see in themselves, or afraid they will "catch" the retardation, take out their own insecurity by condemning her. The retardation is compounded and the retarded child becomes a nonlearner in the classroom. An internal factor which predisposed, but did not predetermine, that a child would encounter a stressful) life experience has led to a stressful experience because of interplay with external environment.

• A learning disabled child, until diagnosed and properly treated, has difficulty integrating its strong and vulnerable areas of cognitive functioning. This child is easily misunderstood and is often taken to be simply "lazy." The child with auditory perception problems may, because it hears incorrectly or gets confused in the face of verbal requests, instruction, etc., appear to be purposely disregarding the adult. Such a child may develop a "wise guy" or clown posture to cover up its confusion and feeling of inadequacy. Such a posture is often misunderstood by the adult who may react punitively. Such a reaction can lead to an even more firmly entrenched negative self-concept. A learning disability can blossom into a serious learning deficit that can range far beyond the limits of the original disability which went undiagnosed and consequently untreated. Again an internal factor has led to a stressful life experience because of interplay with the external environment.

External Factors

External factors are those which come from outside the child and which can be sufficient, in themselves, to cause a stressful life experience. External factors are encountered by the child through direct and indirect contact with the communities in which it lives, with the child's external environment. When the child encounters an external factor directly, the child is a central character in the life experience and, as such, experiences it firsthand. When a child experiences an external factor indirectly, however, it can experience it vicariously through witnessing or hearing about another person's experience. The other person can be a real-life human being or ever a character on television, film, or in literature. There are five categories of external factors:

1. *Family Environment Where Safety and Security Are Central Issues*
   a. Separation
      (1) Hospitalization of self or family member
      (2) Absence of parent due to work, vacation, etc.
      (3) Death of family member or pet
      (4) Divorce
   b. Family discord
   c. Child abuse (mental and/or physical)
   d. Birth or adoption of sibling
   e. Family move to new home
2. *Immediate Outside Community Where Safety and Acceptance Are Central Issues*
   a. Neighbors
   b. Friends
3. *School Where Safety, Security, and Acceptance Issues Are Joined By a Growing Need for Achievement*
   a. Teachers, administrators, ancillary personnel
   b. Academics
   c. Extra-curricular activities

   d. Classmates and schoolmates
   e. Transportation (school bus, public vehicles)
   f. Neighborhoods traveled through; neighborhood in which school is located
4. *Larger Community Where Safety is a Central Issue*
   a. Section of city in which one lives
   b. City in which one lives
   c. State in which one lives (a reflection of a part of the country politically, economically, environmentally)
   d. Country in which one lives politically, economically, environmentally)
5. *World Events Where Safety is a Central Issue*
   a. War (Vietnam, Israel, Lebanon, Afghanistan, etc.)
   b. Sociopolitical uprising (Ireland, Iran, etc.)
   c. Natural phenomena (flood, earthquake, tornado, fire, etc.)
   d. Starvation
   e. Energy-related phenomena (power failures, fuel shortages)

While external factors are sufficient in themselves to cause a stressful life experience, a child's reaction to external factors is strongly influenced by its neuro-bio-psychological makeup. Whether internal factors or external factors contribute initially to a stressful life experience, an interplay of both soon become apparent.

THE CHILD'S PERCEPTION OF AND REACTION TO A STRESSFUL LIFE EXPERIENCE

A child's reaction to a stressful life experience is dependent on its perception of *self* (as one who does or does not possess the ability, power, and control necessary to avoid, minimize, or terminate an anticipated or actual stressful life experience) and on its perception of the *experience* (as one which can or cannot be avoided, minimized, or terminated). The child's perception, of both self and experience, can be accurate or inaccurate based on real strengths or vulnerabilities, or imagined ones. The child's perception is evolved from past encounters with life experiences. These are, of course, affected by the perceptions of others which have been effectively communicated to the child.

The child who perceives itself as vulnerable (one who does not possess the ability, power, and control necessary to avoid, minimize, or terminate an anticipated or actual stressful life experience), may have learned to perceive itself as helpless. Once the child has developed an attitude of learned helplessness, it would see an undesirable state of affairs as not being affected by any response which it might make "and often as a cue for the continued occurrence of such events despite efforts on his part." (Dweck, 1977. p. 136) Dweck's research indicates that fully competent children who ascribe failures to factors beyond their control become demoralized in the face of failure. Their behavior rapidly disintegrates to the point where they become essentially incompetent. Equally competent children who see failure as being the result of easily changeable aspects of their own behavior improve when they fail, using the failure as a signal to try, or to develop, alternative forms of behavior. "The critical variable, then, may be the degree to which childhood experiences have taught one to view aversive events as surmountable." (p. 136–137)

Murphy and Moriarty's research reinforces the importance of past childhood experience indicating that decreases in vulnerability depend on outcomes of interaction between each child and its environment, as well as on the extent to which these outcomes compensate for other deficiencies, or allow for progress in mastery. Increases in vulnerability occur when the interaction between the child and its environment results in new limitations or difficulties, new threats to homeostasis and to integration, new obstacles to learning, increased difficulty in mastering anxiety, or negative expectancies. (1976, p. 202)

A popular psychodynamic conceptualization of depression is "object loss" (i.e., the loss of a significant parenting figure). Recent writing has suggested that "Object loss as a concept has been expanded far beyond that of a literal loss to include distortions in object relationships." (Malmquist, 1977, p. 47) Such a distortion can be the unavailability of a significant parenting figure who suffers from its own depression and emotionally withdraws from the child. (p. 47) The child of such a parent may identify with the parent, thus becoming depressed, or may become depressed by its failure to gain the parental connectedness which is sought.

> Depressive moods are generated by a child's relinquishment of a belief in his omnipotence and a feeling that the parents are withholding power from him. These moods manifest themselves by separation and grief reactions marked by temper tantrums, continual attempts to woo or coerce the mother, and then periods of giving up in despair for a while. In some cases there is impotent resignation and surrender that may have a marked masochistic coloring . . . feelings of loneliness and abandonment proceed to states of despair and general incompetence. (pp. 47, 48)*

* *Depression in Childhood: Diagnosis, Treatment, and Conceptual Models* (Joy C. Schulterbrandt, Ed.) Carl Malmquist. Reprinted with permission Raven Press, New York.

Again, the child's perception of self is one of having little or no control over an aversive event; the child perceives itself as being helpless.

A child's reaction to a stressful life experience is dependent on its perception of self and of the experience and is expressed in the child's ability to cope. There appear to be, roughly, three levels of coping ability:

Exceptionally Good Copers

A few children cope easily with stressful life experiences. They recover spontaneously, grow personally, and integrate the experience into their life style in a positive way. They experience themselves as successful people and build a resource bank of successful alternatives against which they can draw in coping with future stressful life experiences. Their belief in themselves as competent people increases over time with each new success.

Adequate Copers

A majority of children have to work at coping with a stressful life experience. They may or may not manage to integrate it into their life style in a positive way but they do frequently manage to cope with the stressful experience and to get on with life. When they are successful their self-confidence grows, but the successes are less frequent and their resource bank of successful alternatives grows more slowly than that of exceptionally good copers.

Exceptionally Poor Copers

A few children become extremely disorganized by a stressful life experience. They struggle much harder to surmount the experience and seldom manage to build a resource bank of alternatives against which they can draw in coping with future stressful life experiences. Their lack of success reinforces their negative expectations of themselves and/or of life and they become increasingly discouraged.

Children coping at Level 1 are, of course, the least vulnerable; children coping at Level 3 are the most vulnerable. While children generally tend to cope at one or another of these three levels, ability to cope may vary for any given child from one situation to another, presenting the "checkerboard of strengths and weaknesses" described by Murphy and Moriarty. (1976, p. 292)

Most children then are in need, at one time or another, of external resources to help them with the coping process. The more vulnerable the child, the more essential external resources are to its psychological survival.

Should such support not be available, Sula Wolff, in *Children Under Stress,* suggests that overwhelmingly stressful experiences in childhood can result in developmental personality problems and in patterns of repetitive maladaptive behaviors which may prevent the individual from ever achieving full potentiality in adult life. (1969, p. xiii) In the absence of, or with inadequate external resources, vulnerable children may develop self-defeating behavior patterns in an attempt to feel significant and important.

Some examples of these self-defeating behavior patterns and the unconscious, mistaken goals toward which they are directed follow (Dreikurs, 1964, pp. 58–67). It should be noted here that the child is partially or totally unaware of the purpose of its behavior.

Goal 1: *To obtain undue attention*—The child acts as if "I want to belong . . . I have significance only if I am the center of attention . . . At least I will be noticed."

The Child's Reaction	*The Child's Behavioral Cues*
Over-reaction	Crying, tantrums, screaming which indicate the child's feeling of being overwhelmed by a stressful life experience that, in the child's perception seems as if it will go on forever with nothing in the child's resource bank of alternatives to change it. The cry is for assistance from others that the child might be relieved from this helpless state.
Posturing	Counter-phobic "I know it all" or "little adult" attitude designed to deny (to self and world) the helpless, worthless, hopeless feeling underneath and the related anxiety. Additional ways of keeping others busy with self include being unduly pleasing, charming, witty, and coy aimed at winning attention rather than at participation and cooperation.

Goal 2: To obtain power—The child acts as if "I can refuse them . . . I will not be overwhelmed . . . At least I will not be controlled by others."

The Child's Reaction	*The Child's Behavioral Cues*
Negativism	Refusal to comply with reasonable expectations; compliance may be related, in the child's perception, to anxiety about annihilation and, consequently, fought against.

Aggression	Attempt to establish some degree of control over a stressful life experience by bringing it to a halt through disruption of the teacher's lesson, peer's play, or whatever may have caused, or be the anticipated cause, of stress and associated feelings of anxiety.

Goal 3: To obtain revenge—The child acts as if "I can subdue them . . . I can defeat them . . . At least I can strike back when I am hurt."

The Child's Reaction	*The Child's Behavioral Cues*
Intensified Negativism or Aggression	Sullenness, violence and brutality (both physical and verbal).

Goal 4: To demonstrate (or hide feelings of) complete inadequacy—The child acts as if "I have no chance to succeed . . . I am worthless and helpless . . . If I do anything, you'll discover how worthless I am . . . Maybe if I do nothing people will leave me alone and my inadequacy will go undetected."

The Child's Reaction	*The Child's Behavioral Cues*
Withdrawal	General pulling back from, or avoidance of, a potential or actual stressful life experience in an attempt to minimize anxiety.

In addition to the above cited goal-directed behaviors some children may be intruded upon by organically or psychologically based attentional difficulties (e.g., short attention span) or problems with impulse control (e.g., restlessness, so-called hyperactivity). These behaviors may or may not be goal-directed in and of themselves. They may, however, be found to be present in any of the categories of goal-directed behaviors.

Self-defeating behaviors provide the child with "success" experiences relative to the goal they are designed to reach. They serve the child either as a means of avoiding anxiety-producing situations altogether or as a means of moving around rather than through the stressful experience. As such they provide the child with neither a substantive, socially positive sense of accomplishment, nor with a successful coping alternative upon which it can draw in the future. Such avoidance behavior increases rather than decreases the anxiety which the child experiences when the same or a similar stressful life experience arises again. The child's successful avoidance of the situation and temporary anxiety reduction simultaneously increase the liklihood of the recurrence of the self-defeating behavior and decreases the child's self-esteem. In such circumstances the child's feelings of helplessness, worthlessness, and hopelessness can mount to desperate proportions.

RESOURCES AVAILABLE TO HELP THE CHILD COPE WITH THE STRESSFUL LIFE EVENT

Internal Resources

Internal resources derive from the neuro-bio-psychological make-up of the child and may be either actual or potential in nature. Internal resources provide the child with the raw material necessary to cope with internal and external factors contributing to a stressful life experience. Any given experience is exceptionally stressful if the child perceives itself as lacking the internal resources necessary to cope with the experience. The stressful life experience may be either ordinary (e.g., preparation for school, play with peers, school routine, etc.) or extraordinary (e.g., death, abuse, etc.) in nature.

Compensatory efforts on the part of the child may take the form of working harder in a weak area and/or redirecting energy to areas wherein success is more easily achieved. (Ansbacher and Ansbacher, 1964, pp. 24–27) Compensatory efforts can be adaptive (in the interest of self and society) or maladaptive. (pp. 154–157) For example: A child of good intelligence, who has a specific learning disability, may use its intellect to redouble its effort in the areas affected by the disability, to excel in other areas of accomplishment, or to do both. On the other hand, the child may use the same intelligence to figure out ways to avoid relatively difficult academic areas, to inflate its flagging self-confidence by manipulating others to do for it what it cannot do for itself. The former child exhibits power over circumstances; the latter child has directed its effort toward establishing power over people. Left unattended this latter orientation in

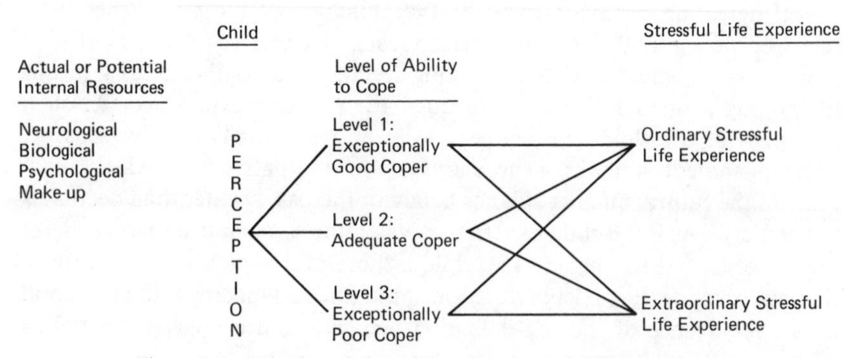

Figure 9–2. Interplay of the child and the stressful life experience.

the extreme can result in the development of a sociopathic personality type. In order to successfully intrude upon the internalization of this type of maladaptive personality development, external resources, or sources of support, must be made available to the vulnerable child.

External Resources

The Mediating Agent. A person who becomes an external resource, or source of support, who intervenes to help a child with the coping process before, during, or after exposure to a stressful life experience, might be thought of as a mediating agent. A mediating agent in an early childhood educational setting can be the child's teacher, the school or center psychologist, counselor, or social worker. The child's off-site therapist is, of course, a mediating agent. Parents, peers, and other persons, in or out of the school setting, who befriend the child (e.g., tutors, lunchroom workers, janitors, relatives, neighbors) can also be mediating agents. The focus of the remainder of this chapter, however, will be on the teacher, recognizing that the management and treatment alternatives suggested can be adapted for use by other mediating agents. The school or center psychologist, counselor, or social worker might also wish to become involved in training the teacher to act as a more effective mediating agent.

In the educational setting the teacher is in a position to be the most valuable mediating agent because of his or her daily relationship with the child, knowledge of child development, of the particular child, of learning theory in practice, as well as observational skills. It is probably the teacher who can most readily notice from the child's cues that support is needed and who can mediate as needed throughout the day, thus enabling the child to benefit maximally from learning opportunities. Irene Josselyn (1955, p. 397) writes that teachers who see children against the backdrop of children their own age are able to evaluate the picture that the child presents and have the opportunity to gain clues as to the child's inner life through spontaneous remarks, writing, and drawing.

It has been argued that a teacher is not trained to be "therapist" and yet teachers are somehow expected to enter the classroom well versed in the intricacies of human relationships. During any given day they are called upon to "motivate learning, encourage autonomy, bolster self-esteem, engender self-confidence, allay anxiety, diminish fear, decrease frustration, defuse rage, and de-escalate conflict." (Ginott, 1972, p. 45) They need a high degree of competence including alternatives from which to draw in helping a child cope with a stressful life experience.

Many of the management and treatment alternatives suggested here are not very different from those developed and implemented by trained therapists. The context in which they are implemented, however, is different, as is the goal of the teacher: learning in an academic setting. Consequently, the application of the management and treatment alternatives is less intense, sometimes more occasional, sometimes more frequent, than that of the therapist. Consider an example of the teacher intervening as mediating agent:

• Peter, a three-year-old, held on to his mother's hand trying to pull her back into the room on his first morning at the day-care center. His teacher asked his mother to come into the room and sit for a while as Peter became accustomed to his new center. This teacher took a step in helping a child cope with a stressful life experience.

It cannot be assumed, however, that the teacher in an early childhood educational setting will act as mediating agent. He/she can also contribute to a existing stressful experience:

• A first-grade child, during Show and Tell, said, "Once I had an aunt. She was sick. She died of cancer." The teacher responded, "That's not a very nice story for Show and Tell. Next week let's have a pleasanter story." This teacher probably contributed to an existing stressful experience.

A teacher can even initiate a stressful experience:

• Leo, a kindergarten child, heard his teacher say, "on your report cards I have said some good things about some of you. But for those who have misbehaved, I will have to tell your mommy." This teacher possibly initiated a stressful experience for Leo who may have known, or wondered if, he had misbehaved.

Another example of when a teacher either contributes to or initiates a stressful experience is when he/she responds to a child with what Ginott (1972, p. 88) calls "destructive 'whys' " "Why can't you be good for a change? . . . Why are you so selfish? . . .Why are you so slow? . . . Why are you so stupid?" Dick Gregory refers to such a teacher in his autobiography *Nigger*: "I never learned hate at home, or shame. I had to go to school for that . . . The teacher thought I was stupid . . . a troublemaker." (Gregory, 1974, pp. 114, 115)

It can be assumed that most teachers want to be mediating agents, want to become a valuable external resource, or source of support, intervening to help a child with the coping process. The ability to do so varies from person to person depending on one's ability to conceptualize and implement a mediating role.

To be helpful the mediating agent must recognize that children experience an interplay of internal and external stress factors, that children react differently to stressful life experiences depending on their neuro-bio-psychological make-up, as well as their perceptions of life experiences. In addition, the mediating agent must see his or her role as (1) that of meeting the child's immediate emotional, social, and cognitive needs by being available and supportive, and (2) that of building a resource bank of alternatives against which the child can draw in coping with future stressful life experiences. In other words, the role of the mediating agent should have as its goal the meeting of immediate needs and the building of resources so that the child can grow toward feelings of self-worth, self-confidence, and hope rather than develop feelings of helplessness, worthlessness, and hopelessness. Sula Wolff (1969, p. xiii) writes that the help provided for children under stress fulfills the double purpose of relieving present anxieties and preventing personality defects later in life.

The mediating agent can help the young child to cope by minimizing the stressful life experiences in his/her environment (their variety, frequency, and duration) and by helping the child to deal with stressful experiences in gradually increasing degrees. Such an approach is not aimed at the elimination of stress, which is neither possible nor desirable, but, rather, the reduction of stress and associated anxiety. Such an environment provides an opportunity for the mediating agent to introduce and support, and for the child to develop effective, socially adaptive ways of moving through anxiety and coping with stressful life experiences.

The Mediating Environment. The mediating enviornment is that space which will be used for management and treatment in anticipation of the child's reaction to a stressful life experience and in helping a child to cope with such an experience during and following its occurence. In an early childhood educational setting the classroom is the site where the teacher and child spend most of their time, with which each is most familiar, and which offers, generally, an array of materials which will encourage the young child to "play out" his/her feelings related to a stressful life experience. If a teacher's interaction as mediating agent with the child is to be brief, if the interaction involves other class members, or if there is a teacher assistant to take over regular classroom tasks allowing teacher and child an uninterrupted block of time, the classroom can well be utilized as the mediating environment. In fact, it may be all that is available.

If other professionals become involved (the school or center psychologist, counselor, or social worker) it may be more convenient for an office or playroom to become the mediating environment. Such an office or playroom might also be available to the teacher. If the child is meeting with a private therapist, his/her office will become an additional mediating environment.

It is desirable for the mediating environment to have some or all of the following: walls and floors that can be cleaned, a sink, a chalkboard, a table and chairs, and play materials. (Axline, 1969, pp. 53–54) Play materials are an essential component of the mediating environment for young children. Ginott (1961, p. 51) explains that the child can show how it feels more adequately through the manipulation of toys than through words. Play materials can be structured or unstructured in nature. Structured materials are the direct facilitators in the expression of feelings. Unstructured materials allow for indirect and diffuse expression of feelings. Moustakas (1959), Ginott (1961), and Axline (1969) each list appropriate play materials including the following:

Structured materials

- Guns, knives, swords (used to express hostility and aggression in a socially acceptable manner);
- Housekeeping equipment (used to test reality and focus on direct expression of feeling through role play);
- Dollhouse and family dolls (used to play through family conflict and crises); puppets can be used for the same purpose;
- Neighborhood buildings and people (used to play through neighborhood conflict and crises); puppets can be used for the same purpose;
- Toy stuffed or rubber animals and puppets (used to express feelings);
- Transportation toys (used in the conventional manner or as disguised people);
- Climbing equipment (used to release the urge for free motility, to test abilities and gross motor coordination);
- Nursing bottles (used to play out ambivalence between wanting to be a baby and grown-up).

Unstructured Materials

- Sand (used in construction, destruction, and aggressive play);
- Clay (used in construction, destruction, and aggressive play; lends itself to symbolic use);
- Blocks (used in construction, destruction, and aggressive play);
- Water (used for easy manipulation requiring no special skills; used at times to soothe or stimulate);
- Finger paint (used for messing and for translating feeling into color and movement; used to encourage spontaneity);
- Easel paint (tempera and water color can be used to express feelings without the messy quality of finger paint)

Other materials can be included in the mediating environment such as toy soldiers and army equipment, large dolls, crayons and paper, peg-pounding sets and wooden mallets, paper dolls, airplanes, toy telephones, newspapers and magazines, pictures of people, games, etc.

Materials in the mediating environment are generally arranged on shelves within easy reach of the child, so that it can freely choose any materials with which to play. The materials should remain consistently available. Some of these can be packaged in a box or suitcase to be carried to whatever space is available for interaction between the mediating agent and child. They can also be kept on a special shelf or in a drawer if such a limitation of space is necessary because of other demands placed on space used only occasionally as a mediating environment.

The Management and Treatment

Anticipatory Support Mediation Strategies. Anticipatory support mediation has two emphases: (1) the general atmosphere of the mediating environment, and (2) the specific preparation for an expected and potential stressful life experience.

1. The general atmosphere of a mediating environment is one which should be typical of every early childhood classroom. It is one in which the ordinary stressful life experiences of childhood can be managed with a minimum of effort on the child's part. In this environment the extraordinary stressful life experiences can be seen as an opportunity for the mediating agent to introduce and support, and the child to develop, effective, socially adaptive ways of moving through anxiety and coping with a stressful life experience. Such an environment can be created by establishing the following:

- A balance between an overall calmness and the availability of a well-planned, stimulating large group, small group, and individual learning experiences and materials;
- A structured and consistent classroom procedure that teaches individual responsibility, that enlists the participation of the children, and that provides:
  1. Clearly communicated expectations (e.g., class rules) which can be easily referred to and periodically reviewed,
  2. Clearly established positive and negative consequences for behavior,
  3. Frequent opportunities for personal success.

A consistently communicated acceptance of, and respect for, the children which Ginott (1972, pp. 70–93) refers to as "congruent communication."Ginott's examples of congruent communication best define the interpersonal component of a successful mediating environment:

• Addressing oneself to a situation rather than judging character and personality;

• Responding genuinely to angry feelings and expressing them without doing damage (without insult, abusive names, attack) by describing what one sees, what one feels, what one expects;

• Recognizing children as complex human beings with strengths and vulnerabilities, capable of a variety of feelings;

• Inviting cooperation through giving a voice and a choice in matters that affect life in school;

• Avoiding commands;

• Conveying acceptance through uncritical statements when responding to a child's plight, complaint, or request;

• Avoiding labeling;

• Correcting by directing or describing processes, not by criticizing;

• Omiting questions which make the child feel foolish, guilty, enraged, vengeful;

• Avoiding sarcasm;

• Avoiding quick reassurances of "hurried help";

• Utilizing brief methods of dealing with minor mishaps;

• Praising by describing what one sees in, and feels about, a child's work rather than by evaluating a child's character.

2. Life experiences which can be potentially stressful to an individual child, or to a group of children, can sometimes be expected and support offered through specific preparation. Such expected events can arise during a school day (a change of the schedule, a fire drill, a test, a new person coming into the room, etc.) or can carry over from home (the imminent birth or adoption of a sibling, hospitalization, death, etc.). When a stressful life experience is expected it is helpful if the mediating agent enlists the help of the children in

• describing the approaching life experience;

• describing feelings about the stressful life experience;

• describing the support available;

• describing alternatives for moving through anxiety and coping with the stressful life experience.

Responsive Support Mediation Strategies. It is often not possible to anticipate a stressful life experience and it is always necessary to respond, as a mediating agent, during or after exposure to a stressful life experience. The teacher can respond by making a concerted effort to identify the stressful life experience and its scope by observing and speaking with the child, with its parents, and by reviewing the child's record and meeting with previous teachers. He or she can also meet with the school or center psychologist, counselor, or social worker. If the child is in therapy, the parent's permission can be requested to communicate with and cooperate with the therapist in developing a helpful approach to the management and treatment of the child's reaction to the stressful life experience.

The following alternatives have been adapted from those described by Woods (McNamee) and Delisle (1977) and can become part of a management and treatment plan. They can be drawn upon by the teacher, or any mediating agent, in response to a child who needs support during and after exposure to a stressful life experience. These alternatives have been sequenced beginning with the nonverbal and moving toward increasingly verbal interaction, an attempt being made to help the mediating agent become involved with the child in the least threatening manner possible. It is possible to implement the alternatives in another sequence, or to implement one or some alternatives and not others; implementation should be adapted to the style of the individual mediator and to a particular child or group of children as well as to a particular stressful life experience.

Recognize the Child's Cues. Regardless of the presence of internal or external resources, the effectiveness of coping style, or the perceptions of self and circumstances, all children experience stress. Although it is not always possible to successfully identify a child who is anticipating or encountering a stressful life experience, the chances of early identification are greatly enhanced if the mediating agent is sensitive to and aware of children's cues. These cues will probably be a change from or an exaggeration of a child's normal behavior (e.g., sad appearance, thumbsucking, trying to sit very close to the adult) or a deviation from normal behavior for a child that age (e.g., an eight-year-old wetting his pants in school, a young child acting the "little adult"). Sometimes the cues are direct and either from the child ("I feel sad/angry" . . . "Why did my Grandpa have to die?" . . . "Why won't these dumb scissors cut right?" . . . "Make Melissa let me play in the playhouse.") or from another person who reports that a stressful event is about to or already has occurred.

At other times the mediating agent may witness an event that is potentially stressful for a child or children (e.g., an accident which can been seen from the school yard, a parent's physical or verbal abuse of a child before school begins, a television program or news announcement). At still other times the child itself may be unaware of the effect a stressful life experience is having on its life but may express possible related symptoms (e.g., a mild physical complaint which has no apparent basis in medical reality, a wish). In more extreme cases the child may respond in a less adaptive fashion and the cues may be more disruptive or regressive in nature (e.g., crying and screaming, hitting another child or an adult, destroying one's own or another child's block tower or art work).

To be able to pick up on and to differentiate between these cues a mediating agent may ask him or herself several questions:

First: Is the child's behavior different today?
Second: How is that behavioral difference manifested?
Third: What is the child's behavioral goal?
Fourth: How do I respond to the child's behavior and what does my reaction tell me about the child's goal?
Fifth: Are there any other cues that may help me to understand the goal of the child's behavior?
Sixth: What can I do to help this child deal more effectively with the stress and associated anxiety which it is encountering?

For the majority of children whose reactions to stress are more or less age appropriate the mediating agent can respond (Sixth Question) after the cues have been identified (First and Second Questions) with other mediating alternatives. Perhap to:

Be Physically Supportive. When a child is experiencing stress-related anxiety being physically supportive can be very helpful. This does not mean creating an artificial environment or a physical relationship between a child and the mediating agent which has never before been experienced and with which the adult or the child would be uncomfortable or threatened (some children find being touched a stressful life experience). It does mean doing what has been physically acceptable in past supportive experiences or what would seem, now, to be supportive. Examples might be stroking a child's hair, face, shoulder, elbow, hands; letting the child be close. This mediating behavior should communicate "I care" though nothing has necessarily been said. When Richard told his teacher that his grandmother has died, she described holding him in her arms and kissing his forehead. He responded, she said, with a "great big smile." Physical support is a way of being helpful even before the mediating agent can think of what to say.

State or Restate the Situation. Stating the situation would occur when the child has verbalized nothing and yet the mediating agent is aware that the child has been exposed to a potentially stressful life experience. The child may look, sad, angry, etc., and has therefore given a cue to its feelings. Restating the situation would occur when a child has verbalized what has occured and what feelings are associated with that occurance. Such stating or restating implies empathy and extends support without evaluation. Consider some examples:

• Richard withdrew to his cubby during the day. He looked sad. In a quiet aside the teacher might have said, "You feel very sad today, Richard. You want to sit in your cubby and not play for a while?"

• If the teacher had been contacted by the parents and told that Richard's grandmother died and that the family attended her funeral over the weekend, the interaction might have gone something like this: "Your mother told me, Richard, that your grandmother died and that you went to the funeral. You're feeling sad and want to sit in your cubby and not play for a while."

• If the child had said, "My grandmother died last week and we went to her funeral" the response might have been, "Your grandmother died last week and your family went to the funeral."

• If the child had asked a question, "Why did my grandmother have to die? the teacher might have responded, "You're wondering why your grandmother had to die."

• In addition to implying empathy and extending support without evaluation, this suggested alternative gives the mediating agent time to determine how best to respond to the child further. It often enables the child to talk, giving the adult information about its perception of the stressful life experience and the child's ability to cope with it.

Share Feelings. It is important for the child to know that its feelings, whatever they are, are acceptable to the adult; that it is okay to feel sad, angry, hateful, etc. It is important for the mediating agent to facilitate the expression of feelings. When Richard came into his classroom stating, "My grandmother died last week and we went to her funeral." his teacher might have asked him to tell her about his feelings. She might have said, "Give me your best guess about how you feel inside." (Looff, 1976, p. 89)

It is important to note, here, that while feelings are always okay, some behavior is not. It is not okay to hit others because of anger or to throw or break toys and materials. The mediating agent must communicate to the child who acts this way, "I know you feel angry and that is okay, but it is not okay to hit me and I can't let you do that." But more about these less adaptive and more disruptive behaviors later.

The child needs to know that adults, too, have feelings. It is appropriate, at times, for children to have an opportunity to share adult feelings. Richard's teacher shared her sorrow over the death he had experienced: "I told him that I was sad about what had happened." She was able to share not only her sorrow at his loss, but her feeling for him as a person when she held him in her arms and kissed his forehead. An adult sharing feelings should be careful not to overwhelm the child with either an emotional or verbal flood. Sharing is meant to be therapeutic time for the child, not the adult. The child is too young to handle adult guilt or anger or grief and should not be placed in a situation which scares or frustrates or forces the child to do so. The adult should not become the child, thereby forcing the child to become the adult.

Give Information. A child attempting to cope with a stressful life experience will need some information to help it feel secure. This information will vary, of course, according to the stressful experience. It should however always be accurate and appropriate to the developmental and experiential level of the child in depth and vocabulary. Information should be concrete and honest, not abstract or euphemistic. It should describe what has happened, what support is available, and what can be done about it. "Your mother will be late today but I will stay with you until she comes. The two of us can wash the table tops, then maybe we'll read stories for a while." Sometimes the child wants to know why something has happened: why grandmother died, "She was sick and the doctors could not make her well"; why Daddy and Mommy are getting a divorce, "Mommy and Daddy are unhappy living together and have decided to live apart." Sometimes knowing the cause of a stressful life experience can help relieve feelings of guilt that the child is the cause. "When your parents fight, that is very hard for you and sometimes makes you cry. But grown-ups' fighting is really grown-up business." (Warren, 1977, p. 22) The adult might go on to say that even when grown-ups are fighting about the child they do so because they are mad at each other and not because of anything that the child did.

Saying nothing is not a solution. Silence at the wrong time can be very harmful. Without information a child is left to its fantasy which is often more extreme and scary than reality. Consider, for example, the four-year-old whose brother died and whose parents thought it best not to tell him about the death. He decided that his parents had gotten rid of the sibling . . . and they might do so to him.

Propose Experiences. A mediating agent can propose experiences which may help to meet the child's immediate needs and contribute to the child's bank of resources. There are many experiences from which a mediating agent can choose. Examples might be:

- To propose interaction, in a quiet place, with play materials such as those which should be available in a mediating environment, saying, "These play materials are for you to use. They will be kept on this shelf (in this box, on this table) each time you come here" (if the mediating environment is a separate room) or "each time you want to use them" (if the mediating environment is the classroom). Any rules which the mediating agent thinks are necessary can be stated, for example: "These materials must stay in this room (or area)." Of particular usefulness in working with one child, or a group, is paper and crayons (or paint, though crayons are the easiest to manage and the least likely to be threatening, of the art materials, in themselves). The mediating agent might say, "I thought you would like to draw about what happened (about how you feel inside)." Should the mediator wish to talk with the child about the drawing, is it best to say, "Tell me about your drawing" rather than "What did you draw?". Play materials are generally available in an early childhood classroom and will often be used by the children with no introduction by the teacher, as they work through a stressful life experience. Such usage, noticed by the teacher, is a cue which he or she might wish to follow up with one or more of the suggested alternatives.

Still other approaches with which mediating agents have had success, which can be implemented with an individual child or with a group of children, and which have the characteristic of being minimally intrusive are:

- To read a story or poem, to show a film/filmstrip, or to listen to a record (or to discuss a television program or film seen outside of the classroom) about specific kinds of stressful life experiences encountered by young children. These can be followed by general discussion that encourages children to share perceptions and feelings about what they have seen and to share similar first-hand experiences. Local libraries furnish lists of children's books related to specific stressful life experiences and often stock related records and films which can be borrowed.
- To share memories of stressful life experiences and ways of coping with them: "I can remember when . . ." The teacher and other adults can also become involved.
- To make universal statements (e.g., "All boys and girls worry about . . .," "Lots of people are afraid of that . . .," "People sometimes get angry and wish that . . ."). (Looff, 1976, pp. 87–88) These statements tend to have a reassuring effect on children who have recently experienced a stressful life experience and are feeling isolated as if they are the only ones who . . .
- To give homework assignments to help a child to think more objectively about its behavior and to clarify its functioning, essential if the child is to learn more effective, socially adaptive ways of moving through anxiety and coping with stressful life experiences. David Looff* describes how the giving of homework assignments might be implemented:

* David Looff, *Getting to Know the Troubled Child.* Copyright © 1976 by The University of Tennessee Press, Knoxville. Reprinted by permission of the University of Tennessee Press.

> . . . You told me that when you get angry, you lose your patience and end up sometimes hitting Sissy. It was your idea to count to a million if she gets you mad, so you can stop yourself from hitting her. . . . Your homework, Charlie, will be (to) . . . keep track of how many times this million thing works and (to) let me know . . . (p. 91)

• To tell mutual stories, a technique developed by Richard Gardner, which has a variety of carefully designed approaches (e.g., word cards about which the child and the adult alternately tell stories; (1976, pp. 72–76) orally presented stories, which can be taped, told first by the child and then retold by the adult who describes additional resolution alternatives (1971, pp. 25–31)). Through these techniques, the child can be encouraged to express its anxiety in story form and to recognize behavior alternatives.

• To hold a class meeting or council, a blend of William Glasser's "classroom meeting" (1969, pp. 122–144) (social-problem-solving meetings geared to solve the individual and group educational problems, educational-diagnostic meetings geared to evaluate whether or not teaching procedures are effective, open-ended meetings geared to the discussion of thought-provoking questions related to the children's lives) and Rudolf Dreikurs' "family council" (1964, pp. 301–305) suggested as a means of dealing with troublesome problems in a democratic manner. Each council group can work out a procedure to suit its own needs, but Dreikurs describes basic principles: the meetings involve every group member and are held at a definite time set aside for the purpose each day or week. Each person has the right to bring up a problem, each has the right to be heard, all seek a solution to the problem, and the majority opinion is upheld. In addition, the adults' voices are no stronger than those of the children, chairmanship is rotated among all council members, and decisions hold for a prescribed period of time and cannot be changed between meetings. Even young children can participate in such meetings.

Whatever the experience a mediating agent might propose to a child, or to a group of children, it should be examined carefully to determine whether it contributes to the children's intellectual, emotional, and social needs and resources. The mediating agent should ask:

Intellectual Needs and Resources. Does the experience, including my own conversation, provide the child with accurate and appropriate information?

Emotional Needs and Resources. Does the experience, including my own conversation, provide feedback that the child is okay to feel as it does, that the child is being taken care of?

Social Needs and Resources. Does the experience, including my own conversation, provide feedback that the child is sharing an experience?

Close the Conversation. There comes a time when the conversation/interaction must be closed. Closure is not harmful, and, in fact, can be helpful as long as the reality of reopening is clearly and honestly offered by the mediating agent.

The timing for closure may be the mediating agent's: Perhaps the conversation/interaction has become more than he or she wishes to (or has the ability to) deal with at the moment. Distance may be needed to adjust feelings and thoughts.

The timing for closure may be the child's: Perhaps the child will change the subject, get involved in other things, or get up to wander off. The child's timing is often limited by attention span. A child cannot deal for very long with any issue and tends to end uncomfortable conversations/interactions abruptly to reintroduce them at a later time.

Whether the time for closure is the adult's or the child's, the promise of reopening is reassuring to both. The mediating agent will have the opportunity to be again supportive, perhaps even more skillfully so; the child will have the opportunity to be again supported in its effort to move through anxiety and to cope with a stressful life experience. If the timing for closure is the mediating agent's, he or she might say: "It's time to stop now but we can talk (draw, play, etc.) again tomorrow during rest time (after lunch)," indicating a specific time, whenever possible, that the child can count on. If the timing for closure is the child's, the mediating agent might say "I think it would be a good idea to stop now. When you're ready to talk (draw, play, etc.) again let me know and we'll work out a time together."

But what of the child whose reactions to stress are not age appropriate and whose behavioral cues are characterized by high degrees of disruptive activity or by almost no activity? The child's unconscious goal in executing these maladaptive behaviors may be obscure precisely because the child has little or no awareness of its misdirected goals. Dreikurs, in fact, warns the adult of the danger in telling the child what is suspected to be the goal of its behaviors. He writes that psychological insight is not to be repeated to the child but rather is to serve as a basis from which one will operate with greater sensitivity and understanding in interaction with a troubled child.

Referring back to the questions which can help guide the mediating agent toward his or her goal of aiding the child with misdirected goals, The Third Question should be considered: What is the child's behavioral goal? To answer this question one need only observe the child's behavioral cue and find the goal with which it is associated as described in Section II of this chapter.

The Fourth Question is more personal: How do I respond to . . . and what does my reaction tell me about the child's goal? For example, if the goal of the child's maladaptive behavior is to obtain attention, one tends to feel annoyed and to experience the child as a pest or a nuisance. If the goal is to gain power over others, one tends to feel defeated, frustrated, angry, that one's leadership is threatened. If the goal is to obtain revenge, one tends to feel hurt and to regard the child as mean and nasty. If the goal is to demonstrate or hide feelings of complete inadequacy, one tends to feel helpless, to feel like giving up, and to think of the child as a dreamer or as being stupid. (Walton and Powers, 1974, p. 7)

The Fifth Question looks for still more information: Are there any other cues that may help me understand the goal of the child's behavior? Walton and Powers (1974, p. 7) suggest that the child's reaction when verbally disciplined or corrected can provide an additional cue to the child's unconscious goal. If the goal it to obtain attention, the child will stop the behavior, but only for a brief time. If the goal is to obtain power, the behavior will continue or actually become worse if corrected. If the goal is to obtain revenge, the behavior becomes a more intensified attack in retaliation for being corrected. If the goal is to demonstrate (or hide feelings of) complete inadequacy, there is no response when the child is corrected.

By being aware of the child's goal the mediating agent can avoid becoming accidentally supportive of the child's maladaptive behavior. It is also possible to help children to change their behaviors. Walton and Powers (p. 9–12) cite some goal oriented intervention strategies that have met with some success:

• If the goal is to obtain attention the mediating agent can ignore the behavior when possible, comment on the helpful behavior of another child so that the disruptive child can hear the interaction, find a way for the child to earn recognition appropriately.

• If the goal is to obtain power the mediating agent can avoid power struggles by admitting his or her limitations and requesting the assistance of the child; since the child is expecting to meet the adult's power, it will be surprised by being respected and the mediating agent can thereby model cooperative behavior. The mediating agent might also find a way to help the child to feel important.

• If the goal is to obtain revenge the mediating agent can help the child to feel loved and accepted as well as valued, perhaps by enlisting its help in reaching a frightened or discouraged classmate. The mediating agent can expect provocation and side-step it when it comes so that the child's expectation of rejection is not fulfilled. The mediating agent can ask someone on staff to try to establish a working relationship with the parents of such a child to help them find alternatives to the physically or verbally hurtful disciplinary measures they must be employing at home.

• If the goal is to demonstrate (or hide feelings of) complete inadequacy the mediating agent can maximize successes for this child without completely sacrificing his or her standards. The child can be helped to find areas in which it can achieve and any positive contribution which it is able to make can be acknowledged but without fanfare which might make the child feel uncomfortable.

SUMMARY

The successful management of stress and related anxiety in the early childhood educational setting is an outgrowth of:

• An interplay of internal and external factors which can contribute to a stressful life experience;

• The child's perception of him/herself and of the experience and resulting reaction;

• The resources available to the child to help develop effective, socially adaptive ways of moving through anxiety and coping with stressful experiences.

Successful stress management can free a child from self-defeating behavior patterns and help maximize the child's learning potential. It is therefore crucial that school personnel increase their awareness of the wide variety of stressful life experiences likely to be encountered by young children. An aware teacher can facilitate early identification, and provide for the needs of the child who requires external support in the classroom or through referral for more comprehensive evaluation and treatment.

BIBLIOGRAPHY

1. Ansbacher, Heinz L., and Ansbacher, Rowena R. *The Individual Psychology of Alfred Adler*. New York: Harper Colophon, 1964.
2. Axline, Virginia. *Play Therapy*. New York: Ballantine Books, 1969.
3. Dreikurs, Rudolf. *Children: The Challenge*. New York: Hawthorne Books, Inc., 1964.
4. Dweck, Carol S. Learned helplessness: A developmental approach, *In: Depression in Childhood: Diagnosis, Treatment, and Conceptual Models,* Joy G. Schulterbrandt and Allen Raskin (eds.). New York: Raven Press, 1977.
5. Gardner, Richard A. *Psychotherapy with Children of Divorce*. New York: Jason Aronson, Inc., 1976.
6. ________________. *Therapeutic Communication with Children, The Mutual Storytelling Technique*. New York: Jason Aronson, Inc., 1971.
7. Ginott, Haim. *Group Psychotherapy with Children*. New York: McGraw-Hill Book Company, 1961.
8. ________________. *Teacher and Child*. New York: Avon Books, 1972.

9. Glasser, William. *Schools Without Failure.* New York: Harper & Row, Publishers, 1969.
10. Gregory, Dick. Nigger: An autobiography, *In: Childhood Revisited.* (Joel I. Milgram and Dorothy June Sciarra, eds.). New York: Macmillan Publishing Co., Inc., 1974.
11. Josselyn, Irene. *The Happy Child.* New York: Random House, 1955.
12. Looff, David H. *Getting to Know the Troubled Child.* Knoxville: University of Tennessee Press, 1976.
13. Malmquist, Carl P. Childhood depression: A clinical and behavioral perspective, *In: Depression in Childhood: Diagnosis, Treatment, and Conceptual Models* (Joy G. Schulterbrandt and Allen Raskin, (eds.). New York: Raven Press, 1977.
14. May, Rollo. *The Meaning of Anxiety.* New York: W. W. Norton & Company, Inc., 1977.
15. Moustakas, Clark. *Psychotherapy with Children, The Living Relationship.* New York: Ballantine Books, 1959.
16. Murphy, Lois, and Moriarty, Alice. *Vulnerability, Coping, and Growth.* New Haven: Yale University Press, 1976.
17. Walton, Francis X., and Powers, Robert L. *Winning Children Over, A Manual for Teachers, Counselors, Principals and Parents.* Chicago: Practical Psychology Associates, 1974.
18. Warren, Ruth. *Caring, Supporting Children's Growth.* Washington, D. C., National Association for the Education of Young Children, 1977.
19. Wolff, Sula. *Children Under Stress.* London: Allen Lane The Penquin Press, 1969.
20. Wolman, Benjamin. *Children's Fears.* New York: Grosset and Dunlap, 1978.
21. Woods (McNamee), Abigail S., and Delisle, Robert G. *Children and Death—Helping Them Cope.* (audio tape). Fairlawn, New Jersey: JAB Press, 1977.
22. ________________. *Helping Children Cope With Death.* ERIC Document, ED 173 787, (1979).

Adolescence is a period recognized as normally associated with emotional problems revolving around a search for identity. Dr. Rudd examines the evidence of numerous case records at an adolescent clinic for children and youth and provides answers from this experience to several pertinent questions: why there is early sexual activity; why there is adolescent pregnancy despite the availability of birth control information and programs; what adolescents think of abortion. Furthermore, she divides adolescence into three major developmental periods, each with its characteristic behavior pattern reflecting a resolution of conflict particular to that period. As a result of this survey, she makes suggestions for management of the sexually active teenager.

10
Pregnancies and Abortions

Lucie Rudd, M.D.

Pregnancy in the adolescent girl represents a major crisis in her life. Whatever the outcome of the pregnancy may be, the stark reality of the event is remembered and consciously or not, will affect the rest of the girl's life.[28]

The developmental process of adolescence can be severely disturbed by pregnancy. The girl has to face it:

- At a time when her physical appearance changes almost overnight, when her nutrition has often become inappropriate, her maturation level is still uneven, and when her body has to contend with her own growth while coping with the growth of the fetus and the anatomical changes brought upon by pregnancy.
- At a time of easy delusion, fantasy building, and day-dreaming, she is asked to make decisions and to plan constructively when she is conceptually unable to plan ahead.
- At a time when sexual identification needs to be established, she deprives herself of all possible parameters except for the ability to become pregnant.
- At a time when she needs help and support, she is often estranged from her family and has only fragmentary sources of help offered to her.

As we enter the nineteen eighties, we are facing an unabated "epidemic" of younger and younger adolescent pregnancies.[33]

MAGNITUDE OF THE PROBLEM

In 1970, there were fifty-eight births per thousand girls aged fifteen to nineteen years in the U.S. This number was higher than in eighteen other countries and lower than in only three other countries.[2]

In 1974, more than a million girls aged 15–19, one-tenth of all women in this age group, became pregnant. Fourteen percent miscarried spontaneously, 27% chose abortion, 59% gave birth. Among the 30,000 pregnancies which occurred that same year among girls below the age of thirteen, 45% were terminated by induced abortion and 36% produced live births. Altogether more than 600,000 teen-agers gave birth that year.

In 1977, the natality statistics from the National Center for Health Statistics mentioned 559,154 births to young women under the age of nineteen.

More recent national statistics are not available as of this writing; nevertheless, most clinics engaged in adolescent health care appear to show an increase in the number of pregnant young adolescents.[28]

It is only recently that natality statistics have used the grouping fifteen to nineteen years of age and below fifteen. It had become quite clear that the younger girl had much less access to early good prenatal care, and more chances to develop toxemia and to deliver prematurely. The morbidity and mortality of their offspring is considerably higher. These statistics become much more meaningful when the grouping of 15–25 years of age, used in the past, was divided into under fifteen, fifteen to nineteen years of age, and nineteen to twenty-five years of age. Even this does not correspond completely to reality. Among the two younger groups, one can distinguish three groups whose maturation level does not always correspond to their chronological ages.

The young adolescent may have seen the occurrence of her first menstrual period, the menarche, anywhere between her ninth and her fifteenth birthday. The present average occurrence of menarche is at age eleven. For the next two or three years, she develops new feelings and new interests. She may remain tomboyish or she may develop more feminine characteristics. She is only beginning the three big tasks of adolescence: the separation from her family (which is so much easier when she is able to criticize her family), and the gathering of her personality, and defining vocational or educational goals. Although the goals remain childish, her thinking is still concrete and down to earth. Nevertheless passions, jealousy, and possessiveness do bring occasional bouts of violence in junior high school age level adolescents.

The middle adolescent, in the following years of junior high school and the beginning high-school years, is exploring and experimenting with her new, deeper heterosexual relationships. She is able to fantasize relentlessly, including fairy tale endings. She separates more and more from her family, usually through deteriorating communication with her mother or through open rebellion. She "knows better than anybody" and remains extremely self-centered. She is still unable to process information in a social context and to make meaningful decisions. For her, acceptance by her peer group is more important than any other consideration and her behavior conforms to her peer group's standards.

The older adolescent, whether in the last years of high school, in college or at work, has not always succeeded in completing these three big tasks of adolescence: the separation from the family or more exactly, taking one's place as an adult in that family, the sexual identification as an adult in one's own right, and the establishment of goals, vocational or educational for the future. For these results, the adolescent needs the help of a supportive, problem solving[18] family and the help of peers in touch with their own feelings.

At all these three maturational levels, girls might start sexual activity. Sexual experimentation might start in an effort to self-define one's self, or to conform to the peer group, or as an act of rebellion. Whatever the reason may be, this experimentation, which even ten years ago started at sixteen or seventeen, is now starting much earlier, sometimes even before menarche.

WHY EARLY SEXUAL ACTIVITY?

Multiple reasons are given, whether anthropological or sociological, economic or emotional, psychological or cultural. Most of them do not mention the fact that each individual's *sexuality* begins in utero,[6] and that parents, physicians and educators refuse to face its importance until a girl "gets in trouble." The religions or cultures which recognize the sexual drives of their adolescents by arranging early marriages still have to face the consequences of pregnancies in the early adolescent: miscarriages, premature births, and small babies for gestational age.

In our present-day mores, many parents do not recognize the big child and adolescent need for cuddling, for physical touching, for expressions, both verbal and physical, of parental love. The idea of self, which is the composite of many inputs—at home, in nursery school, at play, in school, in the doctor's office—is quite often one of inadequacy, of guilt, of self-belittling, of accepting the mother's unflattering judgment. One superb pediatrician, Dr. Edward N. Joyner, III* would always tell each of his patients that he liked them. But most of the adolescents who will get in trouble have poor self-images to start, and very often no nurturing to help them change. The need to be petted and admired, in a society of peers who are

* Chairman, Department of Pediatrics, The Roosevelt Hospital, 1956–71.

vying with each other to attract and to retain the available male, will push some young adolescents into early sexual activity. The need for acceptance by peers is extremely strong in the young adolescent. When sexual activity also satisfies "the longing for intimacy,"[9] even if not always orgasmic, and answers the adolescent need for experimentation, it is doubly attractive.

Pressure occurs not only from the peer group but also from mass media. The media extoll the beautiful complexion as well as the beautiful body. They will both presumably insure (sexual) happiness without bothering with feelings, compatibility, cultural traits, or ability to plan and to survive. The cover of *Seventeen* is not very different from *Playboy's* cover image. Television advertising carries also the hidden message, "use my products to be better and hold your man." Sex is used to sell anything from toothpaste to cars.

Parental attitudes will add to pressure: very often parents do not feel at ease discussing with their children the all important topics of reproduction, birth control, and sexual responsibility. But they will refuse the schools the right to educate, if they could, in the erroneous belief that "if you don't talk about it," it will not exist. As SEICUS, the Sex Information and Education Council of the U.S., states in one of its pamphlets, "By 15, all kids have had sex education in school . . . in hallways, locker rooms and washrooms."[32]

Pressures come from the boys: "if you love me," "I don't like teasing little girls," "You want to be frigid all your life?," "You can't get pregnant the first time," "I don't have any good sperm, I am sterile, honest!" One young man from Ohio stated that 95% of his friends were out to conquer as many girls as they could, for the sake of the hunt.[24]

Pressures are not relieved in schools. Sex education at its best, with its early teaching of comparative reproduction, its early discussions of feelings, its peer discussions of responsibility taking, and of rights of unborn children, is carried out only in a very few schools. Physical activities, team sports, after-school activities are pitifully missing in the urban schools where they could play such a great role. Teaching of honest behavior and of moral values,[31] one of the pillers of American education in the nineteenth century, is missing, even or perhaps especially in contact sports training. Boredom, lack of directed youth activities, lack of education, lack of supervision, idleness and passivity, all will contribute to sexual experimentation.

Finally and essentially, the family of the girl does play a great role. Chaotic families where the only way to obtain attention is to act in a negative fashion produce quite often boys who engage in drug abuse and antisocial activities and girls who experiment very early in sexual activity.

Our experience in Veritas, a drug-free therapeutic community for adolescents, has shown this to be the case in several instances. Intact families who are going through difficult adjustment periods will often see their children deteriorate and seek outside "love," reflecting in their behavior and the familial unbalance.

WHY PREGNANCY?

HEW deemed in 1975 that adolescent pregnancies were all due to "acting out," a professional term for deviant if not pathological behavior.[1] This is an oversimplification. A most interesting study from the Rochester Adolescent Maternity Project (RAMP) reviewed 100 consecutive cases which had entered the project in 1975.[23] RAMP is a comprehensive, multidisciplinary program in Rochester, New York which offers medical and psychosocial services to pregnant adolescents, their families, and their boyfriends. Out of these 100 pregnancies, 4 could be attributed to contraceptive failures; one motivation could not be determined; only 50 of the remaining 95 pregnancies could be attributed to acting out. Twenty-two were due to true anger (usually directed toward parents or other authority figures), 12 to attention-seeking mechanisms (especially if there was a sibling or a mother becoming the center of attention because she was pregnant); ten were indulging in immature, fantasizing behavior ("it can't happen to me"), and a few (six) were trying to pressure the putative father into marrying them. Thus, acting out is not the only reason for an early pregnancy.

Our own experience is taken from the adolescent clinic of a large, comprehensive medical program (C & Y) for children and youth on the West Side of Manhattan. The population we serve is partly Hispanic (Puerto Rican dominating in numbers, Dominican and Columbian in less numbers, a few Indians from Guyana and the West Indies), partly black North American, and Caucasian. The adolescent clinic which was one of the five teams of the C & Y was disbanded five years ago because of economic reasons and the adolescents were apportioned to the other four teams which have different geographical boundaries, and thus serve patients from birth to their twenty-first birthday. In the old adolescent clinic as well as in the present afternoon clinics, we did find acting out (seeking negative attention) as well as anger, but we have mostly seen depression and loneliness, poor self-image, and lack of good role models.

When the young girl has been lacking a feeling of being loved and cared for,[17] and especially if she has been placed in foster homes or institutions, she will often develop the fantasy that a baby of her own will give her the love she has missed and will help her to live happily ever after. Little does she realize the amount of time and care that her baby will require. We also know only too well that a youngster with poor parenting of her own will be a poor parent unless a considerable amount of teaching involving programs, money, personnel and acceptable sites, is spent on her and her offspring.

We try to obtain a good social history from our adolescents regarding the relationships in their family. Is there a father?, If the family is intact, is the father or the mother violent or alcoholic?, Was the patient beaten up or abused? An intact family may be chaotic and communication may have become impossible.

We have learned to ask the pregnant girl if she has had a recent abortion, whether abortion was imposed by her mother or whether the girl was too aggressively counseled; we also ask if an important person to her may have died or disappeared from her life: mourning is an important reason for a pregnancy.

We ask the mother's age. If that mother has given birth to her first child while still in her early teens, she probably will have left school early and produced more children; the more children, the earlier she had started reproducing. That mother had probably remained out of the labor market and perhaps had to be supported by Welfare and Aid to Dependent Children. Her daughter will want to emulate her, equating pregnancy with an affirmation of her biological female role. Once pregnant, she usually does not return to school. She is not prepared or trained for any special job. Her job opportunities are scarce and menial. There is no incentive to further achievements. But she can stay home and take care of her child and become pregnant again as a new career, supported by her culture, her family and the community at large.

Sometimes there may be subtle family pressure on the girl of a welfare family to become pregnant. She would then obtain her own welfare and not be lost to the family's budget. Becoming pregnant, affirming one's own sexual role, supposedly achieving independence from her family by obtaining a welfare check, thus represents an improvement of importance in status. As a younger sister said once in our clinic, "I want to become important to everybody, just like my sister."

On the other side of the economic scale, we have seen the carefully overchaperoned girl who, in rebellious adolescent stages, will become pregnant because of defiance of her family: she wants to prove to her parents that she is not too young or too inexperienced. This, in therapeutic community jargon, is called "to cut off one's nose to spite your mom."

The victims of sexual abuse will become pregnant. We have seen the mother of the abused girl dispensing her own birth control pills to her daughter, not to embarrass the incestuous father or stepfather. We also have seen the eight months pregnant thirteen-year-old girl who had never dared to complain to her mother about her father. Actually, mothers usually disbelieve the child at first. The mother finally noticed her enlarging girth and brought her to the clinic, too late for prenatal care or abortion or education.

Even though these pregnancies are not always planned, some of them seem to respond to deep unconscious needs. It is almost impossible to prevent them. When social work and psychological supports are given to the pregnant girl, both before and after delivery, it is not unusual to see significant maturation occur as well as unsuspected strengths appear.[5]

But the question remains:

WHY NO BIRTH CONTROL?

There was a time when our clinic thought, with the same naiveté as our governing bodies, that offering birth control to adolescents would prevent pregnancies, and the presence of heavy eye make-up of recent appearance, would alert every fellow, nurse, or physician's assistant in our clinic to the need for referral to adolescent family planning. There was a time when a young man in Tanner stage III–IV* would be offered condoms and a referral to the same family planning clinic. Unfortunately we have recently had more first pregnancies. We do not know if it is part of the present-day phenomenal pregnancy "epidemic" or whether it is also related to a change in health personnel and the loss of a team which previously had charge of all the adolescents.

In some cases, pediatricians early in their training could not feel comfortable in inquiring about their patients' sexuality. Sex education classes in medical schools are not always sufficient to sensitize the medical student and to allow him to be concerned and nonjudgmental. It takes a much longer time to consider one's own values and to be able to reject passed-on values and to be guided by those notions acquired by experience, team discussions, and education. It is important that the physician or the nurse be aware of personal feelings, as these feelings, even if they are not verbalized, are unerringly picked up by the adolescent.

The needs of the adolescents led us to start a family planning clinic as part of the C and Y (Children and Youth Comprehensive Medical Project). The clinic does not require parental consent and is free of charge. It is not limited by any catchment area. No adult women are seeking birth control in the same clinic. There is, at first, a one-to-one review of anatomy and

* Maturational stage when male cells are present.

physiology of the reproductive organs and an explanation of the various birth control methods by the family planning counselor of the Department of Obstetrics and Gynecology. The examination and prescription are done another day by a warm concerned woman gynecologist. The waiting period in this clinic is utilized for a discussion of sexual feelings. This group was first conducted by the social worker of the adolescent clinic, and at present, by a social service student in supervision with the same worker. We took special care to make the family planning clinic hospitable. The welcoming clerk was pleasant, the personnel nonauthoritative and nonjudgmental, and we even were able to have cookies and juice in the waiting room. However, the clinic has not stemmed first pregnancies.

Is it due to the adolescent's sense of omnipotence? Those kids will say, "it can't happen to me," and when it happens, they are able to deny it for a long time.

Is it due to the usual lack of involvement of the young male? Whenever we have offered co-ed discussion groups to fourteen or fifteen-year-olds males, it has been accepted with alacrity. Physicians, nurses, and assistants are not all able to pick up those patients who are the most in need of counseling. Some youngsters have to be reassured in their feeling that they are not ready for sex. Others have to be reminded of their responsibilities. Quite often the necessary questions are either not asked or asked in such a way that the patient will lie.

Is it due to all the myths spread by the "misinformation" given by peers? "I can't get pregnant the first time"; Birth control pills are dangerous"; "All you need is a vinegar douche"; "Rubbers prevent orgasm"; "You can't get pregnant in the middle of the month"; and even from a twelve-year-old with a pelvic inflammatory disease due to gonorrhea: "You can't get pregnant once you have your 'menestration'(!)"

Is it due to lack of promotion? It is likely many adolescents will say that they do not know where to go. Their own physicians are not always aware of the need for confidentiality (even though in California it is a misdemeanor for a physician to tell parents what their children told him) and adolescents are afraid that their seeking birth control (and discharging their sexual responsibilities) will be reported in a negative way to their parents. As much of the early sexual experimentation occurs in families where communication is missing, it behooves the physician or the social worker or psychologist to help the patient to discuss his anger at the parent and to re-establish communication through the youngster, not behind his or her back. Mass media can help. Short public interest messages can be televised. The Planned Parenthood chapter in Columbus, Ohio had two such messages created by an advertising agency. Both messages were followed by the Planned Parenthood telephone number [24]

Is it a lack of communication between parents? We have seen that among some adolescents the sexual act does not necessarily involve friendship, feelings, or communication. However, in other cases, the inexperienced girl may think her partner takes precautions while the irresponsible male decides it is up to the girl to protect herself. Many youngsters are too shy to talk to their partners: physical contact appears easier to achieve than serious talk.

Is it the misconception that if one seeks contraception, it implies planning ahead and the "planning spoils it?" It seems evident that all these reasons have been encountered and that some of the most apparent reasons for not utilizing birth control when it is available may be:

1. Common family planning services for adults and teen-agers. This can be circumvented by the young person attending a center away from her neighborhood.[8]
2. Attitudes of nonhealth related personnel, quite often hypercritical of the responsible desire to obtain birth control (in hospitals as well as private offices).
3. Lack of communication and distance between the adolescent health center and the family planning services. This implies lack of follow-up.[8]
4. Attitudes of doctors, usually with teen-agers of their own.[28]

Other reasons based on studies of pregnant teen-agers were given by the patients:[37]

- 43% did not expect to have intercourse (this is the famous unplanned sex which makes it more acceptable to certain girls).
- 10.1% wanted to use something but could not under the circumstances (?)
- 9.3% of partners objected.
- 12.5% believed it was wrong, unnatural, or dangerous to use contraceptives.
- 3.5% only did not know about it or did not know where to get it.
- 7.1% stated sex was not much fun with contraception or that it was too difficult to use.

The so-called difficulties in using contraception are more related to the lack of knowledge of one's own body, the frequent childhood taboos against touching one's genitalia, as well as intolerance of frustrating efforts.

A fairly large amount, 43%,[11] were risk-takers and decided to "take a chance" without contraception. But a certain percentage, 6%, had received correct information about contraception that they chose to discard. This would represent "knowledge without belief." Those who believed various myths about their inability to conceive and could not accept professional information represented "belief without knowledge."[10]

Various authors have shown that the younger the girl is, the less she is apt to use available birth control, and the more chances she has to become pregnant. A study of young adolescents in maternity shelter foster families has shown that these youngsters were passive and had very little ego structure. They had chosen to keep their pregnancy, still fantasizing their future lives with the baby. This study[17] was comparing them with older adolescents who had chosen to request an abortion. These girls who had chosen an abortion to terminate their pregnancy, were more advanced in their emotional and intellectual development: they had formulated goals, either educational or vocational. The pregnancy, unplanned as it was, did not seem to respond to subconscious needs of the girl, and the usually older adolescent decided for abortion.

ABORTION

Abortion, or the intervention to terminate an unwanted pregnancy, must have existed since time immemorial. Pushing a metal object inside the pregnant uterus has been practiced with good intentional results and extremely morbid consequences for the young woman by midwives or old women, or what was called in Paris "les faiseuses d'anges" (the makers of angels). A method of external massage of the uterus was recently described in American literature as the favorite and effective method to produce a miscarriage in Southeast Asia.[16]

Actually the U.S. laws passed in the nineteenth century prohibiting abortion were written to *protect* the health of women and to prevent infection and sometimes death. Nowadays, whatever different methods are chosen for abortion, depending on the number of weeks of pregnancy, they have proven themselves to be easily done and safe. When the New York Department of Health statistics show for the first time *no* mortality following abortions, it appears nonsensical to oppose the U.S. Supreme Court decision that abortion has been judged to be a matter of decision between the pregnant girl and her physician.

It has always been possible in the past for women of means to obtain an abortion whether illegally in the U.S., or by traveling to a country where abortions were easily obtained. The legalization of abortion and its reimbursement by Medicaid has prevented hundreds of young mothers from having to go on welfare; it has prevented thousands of children from being abused or neglected, many babies to be born small for gestational age, or to present developmental abnormalities. The present intimidation campaign against abortion is even trying to get itself legalized by attaching addenda to CHAP legislative measures! Abortion should remain, not a birth control measure but an available option, especially for the teen-ager.

Teen-agers who become pregnant, quite often come from noncommunicating families with little contact with a meaningful health facility. Using varying denial mechanisms: "it can't happen to me"; "we did it only one time"; "I've been skipping two months before, I am never regular," etc., they will not seek counsel and medical evaluation before the fourth month of their pregnancy. Quite often, it there is no adult they can trust and feel comfortable with, they might not reach prenatal services before the fifth or sixth month. An abortion, if desired, at that time is actually the forced delivery of an occasional viable fetus. This experience has occasionally produced severe cripling emotional disorder.[28]

If seen earlier in their proven pregnancy, it behooves the health professional to present alternatives to the pregnant girl, enlisting whenever possible the presence of the punative father. The options have to be very carefully exposed to the girl. It is useless and even harmful to push one's attitudes, moral, ethical or medical onto the girl.

If abortion is not the wish of the pregnant girl, if the mother finds her daughter too young to bring a baby to term, if the unwise physician tries to sell educational goals to a girl too young for conceptualization or anticipatory thinking,[9] this abortion will be followed by another pregnancy within a few months.[28] whether birth control advice is given or not. If the pregnancy fulfills some conscious or unconscious need, the girl will keep the pregnancy and as the government has provided maternal and infant care programs (MIC), she should be referred or accompanied to these services. A great amount of time and effort has to be spent to help the girl reestablish communication with her family, or sometimes with the family of the putative father, as she is and will be in need of support. If the girl has no cultural, ethical, religious, or mass media induced scruples about abortion, if she is able to plan ahead for her life and chooses an abortion, she should be helped to obtain it within the financial limits that she can afford. In any case, the decision is the girl's and should be respected. Emotionally speaking, if the girl is coerced by her mother or overcounseled toward an abortion, it has been our experience[28] that the girl will get pregnant again, whatever method of birth control is used after the abortion. Legally speaking, the pregnancy emancipates the "legal infant" (the girl) and abortion does not require any permission besides the pregnant girl's.

MANAGEMENT

It is important to remember that any adolescent that we call "at risk" is liable to find herself pregnant. We call them "at risk" because their social history shows either a very large or a chaotic family, and a school performance either below par or deteriorating. The lack of satisfactory, successful experiences with either lack of set limits or harsh limits completely out of line with whatever is usual in her school or neighborhood is a danger sign.

The date of the last menstrual period should always be ascertained: this cannot always be accurately determined.** There should be an easy access to a reliable pregnancy test, immunoassay in the first eight weeks, or urine tests after eight weeks. The result of this test should never by given by telephone. Giving the results of the test should not be an impersonal adult-child information, but the concerned interest of a health-care person, trying to establish a trusting relationship with an adolescent in crisis. Several interviews might be necessary to clear up the cobwebs.

If the pregnancy test is negative, it is important to help the youngster determine whether the lack of conception is making her unhappy or happy. Birth control has to be explored, explained and discussed (if possible in the presence of the boyfriend). The rights of an unborn child, to love, shelter and food, have to be mentioned. This crisis has to be utilized to prevent pregnancy.

If the girl is pregnant, one has to probe delicately into her feelings. Does she want to keep this pregnancy, even though it probably will stop her schooling and the possibility of graduating from high school? What are her feelings about abortion, about delivery? What does she know about her body and its needs during pregnancy? It usually takes several interviews before the adolescent can make up her mind, and she might often vacillate from one type of decision to another.

As stated previously, there should be no coercion exerted by the worker, whatever his or her feelings might be. One should get to know the local resources either for adolescent pregnancy care (MIC) or for medically safe abortions. It is mandatory for the girl to be escorted.

If the girl decides to keep her pregnancy, some care should be exercised to either help the girl re-establish good relationships with her family, whose support she will need; we have seen several times the family of the boyfriend shelter the girl made pregnant by their son. The shelters for pregnant girls or foster families for them are few.

If she decides for an abortion, she does not need her parents' permission. Under the age of sixteen, one can still have trouble finding such a facility, even though pregnancy emancipates the girl.

The ideal solution to the problem would evidently be to prevent the pregnancy. The best federal programs of maternal and infant care, the nutritional programs of WICK, can only help to take care of the pregnancy after it has occurred.

** Periods may be irregular, or the girl does not keep track of exact dates.

We have tried to show that early sexual activity has many reasons to exist in our present-day society. Multiple different approaches may be needed if we want to reverse the trend for earlier and earlier coupling.

Parents do not want anybody to teach their kids reproduction. They appear scared of sharing their responsibilities with some agency outside of the family. It brings out hostility. In the meantime, they do not appear to be able to discuss comfortably with their children love, reproduction or sexual drives. Perhaps, as Dr. Mary Calderone plans to do, we should teach the parents.[7]

PTA's, well aware of adolescent pregnancy problems, might be able to make acceptable to school boards the notion of a curriculum on reproduction from kindergarten through the twelfth grade. Information has never, in spite of some parent's fears, made the kinds act out. Peer groups, whether under the aegis of churches, youth programs, boy scouts or girls' organizations, are needed with good, low-key, counseling adult help. The main question still remains: we don't know the answer to "why pregnancy?" One wonders whether neo-natology is going to replace Family Planning and whether the generation to come will include a large percentage of children born prematurely or small for gestational age. Early detection of possible developmental delays in these high-risk babies might help prevent learning disabilities.

Sesame Street is teaching kids letters and numbers, sounds and new words. Mister Rodgers has some excellent programs to prevent natural anxieties of small fry. Which programs will have the courage to compete with violence, human folly, and slapstick comedy, and bring to the screen valid, honest information for the lost adolescent of today?

Perhaps we should be able to better utilize our knowledge of developmental maturation of the adolescent. Perhaps we should involve both sexes in our counseling and stop pushing all the responsibility on the girl's shoulders. Perhaps we can sensitize educators, pediatricians, and legislators to the adolescent predicaments. Perhaps we can educate our prospective parents to the bottomless nurturing needs of the small child.[13] A sense of belonging and approval in early childhood might prevent low self-esteem in early adolescent years.

BIBLIOGRAPHY

1. The Alan Guttmacher Institute. Annual Report, 1976.
2. *Eleven Million Teen-Agers*. Publication of the Alan Guttmacher Institute.
3. Boyce, John, M.D., and Benoit, Cheryl, B.A. Adolescent pregnancy. *New York State J. of Med.* pp. 872–874, May 1975.
4. Brownstein, Gerri, C. S. W. Waiting Room Groups in Adolescent Family Planning Clinic, The Roosevelt Hospital, Unpublished data.

5. Brownstein, Gerri, C. S. W.: Adolescent Mothers' Groups, The Roosevelt Hospital, unpublished data.
6. Calderone, Mary S., M.D., M.P.H. Pre-adolescent sexuality, presented at the Second International Symposium in Adolescent Medicine, Washington, D.C., May 1979, *Jl. of Current Adol. Med.* **1**:5, October 1979.
7. Calderone, Mary S., M.D. Perspectives on today's teen-ager for the physician. *Transitions* **2**:5, October 15, 1979.
8. Cobliner, W. G., Ph.D. Preferred preventive health care facilities in a survey among urban adolescents. *Bull. of the Ac. of Med.* **49**:10, 922–930, October 1973.
9. Cobliner, W. G.: Pregnancy in the single adolescent girl: The role of cognitive functions. *J. Youth and Adolescence* **3**:17, 1974.
10. Cobliner, W. Godfrey, Schulman, Harold, and Smith, Vivian. Patterns of contraceptive failures: The role of motivation re-examined. *Jl. Biosoc. Sci.* **7**:307–318, 1975.
11. Cobliner, et al. Dynamics of contraceptive failures. *Jl. of Psychology* **94**:153–162, 1976.
12. Crovitz, Elaine, Ph.D., and Hayes, Lynn, M.D. A comparison of pregnant adolescents and non-pregnant sexually active peers. *JAMWA* **34**:4, April 1979.
13. Frank, Lawrence: *The Fundamental Needs of the Child.* Pamphlet, The National Committee for Mental Hygiene, Inc., New York, 1968.
14. Freeman, Ellen W., Ph.D., and Rickels, Karl, M.D. Adolescent contraceptive use: Current status of practice and research. *Obst. and Gyn.* **53**:3, March 1979.
15. Green, Cynthia P., and Potteiger, Kate. *Teen-age Pregnancy: A Major Problem for Minors.* Zero Population Growth. Washington, D.C. August 1977.
16. International report from Thailand. *Medical Tribune,* Wednesday, January 9, 1980.
17. Johnson, Thomas: The psychological aspects of out of wedlock pregnancy.
    Werner, Mrs. Georgianna: Understanding the developmental needs of the early childhood level and its effect on later maturity. Presented at the Seminar on Adolescence, Inwood House, 1971.
18. Lewis, Jerry M., M.D. Evaluation of family competence by an M.D. Presented at the Fall meeting of the Society for Adolescent Medicine in Dallas, Texas, November, 1977.
19. Malinovich, Miriam Miedzian: How not to deal with teen-age sexuality. Planned Parenthood Federation of America, 1979.
20. McLean, Roderick A., M.D., Mattison, Ernest T., Cochrene, Nancy E., and Fall, Karen L. Maternal mortality study. *New York State Jl. of Med.,* pp. 226–230, February, 1979.
21. Moran, Alfred F., Executive Vice-President, Planned Parenthood of New York City, Inc. Memo re teen-agers and sexrelated health care. April, 1975.
22. Murray, Linda. First high school birth control clinic. *Hospital Tribune,* April, 1978.
23. Panzarine, Susan, R.N., M.S., Kubis, Joainne, B.S., Elster, Arthur, M.D., and McAnarney, Elizabeth R., M.D. Motivated adolescent pregnancies. *Jl. of Current Adolescent Medicine.* **1**:2, July, 1979.
24. Planned Parenthood, Columbus, Ohio Chapter: T. V. advertisements, as mentioned in Phil Donahue TV program.
25. Planned Parenthood of New York City, Inc. Symposium on teen-agers and sex. Salk, Lee, Ph.D., Liebert, Robert, Ph.D., and Morgenthau, Joan, M.D.
26. Robbins, D. R., M.D., and Harrison, S. I., M.D. Sexual concerns of adolescents. *Med. Aspects of Human Sexuality,* (Quiz), November, 1979.
27. Romm, May E., M.D., M.S. The pregnant adolescent. Presented to the Symposium of the Society for Adolescent Medicine on Teen-age Pregnancy. Los Angeles, May 10–11, 1973.
28. Rudd, Lucie, M.D. Unpublished studies of the Adolescent Clinic of the C & Y Project at The Roosevelt Hospital.
29. Morgenthau, Joan E., M.D., and Rao, P. S. S., M.D., Ph.D., F.S.S. Contraceptive prac-

tices in an adolescent health center. *New York State Jl. of Med.* pp. 1311–1315 August, 1976.

30. Scales, Peter, Ph.D. in collaboration with Sol Gordon, Ph.D. Preparing today's youth for tomorrow's family. Recommendations of the Wingspread Conference on early adolescent sexuality and health care. June 3–5, 1979. *Jl. of the Institute for Family Research and Education,* October, 1979.
31. Seeley, David S.: Virtue at Andover. *The Andover Review,* Fall, 1979.
32. SEICUS: Appeal for contributions to Sex Information and Education Council of the U.S. "By 15, all kids had sex education in school . . . in hallways, locker rooms and washrooms."
33. The Figures on Our Teenagers is Alarming. State of New York, Office of Health Promotion. (Pamphlet). Albany, N.Y. September 1979.
34. Task Force Report on the Pregnant Adolescent. The pregnant adolescent: A very special problem *News and Comment.* American Academy of Pediatrics. **27**:9, September, 1976.
35. Trussell, James, and Meukeu, Jane. Early childbearing and subsequent fertility. *Family Planning Perspectives.* **10**:4, July-August, 1978.
36. Zelnik, Melvin: Sex education and knowledge of pregnancy risk among U.S. teen-age women. *Family Planning Perspectives.* **11**:6, November-December, 1979.
37. Zelnik, Melvin, Kantner, John F.: Reasons for non-use of contraceptives by sexually active women aged 15 to 19. *Family Planning Perspectives.* **II**:5, September-October 1979.
38. Zelnik, Melvin, Young, J. Kim, and Kantner, John F. Probabilities of intercourse and conception among U.S. teenage women, 1971 and 1976. *Family Planning Perspectives.* **II**:3, May-June 1979.
39. Zelnik, Melvin, and Kantner, John F. Contraceptive patterns and pre-marital pregnancy among women aged 15–19 in 1976. *Family Planning Perspectives.* **10**:3, May–June 1978.

The authors point out that in children over the age of five years ingestion of a toxic substance is rarely accidental. They estimate that poison control centers see more than 250,000 intentional self-poisoning cases in children and adolescents each year. But these patients are not attempting suicide; they are using self-poisoning to change an oppressive life situation by playing what the authors call "pharmocologic brinkmanship." It is emphasized that the child's concept of death changes with age and this must be recognized in understanding poisoning as a suicidal gesture. The authors also investigated cases of self-poisoning by administration of a "psychological biopsy" which evaluates nine areas of each subject's life. Case illustrations demonstrate the utility of this instrument and also increase our understanding of the reaction of the adolescent to excessively high parental control, or negative expectations, or overt indifference and rejection. The problem of predicting recidivism is also dealt with because of the increasing lethality of intent which is often found in cases of self-poisoning.

11 The Taxonomy of Suicide and Self-Poisoning—A Pediatric Perspective

Matilda S. McIntire, M.D.
Carol R. Angle, M.D.

INTRODUCTION

Over the past decade we have been concerned with the major problem of childhood accidents, and particularly, accidental poisoning in children. During an early study on the neurological sequelae of accidental poisoning in children,[1] our analysis of 1033 children hospitalized at the Nebraska Poison Control Center at Children's Memorial Hospital from 1948–65 showed that 6% of these children were six years and over. Since accidental poisoning is age related, declining abruptly at age five, the general consensus is that ingestion of a toxic substance by an older child is rarely accidental. Some of these ingestions resulted from improper labeling or prescription errors, some are therapeutic such as cumulative overdoses of dilantin and digitalis, some result from mass exposures such as leakage of chlorine gas at a swimming pool, but most are intentioned self-poisonings. Thus began our inquiry into suicide, suicide attempts and self-poisoning in children—one aspect of the continuum of self-destructive behavior in children and youth.

The socially acceptable diagnosis of accidental poisoning channels many adolescents of suicidal behavior to poison control centers. As noted below, we estimate that poison control centers each year see over 250,000 intentional self-poisonings in children and youth. Along with crisis centers, hotlines, and school counselors, poison control centers are truly one of the "gate-keepers" of suicide prevention and it is through our work in poison control centers that we arrive at some appreciation of the magnitude of the problem.

Over the past generation, drug abuse and alcoholism have extended down to progressively younger age groups with increasing numbers of unintentioned deaths and suicides. The suicide rate for age 15–24 has quadrupled over the past twenty years. Adolescent alcoholism has become a problem of the first magnitude. This has occurred despite the proliferation of massive antidrug and rehabilitative programs in every section of the United States. The bureaucratic and paternalistic structure of these programs has failed to address the basic problems of self-esteem and economic independence and the results are analogous to the treatment of symptoms rather than the causative disease.

In this chapter we view the current scene from the perspective of the practicing physician in primary care, pediatrics, and the emergency room. The epidemiology, the definition of suicide and self-poisoning, recognition of patterns of self-destructive behavior, analysis of predictors of recidivism, family management and results of current modes of therapy are presented.

EPIDEMIOLOGY

Fatalities from suicide in children under fifteen are fortunately low, but in the age group, 15–24 years old, suicidal deaths have increased from 4 per 100,000 in 1957[2] to 13.6 per 100,000 in 1977.[3] Firearms, poisoning and hanging are the major causes of self-inflicted death in the age groups 5–14 and 15–24[4] as shown in Figure 11–1.

Poisoning accounts for only one-fourth of the fatalities under age twenty-five, but it is by far the most common mode of suicide gesture. In adolescents, the ratio of suicide gestures to fatal events is estimated at anywhere from 16:1 to 200:1. In our own collaborative international survey of 1100 self-poisonings, ages 6–18, seen at fifty poisoning control centers, we found an incidence of 220 self-poisonings for every fatality.[5] It is in this circumstance, the emergency room or a crisis service telephone call, that the health professional is most frequently confronted with self-destructive behavior.

Although mortality from self-poisoning is low, morbidity is high and the frequency of symptoms supports the intentional characteristics of poisoning after age five. Each year there are estimated to be at least one million accidental ingestions by children under five.[6] The National Clearinghouse for Poison Control Centers reports that only 8% of these events evoke symptoms and 3% require hospitalization. In contrast, there are an estimated 100,000 self-poisonings annually in the age group five to fourteen

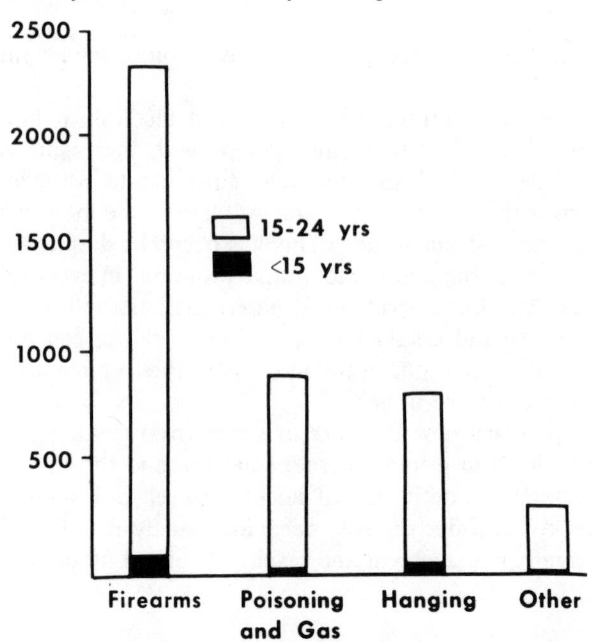

Figure 11-1. Self-inflicted deaths according to mode as cited in the U.S. Vital Statistics of 1975. There were 9 deaths from poisoning and gas, ages 5-14, and 893 in the age group 15-24 years. By 1977 the total deaths, all modes of suicide, had increased from 170 to 190 children 5-14 years old, and from 4736 deaths to 5565 deaths age 15-24 and was second only to accidents as a cause of death.

years and 150,000 in ages fifteen to twenty-four of which 46% cause symptoms and 24% require hospitalization (Figure 11-2). Using the National Clearinghouse of Poison Control Center's data base of 150,000 events in ages fifteen to twenty four, then the 700 poisoning fatalities in 1978, ages fifteen to twent-four, as reported by the National Safety Council represent an incidence of 1:214.[4] It is important to note that these data are from poison control centers which typically see a younger age group than emergency rooms which care for acutely ill, older patients. With increasing age the incidence of symptoms rises sharply and is the usual reason for medical contact.

Although any self-poisoning in a child over five years should be considered to have a major element of intent, the low incidence of fatalities, 1 per 11,000 events in ages five to fourteen years, suggest that the lethality of intent is minimal when compared with ages fifteen to twenty-four where fatalities occur in 1 per 214 events.[4,6]

It is ironically tragic that many of the adolescent suicide deaths are unintentional—the victim did not really intend to die. In our collaborative

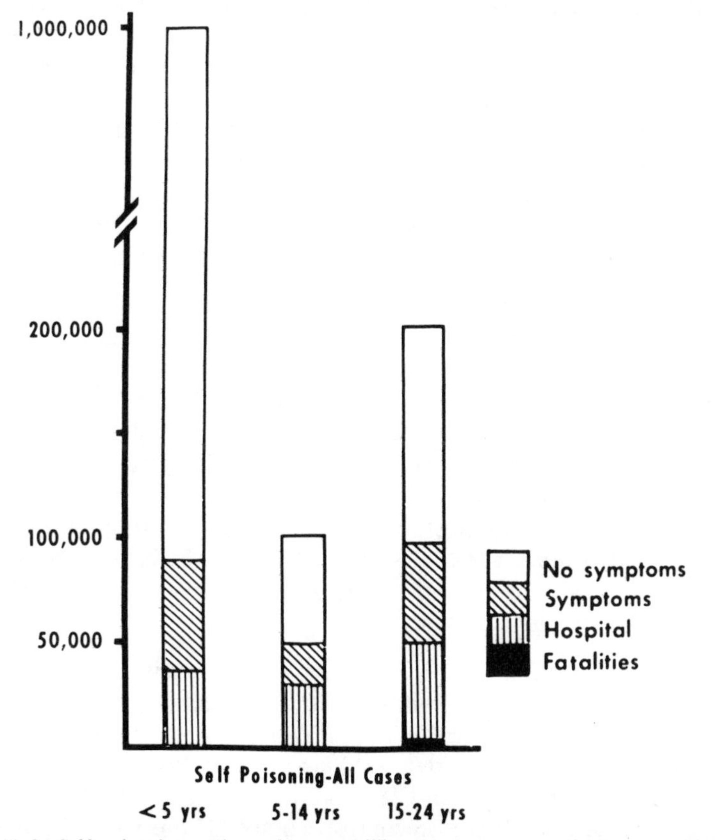

Figure 11-2. Self-poisoning, estimated at one million cases per year under 5 years with an 8% incidence of symptoms and 3% hospitalization. In poison center cases, ages 5 and over, 1976, symptoms are recorded for 46 and 24% are hospitalized and these are extrapolated to the estimated cases for this age group. The 700 poisoning fatalities ages 15–24 in 1977, applied to the estimate of 150,000 events in this age group, suggests a fatality rate of 1:214.

poison study, for example, none of the deaths could be called intended. The adolescents were not victims of poison but of pharmacologic roulette.

LETHALITY OF INTENT

The discrepancies in morbidity and mortality noted in the epidemiologic and demographic data concerning poisoning events in older children and adolescents demonstrates the need for a meaningful classification of the phenomena leading to the event similar to the taxonomy of suicide. A diagnosis of suicide attempt, as contrasted to a gesture or an affect reaction, implies both a lethality of intent and a mature concept of death as an irreversible cessation.[7,8]

Lethality is defined by Shneidman as the probability of an individual's killing himself in the immediate future.[7,8] In addition to classifying all deaths as intentioned, subintentioned, and unintentioned (as opposed to the traditional natural, accidental, suicidal, and homicidal), he has proposed the dimension of lethality to cut across the terms attempted, threatened, and completed suicide. Imputed lethality, ranging from high to absent, or scaled from 4 to 0, may be ascribed to the specific acts and life style of any individual.

High: The subject definitely wants to die and anticipates that his/her actions will result in death.

Medium: The individual is ambivalent, playing some partial, covert, or unconscious role, as in drug abuse, foolhardiness, carelessness, or outright disregard of life-saving medical care.

Low: The subject plays some small but not insignificant role, such as the adolescent "inhalers" who have no conscious wish to die and yet are willing to take unknown risks.

Absent: No lethal intent.

In response to our emphasis on taxonomy of self-poisoning, in 1969 the National Clearinghouse for Poison Control Centers instituted a classification of reported events as accidental, kicks or trips, and self-poisoning as a suicide gesture or suicidal attempt. This provides meaningful data since cases reported to the National Clearinghouse are estimated at 10% of the national total seen at all poison control centers. Of the 147,277 poisonings in 1976, of which 57,522 were over five years of age, there were a total of 40,402 cases classified as intentional self-poisoning; of these 16% were considered of suicidal intent and another 15% were classified as suicidal gestures.[6]

Adolescence is a time of great change, crisis, and pressure with a tendency for impulsive overreaction. The crisis-pressure behavior leads to manipulative and self-destructive behavior. Self-poisoning is rarely of high lethality, as demonstrated by Kessel in his Edinburgh study which concludes that at least four-fifths of self-poisonings are supported by the secure belief that death will not occur.[9] These individuals can go to the brink but not fall off. They are not attempting suicide but attempting to alter their life situation by playing the game of pharmacologic brinkmanship. Unfortunately, they do not know the toxicology of this pharmacologic game and so tragic results can ensue.

The best single correlate of imputed lethality is the probability of rescue.

The probability of rescue is high when the mode of self-destructive behavior is of relatively low toxicity, but even behavior of high lethality is consistent with low lethality of intent if the victim anticipates intervention. The majority of adolescent self-poisonings, for example, occur in circumstances in which the victim will be found soon after the ingestions:

> D., a fourteen year-old girl, is the younger of two children. The family is intact—she is a school dropout and has not been referred to a behavior clinic. She became delinquent in school attendance in the sixth grade and was a member of a gang that gathered in various homes. Her father and mother both worked and seemed to be helpless in both support and placing limits; e.g., when visiting at the hospital, father could not see what they could do. Because of the lack of parental guidance, their minister was instrumental in referring the family to welfare following which she was placed in a foster home by the courts. D. resents the direction she gets from the foster home although there seems to be a real interest in her. D. was home alone as a baby sitter for her foster siblings when she took an unknown amount of the foster mother's sleeping pills. These had been in use for some time, although D. did not realize that the dose form had recently been changed from 30 mg to 100 mg of pentobarbital per capsule. D. became drowsy and called a neighbor who took D. to the poison control center. This was considered a manipulative gesture to draw attention to her plight as an indentured servant. With the help of a counselor, D's subsequent adjustment was good. She resumed junior high school and remained in the foster home.

Another event of low lethality of intent had a tragic outcome:

> A thirteen year-old farm boy had an argument with his father and swallowed a relatively small amount of arsenic herbicide. Although the family found out about this almost immediately, they did not think the amount taken was significant and did not seek medical care until the boy was acutely ill. The boy died almost immediately after entering the hospital and the death was appropriately classified as unintentioned.

CONCEPT OF DEATH

It may be even more relevant to consider what the child and adolescent means when he considers his own death. The concept of death in childhood matures from considering death a sleeplike or reversible state, to a concept of personal continuation with cognizance of the world being left, and then reaches the concept of spiritual continuation or total cessation. Shneidman has emphasized that suicide is an inappropriate diagnosis if the individual does not view death as permanent and irreversible. It would seem that adolescents making suicide gestures would be less likely to view death as irreversible cessation. For this reason we first investigated the maturation of the concept of death, its causes, imagery, and finality of death as expressed by 598 children, ages five to eighteen years, in structured interviews held at a pediatric clinic and at three church schools—Roman Catholic, Protestant, and Conservative Jewish (Table 11-1).[10]

The "why" of death was most affected by socioeconomic status; death as due to violence was seen most often by clinic children. Somewhat surprisingly, the imagery of what happens to the body after death was rarely terrifying, but more realism concerning organic decomposition was tolerated for pets than for self. In all groups, the young child up to age five or six had an immature concept and saw death as reversible. The grade-school child had an awareness of the permanent state with a mature concept beginning to appear at age eleven. By ages thirteen to sixteen, 20% still thought that when dead they would be cognizant, 60% envisioned spiritual continuation, and 20% saw death as total cessation.

Table 11-1. Structured Interview—Concept of Death.

1-4. Age, sex, race, religion
5. Frequency of religious instruction (coded from 0 to daily).
6. Family status (coding includes intact, loss or death of mother, loss or death of father).
7. Have you ever had a pet die?
8. What happened to it (the body after burial or disposal)? (coding includes fantasy, preserved forever, organic decomposition, disintegration to ashes or dust)
9. Do you think it will ever come back to life?
10. Do you think it will ever come back in a different form?
11. Do you think it knows you miss it?
12. Why do people die?

Acquaintance with Death

13. Did you ever know anyone who died? Who?
14. What did they die of?
15. Did you ever see a dead person?
16. Did you ever go to a funeral?
17. If you die, what happens to you? (coded as Number 8)
18. Is dying like going to sleep; can you wake up again?
19. Can people who die sometimes return to life?
20. If the body is dead, does a spirit or soul live on?
21. Can the spirit or soul think just as the living person did?
22. After a person dies, does he know what people on earth are doing?
23. When a person dies, does all life and thought end?
24. Are there times when you really wish you were dead?
25. What kind of things make you feel that way?
26. Which people would care most?
27. What does life mean to you? (coded as simple pleasures, biosocial immortality, theological, transcendental)

In response to the question, "Are there times when you *really* wish you were dead?" 238 (40%) of 598 children replied "occasionally," and 18 (3%) said "frequently," and were considered to have a possible suicidal ideation. The 18 admitting a frequent death wish were all over the age of ten years, were more often Protestant (14/18), came from intact families, and received religious instruction at least once per week. Their concept of death was less naturalistic than that of the total group, with more fantasy of imagery (particularly reincarnation) and they were likely to believe in reversibility of cognizance for themselves after death.

In this group, their formulation of the significance of life was less mature than the entire group and focused on simple pleasures. This supports the concept that youthful integration of the prospect of death into the adolescent personality has profound implications for the individual's mastery of life. This sense of personal insignificance was evident in the frequency of their report that their feelings of a wish for death were most often (10/18) precipitated by family arguments or fear of punishment and most often characterized by anger or sadness.

The professed concept of death, however mature, may obviously differ from the emotional need to believe in the unique immortality of self. In a subsequent investigation of the concept of fifty adolescent suicide attempters we found no difference between the maturity of their concept of death and that held by a control group matched for age, sex, religion and socioeconomic status. The adolescent has a sense of personal immortality no matter what his stated concepts are because his own death is so remote in time; he enjoys the invincibility of youth.

TAXONOMY AS SEEN IN POISON CONTROL CENTERS

To investigate the taxonomy of self-poisoning, a one-year cooperative study was carried out at fifty poison control centers, forty six in the United States plus two in Canada and one each in Scotland and New Zealand.[5]

These poison control centers provided the demographic data on 1103 cases of self-poisoning in children aged six to eighteen. The sex distribution of patients between six and ten (Figure 11–3) showed a predominance of males even greater than that found for poisoning under age five and may represent cases of cognitive immaturity or persistence of the male propensity for accidental injury. The sudden spurt of self-poisoning by adolescent girls at age twelve with a decrease after age sixteen reflects earlier biologic maturation and subsequent social conflicts. In contrast, the events in males continued to increase at ages seventeen and eighteen and would seem to presage the known increase with age of male suicide.

Socieconomic status based on the occupation of the head of the family correlated with the racial distribution. As age increased, blacks accounted

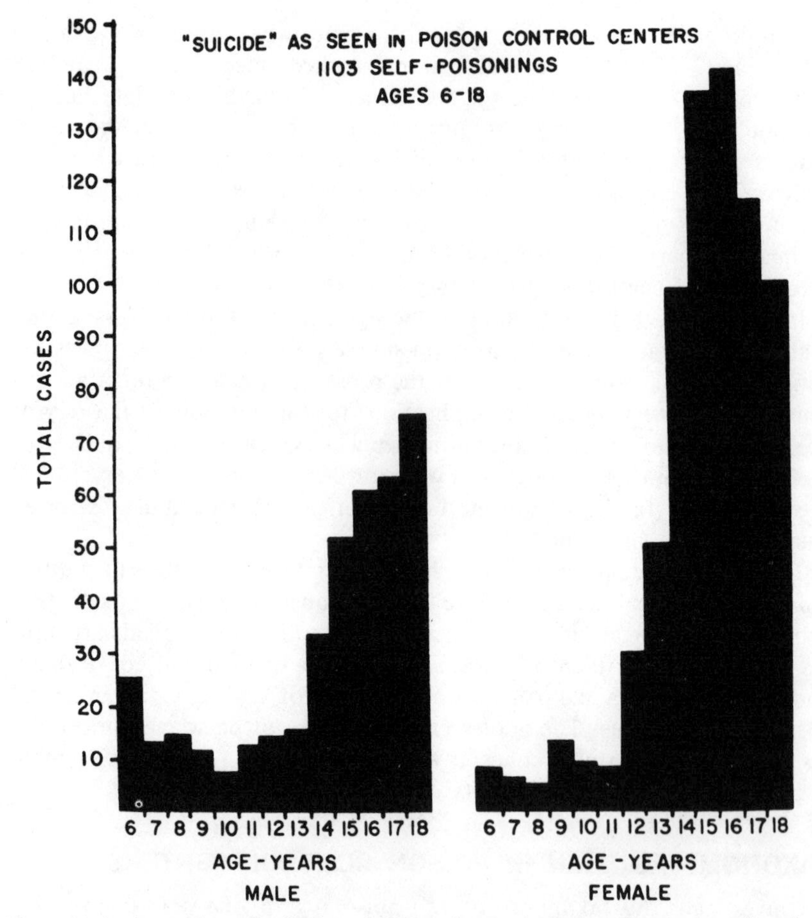

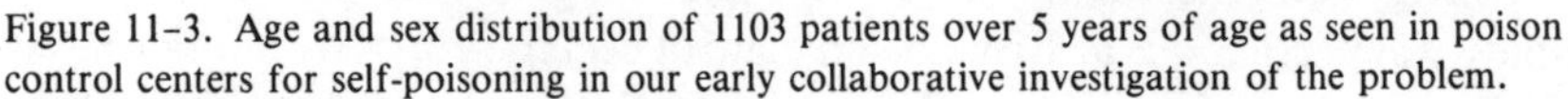

Figure 11–3. Age and sex distribution of 1103 patients over 5 years of age as seen in poison control centers for self-poisoning in our early collaborative investigation of the problem.

for a decreasing percentage. For Hispanics and American Indians the peak incidence was among females, ages fourteen to sixteen, with a subsequent decrease as shown in Table 11–2.

The older conflict between the sociologic and psychiatric evaluation of suicide has receded into a clinical approach that does not attempt to fit patients into rigid categorization of psychodynamics. The diversity of individual problems was apparent in the patients' past history and in the precipitating event. Inquiry was made concerning significant psychosocial disruption: loner, school dropout, juvenile delinquent, character or behavior disorder, brain damage—motor or mental, convulsive disorder, psychoneurosis, psychosis, significant or chronic mental disability or illness

Table 11-2. Race, Age, and Sex of 1103 Self-Poisonings 6-18 Years.

FEMALE	WHITE	BLACK	AMERICAN INDIAN, HISPANIC	OTHER OR NOT REPORTED
6-10	59%	39%*	0%	2%
11-13	61%	27%*	8%	4%
14-16	64%	22%	11%*	3%
17-18	77%**	13%	4%	6%
Total Female	67%	21%	8%	4%
MALE				
6-10	44%	40%**	6%	10%
11-13	60%	33%	2%	5%
14-16	76%	13%	5%	6%
17-18	85%**	6%	4%	5%
Total Male	72%	18%	4%	6%
Total, Male & Female	69%	20%	7%	4%

* p 0.05.
** p 0.005
Analysis of the percent distributions by Chi-square tests shows an increase in black girls aged 6 to 10 and 11-13, and an increase in Hispanic and American Indian girls aged 14-16. Among boys, there was a disproportionately high number of blacks aged 6 to 10 and of whites aged 17 and 18.

(Table 11-3). The 10% incidence of behavior disorders would support adolescent depression and suicide as a late manifestation of an early antagonism between the parent and child.

A history of significant emotional stress at the time of poisoning was obtained from the majority of older patients interviewed, and from 43% of the youngest group (Table 11-4).

These stressful situations were listed on the questionnaire as humiliation, punishment, sense of failure, romance problems, pregnancy, family problems, loss of parent or significant other relative, and "other difficulties."

Table 11-3. "Accidental" Poisoning, Ages 6-18: Past History.

Behavior disorder	10%	Chronic medical problems	2%
Character disorder	6%	Convulsive disorder	2%
"Loner"	5%	Brain damage	1%
School dropout	5%	Multiple problems	7%
Delinquency	4%	No significant problems	31%
Psychoneurosis	4%	No information	20%
Psychosis	2%		

Table 11-4. Age and Precipitating Stress.

AGE	PRESENT	ABSENT	NOT REPORTED
6–10	42%	37%	21%
11–13	73%	14%	13%
14–16	78%	7%	15%
17–18	81%	6%	13%

In the youngest age group, acts of overt aggression, hostility and fear of retribution were the most common difficulties. This is the most transparent expression of suicide as hate. Of the girls seventeen or eighteen years old, 30% were married, separated, widowed, unwed mothers, or unwed pregnant. In boys, homosexuality was frequently reported. Precipitating stress revolved around the "five P's: parents, peers, privation, punctured romance, and pregnancy."

Intent, meaning the deliberate attempt to poison oneself, was assessed by the poison centers (Table 11–5). In children six to ten, 50% of poisoning is called unintentional, but this naive interpretation is not supported by behavioral data; the six to ten year-old selects sedatives twice as frequently as the four year-old; at least 24% of such children are referred to behavior clinics; 26% have a significant history of past difficulties; 43% give a history of current precipitating stress factors. Only 8.6% of the 992 cases in patients aged eleven to eighteen were considered "unintentional" and usually involved errors in prescription medication.

The diagnosis of suicide attempt had been explained to the interviewers as, "did the subject mean to kill himself?" and the frequency of diagnosis is shown in Table 11-6.

The diagnosis of a suicide attempt by any observer was related to, (1) age; (2) drug use—i.e., a "kick" or "trip" was rarely called a suicide attempt; (3) the history of prior psychosocial disruption; (4) precipitating stress; and (5) socioeconomic status, with significantly greater attention be-

Table 11-5. Age and Diagnosis of Intent.

AGE	INTENTIONAL	SUBINTENTIONAL	UNINTENTIONAL	UNKNOWN
6–10	13%	19%	50%	18%
11–13	53%	23%	16%	9%
14–16	64%	21%	7%	7%
17–18	67%	17%	8%	7%
Total	59%	20%	13%	8%

Table 11-6. Age and Diagnosis of Suicide Attempt.

AGE	FINAL DX	CONSIDERED NOT FINAL	NEVER CONSIDERED	NOT REPORTED
6–10	2%	9%	69%**	20%
11–13	20%	29%	42%*	9%
14–16	32%	31%	26%	11%
17–18	28%	31%	34%	7%
Total	26%	29%	35%	10%

* $p < 0.05$.
** $p < 0.005$.
The frequency of the diagnosis of suicide increases with age, but is considered and even diagnosed in children as young as 6 years.

ing given to the possibility of suicide attempt in patients from the upper socioeconomic group.

This study was the first time an attempt had been made, on an international basis, to investigate the dynamics of "accidental" poisoning in an older age group. Considerable regional diversity was evident. Edinburgh, for example, continuing in the clear distinction of gesture from attempts, did not label a single adolescent ingestion as a true suicide attempt. The most important evidence was that only 13% of poisoning at ages six and older were considered true accidents. The fact that intent was evident in three-fourths must redefine the concept of accidental poisoning in school-age children as young as six years old.

The general classifications of toxic substances showed a distinctive pattern for each age group. Intent is suggested by the fact that 27% of six-to ten-year-olds ingested sedatives, or twice as frequently as did four-year-olds. Young thrill-seekers favored alcohol and glue inhalation over other hallucinogens, but drug abuse tripled after age thirteen.

Death occurred in five patients, a mortality of 1:220 self-poisonings. In all cases it appeared that lethality of intent was extremely low and death was the result of a toxicologic mishap.

The results of this initial survey showed that self-poisoning in a child over six years of age is rarely accidental and deserves inquiry by the health professional into the severity and chronicity of prior difficulties and disruptive events, the nature of the precipitating stress, and, most important, the motivation for the act. One needs to know what the child expected to happen to him/her physically as a result of the ingestion and what he/she expected to change in his/her life. The actual self-poisoning may be the end stage of long-standing problems, or it may be an impulsive attempt to control interpersonal conflict by a child or adolescent who sees himself/herself as so lacking in significance that only acute behavior will merit attention.[11,12]

EVALUATION—THE PSYCHOLOGICAL BIOPSY

Given the frequency of initial contact in the emergency room or poison control center, the primary interviewer is a valuable resource for the assessment of self-poisonings, gestures, and suicide attempts in children and adolescents. Systematic examination and evaluation of these adolescents presents the opportunity to study suicidopathic behavior and drug abuse in its most transparent form. Having redefined the concept of poisoning in the older child as an intentional event, our next study was to investigate these children in depth. For this purpose we devised a structured interview and rating system called a "psychological biopsy" and established its validity when administered by health professionals of varying backgrounds.[13]

The interview is conducted as soon as the patient is no longer in danger. In the interim, the rescuers' view of both the immediate event and the past history should be obtained. The adolescent should be interviewed in a private room and assured that the information will not be used against him. Maintenance of confidentiality despite legal pressures and parental concern is important to the adolescent's self-esteem. The three general areas of inquiry are outlined in narrative form in Table 11–7.

The immediate circumstances, particularly information on the probability of rescue, are most useful in estimating the lethality of intent at the time of the self-destructive behavior. The actual event, however, is only one item in a long-term history of difficulties. The family history usually depicts great stress and strife. A history of multiple prior difficulties plus antisocial behavior indicates a low lethality of intent. Rage has been channeled into rebellious rather than suicidal behavior. The exceptional history, in which family perturbation appears low or even absent, is often the first indication of a severe psychiatric disorder.

The "psychological biopsy (Table 11–8) scores nine significant areas of evaluation. Scoring of these items is derived from the initial history supplemented by additional questions as individual circumstances indicate. The goals of the assessment are, (1) diagnosis—"Is this really a suicide attempt?" and, (2) definition of the nature and severity of perturbation.

The final item in the questionnaire, familial expectations and control, overlaps the ratings of stress and of parental reaction. It is included as a separate item because of its critical relationship to adolescent behavior. In adolescents manifesting suicidal behavior the pattern of familial control and demands is often at one extreme or the other. The dominant group of these adolescents comes from families characterized by indifference, low

Table 11-7. Narrative Outline for Evaluation of Adolescent Suicidal Behavior.

Narrative Outline of Event: Tell me what happened. (actual lethality of event) What time of day? What did you do then? Did you tell anyone? Did you think you would be found? How did they find out about it? (probability of rescue) When did you first think about doing this? (premeditation) Have you ever done anything like this in the past? Do you think you will do anything like it again?

Rating of Circumstantial Lethality:

0	1–2	3–4–5–	7–8–9
None	Low	Medium	High

Narrative Outline of Family and Interactions: Tell me about the members of your family, their ages, where they live, how you get along with each. Do you think any of them uses too much alcohol or drugs? Have any of your family or close friends ever attempted suicide? Which people can you talk to when things go wrong? If you could make some changes in your life, what would you change?

Prior Difficulties, Symptoms, and Perturbation: What medical problems have you had? Have you had any school problems? Repeat a class? Dropping out? Suspended? Have you had any trouble with the police? Any trouble because of alcohol or drugs? Ever run away from home? Has a doctor ever treated you for your nerves? Have you had many problems with your boyfriend or girlfriend? Your friends? Marriage problems?

expectations, and sporadic control. These young people are most inclined to act out their hostility and have frequent problems with the law. At the other extreme are those subjected to all-pervasive control and excessive expectations. Some children from this kind of family are incapable of rebellion and have more severe psychiatric disorders. The extremes of parental reaction offer some of the best opportunities for environmental change and supportive encouragement of the patient to recognize the nature of his/her oppression and rejection.

Our first study utilizng this biopsy involved an interview conducted at home by public health nurses of fifty consecutive patients, ages six to eighteen, who had recently been treated at two poison control centers in Omaha along with interviews of fifty controls, matched for age, sex, socioeconomic, and family status.[13] The last was considered particularly important because of the high incidence of single parent, stepparent and otherwise disrupted families.

Long-standing personal difficulties coupled with precipitating stress were found in almost all (Table 11-9). Thirty-two percent of the subjects, but none of the controls, had at least one prior referral to a mental health service. In contrast to 12% of the controls, 88% of the subjects had a past history of significant personal-social difficulties. The most frequent prob-

Table 11-8. Psychological Biopsy Questionnaire.

Name: ____

Age: ________________ Sex: ________________ Race: ________________

Occupation, head of household: ____________________________________

Lives with: ____

Address: ____

Score each category as:

0	1–2	3–4–5	7–8–9	Score (0–9)
None	Low	Medium	High	________

1. Circumstantial Lethality: (___)
   Probability of rescue ___; subject's impression of lethality ___; actual lethality ___; extent of planning ___; plans to repeat ___.
2. Prior Self-Destructive Behavior: (___)
   One or more suicide attempts/gestures ___; suicidal preoccupation ___; "accidental" poisoning after age 6 ___; more than one accident/year requiring medical care ___; drug or alcohol use considered excessive by peer group ___; refuses or denies needs for health care ___.
3. Depression (___)
   Loneliness, hopelessness, exhaustion ___; disorders of sleep ___; appetite ___; chronic illness ___.
4. Hostility (___)
   Feelings of rage, anger, hostility, revenge ___; poor judgment, irresponsibility and impulsive acting out ___; overt belligerence, aggression, antisocial behavior ___.
5. Stress (___)
   Chronicity and multiplicity of conflicts ___; broken or unsympathetic home ___; loss of parent, sibling, or significant other by death, divorce or desertion ___; alcoholic or otherwise irresponsible parent(s) ___; threat of punishment, criminal prosecution, exposure ___; concern over homosexuality ___; other ___.
6. Reaction of Parent or Parent Surrogate: (___)
   Helpless ___; indifferent ___; angry ___; punitive ___; vacillating ___; parent(s) alcoholic ___; other psychosocial difficulty ___.
7. Loss of Communication (___)
   Broken with one or both parents ___; with all adults ___; with most peers ___; all peers ___.
8. Lack of Resources: (___)
   Lack of religious ties ___; lack of availability of professional help-counselor, etc. ___.
9. Parental Expectations and Control: (___)
   Subject feels parental demands or expectations beyond his/her capacity; feels a disappointment to parents ___; parents expect nothing from him/her ___; parent or surrogate demands review of friends, activities ___; refuses any discussion or negotiation of control ___; extreme indifference or neglect ___; vacillates from one extreme to other ___; expectations and degree of control divergent ___.

Table 11-9. Past History, 50 Self-Poisonings, Ages 6-17.

	SUBJECTS	CONTROLS
Prior mental helath referral	32%	2%
Prior behavior problems	88%	12%
Prior suicide gestures	26%	0%

lems were immaturity (38%), school dropout (18%), loner (16%), behavior problem (16%), and delinquency (14%). Prior suicide gestures had been made by 26% of the subjects, but by none of the controls.

The following is a typical example of long-standing perturbation culminating in a precipitous action:

> An eighteen year-old boy, mother a housewife and stepfather a laborer, was a school dropout and had a history of chronic ulcers. He stated he was a failure, had trouble with his girlfriend and feared he might die of kidney disease as did his brother. After his father was killed in an accident his mother remarried and had three more children. At the time of the ingestion of tranquilizers and sleeping pills his mother was filing for divorce. The youth said his mother was crazy but refused psychiatric help. He said his girl-friend was pregnant by him. "I'd had it—my life was a mess—I know what I am, and that's no good. I've thought about suicide many times and finally I really wanted to die". When asked what would be the best thing that could happen he said, "Get married—then my suicide problem would go away." When asked about death, "It's final, you finally have peace, I want to die, I've tried and will probably try again."

Despite the irrationality of his belief that marriage would solve his problems, this boy was clearly asking for relief from overwhelming circumstances.

In contrast, this event may be an acute response to stress in an adolescent whose coping mechanisms had been previously adequate:

> This seventeen-year-old white girl, a high-school student whose father was a technical worker, lived with her mother after the parents' divorce. She had a hearing problem almost all of her life and was embarrassed about it, but nothing had ever been done about it. In the fall, she had acquired a steady boyfriend but had recently had a disagreement with him. One Sunday her mother went visiting while she waited for the boyfriend to call. After waiting all day, with no call, she said she developed a

headache from doing her homework and took some headache pills, three in number, she thought. The mother arrived home later in the evening and found her daughter had difficulty in standing and walking. The bottle of aspirin—phenacetin—caffeine compound tablets was empty and the mother estimated that the daughter took twenty-seven tablets. The medical course ws uncomplicated. Following her hospitalization the hearing problem was evaluated and a therapeutic program undertaken. In view of her previously good adjustment it was not thought that prolonged psychiatric help or counseling was indicated.

One to three weeks after the event the public health nurse made a home visit and in all cases was welcomed as a willing listener. The unlimited time frame and the empathy expressed by the nurse were particularly conducive to revelations of the child's true feelings and the nature of the family problems.

The interview by the public health nurse almost always disclosed information not obtained at the hospital and completely changed the diagnosis in 96% of the cases. The diagnoses based on the psychological biopsy showed only two of fifty events in subjects ages six to eighteen to be accidental:

A seven-year-old girl who followed a neighboring child's lead to fill a small swimming pool with gasoline and was then overcome by the fumes.

A twelve-year-old boy with many areas of maladjustment who, on a dare, put a lump of dry ice in his mouth.

Twenty-two percent of the events were considered intoxications. These were occasionally experimental or convivial in nature, but were frequently just one more manifestation of long-standing problems. A diagnosis of suicide attempt, meaning a high probability that the individual's actions will result in death was made in only one patient, subsequently diagnosed as schizophrenic. The diagnostic value of the structured interview is summarized in Table 11–10.

In one of the fifty cases, the diagnosis was changed to homicide after the interview:

A six year-old boy and his mother had both ingested liquid lye, reportedly thinking it cider. The boy's statement that "Mommy said to drink it—we would live on a cloud in heaven and not have to see Daddy anymore" led to the disclosure of an attempted homicide-suicide resulting from marital conflict.

Table 11-10. Diagnosis, 50 Self-Poisonings Ages 6-17.

Hospital diagnosis	
Accident	58%
Suicide attempt	42%
Biopsy diagnosis	
Accident	4%
Homicide	2%
Trip	22%
Suicide gesture	70%
Suicide attempt	2%

The estimated lethality of intent was plotted against the total score for perturbation, the sum of all nine categories in the psychological biopsy as shown in Figure 11-4. Adolescents classified as intoxications had total scores ranging from 11 to 31, reflecting the frequency of overtly hostile behavior, prior self-destructive behavior and stress in the form of family conflict. The total scores of the adolescents diagnosed as suicide gestures with minimal lethality of intent (0 to 2) were all below 30.

The seven patients considered to have made gestures of moderate lethality of intent all had total scores of 30 or above as did the one subject considered to have made a true suicide attempt. This subject, diagnosed as schizophrenic, illustrates that the questionnaire defines social disruption but is of little value in rating the psychotic subject.

Although the "biopsy" outline used in this study does not clearly define the psychotic subject who may have a high suicide potentiality in the absence of apparent stress or perturbation, it does focus on factors that leave the subject with so few options that the threat of taking his/her own life is the only apparent way to solve his/her problems. It is also recognized that the high intercorrelations for stress, parental reactions, and extremes of parental control/expectation weight the total score as possibly a better index of familial conflict than that of suicidal potentiality.[14]

Scoring in all nine areas of perturbation was significantly higher for the subjects than for matched controls. The estimated lethality of intent had the highest correlation with the scores for depression, hostility and stress.

Hostility was scored as higher than depression in 62% of the subjects, but only 36% of the controls, and is evidence, again, that the depression of the suicide gesture is that of suppressed rage.

Loss of communication in the subjects related to both the extent and the chronicity of the difficulty. Fifty-six percent of the subjects and 48% of the

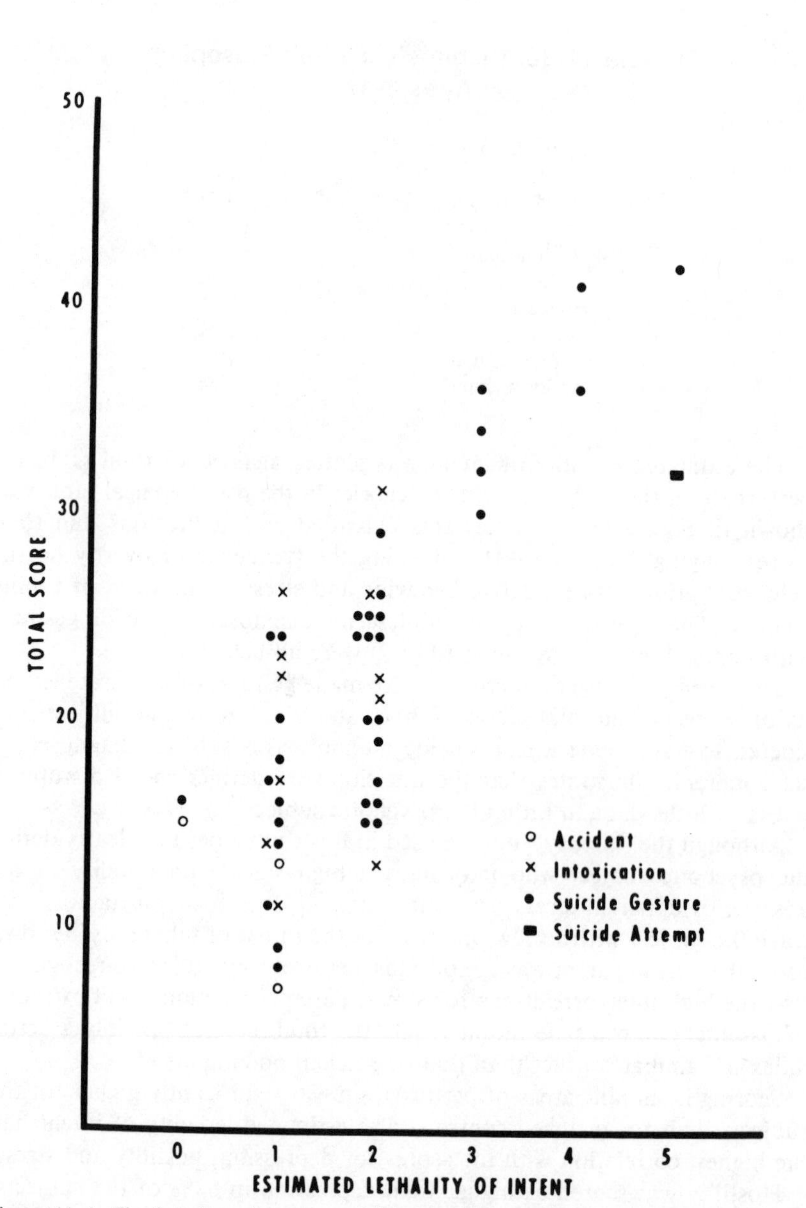

Figure 11-4. The lethality of intent, rated from 0 (none) to 10 (high) for 50 successive adolescents receiving emergency room treatment for poisoning. Lethality of intent was rated as minimal (O-2) for all those diagnosed as intoxications and for the majority of suicide gestures.

controls could not communicate with one or both parents, but the controls retained a more open exchange with peers and other adults.

Parental reaction was seen as negative by most adolescents. Both subjects and controls had encountered stress in the form of divorce, step-parents and economic deprivation, but hostility, indifference and overt rejection by the parent or parent-surrogate appeared the rule for the subjects and the exception for the controls. As shown in Table 11–11, 60% of the subjects, but only 14% of the controls, reported a sense of extremes of parental control and expectations.

The extremes of parental control and expectations encountered in the subjects emerged as a dominant theme. On additional interviews and in subsequent counseling it became clear that these were salient characteristics in the subject's "psychological biopsy" and that peer conflicts and school difficulties were secondary phenomena.

Extreme parental control in the subjects was associated with high depression scores, usually equated with repressed hostility. When pervasive control is coupled with rejection in the form of negative or impossibly high expectations the message to the child or adolescent becomes, "you are incapable," or "you are no good," leading to the progressive loss of self-esteem recognized as a critical factor in the pathogenesis of depression. This repressed hostility and low self-esteem is commonly expressed as a suicide gesture or even a true suicide attempt.

In contrast to pervasive control and excessively high or negative expectations, a more frequent pattern emerged—that of parental rejection expressed as indifference. This pattern of low or inconsistent parental control and low expectations was associated with acting-out behavior as manifested by intoxications and by gestures of low lethality and with hostility scores in excess of depression.

Extremes of parental reaction were seen most commonly in association with parental alcoholism suggesting that these two related forms of self-

Table 11-11. Extremes and Divergence in Parental Attitudes.

CONTROL	EXPECTATIONS	SUBJECTS	CONTROLS
Low	Low	28%	10%
	High	8%	2%
High or Inconsistent	Low	14%	2%
	High	10%	0%
Total Rated as Extremely High or Low in Control/Expectations		60%	14%

destructive behavior, suicide and alcoholism, may be manifest as a self-perpetuating continuum in the parent and child.

These extremes of parental rejection suggest an obvious opportunity for benefit by placing the adolescent in a more favorable environment. The majority of these families are incapable of responding to psychotherapy; they can provide neither structure nor support, and to attempt therapy in these situations is futile.

The observation that 26% of patients already had a history of prior self-destructive behavior and 32% had previous referral to a mental health agency is analogous to the revolving door therapy of the alcoholic. The delusion of the effectiveness of "referral for psychotherapy" is a manifestation of a faulty concept of the dynamics of self-destructive behavior in children and youth. Not only did these subjects have a high incidence of unsuccessful treatment but they themselves predicted therapeutic failure: ten of the fifty patients said they would probably die by suicide at some time. Because of the known and predicted recidivism in these adolescents, an investigation of the critical factors in recidivism seemed essential to define the total spectrum of self-destructive behavior.

RECIDIVISM

Since most self-destructive behavior by adolescents is of low lethality we attempted to arrive at more significant predictors of repeated self-destructive behavior. The goal was to distinguish those at risk for repeated self-destructive behavior of low lethality from those at risk for gestures of increasing lethality of intent.

After the home interview study, an additional group of fifty subjects (forty females and ten males) aged fourteen to eighteen who were successively admitted to three psychiatrc services in Omaha following self-destructive behavior were evaluated by the psychological biopsy.[15] The group had a high mobility but we were able to obtain a follow-up six to twenty-four months after the initial interview in twenty-six subjects (two at six months, thirteen at one year, and eleven at twenty-four months).

The same structured interview was conducted by a paraprofessional with special training in suicidology. The validity of this assessment was established by the concordance of ratings as given by the suicidologist and a psychiatrist. Each subject was rated on a scale of 0 to 9 for: (1) Circumstantial lethality—the probability of rescue; (2) prior self-destructive behavior; (3) depression or negative self-concept; (4) hostility; (5) stress; (6) reaction of parent or parent surrogate; (7) loss of communication; (8) lack of supportive resources; and (9) extremes of parental expectations and control.

Based on the interview and the circumstances of the original event, each subject was then categorized according to: (1) Lethality of intent—low, medium, or high—based on the probability of rescue; (2) diagnostic category—intoxication, manipulative gesture, depressive gesture, true attempt; (3) functional and social incapacitation—none, mild, moderate, high; and (4) estimated risk for repeated suicidal behavior. Risk was rated high if lethality of intent was medium, or high or if a gesture of low intent was coupled with prior suicidal behavior, significant depression, or thought disturbance.

The twenty-six adolescents available for follow-up evaluation were representative of the original fifty subjects. None of the original or follow-up subjects were judged to have a high lethality of intent. Social incapacitation, defined as moderte to severe difficulties in functioning, was noted in 62% of the original group and 70% of those reevaluated. Of the original fifty, 52% had made prior gestures, compared to 50% of the follow-up subjects. Of the original group, 44% had an alcoholic parent, similar to the 50% incidence for the follow-up group. Thought disturbances were present in 10% of the original and 15% of the follow-up group.

Of the follow-up group of twenty-six subjects, risk had been predicted as low for six subjects and high for twenty subjects by both the suicidologist and the psychiatrist (Table 11-12). The six "low-risk" subjects had all made gestures of negligible lethality of intent—predominantly drug and alcohol overdoses. They had a high incidence of social incapacitation with antisocial, delinquent behavior and high ratings for hostility. Only one had made a prior gesture, none were significantly depressed, and none had disturbed thinking.

A prediction of high risk of recurrent self-destructive behavior correlated best with the lethality of intent or probability of rescue in the original event, with prior suicidal gestures and with high ratings for depression or depression-hostility. The presence of moderate to severe functional incapacitation was unrelated to the prediction. Prior suicidal gestures had been made by 60% of the predicted high-risk group and disturbed thought was diagnosed in 20%. The overall recurrence rate was 31%, with eight repeated attempts in twenty-six subjects.

The six subjects considered at low risk had no recurrences. Prediction of risk was 100% reliable in the low-risk subjects of this study. Low-risk subjects were identified by the low lethality of intent, past history of acting-out and delinquent behavior, and relatively high ratings for both hostility and self-esteem. The low-risk group continued to have significant problems, particularly alcoholism and conflict with the law, but half of the low-risk group improved.

Of the twenty high-risk subjects, 40% made repeated gestures—five

Table 11-12. Predicted Risk for Recidivism in 26 Adolescents.

	NO. (%) OF SUBJECTS WITH PREDICTED RISK	
	LOW	HIGH
No. of subjects	6	20
Lethality of intent		
Minimal	6 (100)	—
Low-moderate	—	20 (100)
Depression/negative self concept rating > median	0	13 (65)
Hostility rating > median	5 (87)	6 (30)
Prior gestures	1 (15)	12 (60)
Thought disturbance	0	4 (20)
Alcoholic parent	2 (33)	11 (55)
Social incapacitation	4 (67)	14 (70)

within six months, two more by one year, and one by the second year. Only three were improved. Acting-out and delinquent behavior and alcoholism persisted in three subjects. Three continued to have incapacitating thought disturbances. The dominant response in the other eleven was one of depression and entrapment related to poverty, alcoholic parents, chronic illness (two subjects), unwanted pregnancy (two subjects), homosexual guilt (one subject), and a life-long inability to cope with a multitude of problems.

Recidivism was primarily related to the subjects' failure to change their circumstances or the inability to respond to environmental change. In the six subjects moving to an improved environment, two in their own home and four in foster homes, there were no repeated gestures. The move itself appeared fortuitous since two of six foster homes were unsuccessful. In these two cases, unsuccessful foster home placement led to sequential foster homes and institutions; one of these subjects made a repeated gesture while at an interval youth center.

Institutionalization for nine subjects was even less successful. Three institutionalizations were at reform school or prison, and only one of the three subjects made a subsequently good adjustment at home (Table 11-13).

Any predictive correlation of the duration of therapy with repetition is obscured by the fact that subjects with extreme perturbation in multiple

Table 11-13. Therapy and Recidivism.

	TOTAL NO	NO. (%) OF SUBJECTS MAKING GESTURES
Total	26	8 (31)
Environment		
Worse	9	5 (56)
Better	6	0
Foster home	6	1 (15)
Recurrent institutionalization	6	5 (88)
Therapy > 2 mo	9	5 (56)
Thought disturbance	4	1 (25)

spheres required recurrent therapy. All twenty-six subjects were initially dismissed at two to six weeks. Therapy for more than eight weeks was received by nine subjects, all with severe functional disability, including three with thought disturbances. None of the nine with prolonged therapy were considered improved.

Subjects with a thought disturbance had a poor overall prognosis. Three of the four subjects with a thought disturbance went from one institution to another and one of these made a repeated suicide gesture; one deteriorated after being sent home but then made a surprisingly good adjustment with foster parents.

Overall, the recurrence rate was 31% and the relative risk ratio was highest for the severely depressed, those with thought disturbances and those with a deteriorating environment:

	Risk Ratio
Total	1.0
Thought disturbance	2.4
Depression above 75th percentile	2.8
Environment worse	2.4
Need for continued therapy	1.6

Psychiatric hospitalization with a return to an unchanged environment was uniformly unsuccessful. In many of these cases the degree of incapacitation became more manifest and seems to have been reinforced by repeated institutionalization and failure to improve.

The present methods of management, psychotherapy, and parental counseling are appallingly unsuccessful. In all of our studies, the majority of the families were already known to social agencies, but the suicide gesture precipitated the crucial need for intervention. Frequently, the family situations were beyond repair. In these cases, we found the best results in adolescents who were able to move to a more favorable home situation with a relative or friend. These adolescents, however, are the product of years of familial and socioeconomic stress, and are often unattractive, rebellious, sullen, or withdrawn and foster home acceptance is difficult for the older and more intractable adolescent.[16]

In the changing shift in problems confronting children and youth the child health professional must take the initiative for earlier intervention in the unremitting cycle of self-destructive behavior. We see, for example, training for parenthood courses both at the level of the high school student and the young parent, referral of problem families to such programs at the earliest possible moment, consideration of foster home placement in preadolescence, and most important, earlier implementation of therapeutic programs to help the young child handle the dynamics of interpersonal conflict.

The magnitude of the problem of self-destructive behavior in young children becomes apparent on analysis of the data from poison control centers. By its very size it enters the domain of public health and is the earliest manifestation of three major problems: alcoholism, drug abuse, and suicide. The high incidence of all of these problems in the families of adolescent suicide attempters supports early acquisition of familial patterns of behavior. The correlation of alcoholism and suicide in adults is well known; our own studies show a 40% incidence of confirmed alcoholism in one or both parents. This correlation of adolescent suicide attempts with parental alcoholism demands comprehensive evaluation of the family of the alcoholic. The question of whether this represents a response to erratic parental control or the imprinting of self-destructive behavior warrants further investigation and analysis.

Just as the health professions provided the leadership for early detection and development of needed programs for the retarded and the handicapped during the 1960s, they should, in a like manner respond to the new challenge of childhood decompensation in a disturbed family environment.

REFERENCES

1. Angle, C. R., McIntire, M. S., and Meile, R. L. Neurological sequelae of poisoning in children. *J. Pediatr.* **73**:531-539 (1968).
2. Monthly Vital Statistics Report, Annual Summary for the United States 1975, **24**:5 (1976).

3. Monthly Vital Statistics Report, Final Mortality Statistics, 1977. National Center for Health Statistics, DHEW Publication No. 79-1120, **28,** May 11 (1979).
4. Accident Facts, National Safety Council, Chicago, Illinois (1979).
5. McIntire, M. S., and Angle, C. R. The taxonomy of suicide as seen in poison control centers. *Pediatr. Clin. N.A.* **17**:697-706 (1970).
6. Poison Control Statistics, 1976, National Clearinghouse for Poison Control Centers, FDA; 5401 Westbard Avenue, Bethesda, Maryland 20016, Spring (1978).
7. Shneidman, E. S. Orientations toward death. *In: The Study of Lives,* R. W. White (ed.) New York: Atherton Press, 1966.
8. Shneidman, E. S. Orientation toward cessation: A reexamination of current modes of death. *J. Forensic Sci.* **13**:33-45 (1968).
9. Kessel, N. Self-poisoning. *Br. Med. J.* **1**:1265-1270; 1336-1348 (1965).
10. McIntire, M. S., Angle, C. R., and Struempler, L. J. The concept of death in midwestern children and youth. *Am. J. Dis. Child.* **123**:527-532 (1972).
11. McIntire, M. S., and Angle, C. R. Is the poisoning accidental? *Clin. Pediatr.* **10**:414 (1971).
12. McIntire, M. S., and Angle, C. R. Suicide as seen in poison control centers. *Pediatrics* **48**:914-922 (1971).
13. McIntire, M. S., and Angle, C. R. The psychological biopsy in self-poisoning of children and adolescents. *Am. J. Dis. Child.* **126**:42-46 (1973).
14. McIntire, M. S., and Angle, C. R.: Evaluation of suicidal risk in adolescents. *J. Fam. Pract.* **2**:339-341 (1975).
15. McIntire, M. S., Angle, C. R., Wikoff, R. L., and Schlicht, M. L. Recurrent adolescent behavior. *Pediatrics* **60**:605-608 (1977).
16. McIntire, M. S., Angle, C. R. and Schlicht, M. L. Suicide and self-poisoning in pediatrics *Adv. Pediatr.* **24**:291-310 (1977).

The author investigates the relationship between psychogenic hearing loss and the emotional configuration of the individual as determined by diagnostic psychological test profiles. Drawing upon his years of clinical experience, Dr. Rousey provides insights based upon actual case histories. He utilizes a psychoanalytic understanding to illustrate the function of loss of hearing as a coping effort of the indidivual within the context of family relationships.

12
Psychogenic Hearing Loss

Clyde L. Rousey, Ph.D

INTRODUCTION

Baffling as it may be, there are times in most persons' lives when they do not hear or comprehend what is said despite the anatomical, physiological, and neurological capacity to do so. Such behavior ranges from the commonplace and essentially benign behavior of children who exasperate their parents by not listening to instructions, or the husband who hears not a word said by his wife, to the patient who suddenly loses his hearing following an emotional trauma or gradually becomes deaf or hard of hearing as a coping device in response to intolerable internal or external stress. Although the focus of this book is on children and adolescents, the phenomenon of psychogenic hearing loss is not age or phase specific. As a consequence, in our study we shall use material gathered from work with varying age groups.

Efforts to explain the above range of human behavior have ranged from labeling it as a willful and conscious action to obtain compensation (malingering) to postulating unconscious and dynamically determined factors (e.g., as in a conversion reaction or hysteria). That these two extremes were not completely useful is attested to by a third approach which attempts to be more descriptive and "nonjudgmental" (e.g., using such terms as functional, nonorganic, or pseudohypoacusis). Recent otological and audiological literature has paid increasingly scant attention to the foregoing psychological possibilities—choosing now to focus predominantly on organic reasons for the appearance of unexplained hearing loss (subnamed under such terms as sudden or fluctuant deafness) (Shea).[30]

Because the effective use of sound allows us to understand others, pro-

The author gratefully acknowledges the critical review of this manuscript by Carol G. Rousey, Ph.D. and C. P. Goetzinger, Ph.D.

tect ourselves from danger, and have a sense of psychological contact with the world in varying degrees (Ramsdell),[24] hearing loss which is consciously or unconsciously assumed has obvious self-destructive components. To understand the psychological components which might be involved requires at least a cursory understanding of how and what we hear, how acuity is assessed and a theoretical model which will allow a broad understanding of hearing loss secondary to psychological distress.

AUDIOLOGICAL CONSIDERATIONS

Pathways of Hearing

While it is outside the purview of this chapter to focus on a detailed description of acoustics and physiology, it is appropriate to review for the reader the general facts of how sound is received. Sound is heard by either air conduction or bone conduction. Hearing by air conduction refers to auditory stimuli which enter the external ear canal, vibrate the tympanic membrane (eardrum) with a resulting movement of the ossicles in the middle ear resulting in a subsequent stimulation of the cochlea. In contrast, hearing by bone conduction refers to sound which is sufficient to vibrate the skull with a subsequent bypassing of the external ear canal and middle ear and a resulting primary stimulation of the cochlea. The pathway for auditory stimuli at that point is generally the same for stimuli perceived either by bone conduction or air conduction. That is, from the cochlea sound follows both an ipsilateral and contralateral course through the various synapses of the auditory tract to the temporal lobe.

Measurement of Hearing

Most clinical assessment of hearing uses an audiometer which is capable of presenting pure tones ranging from 125 Hz to 8000 Hz. Intensity variation extends from an arbitrary reference point where the average person can indicate first perceiving sound (labeled as O dB) and extending to 110 dB above this beginning level. A wider range of intensity is available for presentation by earphones from 500 Hz through 4000 Hz than at 125 Hz, 250 Hz or 8000 Hz. In addition, there are instrument limitations which affect and limit measurements. For example, testing sensitivity for sound by bone conduction requires a different transducer from what is used in testing sensitivity by air conduction. The oscillator used for tone or speech presentation by bone conduction requires more power and at levels above 65–70 dB HL often produces tactile, as well as auditory sensations. All of these parameters must be taken into account in any measurement of hearing sensitivity.

In describing hearing problems, any stoppage of sound transmission by air conduction which occurs in the external ear canal or middle ear cavity is generally described as a conductive impairment; while, if the site of difficulty can be localized at or beyond the cochlea, audiologists and otologists will generally call the difficulty a sensorineural impairment. A typical audiogram showing normal hearing for pure tones is found in Figure 12–1. The symbol (O) is universally used to indicate the right ear, while (X) indicates the left ear. A solid line connecting the intensity levels and frequencies measured is used to indicate that the stimuli is presented by air conduction.

Figure 12–2 shows a typical plotting for a conductive hearing loss. Here the reader will note that the dashes and symbols (>)* for the right ear and (<)* for the left ear indicating thresholds for bone conduction are within what is generally regarded as the normal range of sensitivity for pure tone acuity (i.e., between −10 dB and +10 dB at all frequencies tested), while the solid lines indicating air conduction thresholds are at higher intensity levels. A difference of more than 10 dB between air conduction and bone conduction curves with normal sensitivity for bone conduction is the criteria for considering the loss as conductive.

In Figure 12–3, the dashes and solid lines intermingle and show graphically that sensitivity for sound is similar regardless of whether sound is presented by air conduction or bone conduction. The loss is said to be sensorineural since the site of the lesion is probably at or beyond the cochlea.

When a loss is noted by bone conduction and air conduction (but thresholds are still higher than 10 dB and a difference exists between air conduction and bone conduction thresholds), then a mixed loss (i.e., containing both conductive and sensorineural components) as shown in Figure 12–4 is said to be present.

Isolating the site of the transmission difficulty at points past the cochlea becomes extraordinarily difficult although evoked potential and brain stem techniques offer some hope (Davis)[5] and Jewett and Williston).[17]

In all of the above statements we have been talking about the transmission of a pure tone—usually a specific frequency (Hz). Auditory stimuli received by humans are more than just pure tones. Complex acoustic stimuli are involved in what we call verbal language. Although these stimuli travel the same route as pure tone stimuli, there is the added requirement that the cortex be functioning and able to interpret the symbolic meanings of the sounds. Verbal language which is heard and interpreted may be: (1) Redundant and, therefore, easy to understand; (2) easy to understand, but having no redundancy; or (3) difficult to understand. It is more likely that

*These symbols are generally, but not universally, used. In reading an audiogram, the clinician will generally have tables showing the meaning of all symbols used.

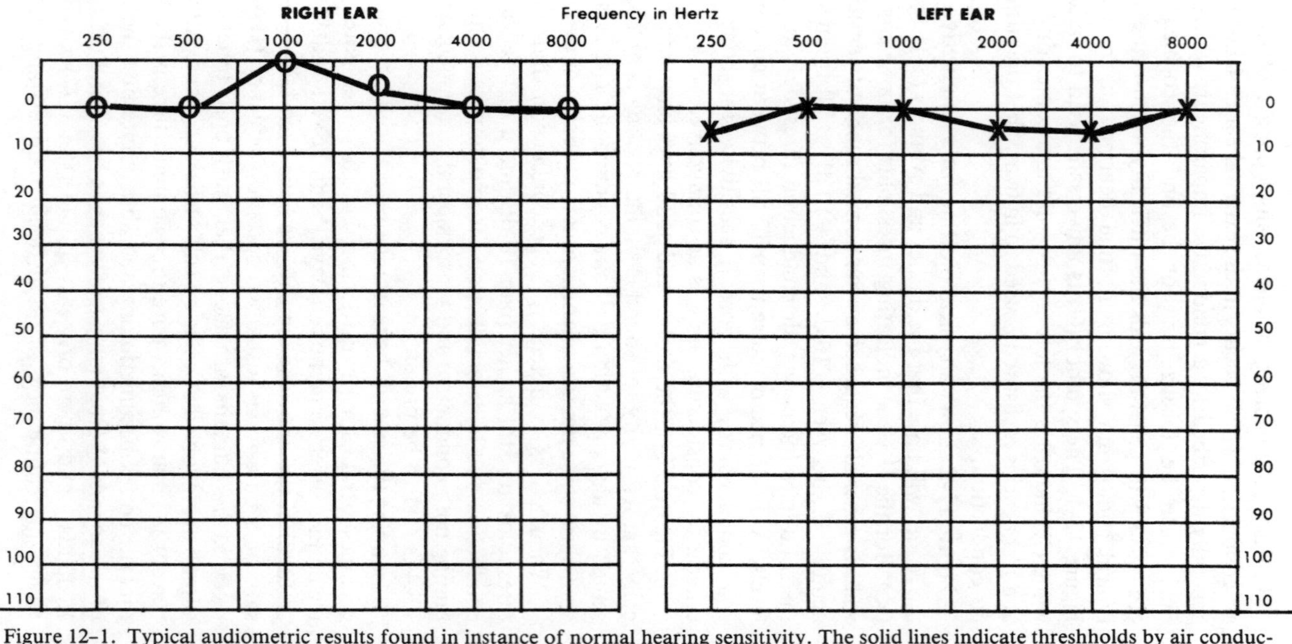

Figure 12–1. Typical audiometric results found in instance of normal hearing sensitivity. The solid lines indicate threshholds by air conduction. No bone conduction testing was completed because of the normal hearing by air conduction.

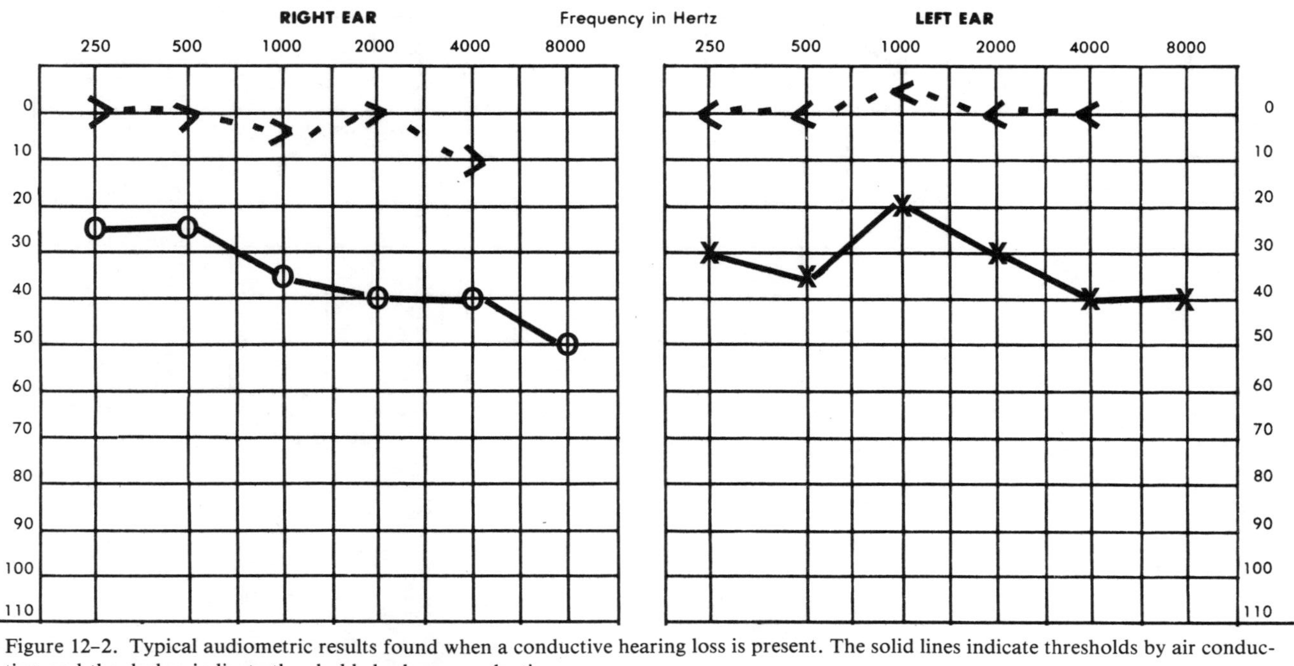

Figure 12–2. Typical audiometric results found when a conductive hearing loss is present. The solid lines indicate thresholds by air conduction and the dashes indicate thresholds by bone conduction.

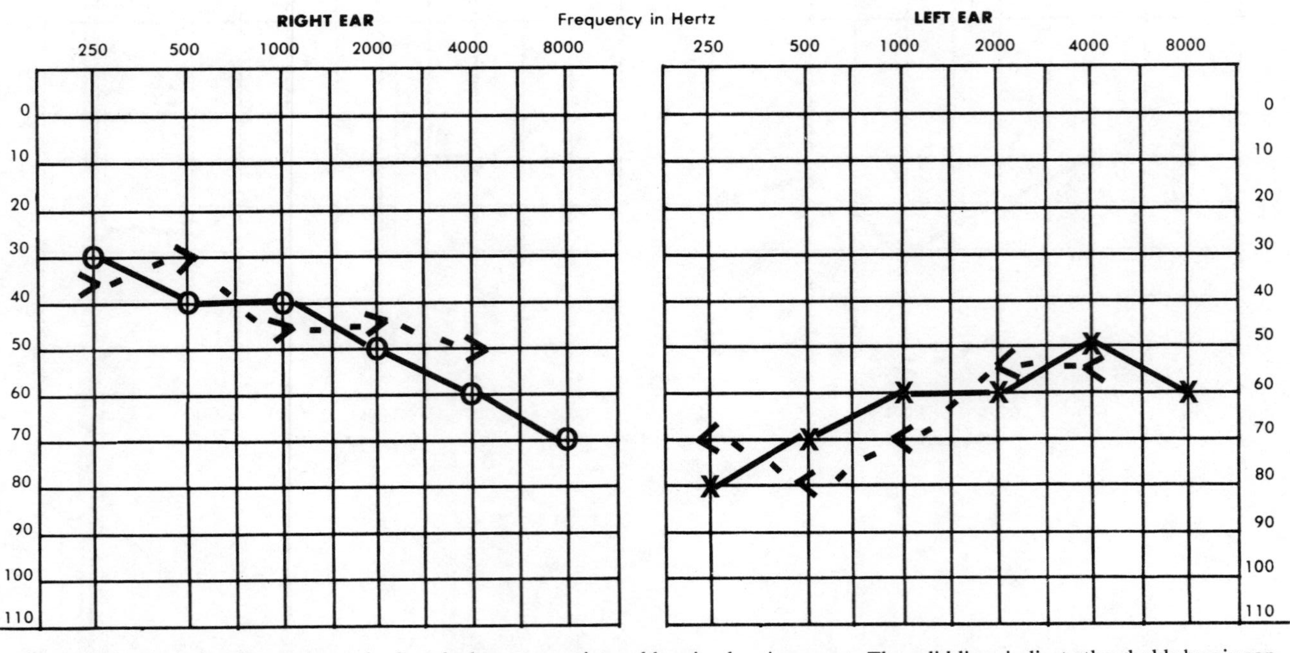

Figure 12–3. Typical audiometric results found when a sensorineural hearing loss is present. The solid lines indicate thresholds by air conduction and the dashes indicate thresholds by bone conduction.

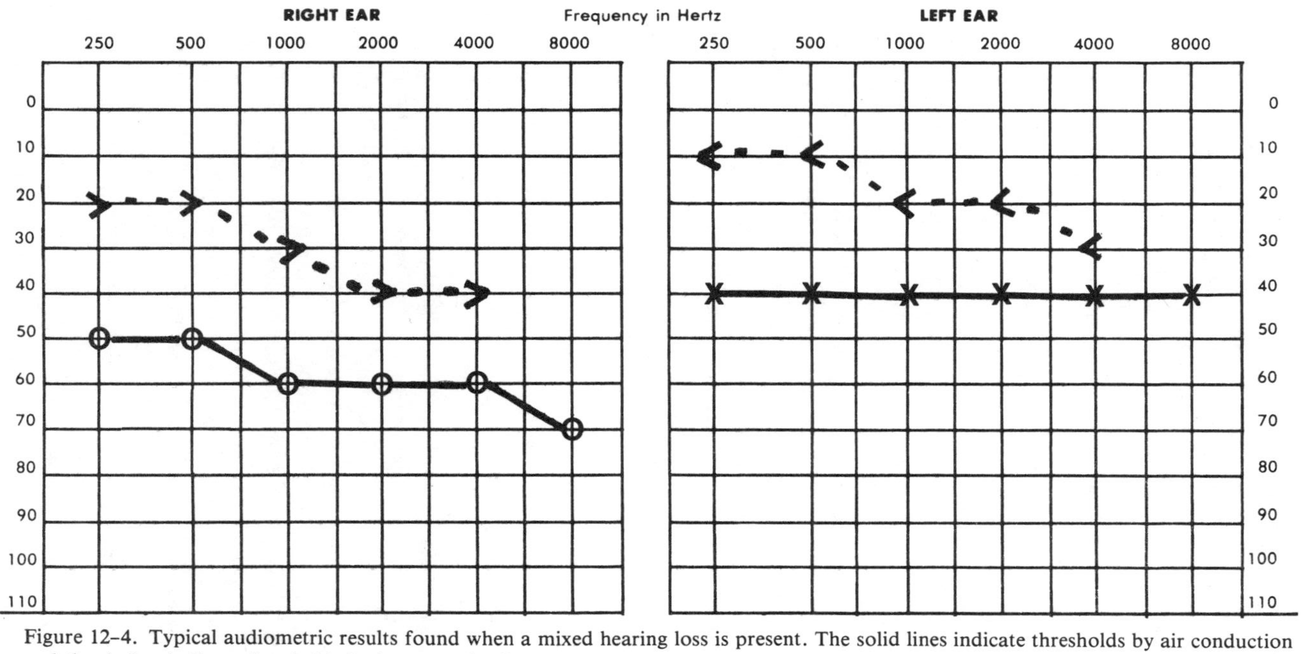

Figure 12-4. Typical audiometric results found when a mixed hearing loss is present. The solid lines indicate thresholds by air conduction and the dashes indicate thresholds by bone conduction.

all, rather than only one, of these elements are involved in a typical listening situation. Thresholds for hearing speech stimuli are determined by use of air conduction and bone conduction pathways. Except in instances where there is a precipitous drop-off in frequency response beginning at or around 1000 Hz, it is usually possible to correlate quite closely an individual's speech reception threshold (i.e., ability to repeat back spondaic words such as hotdog, birthday, etc.) with the average of the pure tone thresholds obtained at 500 Hz, 1000 Hz and 2000 Hz. Since this type of material does not sort out ability to discriminate spoken speech, it is necessary to determine further this aspect by special tests of discrimination. (Goetzinger[12]). Recently, sophisticated tests have been developed which show the effects of cochlear, midbrain, and cortical functioning (Keith).[18]

The importance of the foregoing discussion is to underline for the psychologist the organically determined diagnostic issues which must be addressed along with the psychological possibilities discussed later in this chapter. The history of clinical psychology and psychiatry is replete with examples of where such a basic injunction has been disregarded. Organically oriented clinicians from Freud to the present know that while their long-term hopes are for a reduction of human behavior to pure neurological or physiological explanations, the reality of clinical practice is such that psychological explanations are both useful and necessary.

Indicators of Psychogenic Loss

Hearing loss (secondary to psychological distress) whether called malingering, hysteria, functional, pseudohypocusis, nonorganic, psychogenic, auditory regression, auricular pithiatism, or sinistrosis depends on its detection to certain accepted fixed relationships between pure tone and speech stimuli as well as to the known stability of test results using these parameters. For example, it is well established that an individual's threshold for pure tones heard by air conduction does not vary over ± 5 dB in test-retest situations. When pure tone stimuli are presented by bone conduction, the expected variability in threshold for test-retest situations should not exceed ± 10 dB. With respect to redundant speech stimuli such as in words like baseball, birthday, hotdog, etc., the normal threshold variation is ± 4–6 dB. Normal test-retest performances on easy discrimination tests should not vary over ± 6% (Goetzinger).[13] Thus, purely on a statistical basis, variation which is greater than the above limits is suspect in terms of validity. Even over time, if obvious organic factors (e.g., exposure to noise, toxic reactions, neurological problems, aging, etc.) are excluded, significant variations in thresholds should not occur. When they do, the potential for psychogenic factors affecting hearing threshold should be considered. Observation of inconsistent behavioral responses to sound may also reflect the possibility of psychological factors. While the above criteria were developed for normal and/or neurotic persons, no criteria have been developed for psychotic patients. Hearing loss intertwined with or binding a psychosis offers new and unexplained problems for audiologists. In the author's experience among psychotic patients who have a psychogenic hearing loss, little variability in test results may occur. As a result, for such patients the standard indicators of psychogenic loss become invalid. It is with such patients that tests using indirect physiological indicators of auditory sensitivity are required.

A detailed discussion of specific tests used in the assessment of psychogenic and/or malingered hearing loss is outside the purview of the present chapter. Previous publications by Goetzinger and Proud[14]; Chaiklin and Ventry[4]; Ventry and Chaiklin[32]; Martin[20] and Hopkinson[15] provide a critical summary and evaluation of the usefulness of most such tests. It is relevant to note that most of the tests described by the above authors are constructed with the assumption that the individual's responses are in large part at a conscious level. Consequently, in individuals where preconscious or unconscious factors depress sensitivity for sound, the tests become invalid. The lack of consideration of these topographical features of mental functioning is an example of the price paid by professional groups addressing a complex clinical problem without benefit of knowledge of all the important parameters.

As noted previously, indirect physiological approaches offer the best way to circumvent the complications resulting from the impact of preconscious or unconscious elements in mental functioning. However, even here the extent of mind/body interaction is an unknown factor. Most recently, Reiter[25] and Reiter and Ison[26] have demonstrated that by use of a technique they call reflex modulation, physiologically determined thresholds can be obtained which are equivalent to what individuals voluntarily give. By objective recording techniques they are able to demonstrate that presentation of a pure tone can inhibit the magnitude of the patient's air puff-induced eyeblink reflex. As a result, threshold can be estimated. Another useful approach utilizes specific patterns of respiration which occur at or above, but never below, a person's auditory threshold (Rousey[27]). This technique has the virtue of allowing ongoing internal checks for the validity of the findings. This is done by adding a known level of effective masking noise which will produce a known predicted threshold which can be compared to a threshold obtained under normal conditions. The critical factor in all indirect physiological techniques, in terms of our present topic, is the level of Central Nervous System (CNS) integrity required to elicit a response. The more the cortex is necessary, the greater the potential usefulness in detecting hearing loss secondary to psychological disorganization.

PSYCHOLOGICAL FACTORS

Personality and Intelligence

Gleason's[11] study of psychological functioning of 278 patients whose hearing was tested at Walter Reed Army Hospital gives a good starting point for understanding clinical research in this area. He and his colleagues divided the above group into those who gave consistent audiological responses versus those who gave inconsistent responses (cf. the earlier discussion under basic audiological indicators of psychogenic loss). Having done this, both groups received the Shipley-Hartford, the Cornell Index-Form N2, the PD scale of the MMPI, a sentence completion test and a 10 to 30 minute individual psychological interview. He reports:

1. Inconsistent responders had a significantly lower I.Q. than consistent responders (significant at the .05 level). Of note is that means for both groups were within the average range of intelligence.
2. Inconsistent responders had significantly more psychiatric and psychosomatic complaints (significant at the .01 level).
3. Inconsistent responders showed a greater degree of antisocial philosophy and behavior (significant at the .05 level).
4. Eighty-six percent (72 persons) of the total group of inconsistent responders had a functional overlay of hearing loss on top of a medically diagnosed loss of organic etiology.

Chaiklin and Ventry[4] and Ventry and Chaiklin[32] approached the issue somewhat differently. Their report, which is still the best primary resource for orthodox views and techniques for assessing psychogenic determined hearing problems, was based on work with World War II male veterans whose initial hearing loss was resolved by brief counseling compared to those where this did not occur. They used the WAIS, MMPI, Rorschach and the Cornell Medical Index (CMI). While their findings do not speak to the issue of why the psychologically determined hearing loss occurred in the first place, it does give some clues for our general understanding of the dynamics involved. They found higher mean I.Q.s (Full-Scale I.Q.s of 100.6 vs. 93.3) on the WAIS for veterans who gave up their initial claim of a loss than for those who didn't (significant at the .05 level). On the MMPI, persons who resolved their loss after counseling scored higher on the Pd scale than those who did not (significant at the .05 level). This finding is the only one which was unexpected based on the above noted Gleason report. Both groups had elevations of one standard deviation on the MMPI "neurotic triad" scale. On the Rorschach, affects studied included hostility, anxiety, bodily preoccupation, dependency, and positive and neutral feelings. A greater percentage of hostile affect (significant at the .01 level) was found to occur in the unresolved group. A finding of greater percentage of overall psychopathology was also found for the unresolved group. No significant differences were found between the groups on the CMI. In a related paper by Trier and Levy[31] in the above monograph, it was noted that psychiatrists found a higher incidence of denial (significant at the .05 level) in the group having functional hearing loss than in the control group with no indications of functionally determined problems with hearing. The functional group was also noted to be more isolated socially. Further, more somatic preoccupation (e.g., tinnitus) was found in the functional group. The phenomenon of tinnitus was unfortunately not detailed so we know little in terms of frequency, duration, times of onset, nature, etc. This makes even a preliminary attempt to sort out possible organic vs. psychiatric determinants unfeasible.

Unfortunately, similar studies have not been completed on a comparable large sample of children. This is as true today as it was when Chaiklin and Ventry[4] and Ventry and Chaiklin[32] published their efforts in 1963 and 1965. Chaiklin and Ventry[4] note the predilection to explain children's functional hearing loss on psychological bases, while viewing the phenomenon in adults as an example of malingering. That no further substantive research with large samples has been reported since 1965 speaks eloquently of the neglect of this area by clinical psychology.

Incidence

The incidence of psychogenic hearing loss is largely unknown. In Gleason's military population, the incidence was 30%. In Chaiklin and Ventry[4] and Ventry and Chaiklin's[32] sample of veterans, they noted such hearing losses are more common in females than males. Why this should be is unknown. Adults having functional losses have largely been viewed as malingering for purposes of receiving compensation. Whether in the armed services, veterans' hospital, or on an outpatient basis, the negative affect this arouses in most diagnosticians is such that the focus is on "catching" the person, with little attention being paid to any possible psychopathology involved in attempting to gain remuneration for a nonexistent hearing loss. Indeed, most persons who malinger are not thought of as exhibiting psychopathology. Even further complicating the matter is that with adults, with the exception of frank hysterics, little consideration is given to thinking a hearing loss may be of psychogenic etiology. Given such an orientation, the true incidence with adults will remain a mystery. The only way to evaluate the incidence of hearing loss of psychogenic origin would be to treat every hearing loss as a potential loss secondary to both organic and psychogenic factors and investigate both their actual acuity by indirect physiological techniques and standard techniques as well as studying the actual psychopathology of each individual.

In contrast, children are more often thought of as having hearing losses of psychogenic etiology. However, there have been no careful incidence studies of this age group. The literature contains impressions, but no hard data. There are enough examples of deaf children having remarkable speech patterns or of individuals who should benefit from wearing a hearing aid but do not, to raise the question of whether underlying psychopathology is operative on a broader basis than is generally thought. Currently, successful *vs.* unsuccessful talking and use of language in hearing impaired children and adults is explained by time of onset of loss, discrimination ability, CNS functioning, inadequacies of hearing aids, etc. Significantly, attention is rarely paid to possible interactive effects of psychopathology. Without such attention and consideration, we will never know the true incidence of hearing loss of psychogenic origin in children or adults.

PSYCHOANALYTIC PERSPECTIVES

Few analytic papers have been written about problems with hearing. This is despite Freud's[8] early indication of an "ear" as part of his conceptualization of the ego. While this part of the drawing vanished in his later visual conceptualizations of the ego, he continued to emphasize the role of audition in differentiation of psychic structure. For example, in describing the principal characteristics of the ego, Freud[9] noted:

> . . . It has the task of self-preservation. As regards external events, it performs the task by becoming aware of stimuli, by storing up experiences about them (in the memory), by avoiding excessively strong stimuli (through flight), by dealing with moderate stimuli (through adaptation) and finally by learning to bring about expedient changes in the external world to its own advantages (through activity). As regards internal events in relation to the id, it performs that task by gaining control over the demands of the instincts, by deciding whether they are to be allowed satisfaction, by postponing that satisfaction to times and circumstances favourable in the external world or by suppressing their excitations entirely. (p. 145–146)

Although he refers to stimuli in general, we may take audition as one special case. In so doing, we have a paradigm in his above remarks for explaining what happens to unwelcome, as well as welcome stimuli. Further evidence for the interaction between sound and psychic phenomenon is found in the study of dreams. Freud[6] notes:

> Every noise that is indistinctly perceived arouses corresponding dream-images. A peel of thunder will set us in the midst of a battle; the crowing of a cock may turn into a man's cry of terror; the creaking of a door may produce a dream of burglars. (p. 24)

If this can happen normally during sleep, there is no reason to believe that at some level the same phenomenon does not take place in waking life and is tied to various tones or to verbal language. Castaldo and Holzman[3] have conclusively demonstrated that hearing can influence the quality of one's dream. Elsewhere Rousey[29] demonstrated that relatively little hearing loss occurs even in the deepest stages of sleep. This opens the possibility for structural modification of psychic structures twenty-four hours a day (e.g., through sounds heard at night during parental intercourse, arguments, discussions of feelings about the child, etc.) That hearing also affects superego development is also emphasized by Freud:[7]

> . . . it is as impossible for the superego as for the ego to disclaim its origins from things heard; for it is part of the ego and remains accessible to consciousness by way of these word presentations (concepts, abstractions). (p. 52–53)

Isakower[16] supports this possibility even further when he proposed ". . . the nucleus of the superego is the auditory sphere. . . " With this information in mind, it is possible to understand the numerous variations in processing auditory stimuli which were described at the outset of this chapter. Indeed, the entire gamut of psychopathology occurring as a result of structural dysfunction can be affected as a result of an individual's use of audition. Of special interest are possible variations in superego development which may occur in congenital *vs.* adventitious deafness (Goetzinger[13]). In the present context, it would be reasonable to hypothesize that there might be less feelings of guilt and a development of social mores and standards at variance with hearing individuals. This possibility needs careful and sensitive research because of the implications.

Knapp[19] has written the primary paper on the symbolic psychological meanings attached to the ear. He notes that the external ear canal—being a receptive passage—can be stimulated and penetrated. The resulting erotic and aggressive potential is self-evident. He further summarizes how the ear canal symbolically has served as a pathway for conception (e.g., the entrance of the Holy Spirit into Mary's ear resulting in the conception of

Jesus), a depository for food (to get an earful) and as an act of aggression (e.g., blow it out your ear). In some cases, Knapp[19] contends the ear lobe may also acquire a phallic significance.

Niederland[22] assumes that sound is first felt before it is heard. If this is so, then the infant in his primal state could equate sound as something which enters and is felt. It is interesting that rock music played at a high level of intensity is often described by adolescents as producing a feeling of pleasure, while adults experience distress. In the adult, the distress produces anger while in the adolescent, a surge of ecstasy with decided sexual implications often occurs. The consequences of these two affects are a familiar experience in the relationships between parents and adolescents. If sound produces such meanings, it is theoretically understandable why one coping mechanism of the ego may be a pseudo-deafness. Von Frey[33] has also described the erotic potential of sound. The early difference in sound-making by a child's father and mother may be interpreted by a child in sexual and aggressive ways. Another index of the importance of hearing sound to personality development is documented by Burlingham's[2] description of use of sound by blind children. Here, sound is used for the purpose of recognizing important figures. The resulting object internalization is thus closely tied to and affected by the sounds heard.

A more recent formulation of the psychological meaning of sound has been proposed by Rousey.[28] Although the formulation was with reference to speech defects, the theory has relevance for understanding the psychological meaning which may become attached to heard sound. In this approach, the elements of spoken speech (i.e., vowels and consonants) are viewed as drive expressions and indications of object relationship development respectively. Although there are elements of various frequencies in the formants of both vowels and consonants, the production of a vowel sound is a closer approximation to a pure tone than would be found in a consonant. Thus, a pseudo-deafness for various frequencies has the potential for serving as a signal of drive distress which could then be handled by a person by "turning off" of sound (i.e., becoming psychogenically deaf). In general, front vowels in phonetic theory have higher frequency components than back vowels. Culturally, it is believed low guttural sounds are associated with aggression, whilst the high fine delicate sound of the violin generally is thought of as embodying creativity and sexuality in its broadest sense. Loud sounds are similarly associated with aggression, while soft sounds are experienced as protective and nurturant. Thus, it would be hypothesized that acuity for higher frequencies and sensitivity for low intensities would be most susceptible to psychogenic deafness if the person were conflicted around sexual drives; while acuity for lower frequencies and sensitivity to loud sounds would be involved were the conflict around aggression. That in practice there is often a diminution of many frequencies in persons with psychogenic deafness does not negate the premise. Rather, it illustrates the psychoanalytic understanding of drive expression—that is, that there is a fusion of aggression and sexuality with one drive dominant at one point and the other at some other point in time.

Freud[10] also noted that hysterical deafness is rarely bilateral. He did not comment on the tendency for it to occur in the right or left ear. In the present author's experience, there has been a tendency for such forms of deafness to occur in the left ear. For example, an adolescent patient of the author's lost her hearing for tones and understanding speech in the left ear following a seduction by her stepfather. Therapy revealed the "rupture" of her ability to hear was closely related to her loss of virginity. A definitive statement of dynamics in terms of ear choice in unilateral psychogenic deafness remains open for study.

For their part, consonant sounds give intelligibility to vowel sounds. It is these sounds which may be involved in the experience of not understanding the speech of others. Since understanding what is said requires the presence of another person, deafness of psychogenic origin usually contains elements of early object relationship disturbances. It is a common experience for persons to say I can hear male voices, but not female voices or vice versa, yet have no demonstrable kind of loss which would really explain sex specific trouble in understanding. In line with the present proposal, what is probably meant is that the sound of a male or female voice arouses such conflict over drives that the individual can only deal with it by not hearing a male or female voice.

UNDERSTANDING PSYCHOGENIC HEARING LOSS

With the foregoing in mind, it is clear that sound not only has multiple meanings, but also can affect psychological development in many ways. As evident from earlier remarks, having to designate someone as having a pseudo-loss of hearing has produced clinical problems for audiologists and otologists. This is probably so because of failure of these disciplines to understand that a loss of hearing can be used as a coping device at several levels of psychopathology rather than only reflecting malingering or hysteria.

One approach to ordering our understnading of the interaction of the symptom of not hearing with psychological functioning is to use Menninger's[21] conception of the five levels of dyscontrol which may affect an individual's vital psychological balance. These levels of dyscontrol are to be distinguished from the transient coping behavior used by most people at varying times in their life. Examples of such normal devices are dreams, laughing, crying, fantasy, physical exercise, etc.

First Level of Dyscontrol

When the level of psychological tension increases sufficiently so the above coping procedures do not help, an individual slips into the first level of dysfunction. Common psychological maneuvers found at this level are hypervigilance, hyperemotionalism, hyperkinesis, hyperintellection, and hypercompensation. The psychological defense of denial is also used at this level. Indeed, the insistence that no sound is made when it, in fact, is present is about as clear an operational definition of denial as can be found. Thus, selective—albeit transitory—deafness between husband and wife or parent and child is seen as an early indication of dyscontrol on this first level. The frequency and intensity of this type of hearing problem depends on the level of affect attached to the relationships as well as the individual's internal stability. Not hearing is then a symptom. Inasmuch as all psychological symptoms represent a compromise between an internal wish and reality, contain pleasurable and aggressive elements and serve as a form of self-punishment (Menninger),[21] we have available for psychological study a simple form of psychogenic hearing loss. Although formal audiological tests would probably fail to reveal a loss, it is real for the people involved. The resulting affect is real and, depending on the frequency and intensity of this behavior, the net result for the parties involved may be quite destructive; for example, child or spouse abuse, separation, divorce, etc. Because such a psychological situation is infinitely easier to understand than the more complicated levels of dyscontrol described in the following paragraphs, it can serve as a point of interface for the disciplines of psychology, audiology, and otology in their training to understand the dynamic factors involved in hearing loss.

Second Level of Dyscontrol

It is in the second level of dyscontrol that we find the psychological behavior most likely observed in cases of psychogenically determined hearing loss which come to the attention of the audiologist or otologist. This stage is characterized by a person having a slight detachment from reality and his environment. Both sexual and aggressive instincts show dyscontrol at this level. Because these drives may be expressed through speech and sound, they readily become entwined with disturbances in hearing.

Psychosomatic Problems and Psychogenic Hearing Loss Superimposed on Hearing Loss Caused by Organic Factors.

While psychosomatic medicine has made singular advances in understanding mind/body interrelationships (e.g., understanding the psychological origin of ulcers), little is known of somatization as it pertains to the hearing mechanism. Occasionally one sees articles relating to Ménière's disease, Bartemeier[1]. This disorder characterized by vertigo, tinnitus, and fluctuating hearing loss affects the cochlea. Given the current knowledge obtained by biofeedback experiments, it seems plausible that psychologically induced vasomotor constriction or dilation could affect the cochlea. Another type of hearing loss which may well be psychosomatic in etiology is that ascribed to pregnancy. A possible dynamic explanation is that the woman's anger over her pregnancy is displaced onto the act of hearing. We have already seen the symbolic connection of the ear with fertility as detailed by Knapp.[19] Thus, by becoming deaf, the superego of the mother who gives birth to an unwanted child is served by symbolically punishing her through reduction of her capacity for further auditory "conception." Another example of such displacement of anger and guilt to one's body can be illustrated by a patient where a unilateral loss of hearing followed the death of a sibling. In the mind of the survivor, there was a penalty to be paid for feelings of anger and jealousy which, in a childish sense, were seen as causative factors in the death of the sibling. The penalty paid by becoming unilaterally deaf was behaviorally and economically a sound sacrificial compromise. Only a careful psychological evaluation would uncover such features of psychological functioning. Consequently, deafness related to dysfunctional handling of aggressive drives will usually go undetected.

Problems with aggression can be controlled by dissociation and disavowel, displacement to one's body and use of magic, symbol or ritual. Such maneuvers are most easily seen in some aphasic patients. In such individuals, true difficulty in hearing (i.e., understanding) is based on cortical or midbrain dysfunction rather than cochlear dysfunction. Psychogenic factors can simulate the same overt behavior. How psychological problems become involved with hearing and understanding can be illustrated by the behavior of a patient who was having an extramarital affair and subsequently became involved in an accident. Because of head trauma sustained in the accident, he was first thought to be aphasic. It could be demonstrated that his acuity for sound was normal and that he understood his doctors, yet he maintained the role of being unable to hear his wife when she asked what happened. In another instance, a young adolescent girl involved in a hit-and-run accident lay for days in a coma seeming not to hear. There was reason to believe she felt somehow she had caused the accident. By staying silent—not seeming to hear or speak—she dealt with her feelings and also punished herself. In this instance, merely by recognizing in front of her and her physician the affect which was involved allowed her in a day's time to recover her hearing and speaking. Such intervention occurred early in her hospitalization, thus preventing any role being adopted which would have been psychologically difficult to abandon.

The second level of dyscontrol may require the individual to make compensatory adjustments or use devices (often expensive) in order to keep some semblance of comfort. One clinical example of this is found in the adolescent who, overwhelmed with psychological distress, is suddenly found to have a mild to moderate impairment of hearing. When subsequently fitted with a hearing aid, she hears well. It could be demonstrated that she had no real loss of acuity, but through wearing a hearing aid, she elicited enough pity and support to at least temporarily quell her psychological distress. Fittings without the confirmation of definite medical problems were more possible in the past than now because of current federal emphasis on having a complete otological examination prior to a hearing aid fitting. However, it still remains possible for the adult or child who is lonely and feeling cut off from the world to be fitted with a hearing aid even though the loss is psychogenically determined. This use of a hearing aid should not be too startling if one considers the positive effects of the numerous trips made to physicians by lonely people with psychosomatic illnesses who need nurturance and recognition as opposed to orthodox medical intervention. Intermittent or inconsistent wearing of a properly fitted hearing aid can be a behavioral manifestation suggesting possible hearing loss of psychological origin. The previously noted current tendency to ignore psychogenic factors as a result of training and/or orientation obviously is complicated further by the above noted realities of our daily lives. The prevalence of persons who fall in this category is unknown, but needs careful study.

Neurotic Problems. A related phenomenon is deafness subsequent to hysterical factors. It is this area of psychological functioning which, next to malingering, has received the most attention from audiologists and otologists. A major complicating psychological factor is the correct assessment of hysteria. In this regard, Zetzel's[35] description of levels of functioning labeled as hysteria is relevant. She speaks of true good hysterics (persons who have experienced a genuine triangular conflict, yet have been able to retain good preoedipal object relationships); potentially good hysterics (persons who are younger, less mature, more passive, less successful in achieving and who have trouble in the establishment of a stable analytic situation); persons with hysterical symptomatology which disguises an underlying depressive character structure and, finally, persons whose overt hysterical symptomatology proves to be pseudo-oedipal and pseudo-genital. Thus, persons with a hearing loss thought to be hysterical in nature, but in reality related to personality features found in her third and fourth groups, present difficult treatment problems. When they do not respond to psychotherapy based on the diagnosis of hysteria, it would be tempting to try to find some organic factors. Undoubtedly, this is one factor involved in the current turning away by audiologists and otologists from study of psychogenic deafness. The issue is further complicated by use outside of the disciplines of clinical psychology and psychiatry of the terms psychogenic and hysterical as meaning the same thing. Precisely how deafness is symptomatic for what Zetzel[35] terms "true good hysteria" has never been clinically dilineated. Little help is given in this regard by Breuer's (Freud)[7] description of Fraulein Anne O.'s hearing loss. He noted not only that his patient did not appear to hear when alone and spoken to; but that she also did not hear when someone came in, when several people were talking and when she was frightened or there was movement. Since most hysterical patients are not blatantly psychologically ill, it is not surprising that the examining audiologist or otologist overlooks this possibility. Further, if a patient hears normally in one ear, it could be quite likely there would be no complaint of hearing difficulty by the patient or observation of a handicap by the psychologist or psychiatrist treating someone with the diagnosis of hysteria. The resulting "catch-22" situation prevents both an accurate estimate of the prevalence of hearing loss subsequent to hysteria as well as an intensive exploration of dynamics which might be operative.

Character Problems. It is hearing loss in persons with personality deviations which have been most comfortably approached by the otologist and audiologist. Such persons are likely to be labeled as malingerers. Among many professional people, malingering has never been considered an illness, but rather a behavior—almost criminal—which needs to be detected and announced to the world. Yet the personality deviation which allows this to occur represents a longstanding structural deformity of the ego. The orientation which allows aggressive and inappropriate acquiring of others' money as a result of malingering is usually ego syntonic. In Menninger's[21] words:

> No healthy person, no healthy-minded person would go to such extremes and take such devious and painful routes for minor gains that the invalid status brings to the malingerer. (p. 208)

That previous psychological studies and views of psychogenic hearing loss do not conceptualize malingering in such serious terms probably reflects the current popularity of the statistical *vs.* dynamic approach to psychiatric diagnosis.

Third Level of Dyscontrol

Menninger's third order of dyscontrol centers around more frank outbursts of aggression and divergence from reality testing. Because of the nature of the symptomatology (i.e., more open expression of raw agression), relatively little hearing dysfunction has been reported. It is likely that a great deal exists.

Fourth Level of Dyscontrol

In the fourth order of dyscontrol, one may see severe depression, manic behavior, autistic regression, delusions, and confused disorientation. Such behavior may occur in psychologically determined deafness in, for example, students who have been used to structure and identity provided by schools for the deaf, but which are lost upon graduation. It may erupt in students in schools for the deaf who cannot adjust or make use of the schooling and who are expelled. In the past, such ego ruptures have been understood in part as a consequence of lack of adequate language or the intolerance of the hearing world. Explaining such behavior solely in this way violates the principles of overdetermination of all behavior. One consequence has been to obscure the psychological understanding of persons whose deafness is of psychogenic origin.

Some illustrations of psychopathology which occur in such instances will underline the destructive consequences of not recognizing deafness of psychogenic origin. One such "deaf" person was so inept in school, he was expelled and went to live with his parents. His basic disorganization was so great that, overwhelmed by inappropriate sexual stimuli in his home environment and deprived of the identity of a "deaf person," he borrowed the family car and, while taking a drive, stopped indiscriminately at a farm home and stabbed the woman who answered the door. In another case, upon graduation from a school for the deaf and subsequent difficulty in comfortably relating to the deaf community, the person went berserk and was hospitalized in a state mental hospital. Because the staff thought him deaf, treatment of his mental illness—a psychosis—was subverted for a time. His use of deafness during his early years can be said to have bound his psychosis. When this mode of adaptation (i.e., being accepted as a deaf student) was taken away, his mental illness predominated.

Fifth Level of Dyscontrol

In the fifth order of dyscontrol which Menninger[21] characterized as "beyond psychosis," whether there is psychogenic deafness is beside the point. For it is at this level that psychogenic death (aphanisis) and suicide attempts and completions are seen.

FINAL REMARKS

By now it is clear that the author takes issue with current conceptualizations of the relationship between auditory problems and psychological factors primarily because there has been an attempt to group the symptom (hearing loss) under the simplistic categories of malingering or hysteria. This has occurred because few otologists or audiologists have any indepth training in psychiatric problems—let alone, psychoanalysis. There are even fewer psychiatrists, psychologists, or analysts who treat the deaf. It has only been in recent years that the psychotherapy with the deaf received any attention (Rainer and Altschuler)[23]. In a recent article published in Europe, one otologist (Wind)[34] cautiously advanced thoughts on what he termed the borderland between psychiatry and otorhinolaryngology. In this article, he notes only that hearing loss may be a form of conversion hysteria and that a slight impairment may be associated with a neurosis; thus, perpetuating the errors in conceptualization addressed earlier in this chapter.

Probably it is best to continue to use the term psychogenic deafness to initially categorize the clinical problems covered in this chapter. The turmoil over terminology (e.g., malingering, hysteria, functional, nonorganic, psychogenic, auditory regression, auricular pithiatism, sinistrosis) will continue among audiologists and otologists until they recognize the broader psychological issues described in this chapter. The suggested use of Menninger's[21] level of dyscontrol, as expostulated above, would offer a way of clarifying the true meaning of psychogenic deafness for any one individual.

Finally, one controversial implication of the material advanced here is the possibility of a high and unrecognized incidence of psychogenic hearing loss in students in schools for the deaf, among hearing aid users, and in the general population without confirmed organic antecedents. Of course, the possibility remains even where organic factors are present that there may also be a psychogenic overlay. The validity of this assertion will have to await carefully controlled clinical studies where not only physical, but also psychological factors are studied.

REFERENCES

1. Bartemeier, L. Ménière's syndrome revisited. *Bulletin of the Menninger Clinic,* **42**:350–51 (1978).
2. Burlingham, D. Hearing and its role in the development of the blind. Psychoanalytic Study of the Child, **19**:95–112 (1964).
3. Castaldo, V., and Holzman, P. The effects of hearing one's voice on sleep mentation. *J. of Neurological and Mental Disease,* **144**:2–13 (1967).
4. Chaiklin, J., and Ventry, I. Functional hearing loss. In: *Modern Developments in Audiology,* J. Jerger (ed.) New York: Acdemic Press, 76–125 (1963).
5. Davis, H. Principles of electric response audiometry. *Annals of Otology, Rhinology and Laryngology,* **28**(85)#3-part 3 (1976).
6. Freud, S. *Standard Edition—Vol. 4.* London: Hogarth Press, 1953.

7. Freud, S. *Standard Edition—Vol. 2*. London: Hogarth Press, 1955.
8. Freud, S. *Standard Edition—Vol. 19*. London: Hogarth Press, 1961.
9. Freud, S. *Standard Edition—Vol. 23*. London: Hogarth Press, 1964.
10. Freud, S. *Standard Edition—Vol. 1*, London: Hogarth Press, 1966.
11. Gleason, J. Psychological characteristics of the audiologically inconsistent patient. *Archives of Otolaryngology*, **68**:42-6 (1958).
12. Goetzinger, C. Word discrimination testing. In: *Handbook of Clinical Audiology*. J. Katz (ed.) Baltimore: Williams and Wilkins Co., 157-179 (1972).
13. Goetzinger, C. Personal communication, 1979.
14. Goetzinger, C., and Proud, G. Examination techniques for evaluating malingering and psychogenic disabilities. *J. of Kansas Medical Society*, **LIX**(3)95-101 (1958).
15. Hopkinson, N. Speech tests for pseudo hypacusis. In: *Handbook of Clinical Audiology*, Second Ed. J. Katz (ed.) Baltimore: Williams and Wilkins Co., 291-303 (1978).
16. Isakower, O. On the exceptional position of the auditory sphere. *International J. of Psychoanalysis*, **20**:340-48 (1939).
17. Jewett, D., and Williston, J. Auditory-evoked far field averaged from the scalp of humans. *Brain*, **94**:681-96 (1971).
18. Keith, R. *Central Auditory Dysfunction*. New York: Grune & Stratton, 1972.
19. Knapp, P. The ear, listening and hearing. *J. of American Psychoanalytic Assn.*, **1**(4)672-89 (1953).
20. Martin, F. Nonorganic hearing loss: An overview and pure tone tests. In: *Handbook of Clinical Audiology*, J. Katz. (ed.) Baltimore: Williams and Wilkins Co., 357-73 (1972).
21. Menninger, K. *The Vital Balance*. New York: Viking Press, 1963.
22. Niederland, W. Early auditory experiences, beating fantasies, and primal scene. *Psychoanalytic Study of the Child*, **13**:471-504 (1958).
23. Rainer, J., and Altschuler, K. *Comprehensive Mental Health Services for the Deaf*. New York: New York State Psychiatric Institute, 1966.
24. Ramsdell, D. The psychology of the hard of hearing and deafened adults. In: *Hearing and Deafness*, H. Davis and S. Silverman (ed.). New York: Holt, Rinehart and Winston, Inc., 459-76 (1960).
25. Reiter, L. Experiments re: clinical application of reflex modulation audiometry. Accepted for publication in *J. of Speech and Hearing Research*, 1979.
26. Reiter, L., and Ison, J. Inhibition of the human eyeblink reflex: an evaluation of the sensitivity of the Wendt-Yerkes method for threshold detection. *J. of Experimental Psychology: Human Perception and performance*, **3**:325-36 (1977).
27. Rousey, C. *Indirect Assessment of Hearing Sensitivity by Changes in Respiration* (Report No. 6-1572). Washington DC: U.S. Dept. of Health, Education and Welfare, Bureau of Education for the Handicapped, May, 1969.
28. Rousey, C. *Psychiatric Assessment by Speech and Hearing Behavior*. Springfield, Illinois: Charles C Thomas, 1974.
29. Rousey, C. Auditory acuity during sleep. *Psychophysiology*, **16**:363-66 (1979).
30. Shea, J. *Fluctuant Hearing Loss*. Philadelphia: W. B. Saunders, Co., 1975.
31. Trier, T., and Levy, R. Social and psychological characteristics of veterans with functional hearing loss. In: *Multidiscipline Study of Functional Hearing Loss. J. of Auditory Research*, **5**:241-56 (1965).
32. Ventry, I., and Chaiklin, J. Multidiscipline study of functional hearing loss. *J. of Auditory Research*, **5**:179-272 (1965).
33. Von Frey, M. *Vorlesunger über Physiologie*. Berlin: Springer, 1920.
34. Wind, J. On mental conditions: A review of the borderland between psychiatry and otorhinolaryngology. *Minerva Otolaryngologica*, **27**:39-46 (1977).
35. Zetzel, E. *The Capacity for Emotional Growth*. New York: International Universities Press, 1970.

Family relationships are viewed by the author as the critical factor in cases of suicidal children and adolescents, and treatment of these cases by means of conjoint family therapy is described. Characteristics typical of families at the time of the suicidal crisis are noted and the way in which the achievement of autonomy by the child is impeded. Disposition decisions are discussed as a logical consequence of the assessment of the family and criteria for hospitalization or outpatient treatment are indicated. Qualifications for therapists for this type of work are discussed, and in conclusion the author comments on the need for more education about suicide and its prevention.

13 Family Treatment of Suicidal Children and Adolescents

Joseph Richman, Ph.D.

Suicidal behavior and more broadly self-destructive behavior, has become widespread among the young, the varied forms ranging from drug abuse and reckless driving to direct and completed suicide. The increasing incidence of such acts has become a focus of growing social concern, among both the families of the young and within the larger society. This chapter is primarily concerned with attempted suicides, that is, survivors of deliberate infliction of harm upon the self for the purpose of causing death or damage. But the implications extend to other forms of self-harm.

In addition, while I shall deal primarily with those who have attempted suicide and survived, the problem of completed suicide cannot be ignored. Suicide is the second most frequent cause of death among adolescents and young people (accidents are first); and it is likely that many deaths officially listed as accidents are suicides in disguise. Moreover, the actual suicide rate is undoubtedly higher than the official one, since many suicides are concealed, primarily due to the stigma attached to the act.

THE NATURE OF SUICIDE IN THE CHILD AND ADOLESCENT: FIVE CASE VIGNETTES

How does suicidal behavior come about, and who are most vulnerable to its manifestations? The literature indicates that the suicidal impulse touches members of every class of society, and can begin as early as three years of age. Although for most people, childhood can be considered a time of hope, developing friendships, dawning school interests, and pleasure in activity, pain and despair also exist in that period. Rudyard Kipling, in his autobiographical short story, "Bah, Bah, Black Sheep," described the suicide attempt of a six-year-old boy after he was taken from his home and parents in India, to be boarded in England with a brutal and insensitive family.

Different, but within the same unhappy and self-destructive framework, was the case of an eight-year-old girl admitted to Jacobi Hospital, who attempted suicide after her depressed mother had gone to a hospital for an abortion, leaving her child with the frightening message that she might never return, and putting her in the charge of a twelve-year-old brother, who beat her unmercifully.

While suicide and other disturbed behavior during latency may be a surprise to some, the trials and tribulations of adolescence are well known. Adolescence is traditionally a time of extremes—of life, hope, and expanding horizons on the one hand; serious emotional storms and stress on the other. Everything is possible; yet the problems of life may appear insurmountable.

Martin Buber (1955), for example, described how he as an adolescent almost ended his life because he was unable to resolve a philosophical problem: "When I was about fourteen years of age I myself experienced this [the danger of trying to conceptualize both finite and infinite space] in a way which has deeply influenced my whole life. A necessity I could not understand swept over me: I had to try again and again to imagine the edge of space or its edgelessness, time with a beginning and an end or time without beginning or end, and both were equally impossible, equally hopeless—yet there seemed to be only the choice between the one or the other absurdity. Under an irresistible compulsion I reeled from one to the other, at times so closely threatened with the danger of madness that I seriously thought of avoiding it by suicide" (p. 136).

Was young Buber's life really in danger because of an insoluble philosophical problem, or were there more personal reasons? In that period of his life, he was sent from Germany to his grandfather's house in Galicia and back to his parents again. His parents then divorced. The unanswerable questions about the nature of space and time may have been a metaphor for the sense of being in an impossible human and family situation.

Arthur Rubenstein (1973) also described how he seriously attempted suicide at the age of nineteen, and his subsequent rebirth experience. His career had come to an end, or so it seemed to him; he was penniless, literally starving, facing eviction from his hotel room, and estranged from his family. In a state of complete despair, he hung himself with his bathrobe belt. But the belt broke, and he fell to the floor with a crash. Stunned, he lay there in a state of shock. Finally, he cried bitterly, or, as he put it, cried himself out in music. After he stopped crying and went out, he saw the world anew; he had been reborn.

Buber and Rubenstein resolved their suicidal episodes, and went on to grow and mature in life. However, not all children are as fortunate. A famous and more unusual example is Thomas Chatterton (Meyerstein, 1972), whom scholars consider to be one of the precursors of the romantic school of English poetry. He killed himself at the age of seventeen when some remarkable poems which he claimed were newly discovered medieval works, were correctly suspected as having been written by himself.

These suicidal children and adolescents were very different and at the same time so very much alike, whether one is referring to Kipling, a future gifted writer at the threshold of latency; or a little eight-year-old black girl on the psychiatric ward of a city hospital. Both had something in common: they were separated from their parents, and at the mercy of cruel guardians. Rubenstein, too, was separated from his parents, and he also dated the problem to an earlier separation in latency. "I suppose that the main reason for the estrangement from my family," he wrote, "lay in the fact that my parents sent me to live among strangers . . . at an age when I was most vulnerable" (1973, p. 72). Chatterton was also alone and without his family. Shortly before his suicide, he wrote a poem to Peter Smith, a close friend who had also killed himself, in which he savagely blamed the family. Finally, Buber, as we saw, was shuttled between his parents' and his grandfather's home, while facing the loss of his parents through divorce.

These five cases were chosen at random; yet all of these children were separated, estranged, or facing the dissolution of their families. This, I suspect, is the conceptual unifying thread running through the stories of suicidal children and adolescents, and the relationship between their self-destructive act and family relationships. It, too, is the clinical basis for treatment and rehabilitation of the troubled, self-destructive child. As such, this paper shall explore the nature of suicide in the child and adolescent, in particular its roots in family processes and crises; and its treatment through activating the healing powers of the family.

CONCEPTUAL ORIENTATION: FAMILY PROCESSES AND CRISES

All modern understanding of suicide, in my opinion, is built upon the pioneering contributions of Freud (1917) and Durkheim (1897), Freud for the understanding of the individual, including the vicissitudes of drives and object relationships, and the ego changes attendant upon suicide; and Durkheim for his masterful contribution to the sociology of suicide, which has major implications for the social and family systems approach to treatment. The essence of Durkheim's theory is condensed in his aphoristic summary: "Suicide varies inversely with the degree of integration of the social groups of which the individual forms a part" (1897, p. 209).

With a shift in emphasis, this formulation can be applied to the suicidal individual: "Suicide varies inversely with the degree of integration between the individual and the social groups of which that individual is a part." Therefore, whatever fosters social alienation contributes to suicide, given certain facilitating conditions (to be described later), while whatever fosters social cohesion contributes to life rather than suicide.

While Erikson (1963) did not deal directly with the problem of suicide, his description of "The eight ages of man" has provided a host of fruitful clinical insights into the concrete internal and external pressures and crises that have impelled persons towards suicidal acts at different periods of their lives. By and large, suicide in the child and adolescent can best be understood as an interconnected reaction to developmental tasks and family pressures.

In the child, the major developmental tasks incldue the establishment of interests outside the home, especially in school and peer relationships. The capacity for future intimacy may be laid down at this time (Sullivan, 1953). These tasks may then conflict with an overly close identification with a depressed or suicidal parent, combined with an arousal of feelings of threat or anxiety in the parents and child over leaving the home—which symbolizes the first step toward leaving the familial rest.

The developmental demands of adolescence call for still more expanding horizons: the establishment of autonomy and a clear ego identity; the development of friendships outside the home; sexual relationships (hopefully, also outside the home); the achievement of success at school, work, the beginnings of a career, and the first steps toward leaving the family of origin and setting up a family of one's own. All of these tasks are occasions of pleasure to most families. However, they are experiences of deep pain and the threat of loss to some. Such families therefore see the outside world as an enemy, and set up protective barriers to shield themselves. The family thus becomes a closed system and tries to avert these necessary changes of adolescence. In addition, the family is very ambivalent; it wishes the adolescent to succeed in the very tasks that are seen as a danger.

The family, then, is at risk at the time the troubled adolescent becomes suicidal. In a series of studies by Rosenbaum and myself (see refs.) the following characteristics are noted as typical of the family at the time of a suicidal crisis in one of its members:

1. An inability to accept necessary changes, including an intolerance for separation, a symbiosis without empathy, and infantile fixations (Richman, 1978);

2. Role disturbances (Richman and Rosenbaum, 1969);
3. Affect disturbances, including a one-sided handling of aggression, a family-based depression, and sexual difficulties with incestuous overtones (Rosenbaum and Richman, 1970);
4. Interpersonal difficulties, including a reliance upon scapegoating, double-binding, and sado-masochistic relationships (Richman, 1971);
5. A closed family system which is dominated by a fragile family member (Richman, 1979);
6. Communication disturbances (Richman, 1973);
7. An intolerance for crises (Richman, 1980).

Clearly, there is a meshing of these family characteristics with the adolescent task of achieving autonomy and moving out of the home. Therefore, adolescence is a time of particular susceptibility to such conflicts, and suicide is one extreme outcome of the unresolved interaction between developmental demands and family factors.

CLINICAL IMPLICATIONS: FAMILY TREATMENT

It follows from the above that family therapy is the treatment of choice for suicidal children and adolescents. This derives from its ability to foster cohesion with the suicidal person's primary group, while at the same time setting the groundwork for autonomy and independence. Family therapy is consistent with the Durkheimian emphasis upon social factors. It is also compatible with Freud's formulation. Through family therapy, there is a major opportunity to help activate the ego reparative functions of the suicidal individual, arrest and reverse the regressive processes of the instinctual drives and object relations, and help alleviate the melancholia that occurs in suicidal persons, which is intimately related to alienation.

Assessment

A comprehensive individual and family assessment is required for evaluation of suicidal potential, as well as planning for treatment and management. Evaluation of the family system includes its potential to heal and build up as well as to break down and destroy its members. Consequently, the relatives of the child as well as the suicidal child or adolescent, are seen. The most effective procedure is first to see each member of the family alone in order to obtain his/her individual perception of the situation, establish rapport, and invite his/her respective collaboration in the therapeutic endeavor. This is best followed by a family interview (Richman, 1979).

Figure drawings are extremely valuable diagnostic aids (Richman, 1972;

Richman and Pfeffer, 1977). Such drawings are obtained from all participants, including the suicidal child and each relative. They serve as a quick screening device to evaluate personality factors in general and suidical impulses in particular. The majority of the figure drawings of the suicidal persons contain slash-like lines, especially at the neck and wrists, but sometimes in other areas. These seem to represent a nonverbal communication of an angry or destructive impulse, turned against the self.

It is noteworthy that the drawings of the family members also contain these slash lines, often in individuals who disclaim any suicidal impulses of their own. The implication is that the overtly suicidal member may be acting out the destructive and self-destructive impulses of the whole family system.

The most crucial assessment procedure, however, is the conjoint family interview, when the family members are all seen together. At the beginning of the interview they are told: "I have seen each one of you individually and obtained your perceptions of the situation. Now, your job is to face each other, talk about what happened, share your understanding, and discuss what can be done so that this need not happen again." The therapist then sits back and lets the family interact with one another. During the second half of the session, the therapist is more active and directive. For this more structured segment, Wells and Rabiner's "Index of Family Tensions" (Wells and Rabiner, 1973) is very helpful. The Index is part of a complex, structured family diagnostic interview, one part of which consists of a systematic inquiry regarding areas of family tension, and a rating of the degree of disagreement or conflict in each area. The nine areas cover the most frequent sources of family tension, such as employment, living arrangements, maintenance of the home, financial matters, social matters including choice of friends and activities, religion, health, parent-child relations, and sexual relations. Although there is not always time to utilize their method in as systamatic a manner as would be optimally desirable, it still serves as a valuable guide.

Disposition

A major question to be answered by the assessment is that of disposition. In the emergency room, for example, should the patient be sent home, referred to an outpatient clinic or crisis center, or admitted to the hospital? Should there be a question of hospitalization, the criteria are fourfold:

1. The degree of stress or distress, and of the decompensation of resources and defenses in the suicidal individual. Indications of failing defenses include evidence of losses of control over impulse, severe

depressive manifestations, psychosis, and an inability to function socially. In someone who is or was actively suicidal, these are all major indicators for hospitalization.

2. The degree to which hospitalization will disrupt rather than facilitate ongoing functioning. Hospitalization would be much more desirable for a suicidal adolescent who has dropped out of school, is not working, and remains at home, for example, than for one who has managed to maintain these functions.

3. The availability and cooperativeness of the family. If the family members are falling apart and showing evidence of decompensation, especially if the presence of the suicidal child or adolescent is perceived as endangering the integrity of some key member of the family, hospitalization is much more likely to be recommended. Such a step, however, contains its own dangers, and is neither to be undertaken lightly, nor to be acted upon without the participation of the family.

One suicidal young man, for example, swallowed poison and was hospitalized. The parents were mainly concerned with concealing this from the maternal grandmother who lived with them and was very "nervous." They also believed that the grandmother should not know of the hospitalization, since it was considered a stigma. A double-bind was thus created, in which the patient could not be home; yet hospitalization was seen as a disgrace to the entire family. Eventually, the patient was discharged, returned home, and killed himself.

Perhaps such incidents are inevitable. However, it may be noted that this patient was treated purely in individual treatment, and it is conceivable that working with the family might have resulted in a less tragic outcome.

4. The availability of adequate outpatient resources. The disposition may sometimes depend upon whether an experienced therapist is available to see the suicidal patient. It has been my personal experience that the psychiatrist in the psychiatric emergency room call and ask if I, or someone else who is knowledgeable about suicide, can see a patient. If the answer is yes, the doctor will arrange an immediate referral; if no, the doctor will admit the patient.

A comprehensive suicide prevention center is to be preferred over such individual recourses. This type of center can provide a wide variety of services, including crisis intervention, long-term therapy, a telephone hot line, and follow-up arrangements.

There is some evidence in favor of the outpatient treatment of suicidal patients, by therapists experienced in suicidology and with hospital backup available. Langsley and Kaplan (1968) in Denver successfully provided outpatient family crisis intervention in place of inpatient hospitalization. Although they were not dealing with suicidal patients per se, over 40% of their population actually had significant problems with suicidal and/or homicidal impulses.

What the individual clinician chooses depends upon his theoretical orientation, combined with his training, experience and comfort with such patients. In my own practice, I most often prefer to see the suicidal patient in outpatient therapy. My inclination is to take a calculated risk and see the adolescent and his family conjointly in outpatient crisis intervention, provided that they all agree to this, and a clear therapeutic contract and alliance has been achieved. In place of the hospital, then, the therapist offers himself and an alliance with the family.

Case History

The following is a selection from a wealth of rich data that emerged from a combined individual and family assessment.

The patient was an eighteen-year-old male high-school senior, with epilepsy, who was hospitalized after taking an overdose of phenobarbital. Individual and family diagnostic interviews were conducted with him, his twenty-three-year-old sister, and sixty-two-year-old father. The reason given by the patient for his suicide attempt was failure in one of his high-school courses, resulting in failure to graduate. His father attributed the attempt to the patient's epilepsy and overall violent temperament. Father in fact reported that he was afraid to fall asleep, lest the patient enter his room and kill him. The young man's sister thought, rather, their mother's death two years ago from cancer was most important. In the family interview, father reported that his son had stopped studying, played hookey, and slept up to sixteen hours a day. The patient explained that he felt depressed, and "I want to join my mother."

In the course of the individual interview, each of the family members were asked to draw a picture of a person; and these were utilized as a screening personality device. The figure drawing of the patient suggested many neurotic, characterological, and impulse control disturbances, as well as depression, marked immaturity, and strong dependency needs. A hysterical quality was also apparent. The father appeared intelligent, markedly compulsive, furiously angry, and evidenced strong underlying oral dependency needs of his own. The sister emerged as obsessive and ideational, matching her father's compulsivity.

Dynamically, the drawings suggested a pattern of dependency in the patient, punitiveness and pseudo-masculinity in the father, and anxiety and avoidance in the sister. It is interesting, in light of the similarities of defenses and character, that the family interview indicated an alliance between father and sister, countered by one between mother and son (the patient). It is also of interest that the drawings of the father and sister contained "suicidal slashes" on the wrists and, questionably, on the neck; but they were not present in the patient's drawings, the one who actually acted out the suicidal impulse. It is not an infrequent pattern, however, for the drawings by relatives, rather than those by the identified patient to contain suicidal indicators. In short, hypothetically, this patient was a dependent and suggestible youngest child, who was acting out the depression, unresolved grief, frustrated rage, death wishes, and self-destructive impulses of his entire family.

Nevertheless, I saw no evidence of psychosis in the drawings. Consistent with this impression, the communication during the family interview was less devious and more direct than in more seriously disturbed, high-risk suicidal subjects and family. The patient did look as though he could function on the outside with support. I thought that family therapy could be feasible, with the goal of helping the patient and father, in particular, to accept or at least to tolerate each other, and to help them to decide whether to live alone or separately. However, both the father and sister were under too great a strain. Therefore, it was appropriate for the patient to be hospitalized, as he had been.

In the family interview, it was also disclosed that the entire family turned away from the patient after the mother's death. The sister married four months later and left the house. She became increasingly detached from her brother, their contacts consisting primarily of telephone calls scolding him for doing so poorly in school. In addition, the patient's initial, very positive and friendly relationship with his sister's fiancé/husband ceased as the sister removed herself.

The patient and his father were thus left together, and the relationship between them, which had always been antagonistic, worsened. After an extensive telephone talk with his sister, during which she criticized the patient for over an hour, his father started scolding him, taking off where his sister had stopped. The patient then picked up a knife and went after his father, but stopped short of an actual attack. The next day, he made his suicide attempt.

This pattern, in which the sister removed herself while the patient became centrally involved in the family conflicts, was the prevailing one of the family. Mother and father had fought bitterly. The patient was strongly identified with his mother, and was seen as her surrogate by the entire family. In the fights between mother and father, mother used to call out to the patient for help, crying "See what he's doing to me!"; and he felt scarred by these verbal and physical altercations. His sister, on the other hand, to quote father, "built a wall and didn't hear it, so to speak; closed herself in her room. But he saw all that and it preyed on him."

The patient added, "I remember when I was four year old, and you (father) picked me up and threw me down."

Sister came to father's defense at this point, saying that their mother used to hit the boy too, but that he only remembers what father did.

Father then added, "I'm in constant fear for my life now."

Most striking in these interchanges was the intensity of the feelings that were present. Farberow and Schneidman (1970) concluded that suicide in the elderly is based upon the wish to die, while in the young it is the wish to kill or be killed. The extreme intensity of the rage behind the suicidal impulses of a young person is hinted at in this case history.

To summarize the diagnostic interview, the disturbed family pattern interacted with the patient's ailment (epilepsy) and the failure of his age-appropriate strivings for success and autonomy. The result was a crisis, which the patient tried to resolve by his suicide. The immediate crisis was his failure in school. A major goal of treatment, therefore, would be to help him to obtain a diploma, and either to begin to work or learn a trade. However, the more central crisis was the death of his mother, still active and unresolved after two years. The goal of therapy here would be to help the family mourn; to detach the patient from his role of surrogate for the unfinished conflicts surrounding the mother; and to fill the role hiatus left by her death (Richman, 1977).

Follow up: The patient was discharged from the hospital and entered individual therapy. He did graduate from high school, began to work, and was discharged from treatment. The further fate of this young man and his family is unknown to me.

Therapy and the Therapist

Treatment of the suicidal child and adolescent is a challenging task. In addition to its promise of relieving pain in the patient, it offers intrinsic rewards to the therapist, in terms of enhanced growth, the pleasures of learning, and the application of professional skills. The application of these skills form the major thrust of this section.

First, suggested qualifications of the therapist deserve mention. These include certain personal qualities, such as warmth and empathy, which at best can be but partially learned; and a special background of training and experience which can be learned, and in the opinion of this author is necessary for the successful pursuit of family psychotherapy with the youthful suicidal patient. In summary form, these qualifications include the following:

1. The therapist should be a developmental psychologist, possessing a broad knowledge of development and personality in the child and adolescent.

2. The therapist should be a suicidologist, with a knowledge of suicide in its biological, psychological, family, and social aspects.

3. The therapist should be a family therapist with a knowledge of family processes and treatment (A description of this aspect in the suicidal young person is the broad purpose of this chapter), a prerequisite of which is knowledge of family theory and the therapy field in general.

4. The therapist should work in a private or clinical setting characterized by good morale, adequate supervision, and a supportive atmosphere.

An effective beginning for treatment is the combined individual and family assessment procedure (described in the previous section) whether as preparation for individual, group, or family therapy. This initial family session is not only diagnostic; it is simultaneously therapeutic. Beck et al. (1979) stated, for example, that they try to "play for time" during a crisis, until the suicidal danger is past. In contrast, I strive to increase cohesion, which can best be accomplished with the family present. Paradoxically, I permit and even encourage the voicing of seemingly divisive expressions of anger and destructive impulses. Their meaning in the presence of a therapist who can deal with such expression changes from a suicidal communication to the communication of a problem. In addition, the fact that no one dies or is destroyed, and that the outcome is often the emergence of positive feelings by the end of the session, increases the therapeutic effect.

It is desirable to see the patient and his/her family as soon as possible after the suicide attempt or the onset of suicidal impulses. In the beginning, the usual family crisis intervention procedures apply. These include the following tasks: (1) Establishing rapport; (2) determining the degree of suicidal risk that may still be present; (3) deciding upon the disposition, including the question of whether to hospitalize or treat on an outpatient basis; (4) identifying the major crisis or crises that precipitated the suicidal situation; and (5) selecting the most effective intervention.

Thus, the initial tasks are to deal with the immediate crisis and prevent further suicidal behavior. These goals apply to all crisis intervention attempts with suicidal patients. Once these are accomplished, then further treatment can take place, with the additional goals of promoting personal growth and social cohesion.

Some general considerations in the family treatment of suicidal patients should be emphasized at the outset:

1. Timing is of the essence. In particular, premature efforts to separate or interrupt a longstanding symbiotic relationship, no matter how pathological, can precipitate another serious crisis or even actual suicide. One must proceed at a pace the family and patient can tolerate. The patient and

relatives are told that they need not separate until they are ready. The message is thus twofold: first, that the long-range goal is that of autonomy and individuation; and second, that there is no urgency. They are further told that the therapist and the family will all work together, and that homework assignments may be given.

2. It is essential that the therapist avoid all imputation of blame or scapegoating, no matter how disruptive or scapegoating the family members may be. The relatives, especially the most significant other for the patient, are characterized by an extraordinarily primitive and punitive superego. They are, therefore, overly sensitive to any hint of blame or guilt. Their perception of such an attitude in the therapist will consequently signal the failure or termination of treatment.

An example, early in my experiences with the families of suicidal persons, was a meeting between a thirty-year-old suicidal woman and her mother. Mother said, near the beginning of the session, "If my daughter is happy, I am happy." "How does that make you feel?" I asked, turning to the daughter. "It's a burden," she replied, "being responsible for her like that." The mother's response was a heartfelt, "I wish I was dead." And her daughter's response, in turn, was, "I'm not coming to therapy anymore."

The intended communication by the therapist was that the relationship is part of the situation; but it was received by the mother as blaming her for her daughter's depression. It was also a warning to the daughter and the therapist of the life-threatening consequences of trying to change their relationship. My response to the mother would now be, "You care for your daughter very much;" or, "You are very concerned about your daughter's welfare;" or a sympathetical acknowledgement of her caring in a nonverbal way. The significant other is often covertly or directly suicidal; and his or her harsh and primitive superego can be turned against the self. Therefore, I maintain a very benign attitude and am very tolerant of scapegoating, projection, and dichotomous thinking (e.g., "I am blameless; you are totally to blame") until the time for confrontation is appropriate. The above vignette was also an example of the effect of confronting the family or the pathological other too soon.

3. Finally, family therapy of the suicidal person is characterized by particular and predictable processes. It begins with blaming and scapegoating; and is followed by a period of quiescence and reduced anxiety, during which time the suicidal child or adolescent begins to function more effectively at school, with peers or at work. Then the family, including the suicidal patient, seems to realize what is happening. The result is a blowup, or a crisis in therapy. The therapist should continue to see the family through the crisis; and the process continues. A period of resolution and

acceptance follows, and ultimately therapy is ready to be terminated. In the later stages, the therapist becomes more active and interpretative, and prescribes homework and other forms of intervention. (These are generally not effective early in treatment).

The above process, I suspect, is characteristic of the successful psychotheraphy of suicidal subjects in general, not only those in family treatment. Medard Boss (1963) described a similar sequence, in his account of the individual treatment of a suicidal schizophrenic woman. After describing a psychotic and self-mutilating episode which he helped her to get through, and then her eventual recovery, he continued:

> But it was to happen again *dozens of times* that these two opposed phases—the state of the happy, symptom-free child, and that of the tormented psychotic—alternated with and followed one another. The pathological phase could be predicted with empiric certainty each time the patient was confronted with the realm of her sensual and emotional grown-up feminity (p. 23).

Similarly, with the suicidal child and adolescent (more so with the adolescent), periods of growth in the patient and harmony in the family alternate with periods of extreme turmoil and rage.

In summary, in the light of these observations, I see the therapist of the suicidal person primarily as a catalyst who helps precipitate and maintain the healing processes intrinsic to the patient and family.

Case History

Cathy, an eighteen year-old girl with a five-year history of drug abuse, took a massive overdose of pills in the contest of an intense quarrel with her parents after her boyfriend brought her home high. She was in a coma for eight days.

The therapist first saw the parents while the patient was on a respirator in the intensive care unit of a hospital. They agreed to enter therapy in order to help their daughter. A diagnostic interview with the entire family was scheduled after Cathy recovered and was able to attend.

The family was white, middle class, and Catholic. The father was a professional, an engineer; the mother worked as a secretary. Cathy was the youngest of four children. Her next older sibling, a brother, had been heavily involved with hard drugs, and had been away for a year at a drug treatment facility. It was during his absence that Cathy entered the drug scene. The two older children were "straight" and socially conservative.

Seen individually before the initial family interview, they all described

Cathy as a loser who failed in school and never held a steady job. The mother appeared as a severely anxious woman who was prone to extreme temper outbursts, very hysterical in nature, but often reaching an almost catatonic intensity. The father emerged as a genial but rather slippery character, who closely followed his wife's lead during the sessions, and presented a life philosophy of being careful and watchful, and fitting into what others expected of him.

In the initial interview, the family was united in being uniformly critical of Cathy. They were especially angry at her causing the mother's social and personal difficulties, with her former drug addict brother a central figure in the attack. Cathy fought back with much hostility towards the father and siblings, which was markedly less towards the mother. She insisted she wanted to leave home, go on welfare, and live in an apartment on her own. The therapist commented, "I don't think you're ready for that, yet."

During the second meeting a week later, the attacks continued. At that time, it was agreed to continue treatment with Cathy and her parents, and for the others to come in from time to time.

At the third meeting, Cathy announced that she was returning to school to become a doctor's assistant. Her parents had no reaction. She began class, and did very well. A month passed; and one evening the therapist received an urgent call. Cathy had come home high. Mother was screaming in the background, father had locked the door and would not let his daughter out, and Cathy was threatening to jump out the window.

The therapist arranged an immediate family session in his office. The parents were angry at both Cathy and the therapist, and labeled the treatment a failure. They insisted that Cathy terminate school. Cathy refused. The therapist commiserated with how difficult this was for everyone. They went home.

This crisis subsided, and Cathy continued to do well at school. She also stopped seeing her boyfriend, who was a drug addict. The family continued to complain at meetings, and to discount Cathy's successes. Her father said, for example, "What a pity Cathy did not do well in school when she was young, instead of waiting until she was 19." Mother harped on her anxiety lest Cathy return to drugs, and how the strain was too much for her. She said, too, that she would prefer Cathy to be dead, "rather than see her like this."

Asked for her reaction, Cathy replied that she was used to such statements. I recognized that mother was speaking out of anger, because she was caring and troubled. I also assigned some homework, instructing mother to write down all the reasons she wanted her daughter dead and all the reasons she wanted her alive.

Meanwhile, mother and father began to move out of the withdrawal and isolation which had characterized their existence since their son became a drug addict, and to resume their social life. Cathy continued to do well in school.

I became more active, directive, and confronting after the first six months of treatment. In particular, I worked upon their negative attitudes and belief that praise is undesirable, and discussed the desirability of positive feedback.

Periodic blowups continued to occur, and I saw the family through these. Cathy graduated school and began working steadily for the first time.

A major turning point occurred when Cathy's eighty-eight-year-old maternal grandmother became gravely ill. Cathy took over, relying upon the skills she learned at school and work. She took care of grandmother and advised the rest of the family what to do. A new respect for her emerged.

The treatment lasted about a year and a half, with a gradual tapering off during the last six months.

Cathy is now married and has a child. Problems are still present, some of them severe. But she is not suicidal, not on drugs, and her relationship with her family has remained positive.

In summary, as seen in this example, the presence of periodic crises is a typical pattern in the family treatment of suicidal persons. Essential ingredients are the therapist's ability to avoid taking sides; to tolerate seemingly destructive interactions; and to realize that these are part of the illness to be treated, rather than immoral acts to be condemned.

Termination

The question of termination and the relationship between the therapist and the family are interrelated. Termination is prepared for from the beginning. This is especially important because the suicidogenic family is so sensitive to separation.

As for the relationship between the therapist and the family, the therapist does not exaggerate his or her importance. The attitude is, he will miss them after termination, but after all, he is only a therapist, not a member of the family; and they may keep in touch. Cognitive behavior techniques, as described by Beck et al. (1979) are strongly recommended. They are very compatible with family treatment, and they may be particularly fruitful when dealing with termination. Homework and readings can be assigned, to be continued after the sessions have concluded. The termination is then less of a loss, and the patient and family take something of the therapist away with them.

In many cases the family drops out of treatment after the immediate crisis has been resolved, which is not necessarily undesirable. The last meeting, however, should be a positive one, so that the family may feel free to return should the occasion arise. Some follow-up is also desirable.

Most suicidal patients can benefit from a longer term therapeutic experience beyond crisis intervention. For them, the therapeutic process only begins with the resolution of the immediate crisis because the family continues to take steps to return the suicidal person to the earlier status quo. In addition, the periodic blowups which continue to occur after the crisis, are crucial. Their effects can continue to be destructive and regressive without professional help, but the therapist can help the family towards a constructive and growth-inducing resolution. A major problem, however, continues to be the paucity of qualified therapists to see the suicidal patient, especially in family-oriented treatment. Hopefully, more people working in suicide prevention will become interested in working with the family.

CONCLUSIONS

It is essential that knowledge of suicide and its prevention be as widely disseminated as possible. While therapy, especially family therapy, for the suicidal child and adolescent, requires specialized training and experience, and is therefore not for everyone, suicidal behavior in the young inevitably involves a great number of people. These include teachers and counselors, physicians, social workers, police, and many other lay and professional persons who are confronted with the troubled teenager. These groups need more knowledge about the problem of suicide in the young, information concerning how to recognize the danger signs, and how to help or to refer for help, if these are called for.

In addition, suicide prevention involves all of medicine, not only psychiatry. Large numbers of suicidal children and adolescents first come to professional attention on the medical wards and clinics of a hospital. In a recent study at the Bronx Municipal Hospital Center, Pfeffer and Beratis (1980) found that 40% of the child and adolescent suicidal population was first seen on medical services.

A major problem confronting the pediatrician is the anxiety aroused when dealing with such a patient. This anxiety, in turn, is largely a function of lack of training and experience. The implication is that more inservice training programs in suicide prevention are needed in pediatrics and general medicine. The problem, of course, is one that involves considerably more than the medical profession. Therefore, more inservice training programs in suicide prevention are also needed in the teaching field, social work, psychology, and the other mental health professions. Indeed, the task of saving lives recognizes no status or jurisdictional boundaries.

The suicidal child or teenage may or may not be a potential Kipling,

Buber, or Rubenstein. He/she may be only an unhappy person who is stuck in developmental time and needs to become unstuck. To help such an individual accomplish that task and enable him/her to live a constructive and meaningful life is a greatly rewarding and fulfilling task.

REFERENCES

Beck, A. T., Rush, A. J., Shaw, B. F., and Emery, G. *Cognitive Therapy of Depresssion.* New York: Guilford, 1979.

Boss, M. *Daseinanalysis.* New York: Basic Books, 1963.

Buber, M. *Between Man and Man.* Boston: Beacon Press, 1955.

Durkheim, E. Suicide. (Tr. by J. A. Spaulding and G. Simpson). New York: The Free Press, 1951 (Original 1897).

Erikson, E. H. *Childhood and Society.* New York: W. W. Norton, 1963.

Farberow, N. L., and Shneidman, E. S. Suicide and age. *In: The Psychology of Suicide* E. S. Shneidman, N. L. Farberow, and R. E. Litman, (eds.) New York: Science House, 1970. pp. 165–174.

Freud, S. Mourning and melancholia. *Standard Edition,* Vol. 14, 237–258. London: Hogarth Press, 1957 (Original, 1917).

Langsley, D. G., and Kaplan, D. M. *The Treatment of Families in Crisis.* New York: Grune & Stratton, 1968.

Meyerstein, E. H. W. *A life of Thomas Chatterton.* New York: Russell & Russell, 1972 (Original, 1930).

Pfeffer, C., and Beratis, A. A study of children and adolescents presenting on the medical and psychiatric services of a city receiving hospital. Submitted for publication, 1980.

Richman, J. Quais-courtroom procedures in suicidal families: One form of scapegoating. Presented at the Third Annual Meeting of the American Association of Suicidology, Washington, D. C. March 20, 1971.

Richman, J. The communication of suicidal intent within the family. Presented at the Sixth Annual Meeting of the American Association of Suicidology, Atlantic Beach, Florida, April 25, 1974.

Richman, J. Familial and environmental aspects of suicide. *In: Suicide and Bereavement,* B. L. Danto and A. H. Kutscher (eds.) New York: Arno Press, 1977.

Richman, J. Symbiosis, empathy, suicidal behavior, and the family. *Suicide and Life-Threatening Behavior.,* 1978, **8**(3) 139–149.

Richman, J. The family therapy of attempted suicide. *Family Process,* 1979, **18:**131–142.

Richman, J. Suicide and closed family system. *Proceedings, 10th International Congress for Suicide Prevention and Crisis Intervention,* Ottawa, Canada, 329–330, 1979.

Richman, J. Family aspects of the suicidal crisis and its management. Presented at the 13th Annual Meeting of the American Association of Suicidology, Nashville, Tennessee, April, 1980.

Richman, J., and Rosenbaum, M. A clinical study of role relationships in suicidal and non-suicidal psychiatric patients. *Proceedings, 5th International Conference for Suicide Prevention,* London, 1969.

Rosenbaum, M., and Richman, J. Suicide: The role of hostility and death wishes from the family and significant others. *American J. of Psychiatry,* 1970, **126**(11),:128–131.

Rubenstein, Arthur. *My Young Years.* New York: Alfred A. Knopf, 1973.

Sullivan, H. S. *Conceptions of Modern Psychiatry.* New York: W. W. Norton, 1953.

Wells, C. F., and Rabiner, E. L. The conjoint family diagnostic interview and the family index of tension. *Family Process,* 1973, **12:**127–144.

The authors, Dr. Fishman and Dr. Rosman, present their more recent approaches to self-damaging behavior in children and adolescents from their experiences in a clinic specializing in problems of these age groups. They emphasize the approach of structural family therapy through case illustrations. Suggested therapeutic techniques for altering the structure of family pathological interractions, where drug abuse, suicide, and anorexia nervosa are salient features, are extensively detailed.

14
A Therapeutic Approach to Self-Destructive Behavior in Adolescence: The Family as the Patient

H. Charles Fishman M.D.
and
Bernice L. Rosman, Ph.D.

The goal of this chapter is to describe an approach to adolescent self-destructive behavior in which the family, rather than the individual child, is the patient. This approach has been utilized in numerous cases of anorexia nervosa, as well as in over forty cases of substance abuse with adolescents ranging in age from thirteen to seventeen.

The family approach to psychiatric problems evolved in the late fifties and early sixties. During the sixties there was more emphasis in the culture at large on seeing people in context. Ecology achieved prominence as a part of biology. We in the United States saw ourselves as much subject to the forces in the world-at-large as everyone else—by no means are we the sole rulers of our own destiny. Instead we both shape and respond to a collective, worldwide organism.

Our treatment of self-destructive behavior similarly reflects a changed concept of the person in context. Rather than seeing the individual as the hero(ine) who is both the locus of his/her difficulties and his/her own rescuer, we view him/her as a part of a larger system, both reacting to and shaping his/her context.

This treatment model is based on a different scientific paradigm. Edgar Levenson in his book, *Fallacy of Understanding* (1972), talks about the change in paradigms of psychiatry over the last decade. The first, that of Freud, involved man as a work machine, modeled on the steam engine. For Freud, man was a machine, run on energy. In his mechanical model, processes were precise, measurable, like clockwork. Events were lawful, following rules. Even Freud's metaphors such as displacement, sublimation, pressure, bespeak his model of mind as energy and are indices of hydraulic flow.

The next paradigm which captured the imagination of psychiatry was that of communications, the information machine. This paradigm was ushered in with the telephone and with guided missile systems. In this model, problems result from a failure in understanding of communication between people. Relief from symptoms comes when people make their messages and feelings clear to one another. Problems result when there is a lack of clear communication.

The third model, and the one that we follow in our work with self-destructive children, follows from the biological understanding of life itself and, unlike the two paradigms noted above, does not result from man's tools. It derives from "the biological processes that can be directly observed in the living organism." For the work machine paradigm, the concept is energetic; for the electronic machine it is communication. For this third paradigm, the organismic model, it is life itself; it is the *world as organization*. The structural family therapist is not interested in a model of mind which represents machinery, or in displacement, or repression, or even the failure of communication, but instead in *patterns of consequence* which occur between people and which maintain people as symptomatic.

These patterns of consequence are seen as occurring between the individual and his/her interpersonal context. As clinicians, we examine the network of relationships to ascertain these patterns of relationship. We do this because following this new paradigm results in a different unit of therapuetic intervention. Since the person is not seen as distinct from his/her context, but as a part of it, treatment which is to be effective must involve a larger unit—the individual plus his/her context and patterns of relating.

In other words, in the contextual approach the individual is seen as imbedded in a social context. According to the interactions within this context, certain aspects of the individual's repertoire of behavior, which is at any given moment larger than those that are being expressed, are called into prominence. Other facets of the personality remain unexpressed and are quiescent. The assumption is that people have a greater potential for behavior than they are manifesting. By this reasoning, the self can be seen as not only existing in the individual, but existing also in those interactions between the individual and his context which result in the expression of certain kinds of behaviors, cognitions, and affects. Treatment hinges on changing those aspects of the context that call forth dysfunctional aspects of the individual.

The symptomatic child is seen as one part of a larger dysfunctional unit—the child and the family—which together form an organism. For example, an orchestra is a multibodied animal. All of the instruments play together in extraordinary coordination to form an entity which is larger than the sum of its parts. But imagine the oboe is practicing alone on Monday morning. There might be a long silence at the beginning (for the violins), then one would hear the oboeist, who in his mind is hearing the other instruments as he reads the score. For an uninitiated observer, however, the solitary staccato "symphony" of the oboe would seem quite strange.

In the same way, we see the symptomatic identified patient as the oboe—responding to what seems to us like silence, but in his or her experience it is really the forces of the context. Our treatment approach entails bringing this multibodied organism (the family), the silent symphony, into treatment.

There is empirical data to support the concept of the family as an organism which functions not as so many independent people, but as a whole. Work done with psychosomatic youngsters at the Philadelphia Child Guidance Clinic has demonstrated this concept. (Minuchin et al. 1978)

These children, whose medical symptoms are exacerbated by emotional factors, were found to be actually involved in their families' dysfunctional patterns of relationships. While individual modes of treatment employed previously had failed, intervention in the child-plus-family context succeeded in alleviating both emotional and medical problems.

FAMILY STRUCTURE

In working with dysfunctional families we utilize the structural family approach developed by Minuchin (1974). Family structure is defined as the organization of relationships between family members. Structure is assessed by observing family interactions and noting patterns. Specifically, we look for patterns which reveal proximity and distance between family members. For example, a mother and son who talk for each other—

"Bobby (age seventeen) doesn't agree with you" or a son who says to his father, "I'm thinking what you are." Continual eye contact or physical contact may reveal too great proximity. At the other extreme, where there is emotional disengagement, one would observe a paucity of appropriate responsiveness and attention.

This is an analysis of family interaction on a *micro*transactional level, that is the moment-to-moment sequence of interactions. Another way of describing transactions is the *macro*structural level where one looks at more general patterns. On the basis of our observations we extrapolate rules which govern the family behavior. These rules, which are obeyed by family members, reflect the structure. For example, mother and daughter may always be close regardless of circumstances while father is always odd man out.

There are certain structures which are considered on the basis of systems theory to be functional. To operate effectively, a family needs to have subsystems which are protected by fundamental boundaries. The subsystems in families are: the parental, the marital, the siblings, and the individual. Occasionally other subsystems form, such as when the men in the family go fishing.

The presence of alliances or coalitions across subsystem boundaries are considered dysfunctional. Alliances are people in affiliation, while coalitions are people working together across boundaries against another person. For example, the mother who is overly close to her seventeen-year-old son may side with him when conflicts arise between son and father. The husband/father, distanced from his wife, is overly attentive to the boy and emotionally unavailable to him. The appropriateness of proximity and distance between family members is judged according to how subsystems function. The son cannot adequately develop peer relationships if he is spending his entire weekend with his mother. The spouses will have difficulty being close and resolving problems if their son is present and siding with mother.

INDIVIDUAL DEVELOPMENT WITHIN THE FAMILY CONTEXT

But where is the individual in this schema? Certainly the adolescent, even though part of a larger unit, is himself a unit. There are certain well-described developmental sequences in adolescence which appear to be relatively constant, at least within our culture. The struggle for separation and individuation, the search for identity, the search for vocation competence, increased importance of peers, and making the transformation from childhood friendships to heterosexual pairings all represent important developmental issues for the adolescent.

However, processes occurring within the individual, such as adolescent developmental needs for more autonomy, must affect the family. An earlier family structure which allowed for mom, dad, and child to spend large amounts of time together is threatened. Other developmental events in family members may similarly shake the accustomed family patterns of interaction. Father's midlife crisis may cause him to become depressed and withdrawn. At this point his eleven-year-old daughter, with whom he had previously spent much time may become suicidal. The entrance of the last child in the family into kindergarten may precipitate an acute identity crisis in the mother—leading her to demand much more from her husband. He in turn may be increasingly unavailable because his father, who is his partner in the family business, had a stroke. Both parents, tense and overwhelmed, fight more—a sequence which activates their eleven-year-old daughter to act out. She feels her parents are too tough on her—since they pay more attention to her in their efforts to avoid confronting each other. Their attentiveness and ensuing strictness is anathema to their daughter who developmentally needs more space and autonomy. And so on.

The developmental demands of the individuals involved therefore impinge upon the family. Similarly, the developmental passages of the family unit—such as the leaving home of one of the children, or sickness and death of the parent's parents also impinge. The result of these changes is that the family stability is upset. The rules, which govern transactions become inadequate. The family is thrown into a "crisis."

The term crisis is used here in a very specific way—it describes any point at which the rules, which had governed transactions in a system, lose their hold. At the very least, uncertainty ensues—at most, chaos is loosed.

From our point of view, the self-destructive youngster's symptoms develop at a point of crisis in the family. The "crisis" emerges from a conflict between the demands of development on the family and its structure. Crisis can be seen as a conflict of the forces of morphostasis ("maintaining structures") and morphogenesis ("creating of new structures"). The developmental demands are clamoring for morphogenesis whereas the maintenance of the structure calls for the opposite, morphostasis (stability of the present structure).

This schema helps us to understand the symptom. Traditionally, in family theory the symptom is seen as a way in which the family stability is maintained. For example, as conflict arises between the parents in a family in which a sixteen-year-old abuses drugs, the abuse becomes more flagrant as tension between the parents increases. The parents focus their attention on the daughter, their conflict forgotten. They then deal with the daughter's problems with varying degrees of ineffectiveness, since they have unresolved conflicts. The result is that the youngster's behavior is not effectively changed. At the same time it is a circular pattern in that the parents' focus on the daughter does not allow them to focus on their difficulties long enough to resolve them. The symptom, thus, can be viewed as maintaining the family pattern and vice versa.

Beyond this, however, the symptom provides a partial solution to the developmental needs of the individual. Not only does the acting-out youngster achieve a function in the family by helping the family to maintain the family equilibrium, it also allows, in the example of a delinquent adolescent, for more freedom, thereby partially satisfying age appropriate needs for autonomy. What results then is a solution that is partially satisfactory to all involved. The difficulty, of course, is that a solution is maintained at great expense to everyone.

Furthermore, continuing developmental demands put increasing pressure on the dysfunctional structure. Having provided a partial solution to difficulties at one point, the configuration becomes increasingly unsatisfactory. For example, the youngster makes greater demands for individuation and autonomy. Or, as drug use escalates, legal authorities become involved.

TREATMENT

The therapist's goal is to challenge the rules that govern transactions in the family. The structure is dysfunctional for not only the index patient, but for the entire family. The therapist may do this by creating a crisis, that is, a period in which the rules cease to function so that new, more functional rules may be arrived at. An artificially induced crisis simulates those that occur naturally through the pressures of development. The goal is to provide new rules that are more adaptive to the needs of the family.

Of course, much more is involved in therapy than creating a crisis. The overall goal is to restructure the family. To do this, the therapist uses numerous techniques such as enactment, intensity, cognitive reframing and many more. Rather than describe these theoretically, it is more useful at this point to give a clinical example which demonstrates both the concepts and techniques of change.

Nicole, a fifteen-year-old girl, was brought to therapy by her parents because of her uncontrollable and self-destructive behavior for one year. She was drinking, using marijuana heavily, running around with a wild crowd, and her academic work was deteriorating. When her parents tried to punish her or to enforce a curfew, she would leave home. She would then stay out all night, often with whereabouts unknown to her parents. She smoked marijuana numerous times a day, frequently alone in her room. Nicole has two siblings, ages eighteen and thirteen. Her father is a lawyer and her mother is a housewife. The family was overwhelmed by their inability to control their youngster. They asked Nicole to either follow the family's rules or move out. Nicole chose the latter and went to live with a nineteen-year-old boy in a ghetto neighborhood.

In the first session the family presented a striking picture. Each person looked more dejected than the other. The parents sat solemnly facing their daughter while the children sat silently. The parents began by talking about the difficulties and stated that they had come to therapy because they wanted someone to "mediate" between them and their daughter. They said they recognized her legitimate right to freedom, but they felt that the two sides had been unable to work out a satisfactory compromise. The parents said they had solved the problem by asking her to move out, a request which she complied with. At that point, the oldest child, a freshman in college, said that they had not resolved the problem. They had only avoided the conflict. At one point, midway through the interview, the father began to cry. The mother looked up at him and said, "Bob, why don't you excuse yourself until you get more control."

In the session, the following was revealed: The middle-aged father had been reevaluating his life goals. In fact, Nicole's symptoms began when he had changed firms and had run into a work block. In addition, the oldest child in the family had entered college, while the youngest had begun high school. The mother, well educated but not working, was floundering. Her future was uncertain. Furthermore, the grandparents had become ill over the last few years and were taxing the family's resources.

This is clearly a family that is experiencing a great many developmental pressures. The family has four adolescent children, all of whom are struggling for individuation. Nicole, however, was experiencing the most pressure from her peer group to separate from her parents. In addition, the oldest child starting college and the youngest beginning high school had left the parents, especially the mother, at sea. The children required less from them. The father's midlife crisis, his self-doubts as far as his career and his relative paralysis in terms of his productivity in work further contributed to the pressures on the family. And finally, the demands from the grandparents were sapping the family resources and challenging the status quo.

The family transactions were dysfunctional in a number of areas. People were overinvolved, especially mother and Nicole. The parents were distant from each other—they would start to interact, have a difference of opinion, and retreat. They did not bring differences to the point of resolution. Frequently, when the parents disagreed, one of the youngsters (frequently Nicole) would misbehave and draw the parents' attention to themself.

The sequence just described, like all manifestations of systems, is circular. The children's activation not only serves to diffuse the parents' conflict, but keeps them from resolving their difficulties. The next time a conflict arises the parents, not having resolved the last difference, are even more unstable and need all the more to involve a third person. And so on.

The participation of a child to stabilize the marriage represents a breach of generational boundaries. Such breaches like all repetitive family interactions, are rule-governed behavior. The rule governing this violation of generational boundaries prescribes the pattern which maintains Nicole's self-destructive behavior. Mother, overly close to Nicole, sides with her against father. This transgression of hierarchies is instrumental in keeping the parents from being effective with Nicole.

We conceptualize a feedback loop between Nicole's misbehavior and the parents' response. The parents' behavior is as instrumental in maintaining Nicole's misbehavior as Nicole's is in maintaining her parents' response. We can attribute the family ineffectiveness to its dysfunctional structure. For example, Nicole comes home after staying out all night. The father gets extremely angry. He sends her to her room without dinner. The mother, feeling that her daughter is misunderstood, goes upstairs and spends hours talking with her about her difficulties. This functions as a reward for the youngster, and undermines the impact of the father's punishment while weakening his resolve. The consequence of this sequence is that father's punishment undermined by mother is ineffective in changing Nicole's behavior. Furthermore, he loses his wife's company, frequently for the remainder of the evening. The effect is Nicole and mother get closer, and father, all the more taciturn and brooding, distances from both of them.

There is another important consequence of Nicole's misbehavior. Mother and father focus on their daughter, and are less available for truly mutual I-Thou intimacy, which would, given their difficulties, lead to fighting. In this way, Nicole's misbehavior helps to stabilize their relationship and hence, the family.

Therapy seeks to change the family structure. In structural family therapy interventions consist of creating new experiences for the family members which will enable them to perceive each other and interact in new ways. One way this is done is by redefining behaviors which puts a different framework and conceptual understanding on the behavior. For example, Nicole's behavior is described as not a manifestation of an illness, as perceived by the parents, but instead as a result of a delinquent "unacceptable behavior" pattern. Framing her behavior in this way frees the parents to achieve enough distance from her to react more effectively.

Enactment is another important technique in structural therapy. New transitions are introduced directly into the session in a variety of ways. In this case the parents were asked to discuss and agree what they will do the next time Nicole misbehaved. As they talked, and began to disagree, Nicole began to misbehave. She began smoking a cigarette, even though the parents forbid this behavior in their presence. Father stated that he thought they should take the cigarette while mother said that Nicole probably could not help herself since she had a very bad addiction to tobacco. The therapist pressed the parents to agree on what they were going to do *right now*. "Whatever you decide to do is acceptable, as long as you work together." If they operated discordantly, then no effective resolution would be arrived at. The parents, after a considerable struggle, decided that they would take the cigarette away from her. They did so and Nicole, much to their amazement, acquiesced readily.

The next issue that came up in the first session was whether they were going to continue to allow their daughter to live "on the street." The therapist, rebuking their egalitarian model of child raising said that since Nicole was only fifteen and needed their protection she was their responsibility. The father agreed but both parents were afraid she would run away "to New Orleans to become a hooker." The father then became stronger and the mother demurred. Then mother strengthened and father demurred.

This flip-flop pattern is often seen in family therapy sessions. If one says black, the other says dark gray. The first then counters with, "You're looking at the wrong part . . ." This pattern, a stand-off, tends to escalate and threaten the system with instability. A third person is obliged to activate to diffuse the tension.

To change this sequence represents a central therapeutic task. The therapist needs to transform the systemic patterns without allowing himself to be inducted into following them. For example, when Nicole's parents began to escalate their conflict, had the therapist allowed himself to be activated to diffuse their conflict there would be a change in content but not process. Participants would be different but the pattern or structure would be unchanged.

One therapeutic technique for changing such patterns is "unbalancing." It represents an important use of self in which the therapist differentially sides with one member part of a subsystem over another. Unlike the triadic activation described above which diffuses the conflict, here the therapist's support is to empower one member of the deadlocked couple, thus moving things off dead center.

When unbalancing is successful the response of the system is transient instability. The rules suddenly do not hold. In the couple described above, the rule is that no one is supposed to win. Each disqualifies the other in what has become a game without end. But the therapist by supporting one side, has changed things. The one who is supported must change to both keep the therapist on his or her side and to maintain a relationship with the spouse. After all, they must drive home together. For the other spouse, the therapist's support changes the way the supported spouse is perceived. Heightened salience and power is bestowed by the therapist's support on the supported member and a change in the way the family interacts with this person ensues.

In Nicole's family, the therapist unbalanced the system by siding with the father. In the process of supporting the father, the therapist deferred to him, challenged him to be strong and took his side in disagreements with his wife. In terms of the content of the session, the therapist stated that the father was correct; the parents needed to take control of Nicole who was living in a delinquent way. Furthermore, father, being the man of the house, needed to bear the burden. He had to convince his wife that the youngster should be brought home.

This intervention produced a transformation of the family system. The father, who had previously been a low status member of the family assumed new authority. The alliance with the therapist gave him new salience, and provided him with more certainty. Not only did the other children see him in a different way, so did his wife. In his enhanced position, the father prevailed upon his wife. The two of them decided that they would insist that Nicole come home that day. Nicole then came into the session and they told her. Much to their amazement, Nicole began crying like a much younger child but protested only mildly.

The important therapeutic change is reflected not in the content of the parents' message but in the modification of the family process. The parents are together in their position. This allows for a clear message to Nicole—neither parent will support her in disobeying. Being together, the parents are not involved in the escalation of conflict—a sequence which ordinarily paves the way for mutual sabotage as well as the need for Nicole to activate her delinquency to diffuse their animosity towards each other.

The treatment proceeded for six months even though Nicole returned home after the second session. After session three the parents, having newfound closeness, began to focus a good deal of attention on each other. Conflict arose. Nicole's acting-out behavior exacerbated.

The therapist continued to support the parents in their need to appropriately control their daughter. At the same time, he joined Nicole in her developmentally appropriate desire for increased, although properly modulated, differentiation and autonomy. (For example, her parents had continued to choose the TV programs their children, even the older ones, were able to watch. The therapist supporting the youngsters in their need for increasing autonomy, helped them to negotiate the freedom to choose their own TV as well as books, movies, and friends.)

Therapy directed at the structural goals described above was continued with a dramatic decrease of symptomatology. Soon Nicole was no longer a problem. She became a better citizen. Therapy was then directed at Nicole's sixteen-year-old sister, Jennifer. This youngster had taken the opposite solution to her stymied developmental needs. Rather than be rebellious, she was the opposite. She spent all her time at home. Her only social activity was working after school, which she did to the exclusion of any other activities. She had no friends. We saw her difficulties as being maintained by her extremely overprotective family. Her parents planned Jennifer's every activity. The initiative for her daily life and even her plans for the future lay not with her, but with her parents. To the extent that her parents were overly responsible about her activities and her future, she was under responsible. She took a reciprocal position to her parents overactivity and overconcern—indolence and insouciance. She knew very little about social life because her parents planned for and maintained her social life, although not with her peers. She shied away from peers since she had limited experience and low self-confidence in dealing with children her own age.

The parents' overresponsibility and concern gave Jennifer the message that she was incompetent. If people had to do so much for her, she must not be able to do enough for herself. Thus, when stressful social situations came up with her peers, she fled. At the same time, since she spent so much time with her parents, she had inappropriately mature interests and vocabulary which tended to isolate her. Her skills and experience relating to other kids her age were limited—which further stunted her desire and ability to relate to age-mates. Thus, a vicious circle ensued.

To resolve these difficulties, therapy was directed toward changing the family rules which maintained these patterns. Specifically, the rule of overprotectiveness was changed. This change required the parents to function adequately as a dyad so that they did not need sixteen-year-old Jennifer always at hand being treated like an eight-year-old. At the same time, the therapist worked individually with Jennifer to help activate alternative behaviors, to give her the experience of herself in the world, relating in a competent manner to a nonfamily member. Sessions with just the siblings were held to emphasize norms of separation and individuation as well as to increase peer pressures toward extrafamilial experiences. The goal of these interventions was to give Jennifer a different experience of herself and the world as well as to allow the family members to see and interact with her differently.

This example further demonstrates this family's "developmental delay." The rules of the system were adequate to handle issues of school age children but they had not evolved with the growth of the kids. The rules were not appropriate to the new stage, adolescence. Something had to give, either the continued development of the children or the family rules. For

Nicole it was more the unwritten code of the family which was changed. For her sixteen-year-old sister, Jennifer, development was impeded while she remained an overly dutiful daughter. These were only relative differences—since, for the entire family, both the intrapsychic development of the individuals and the evolution of the family structure had been impaired.

Finally, as the sequence of involving a third person to diffuse spouse conflicts was continuously blocked, increasing difficulties came up between the parents. It was revealed that they had an extremely dysfunctional sex life and had not slept together for four years. The therapeutic contract was renegotiated and marital therapy was begun.

One way of looking at the therapy is that it artificially induced, in a compressed time period, the developmental progress of the family. The youngsters' processes of separation were supported and augmented, although within limits. The spouse dysfunctions were brought to the foreground in a relatively short time so that they could be helped to function better as a dyad. These things might have transpired in the future but much later and at a greater cost to the family members.

The next example we are going to look at is that of Rick. Rick is a sixteen-year-old boy who is mildly retarded and epileptic and who was brought to therapy by his parents after he had taken a large overdose of phenobarbital. Rick is the youngest of four children and the last living at home. He had no problems while attending an educable retarded class. He was increasingly related to peers and participated in the activities with the other kids in his school although, due to his intellectual deficits, did so in a stilted and somewhat "as if" fashion. In spite of this, he was increasingly accepted by kids his age. His parents in an appropriate way began to decrease the amount of control they kept on Rick. At one point, however, they left him by himself on a Saturday and Rick pressured by the "mainstream" kids, decided to have a huge party. The party soon grew out of control and the police were called, much to his parents' shame and indignation. His parents became increasingly restrictive with Rick, to the point of severely limiting his access to peers.

Following this, the parents' life became even more organized around their son who became the central focus of their lives. This coincided with a change in roles for the parents. Mother had recently gotten a job while father, a blue collar worker, had been laid off. He stayed at home and busied himself by taking extremely close care of Rick. The reciprocal of this was the mother, who having recently shed the role of full-time housekeeper became increasingly distant toward Rick in a fashion complementary to her husband's increasing overconcern with the boy.

The family therapist would understand Rick's symptoms in the following way: Developmentally, he clearly needed more autonomy. His developmental stage was one in which increased peer relationships and increased concerns with differentiation were major issues.

Rick's symptom clearly served a function in the family by giving father a vocation. He now had a reason for being home, helping greatly to mitigate his depression and shame at being unemployed and living in a family in which his wife was the breadwinner. Furthermore, Rick's behavior took pressure off the parental relationships arising from the role reversal. On a microtransactional level, as seen in the therapy sessions, the interactions between family members revealed a structure in which there was extreme enmeshment. The parents both sat looking at Rick expectantly. When he would be asked a question at least one, and frequently both parents answered. They would finish his sentences for him. Rick for his part didn't bother answering certain questions, sure that his parents would respond for him.

On a macrotransactional scale, as described above, the parents' lives were organized around their son. Spouse activities were strictly limited. The parents had not even gone out alone together at night in some years.

Therapy involved creating a "crisis" in the sense described above. That is, the therapist through his intervention threw the family's reliance on their customary rules into question. He did this by demonstrating that the established rule that "Rick is incompetent" was not the case. He interacted with him in the family's presence and found him much brighter, more loquacious and much better informed and effective than the family gave him credit for. This threw the family's pattern of extreme overprotection into uncertainty.

The therapist then more specifically challenged the enmeshment. On a microtransactional level the therapist got the parents to stop talking for Rick, to let him finish his own sentences and to let him do more for himself both in the session and at home.

In the process of increasing the space between Rick and his parents the therapist, recognizing the intricately balanced patterns within the family knew that it would not be enough to help the family to give Rick more space without introducing alternatives that would allow the family members to grow beyond their own developmental impediments. The father was encouraged to continue with his life—to seek a job, to continue in the bowling league, and to return to his hobbies. He did this with reluctance at first, but when seeing that Rick did not falter but actually began to thrive, he began to resume his usual activities.

The symptom, however, also played a part in the parents' marriage. It allowed the parents to focus on their son and avoid intimacy. The therapist addressed this issue by encouraging them to spend time together, to try to share interests and in the session sought to strengthen their relationship by having them bring conflicts to the point of resolution.

Unlike the first example, Rick's symptom was a one-time occurrence.

Nonetheless, it was of sufficient gravity that it profoundly affected the organization of the family. The symptom of the overdose, however, structurally had the same implications as the party, for the family. That is, as a result of either bad judgement or self-destructive behavior, Rick endangered himself. Both events, the overdose and the party resulted in the same structural change in the family—increasing proximity between Rick and his parents; especially between the youngster and his father. In this example the developmental demands on Rick and the family are clear. For Rick, it was less the symptom per se and more the fact that it obliged the family to seek therapy that allowed Rick to better achieve his developmental needs. Therapy allowed Rick respite from the tremendous overinvolvement with his parents which was stunting his psychological growth and expansion of peer relationships. Therapy enabled the parents to adapt in a more constructive way to the new roles and rules associated with their changes in occupational status, and to develop spouse relationships based on mutual gratification rather than on over-parenting a defective child.

We have observed many similar patterns in the families of anorectics. Anorexia nervosa can be viewed as self-destructive behavior. Although psychosomatic persons suffering from this syndrome have control over their food intake they willfully refuse to eat in spite of the exhortations of everyone around them. From this perspective, the self-starvation, like drug overdose, represents behavior directed against the self.

At the Philadelphia Child Guidance Clinic a large number of anorectic youngsters have been treated using family therapy (Rosman et al. 1977). We will describe the treatment of Bonnie to demonstrate the application of this model to anorexia.

Bonnie was fourteen at the point of the initial contact. The only girl and the youngest of three children, Bonnie had been diagnosed anorectic one year before. She had been in individual treatment with poor results except for a one-month hospitalization period which enabled Bonnie to gain some weight which she quickly lost on discharge. At the first family interview, Bonnie, 5′2″ tall, weighed 78 pounds.

The family consisted of Bonnie, her brothers, ages seventeen and nineteen, and her parents. The marriage was chronically conflicted with Bonnie and her mother in a coalition against her father. The parents agreed on nothing while mother and Bonnie made frequent eye contact, smiled knowingly when father talked and took turns answering him disrespectfully. At the time of the first interview the brothers seemed appropriately disengaged from the family, considering their ages. The older brother, in college, was working two jobs while the younger, a poor student, was asserting his autonomy by becoming a laborer, unusual for this family.

Bonnie's development had clearly been hampered. She performed well in school, usually at an A level, but had few friends. She rarely went out except with her mother.

In anorexia nervosa, we assume that dysfunctional family interactions maintain the problem. Specifically we usually observe chronic conflict between the parents, as they undermine one another in their efforts to get their child to eat. The child usually is overinvolved in the parents' marriage, tends to participate at least implicitly, and frequently explicitly in diffusing family conflict.

Central to our therapeutic approach with these families is the concept of enactment. Since the problem is seen as residing in the interactions between family members, then the most certain way of treating them is to elicit and change the dysfunctional interactions in the therapy sessions. Since the problem in anorexia is not eating, then the logical problem to introduce into the therapy session is a meal. The family is asked to bring lunch. The therapist and family set about eating. Usually everyone eats except the anorectic youngster. The parents are then told that their child must eat to live. It is okay if she rebels, rebellion within limits is normal for teenagers, but refusing to eat is not acceptable. She will die if she does not eat.

When this task was presented to them, Bonnie's parents set about getting their child to eat. Each tried in turn only to be undermined by the other. The therapist increased the intensity: "If you fail, she might die." The parents failed. Bonnie did not eat.

A second lunch session was held the next day. Midway through, Bonnie said to her father: "You promised that if today's session did not prove a success, you would let me go back to the hospital." The experience of hospitalization had been extremely pleasant for Bonnie even though it had only transiently ameliorated her anorexia. The therapist had assumed that Bonnie and mother had an alliance and this pattern maintained Bonnie's food avoiding behavior. The therapist had made a special effort to join with the woman so that she would support the efforts to get Bonnie to eat. Bonnie's mention of her father's promise made it clear that father was indeed supporting Bonnie's refusal to eat. The therapist had to change his notion of the structure. Instead of rigidly maintained overinvolvement between mother and Bonnie there was a pattern of shifting alliances. Now mother supported Bonnie, then father, but never both at the same time. Supporting father, the therapist got the parents to work together to get Bonnie to eat. Faced with unified parents, Bonnie ate lunch and from this point on, the anorexia was no longer a problem.

The older brother, Peter, turned out to have problems which, while very different from his sister's, had the same effect on the family. Socially isolated, always at home, he presented difficulties which riveted the parents' attention thereby further diffusing their need to deal with intimacy and conflict between themselves.

While Bonnie has completely recovered, the family is still in treatment dealing with developmental issues for Peter and with the family interactional patterns that maintain him as dysfunctional. For example, the father insists that Peter go to college, where he is a poor student, as a way of proving his wife wrong in her position that Peter should get a job instead. When Peter, speaking in an obsessive and at times idiocyncratic way, fails to communicate, his family, consistent with overprotectiveness, pretends to listen rather than tell him that they don't understand. The family inappropriately supports Peter's working two jobs which results in exacerbating his social isolation. Overinvolved with father, Peter embraces his father's practice of avoiding debt at all costs. He refuses to take out student loans, making two jobs necessary. The family rule against autonomy militates against Peter doing things another way. Instead, he is supposed to do things Dad's way.

The question arises as to just what developmental solution is served by Bonnie's and Peter's symptoms. Via her anorexia, Bonnie was able to assert her autonomy and to rebel. Furthermore, she was able to avoid stressful, albeit growthful peer relationships through her too great closeness with her mother. Had her mother been less needy and less available to her, Bonnie would have been obliged to seek kids her own age. For Peter, the developmental needs that are being satisfied are less clear. No doubt satisfaction of his need for autonomy is derived through his jobs and self-support. Certainly the needs for socialization, as with Bonnie, are at least partially fulfilled by the family for him.

To sum up, we have presented a conceptual model for understanding and treating self-destructive behavior in adolescents by looking at the individual in context. Important implications of this model include a more generic approach which is not limited to specific modes of self-destructiveness; these may include suicidal acts, drug abuse, self-starvation or other self-damaging behaviors. The family approach does not deny the validity of conceptualizations about the individual. Rather, by broadening the focus to include the family context in which the individual lives and develops, we expand our understanding of the significance of the pathology and the interpersonal forces which serve to maintain it. By bringing this significant interpersonal context into the therapy session, we increase our effectiveness as agents for change.

REFERENCES

1. Levenson, E. A. *The Fallacy of Understanding,* New York: Basic Books, 1972. pp. 72–73.
2. Minuchin, S., Rosman, B. L., and Baker, L. *Psychomatic Families: Anorexia Nervosa in Context,* Cambridge: Harvard University Press, 1978.
3. Minuchin, S. *Families and Family Therapy,* Cambridge: Harvard University Press, 1974.
4. Rosman, B. L., Minuchin, S., Baker, L., and Liebman, R. A family approach to anorexia nervosa: study, treatment, and outcome. *In: Anorexia Nervosa,* R. A. Vigersky (ed.) New York: Raven Press, 1977. pp. 341–348.

For a number of years now behavioral approaches have been used in the treatment of pathological behaviors in children. In this chapter the authors describe the application of behavior modification methods to self-destructive behaviors such as head banging, self-biting, and face slapping in children. The basic principles and elements of the behavioral approaches are presented and case material is used to illustrate the various specific techniques that may be used with different symptoms. A vital component of the behavioral approach is the use of systematic ongoing evaluation; and the authors discuss various designs that may be used appropriately to evaluate the efficacy of treatment.

15
Behavioral Approaches to the Management of Self-Destructive Children

Francis J. Keefe, Ph.D.
Eric M. Ward, Ph.D.

Self-destructive behaviors in children have generated a great deal of concern in mental health specialists. These behaviors have frustrated and baffled clinicians. The maintenance of behaviors that seem inherently aversive to the individual and sometimes life threatening is particularly puzzling. Over the years, a variety of treatment approaches have been developed to help change self-destructive behavior patterns. These treatment approaches are largely based on a psychodynamic model. In this chapter, we consider a number of treatment procedures based on an alternative model—the behavioral or social learning model. Behavioral treatments for self-destructive children have emerged as a viable treatment only within the past fifteen to twenty years.

Behavioral conceptualizations of self-destructive behavior differ fundamentally from intrapsychic ones. Psychodynamic theories view abnormal behavior as a result of intrapsychic conflict, as a symptom of underlying disease or quasidisease, or as a sign of a relatively permanent personality characteristic or trait. In the behavioral approach, the development of abnormal behavior is thought to be governed by the same principles and processes that govern the development of normal behavior. Abnormal behavior is viewed more directly as a problem in day-to-day living than as a sign of an inferred trait or symptom of an underlying pathological condition. The behavioral approach emphasizes the current determinants of behavior and as a result focuses on the current *function* rather than the historical *cause* of the behavior.

Early behavior analysis and modification efforts focused on the most common forms of self-destructiveness in which the risk of tissue damage was clear and imminent. The face slapping, head banging, or eye gouging of retarded or psychotic children, or the chronic vomiting in infant rumination syndrome are well-known examples reviewed recently by Russo, Carr and Lovaas (1979).

In focusing on such behaviors the organism remained something of a "black box." The child's perceptions, cognitions, and physiological responses were essentially ignored. Despite this, these early behavioral techniques yielded surprising explanatory power and clinical utility. The child's environment, long viewed as a virtual "black hole" of noninfluence was found to be a rich source of currently operating factors. A taxonomy of physical and social determinants that set the occasion for self-injury or strengthened it were identified. This early research also highlighted the importance of learning in the maintenance, if not the etiology of self-destructive symptoms.

More recently, there has been an extension of behavioral theory, assessment and therapy to cognitive and physiological response systems. These behaviors can be anchored to environmental factors and increasingly are seen as subject to the same laws of learning that govern more overt behaviors. As extensions of the behavioral approach are made to a wider variety of health-related problems, more subtle forms of health-threatening or self-destructive behavior are being considered as valid targets for behavioral intervention. Less immediately health-damaging behaviors often mediated by cognitive and physiological variables are being analyzed and treated. Examples of such behavior include noncompliance with medical therapy regimens and substance abuse.

Thus, behavioral approaches to self-destructive behavior are being applied to an ever-growing number of behaviors and with an ever-widening range of treatment procedures. The purpose of this chapter is to provide the reader with an introduction to the behavioral treatment of the self-destructive child. The chapter begins with a review of the basic elements of the behavioral approach. We then discuss how these elements are applied in the clinical setting by reviewing in detail two case examples.

BASIC ELEMENTS OF THE BEHAVIORAL APPROACH TO SELF-DESTRUCTIVE CHILDREN

There are five basic elements inherent in any behavioral management program utilized to modify self-destructive behaviors. These are: (1) Presenting problems are defined in measurable terms; (2) measurements are repeated over time; (3) treatment is matched to the patient's needs; (4) ongoing evaluation is systematic; and (5) maintenance and generalization of behavior change is planned.

Presenting Problems are Defined in Measurable Terms

"John is always banging his head on the floor"; "Sam keeps pulling out his intravenous tubing"; "I know that Jill is scratching that eczema again." Complaints such as these are common among those working with the self-injurious child. Parents, teachers, nurses, and ward personnel tend to describe and think about self-injurious children along such lines. However, on careful inspection, these terms are often very imprecise and inaccurate. For example, careful observation of a child who headbangs usually reveals that the headbanging is quite frequent under certain conditions, less frequent under other conditions, and absent under still other conditions. Behavioral approaches to treating self-injurious behavior attempt to overcome these problems by insisting that the only meaningful way of defining self-injurious behavior is in clearly observable and measurable terms. Vague and diffuse complaints are thereby redefined in such a manner that permits precise and accurate observation. Self-injurious behaviors are often highly visible and, therefore, easy to define in behavioral terms. Headbanging, poking the eye with a finger, biting an arm or hand are behaviors which are quite discrete and can be easily defined and counted. Behavioral clinicians working with self-destructive children have tended to define the presenting problems in terms of overt motor behaviors. While other response systems (for example, the physiological or subjective response systems) are considered to be important, they are less frequently chosen as targets for modification. This is because movement artifacts involved in most self-destructive behaviors invalidate physiological measures. In addition, many self-destructive children lack the skills and resources to systematically monitor subjective responses. Finally, in most instances the self-destructive behavior that is most salient is some type of motor response.

Self-destructive children are usually identified by either their parents or institutional staff. The behavioral clinician works closely with these individuals to arrive at a definition of the problem behavior. Several steps are typically followed. First, parents or staff members are asked to describe the child's behavior in detail. They might be instructed, for example, to describe a typical incident of the self-destructive behavior or to discuss the child's typical day, starting from the moment he/she gets up to the moment he/she goes to bed. Analysis of this description helps the clinician form a relevant definition. On the basis of such verbal descriptions it is often easy to pinpoint the relevant characteristics of a particular self-injurious behavior. These data help the clinician determine whether the particular behavior is problematic because it occurs with high frequency, (for example head banging) high intensity, (for example eye touching) or prolonged in duration, (for example thumb sucking). In the next step, the behavioral clinician performs a preliminary observation of the child. This is usually very helpful in (1) helping the clinician eliminate irrelevant aspects of the behavior, and (2) suggesting other behaviors to be modified. For example, an initial observation of a child whose self-destructive behavior consists of burning himself probably will reveal no examples of this behavior. Such low frequency, yet very salient, self-destructive behaviors do not lend themselves to easy observation. In such cases, observation usually reveals other behaviors which are functionally related to the problem behavior. In some cases, behaviors such as failing a test in school, fighting, temper tantrums, etc., may trigger an episode of self-injurious behavior or, on the other hand, certain appropriate behaviors, such as cooperative play or sports activity, may be associated with an absence of self-injurious or destructive behavior. In such instances, the problem is redefined so that, in addition to the relatively low-frequency self-injurious behavior, other important behaviors are monitored. Whenever possible it is wise to focus parental and staff attention on some aspect of the patient's behavior which is appropriate. In this way, a self-destructive child who is usually considered by everyone to be a "problem" is viewed in a different light. This may help break a downward spiraling series of negative and coercive interactions. The final step in arriving at a definition is to have the parents or staff actually try out the definition. Usually two observers are asked to use the definition and to record the behavior simultaneously. Differences in definition are thereby made explicit and reliability is enhanced. Behavioral treatment of the self-injurious child is strongly rooted in empiricism. The development of a precise, accurate, and scientific definition of the target behavior is thus considered paramount. Without such a foundation behavioral treatment procedures lose their unique character.

Measurements are Repeated Over Time

A second basic element of the behavioral approach is the use of repeated observations. Measurements of the target behavior are taken on numerous occasions *before* any treatment procedure is instituted. These pretreatment observations form a *baseline* against which future changes in behavior can be compared. While a minimum of three observations is considered necessary, baseline measurements are usually continued until a stable pattern is achieved. The one obvious exception to that rule, however, is when the self-injurious behavior is increasing with frequency or severity.

Measurements are usually carried out by those who spend most time with the child. A practical recording procedure is thus essential (c.f. Keefe, Kopel and Gordon, 1978). For example, a mother might be asked to record episodes of self-biting occurring in her mentally retarded child from the hours of eight to eleven every morning.

The use of such repeated observations has several distinct advantages. First, it permits both the clinician and the mediators to accurately assess the level of behavior. Parents are often surprised to learn that the arm biting, which they thought *always* occurred, in actuality occurs ten to twelve times a day. Second, such observations help one identify the variability in the target behavior. Children whose self-injurious behavior varies from very low to very high frequency daily are more likely to be under the control of important environmental events and as a result more open to change. A third advantage of measurement is that it provides the opportunity to look for correlations between the problem behavior and the environmental antecedents and consequences. The face slapping response of a five-year-old may occur much more frequently when the child's father is in the room than when the child's father is absent. Such initial observations provide clues as to possible interventions to be used in the future. In order to summarize data gathered over repeated observations, simple graphs are typically used. For example, data might be gathered on three self-destructive behaviors in a seven-year-old autistic child: lip biting, anal poking, and head banging. When viewed on a graph, these behaviors vary in frequency from day-to-day. Two of them, lip biting and head banging, may even be found to covary. Such data are essential in suggesting treatment alternatives. For example, when behaviors covary reliably, treatment of one may decrease the other.

Treatment is Matched to the Patient's Needs

In the important task of matching treatment to child it is necessary to consider not only the definition of the problem and its observed occurence but also the resources of the child and his/her family, and the range of available treatments. The child's motivation, mental and physical deficits, and behavioral strengths will need to be considered in planning interventions. Treatment of children with limited language or intellectual abilities or children who are poorly motivated normally requires a mediator (parent, teacher, child-care worker) who is interested and able to ensure that decided upon changes in environmental consequences are implemented.

A "reinforcement survey" (Cautela, 1977) of the child's favorite activities, foods, adults, peers, etc., is useful in identifying motivators to strengthen new behavior.

If a child's self-injurious behavior appears to function primarily to avoid or terminate adult demands, time out from all adult attention (includes demands) is likely to exacerbate the problem. Reinforcement of alternative behavior or contingent aversive stimulation is likely to be more effective. Reinforcement of competing behavior, on the other hand, may be impossible in situations in which extremely frequent self-injury dominates the child's behavioral repertoire. Aversive stimulation may initially be required in such cases.

For both child implemented or mediator assisted treatments the simplest, least disruptive treatment which is still potentially effective is obviously the treatment of choice.

Two broad classes of treatment techniques are used. Those which promote new relationships between overt behavior and consequences (largely independent of consideration of the individual's internal cognitions and physiological responses) fall under the general heading of *contingency management* procedures. Those which promote new relationships between antecedent events and behavior fall under the heading of *self-control* procedures.

Contingency Management Procedures. In their review of self-injury among mentally retarded and schizophrenic children, Frankel and Simmons (1976) report that experimental evidence strongly supports the contention that self-injury is learned in low-functioning children as a coercive means of modifying adult attention. Self-injury is more prevalent among schizophrenic children who are language deficient (Shodell and Reiter, 1968) and among children with severe mental retardation (Baumeister and Forehand, 1974). Self-injury may produce positive adult attention and thus serve as a primary means of interacting with adults (Risley, 1968) or, in high-demand situations, serve to reduce adult attention (Russo et al., 1979). In contingency management programs there is an attempt to modify the relationship between a self-destructive behavior and its consequence. This approach is based on an operant conditioning model of behavior (c.f. Skinner, 1953) which has shown that the likelihood that a behavior will occur is increased if that behavior is followed by positive consequences (i.e., positive reinforcement) and decreased if followed by aversive consequences (i.e., punishment). Applications of these principles in clinical settings require the systematic management of environmental contingencies. The naturally occurring contingency for head banging for a retarded child might be an increase in adult attention. In a contingency management program, staff might be instructed to make their attention contingent upon other more appropriate behavior, e.g., constructive play. Contingency management procedures are usually used with such dramatic self-destructive behaviors as face hitting, eye poking, skin biting and head banging.

Treatments which change the contingencies between self-destructive behaviors and their environmental consequences include "extinction" and "time out" procedures in which specific or all normally occurring consequences, respectively are interrupted or withheld following self-injury. Adult attention or other events (food, toys, etc.) noted during assessment and functional analysis to be probable consequences are consistently programmed *not* to occur. While the effectiveness of the techniques is documented, (Bucher and Lovaas, 1967; Jones, Simmons and Frankel, 1974) there are several contraindications to their use. The temporary increase in intensity and frequency of self-injury that initially occurs and the long numbers of treatment sessions often required for gradual reduction may result in serious harm to the individual. To intervene with adult attention during treatment can make matters worse as the child may learn that higher frequencies and intensity of self-injury are required to win back adult attention.

Alternative behaviors that potentially can compete with self-injury are sometimes established by making adult attention and other potential reinforcers contingent on them. Treatment programs in which several competing behaviors such as holding the hands at the sides, playing with toys, and making verbal requests were followed by praise and other reinforcers can lead to complete suppression of self-injury (Allen and Harris, 1966). More often this procedure only partially suppresses the behavior and must be used in combination with other techniques to produce significant change.

Aversive consequences such as a loud "No," noxious tasting substances, the noxious odor of ammonia capsules, and peripheral electric shock programmed to follow each occurrence of self-injury are occasionally used. The use of contingent shock procedures is credited with a number of rapid and dramatically successful outcomes (Lovaas and Simmons, 1969; Bucher and Lovaas, 1968; Romanczyk and Goren, 1975; Corte et al., 1971). Reductions are, however, often highly situation specific to the treatment setting. Legal (Martin, 1975), ethical, and professional competency concerns place constraints upon the widespread use of the technique. The National Association for Retarded Citizens (May et al., 1975) has published guidelines that aid the practitioner in making ethical, legal, and specific clinical treatment decisions on the use of aversive procedures. In general, aversive procedures are used only when other treatment alternatives are exhausted and only if the behavior is life threatening.

Overcorrection involves components of all of the above techniques. This technique requires that the child repeatedly practice exaggerated or overly correct alternatives to self-injury after each episode. It is thought that the positive practice of such movements (i.e., holding the arms to the sides or behind the back) functions as a timeout from other reinforcers and as aversive stimulation while competing responses are being established. Recent evidence suggests that overcorrection techniques are a particularly effective way to change self-destructive behavior (Foxx and Azrin, 1972; 1973).

Self-Control Techniques. Behavior therapists have used a variety of self-control procedures in the treatment of self-destructive behavior. These different techniques place primary responsibility for behavior change on the patient himself. Because of this, they are not appropriate for many children whose own skills and resources are quite minimal; for example, an autistic head banger. In addition, they are not appropriate techniques to use whenever the particular self-destructive behavior is so high in frequency or intensity that it is life-threatening. Self-control techniques help patients learn to identify the relationship between their own behavior and certain environmental triggers or antecedents which elicit that behavior. Once patients can learn to identify such a response pattern, they are then instructed in some technique which allows them to break the almost automatic pattern of self-destruction which follows from certain antecedents.

In treatments of less health threatening but painful and cosmetically damaging behaviors, such as hair and eyelash pulling, skin and fingernail picking and biting, change in these overt behaviors has been aided by self-instructions and self-delivered rewards as well as by relaxation (Azrin and Nunn, 1978). In theory and practice, it is assumed that while covert processes remain essentially unobserved, they too are functionally related to current environmental determinants and follow the same laws of learning as overt behavior (Kazdin and Wilson, 1978).

Biofeedback in which the child is given a means (i.e., visual display, auditory feedback) to externally monitor a variety of internal physiological responses (heart rate, blood pressure, skin temperature, respiration, brain waves, muscle tension, sphincter control) has led to varying degrees of improvement in a variety of medical disorders (arrythmias, hypertension, Raynaud's disease, seizure disorders, headaches, fecal incontinence). While it is not always clear exactly what new responses children learn to use, changes are often maintained when the feedback is withdrawn. Relaxation training using a variety of methods (progressive muscle relaxation, autogenic training, meditation) has been used to alter similar disorders. Children are carefully weaned from therapist or tape recorded inductions and taught to use relaxation in general and specific problem situations throughout the day.

Improved child compliance with the aforementioned treatments and with life-saving medical regimens, such as dialysis, exercise, dietary and medication schedules has been achieved by simple rearrangements of external rewards and punishments. Additionally, children have been taught to provide their own potential reinforcers for compliance via self-charting and positive self-statements.

Ongoing Evaluation is Systematic

Before a self-destructive child is seen in behavioral treatment many attempts have usually been made to change his behavior. The child may have been threatened, cajoled, spanked, physically restrained, bribed and sometimes even shocked. Parents or institutional staff often are frustrated by their own inability to help the child. A typical complaint is "no matter what we try, nothing seems to work." However, it is often true that the interventions used are not to blame for this state of affairs, but rather, the *way* in which they are used. Faced with a self-destructive child most people will try to do anything to stop the behavior. As a result, many different interventions are introduced in such an unsystematic manner, that it is impossible to determine what works and what doesn't work. For example, a child who is head banging, may be both rewarded with marshmallows for failing to bang his/her head and also physically restrained for engaging in head banging at the same time. On a subsequent day, a totally different intervention such as delivery of an aversive shock might be used. At a later date, perhaps even a different combination of these techniques might be employed. Although such an unsystematic approach may, at times, seem optimal to the clinician faced with an extremely difficult problem, this approach does not facilitate learning on the part of the child. In this case, the consequences for head banging vary from day to day. In addition, when interventions are introduced in this way, the clinician is unable to tell what effect any particular technique has. Self-destructive children do not change rapidly. Usually self-destructive behavior decreases gradually over time and, in the absence of systematic ongoing evaluation, there is no way to determine whether change is actually taking place.

In view of these problems, the behavioral approach to changing self-destructive behavior strongly emphasizes the need to be systematic in both introducing treatment techniques and evaluating their effectiveness. Whenever possible a single treatment technique is instituted at a time. Single case experimental designs (Hersen and Barlow, 1976) are usually employed to evaluate therapy outcome. Several designs are appropriate for analysis of self-destructive behavior. The two most common are the A–B design and the multiple baseline design.

A–B Design. The A–B design involves a comparison between repeated measurements taken pretreatment to those made post-treatment. The A phase of the design consists of repeated observations taken during baseline conditions. The B phase consists of identical observations made under treatment conditions. Treatments are introduced, therefore, at the start of the B phase and used continuously throughout the B phase without modification. For example, a child who is having problems with head banging showed the following rates of head banging on four separate thirty-minute observations: 22, 10, 18 and 25 head bangs per observation. This yielded an average of 18.75 head bands over the A phase or baseline. Observations made during this baseline phase suggested that this child might be very responsive to attention from the teachers and aides working with him. The primary intervention technique, therefore involved having these mediators ignore head banging and positively reinforce, with attention and praise, the child's participation in nonhead banging activities. This intervention was introduced on day one of the B phase and carried out systematically for four days. During the four thirty-minute observation periods carried out over those days, the child showed rates of head banging of 13, 10, 8 and 3 head bangs per period. The resultant decrease in head banging episodes during the B phase suggested that this treatment procedure was effective. This information was helpful in motivating those working with the child to continue the approach over a long time period and follow-up observations made indicated that head banging continued to decrease and after two weeks reached near zero levels. This example shows that data collection is not only part of the behavioral assessment process, but is an integral element in treatment. Outcome data help maintain the whole process of behavior change efforts being used by mediators. In self-control programs similar data can enhance the motivation of the child himself.

The A–B design is very simple and is easily adapted to almost any clinical setting. While it does permit evaluation of baseline *vs.* treatment effects, it is not as methodologically sound as other experimental designs. A variation of the A–B design, the A–B–A–B or withdrawal design, although commonly used by behavior therapists is inappropriate for self-destructive behavior. This design involves withdrawing treatment and determining whether the self-destructive behavior increases in frequency or severity (the second A phase) and then once again reinstituting treatment (the second B phase). The major advantage of this design is that is allows the clinician to rule out important factors other than treatment that may have been responsible for the initial success of that treatment, for example, maturation, coinciding extraneous events, etc. Some might question "if the self-destructive behavior is reduced or gone, why worry about whether the treatment is responsible for that?" The answer to this is, that without knowing the essential elements responsible for behavior change, it is unlikely that change will be maintained and it is also unlikely that any changes could be generalized to other settings. The multiple baseline design does provide a viable yet methodologically sound way of confronting these issues.

Multiple Baseline Design. In the multiple baseline design a single treatment is applied systematically across several target behaviors, several patients or several environmental settings. For example, if one were dealing with a group of autistic children all of whom showed head banging, a positive reinforcement procedure such as the one described above, could be introduced after three days of baseline for subject #1, after six days of baseline for subject #2 and after nine days of baseline for subject #3. If the frequency of head banging showed a marked decline immediately following introduction of treatment for each of these children, then one would conclude with more justification that this is an effective treatment. The resulting behavior change would not appear to be due to extraneous events, since one would expect these events to effect the behavior of all simultaneously, since they are in the same setting and not precisely at the point of introduction of therapy.

When ongoing evaluation of treatment is as systematic as is outlined above, the impact of any given treatment procedure can be thoroughly evaluated. If this treatment is found to be ineffective, modifications are introduced. It is important to point out that this type of systematic, ongoing evaluation is the essence of the behavioral approach. Treatment programs which do not use such systematic approaches should *not* be considered behavioral treatment programs. Although these programs may use certain behavioral treatment techniques, such as positive reinforcement, aversive conditioning, relaxation, etc., their failure to measure the resultant impact of these techniques puts them in the realm of more traditional therapy approaches. This is not to say that these programs may not work or that traditional treatment of the self-destructive child is never effective, but rather that these programs are simply not embodying the basic principles of behavioral approach and, therefore, do not represent an adequate test of behavioral treatment of the self-destructive child.

Maintenance and Generalization of Behavior Change is Planned

Historically, the maintenance of behavioral treatment gains was often unplanned. The "train and hope" method (Stokes and Baer, 1977) was common. No specific provisions were made to ensure that behaviors treated intensively in one setting would be maintained in other settings. Generalization of gains sometimes occurred, but unpredictably. Increases in toy play, social responsiveness to adults and peers, and reductions in the necessity for restraint following use of a variety of positive and aversive behavioral treatments, in general belied the notion that other problem behaviors would be substituted if the "symptomatic" treatments of the behavioral approach were used (Bucher and Lovass, 1968; Epstein et al., 1974; Risley, 1968; Sajwaj, Twardosz and Burke, 1972; Tate and Baroff,

1966). One assumption that is no longer made by sophisticated behavioral clinicians is that treatments will automatically generalize across behaviors and settings. It is widely agreed that generalization must be programmed into treatment in order to occur reliably. A number of strategies are employed by behavior therapists to directly promote carryover of gains (Stokes and Baer, 1977). Treatments found to be successful in one setting such as clinic or hospital are applied sequentially in other settings such as home or school by parents and teachers. The structured and intensive procedures often required to produce change during initial stages of treatment when self-injury is severe can be carefully faded to approximate conditions available in more normalized settings. For instance, powerful but inconvenient rewards for alternatives to self-injury such as candy given numerous times per hour can be gradually replaced with more naturally occurring rewards such as praise and access to toys made available less frequently and less predictably over time. The use of peers, siblings, parents, and teachers in addition to the therapist to carry out some aspects or all of the treatment plan can enhance carryover by making it difficult for the child to discriminate when the treatment regimen is and is not in effect. Also helpful are procedures which train individuals to mediate carryover themselves. Appropriate children may be taught to monitor their own problem behavior outside of the original treatment setting by recording its occurrence and by delivering their own rewards for progress.

APPLICATIONS OF THE BEHAVIORAL APPROACH

In this section we consider the practical application of the basic elements of behavioral approaches reviewed above. We consider two typical cases: one in which a contingency management approach was used and one in which a self-control approach was used.

CASE 1: REDUCTION OF FACE SLAPPING USING CONTINGENCY MANAGEMENT TECHNIQUES

Jane was an eleven-year-old, institutionalized, severely retarded child, who repeatedly slapped her face. Face hitting, which did not break the skin, left her cheeks reddened and bruised and was normally accompanied by crying or screaming. There was no known etiology for her retardation but she was partially blind with one eye removed and cataracts on the other. She had no expressive language and required pointing cues to follow simple instructions. Her participation in an intensive, waking hour, self-help training, and socialization program during the six months prior to this intervention had led to an increase in some thirty-three new skills measured on an adaptive behavior checklist (Gunzburg, 1966) in the areas of dressing, feeding, and toileting. Rates of self-injury which were ignored by clinical, educational and child care staff appeared unaffected during this period. Self-injury seemed to interfere with further gains in self-help and fine motor skills.

To determine if rates differed, self-injury was assessed in two settings. In the first setting, a teacher worked on fine and gross motor tasks individually with the children for forty minutes twice each day. In the second setting an interested child-care assistant supervised the child ten minutes each day in a living area furnished with chairs, a couch, rug and toys. To determine if rates of self-injury increased when the child was required to follow instructions, observations were taken while the child was engaged in free-play and while simple instructions were given in both settings. Jane's face hitting was extremely frequent (several hundred per hour) and was interspersed with a rapid, stereotypic behavior in which she tapped her chin with her finger. This behavior was included in the definition of self-injury since it too interfered with learning and appeared to be functionally related to face hitting.

Measurement of these extremely frequent behaviors was also simplified by recording the occurrence or nonoccurrence of the behavior during successive intervals rather than by counting actual frequencies. The percent of ten-second intervals in which the behavior occurred was the primary measure. On analysis, the data gathered indicated that the child was receiving no apparent positive consequences for alternative appropriate behaviors that did occur. However, given the low rates of alternative behavior relative to self-injury, reinforcement for appropriate behavior may have been too infrequent. During pretesting, the response occurred during some 80% of the intervals during free play but was actually *lower* during structured play when instructions were given. The rate during structured play was 50%. Interestingly, appropriate play, defined as contact with toys during each ten-second interval in free play and, more stringently, in structured play as compliance with toy-related teacher instructions (pull the wagon, bounce the ball, etc.) given every ten seconds, occurred only during structured play.

Staff were instructed to continue ignoring self-injury but to follow appropriate free play and instruction for purposes of intervention, with much more powerful rewards (candy, sips of juice, enthusiastic praise) every thirty seconds these behaviors were observed. After one week of twice daily, 40-minute sessions with the classroom teacher this intervention decreased self-injury to 40% and 20% in structured and free play respectively. Rates during shorter ten-minute sessions in the child's living unit were unaffected. It was decided that this positive program of rewards while effective was not enough. Thus, during the next two weeks an *overcorrection procedure* was combined with the reinforcement program in the classroom only. Immediately following each occurrence of self-injury, the child was told "No, hands down!" in a firm voice. The teacher briefly restrained the child's hands and then, holding her forearms, moved the child's arms to one of three positions: above the head, out from the sides and down at the sides (Foxx and Azrin, 1973). Arm positions were changed, in random order, every ten seconds until two minutes had elapsed. No other verbal or gestural prompts were given.

With the addition of the overcorrection procedure, self-injury reached zero percentages during structured play after nine sessions and occurred only twice during the following sixteen sessions. During free play, some fifteen sessions were required to achieve zero percentages and occurrence varied between zero and 5% thereafter. To determine if the improvement would be maintained when overcorrection was unavailable, the procedure was not used during the next five days. Since self-injury increased to former rates the treatment procedures were reapplied and used continuously in the classroom. Percentages remained at or near zero during the next ten sessions in which data was collected. Simultaneous with the decrease in self-injury, appropriate play was found to increase to near 90% in structured play and 66% in free play. The procedure was recommended for continued use during classroom activities.

Unfortunately, despite these successes self-injury in the child's home living unit remained at high levels. Overcorrection was subsequently tested in the home living unit, with the result that face hitting dropped to an average of 8% in structured play and 5% in free play. While data was kept during only brief ten-minute test sessions, it was reasoned that percentages would reach zero if longer sessions were used. The procedure was recommended for use during longer periods and eventually throughout the day.

The above case illustrates several points discussed earlier. Jane's self-injury interspersed with self-stimulatory behavior, appeared to be unaffected by the withdrawal of adult attention and was found to be only partially suppressed when social and appetitive rewards were made contingent on competing play and instruction-following behavior. Near complete suppression of self-injury and a positive side effect in the form of a dramatic increase in appropriate play was found when a mildly punishing consequence was used. The treatment failed to generalize to a second setting and, therefore, had to be applied by a child care worker for change in that setting to occur.

CASE 2: REDUCTION OF PRURITIS USING SELF-CONTROL TECHNIQUES

Sandra B is a thirteen-year-old girl with a history of dermatological problems dating back to age four. Her current diagnosis is that of atopic dermatitis. Her symptoms include persistent itching and superficial inflammation of the skin. Because of her tendency to scratch and rub inflammed areas, she is often bothered by excoriations. The areas infected include her face, neck and popliteal spaces. Associated with her dermatological problems is a marked behavioral problem consisting of chronic scratching. In Sandra's case the scratching is so prominent that she has developed sores which crust and ooze. As a result, she often develops secondary infections. Sandara has been managed primarily through the use of a variety of ointments, lotions, and topical steroids. Over the years she has been admitted frequently to the hospital, has managed to show marked improvement with medication, but upon discharge she resumes scratching and the problem flares up once again.

During an initial interview, Sandra did not scratch any of the affected areas. However, she scratched and touched many other body areas, her hair, legs, shoulders, etc. Sandra also reported that her scratching tends to increase when she is tense, upset, angry or frustrated and decreased if she is distracted or relaxed. In an interview with Sandra's mother, she revealed that Sandra's scratching problem has been the focus of many negative interactions between them. Sandra's mother reported that she "constantly" has to remind her daughter to stop scratching and feels frustrated by the fact that this doesn't seem to work. She stated that if she doesn't "keep after her," Sandra does not seem to try.

These initial interviews suggested that Sandra was an intelligent, young woman who was motivated and had the skills to adopt behavioral self-control procedures for controlling scratching. It was also felt that her mother's negative attention may, in some way, be functioning to maintain the problem and that instructing the mother to let Sandra carry out the program on her own, might help eliminate this source of possible reinforcement. It was also reasoned that touching of other nonaffected areas of the body was a habit for Sandra which was topographically similar to scratching and probably functionally related. As a result, a broad definition of scratching was arrived at by the therapist and Sandra. Briefly, scratching was defined as any touching of an area of exposed skin. A three-phase behavioral approach program was instituted.

During the first phase, baseline, Sandra was asked to keep daily records of the frequency of her scratching. She was given a 3" x 5" card and asked to make a mark on the card each time that she scratched. She was also asked to rate her itching three times a day, at breakfast, lunch and dinner. Data on both scratching and itching were displayed on simple graphs placed at her bedside. In the course of this phase of treatment, Sandra was encouraged to become as aware as possible of the relationship between scratching and various environmental events.

The goal of the second phase of training was to teach Sandra to relax those muscles in her arms involved in the scratching response. She was initially trained in progressive muscle relaxation, given a relaxation tape and asked to practive with this routinely. She was then trained to use brief, one-minute periods of profound relaxation of the wrist flexors and extensors as a response incompatible with scratching. Each time Sandra had the urge or actually began to move as if to scratch, she was instructed to place her arms in her lap and relax the forearm muscles as deeply as possible. She continued to keep records during this phase.

During the final or maintenance phase of training, Sandra was given instructions to continue with the program on her own as an outpatient. She was asked to continue keeping daily records of scratching and itching and to continue practicing with the relaxation tape and brief relaxation periods. Phone call follow-ups for the purpose of data collection and discussing treatment progress were made at weeks two, four, eight and twelve.

Our results showed that Sandra decreased scratching by 90% and maintained very low levels of scratching following the introduction of the treatment procedures. Along with this behavioral change, there was also a pronounced reduction in the attendant costs of the various medications which she had been relying upon. Sandra has maintained these changes at six month follow-up and the physicians working with her report that this is the longest period of time that she has been asymptomatic in years. Sandra takes great pride in her progress. Her mother is quite pleased and has welcomed the change in their relationship brought about by this program as well.

This case illustrates the potential of simple, inexpensive self-control procedures in reducing long-standing habit patterns. Such programs can be applied to help change numerous self-destructive behaviors. We often find that even in cases in which a contingency management program is needed, that combining that program with a self-control program facilitates behavior change.

DISCUSSION

What may now be obvious to the reader is that the stereotype which suggests that a behavioral approach to self-destructive behavior relies on aversive methods is inaccurate. From the perspective of current theory, research and practice, the image of a cadre of unfeeling "behavior modifiers" wielding cattleprods on the neglected back wards of a state institution simply does not hold up.

Applications of behavioral technology in the early 1960s did include some use of peripheral electric shock to control self-injury. While comparative figures on the use of these procedures are unavailable there are several reasons why use of shock may have been more frequent then than now. As purveyors of a new treatment technology, behavior analysts often found themselves treating patients with severe disorders that had not yielded to other forms of therapy. They had, at that time a more limited number of techniques available and often were without staff resources to consistently carry out positve reinforcement programs. It is not surprising then that the relatively brief treatment normally required to decelerate self-injury with shock was chosen. In addition, the specificity in target behaviors, treatment methods and outcome measures (Stolz, 1977) of the behavioral approach opened it to easy scrutiny and possible criticism. Similarly, both the failures as well as the successes of behavioral treatment may have been identified with deprived institutional environments in which violations of patients' human and treatment rights were common long before behavioral approaches were ever introduced. While aversive treatments have freed many individuals from lifelong regimens of physical or chemical restraint, the use of such treatments with individuals too mentally impaired to give consent appeared to some as more dehumanizing than restraint.

In contrast, currently armed with a much expanded repertoire of available interventions, operating in better staffed residential programs, schools, medical centers and community clinics, behavior analysts are treating individuals competent to make informed decisions or represented by well informed advocates or guardians. In many settings aversive procedures take their place in a hierarchy of possible treatments in which the least intrusive is normally recommended. While the commitment to a thorough behavior analysis of the problem as a means of matching the best treatment to the client remains strong, it is now done in the context of legal and ethical concerns which balance the patient's rights to the most effective and least restrictive treatment. For example, behavior analysts have participated in the establishment of regulations for the use of aversive and deprivation procedures in several states (Thomas, 1979). These documents set standards for use of any procedure with an aversive or deprivation component regardless of the professional discipline or treatment approach from which they were derived (Stolz, 1977). In these regulations and in guidelines published by the National Association of Retarded Citizens (May *et al.,* 1975; Sajwaj, 1977) it is characteristic that procedures are grouped in three to four levels according to intrusiveness and risk. Each level has progressively more stringent requirements for paraprofessional staff training, monitoring by supervising professional staff, the timing and extent of approval by patient's rights committees, patient or guardian consent if necessary and documentation of the prior failure of more benign techniques.

In conclusion, it appears that behavioral clinicians have much to offer in the treatment of self-destructive behavior. The behavioral approach is a comprehensive one that provides the practicing clinician with specific guidelines for both assessment and treatment. Over the past two decades this approach has become increasingly more sophisticated and attuned to the needs of children and their families. We expect this trend to continue with resultant benefits not only to self-destructive children but to society as a whole.

REFERENCES

1. Allen, K. E., and Harris, F. R. Elimination of a child's excessive scratching by training the mother in reinforcement procedures. *Beh. Res. Ther.* **4**:79–84, 1966.
2. Azrin, N. H., and Nunn, L. G. *Habit Control in a Day*. New York: Pocket Books, 1978.
3. Baumeister, A. A., and Forehand, R. Stereotyped acts. *In: International Review of Research in Mental Retardation* (Vol. 6), N. R. Ellis (ed.) New York: Academic Press, 1974.
4. Bucher, B., and Lovaas, O. I. Use of aversive stimulation in behavior modification. *In: Miami Symposium on the Prediction of Behavior*. 1967: *Aversive stimulation*. M. Jones (ed.) Coral Gables, Florida: University of Miami Press, 1968.
5. Cautela, J. R. Behavior Analysis Forms for Clinical Intervention. Champaign, Illinois: Research Press, 1977.
6. Corte, H. E., Wolf, M. M., and Locke, B. J. A comparison of procedures for eliminating self-injurious behavior of retarded adolescents. *J. App. Beh. Anal.* **4**:201-213, 1971.
7. Epstein, L H., Dole, L. A., Sajwaj, T. E., *et al.* Generality and side effects of overcorrection. *J. App. Beh. Anal.* **7**:385–390, 1974.
8. Favell, J. E., McGimsey, J. F., and Jones, M. L. The use of physical restraint in the treatment of self-injury and as positive reinforcement. *J. App. Beh. Anal.* **11**:225–241, 1978.
9. Foxx, R. M., and Azrin, N H. Restitution: A method of eliminating aggressive disruptive behavior of retarded and brain damaged patients. *Beh. Res. Ther.* **10**:15-27, 1972.
10. Foxx, R. M., and Azrin, N. H. The elimination of autistic self-stimulatory behavior by overcorrection. *J. App. Beh. Anal.* **6**:1–14, 1973.
11. Frankel, F., and Simmons, J. Q. Self-injurious behavior in schizophrenic and retarded children. *Am. J. Men. Def.* **80**:512–522, 1976.
12. Gunzburg, H. C. Primary progress assessment chart of social and personal development. Birmingham, England: SEFA Publications, 1966.
13. Hersen, M. and Barlow, D. Single case experimental designs: Strategies for studying behavior change. New York: Pergamon Press, 1976.
14. Jones, F. H., Simmons, J. Q., and Frankel, F. An extinction procedure for eliminating self-destructive behavior in a 9-year-old autistic girl. *J. Aut. Child. Schizophren.* **4**:241–250, 1974.
15. Keefe, F. J., Kopel, S., and Gordon, S. B. *A Practical Guide to Behavioral Assessment*. New York: Springer, 1978.

16. Kazdin, A. E., and Wilson, G. T. *Evaluation of Behavior Therapy: Issues, Evidence and Research Strategies.* Cambridge, MA: Ballinger, 1978.
17. Lovaas, O. I., and Simmons, J. Q. Manipulation of self-destruction in three retarded children. *J. App. Beh. Anal.* **2**:143–157, 1969.
18. Martin, R: *Legal Challenges to Behavior Modification.* Champaign, Illinois: Research Press Inc, 1975.
19. May, J. G., Risley, T. R., Twardosz, S., et al. Guidelines for the use of behavioral procedures in state programs for retarded persons. M. R. Research, 1975.
20. Risley, T. R. The effects and side effects of punishing the autistic behaviors of a deviant child. *J. App. Beh. Anal.* **1**:21–34, 1968.
21. Romanczyk, R. G., and Goren, E. R. Severe self-injurious behavior: The problem of clinical control. *J. Cons. Clin. Psych.* **48**:730–739, 1975.
22. Russo, D. C., Carr, E. G., and Lovaas, O. I. Self-injury in pediatric populations. *In: Advances in Behavioral Medicine,* J. Ferguson and C. B. Taylor (eds.), Holliswood, New York: Spectrum Publications, 1979.
23. Sajwaj, T.: Issues and implications of establishing guidelines for the use of behavioral techniques. *J. App. Beh. Anal.* **10**:531–540, 1977.
24. Sajwaj, T., Twardosz, S., and Burke, M. Side effects of extinction procedures in a remedial preschool. *J. App. Beh. Anal.* **5**:163–176, 1972.
25. Shodell, M. J., and Reiter, H. H. Self-mutilative behavior in verbal and non-verbal schizophrenic children. *Arch. Gen. Psychiat.* **19**:453–455, 1968.
26. Skinner, B. F. *Science and Human Behavior.* New York: Macmillan, 1953.
27. Stokes, T. F., and Baer, R. M. An implicit technology of generalization. *J. App. Beh. Anal.* **10**:349–267, 1977.
28. Stolz, S. Why no guidelines for behavior modification. *J. App. Beh. Anal.* **10**:541–547, 1977.
29. Tate, B. G., and Baroff, G. S. Aversive control of self-injurious behavior in a psychotic boy. *Beh. Res. Ther.* **4**:281–287, 1966.
30. Thomas, D. R. Certification of behavior analysts in Minnesota. *Beh. Analyst* **2**:1–13, 1979.
31. Williams, R. B., and Gentry, W. D. (eds.) *Behavioral Approaches to Medical Treatment.* Philadelphia: Ballinger, 1977.

In an instructive manner, the authors investigate the core of a problem familiar to all therapists. Premature interruption of therapy and deterioration effects in either patient, parents, or both, have thwarted efforts to carry therapy to a successful conclusion and represent self-destructive behavior. Reviewing pertinent literature on negative therapeutic reactions, Drs. Keith, Curry, and Autry proceed to illustrate through case material empirical behavioral evidence supporting their conclusions. No small satisfaction with their presentation of this material lies in the suggestions they make for handling common problems of the therapist and patient in this area.

16
Self-Destructive Forces in the Psychotherapy of Children: The Negative Therapeutic Reaction

Charles Keith, M.D.,
John F. Curry, Ph.D.,
Bess Autry, ACSW

INTRODUCTION

The tendency to romanticize the past often combines with the repressive focus of childhood to cloud the fact of self-destructive forces within children. Child therapists can fall prey to this romanticizing as they begin their child therapy cases, only to be brought up short as the child patient attempts to defeat the therapy and the therapist's good intentions through destructive, resistive processes which often are manifested by self-destructive activity. In this chapter, we will focus on one particular form of that behavior, namely the negative therapeutic reaction discussed at length by adult psychotherapists but rarely mentioned in the child psychotherapy literature.

Since any self-destructive activity has both intrapsychic and interpersonal symbolic determinants, we must include in our discussion the role of the parents who make child therapy possible and yet may defeat it through their own needs, fears, and guilt. The third party in this "tripolar" therapeutic field is, of course, the therapist who is always drawn either wittingly or unwittingly into the self-destructive processes and whose interventions are intended to reverse the repetition of those patterns within the child and family unit.

Although our case examples will focus on individual child therapy with concomitant parent work, the same self-destructive forces in the therapeutic field take place in other child treatment modalities, e.g., family and group therapy.

A PROPOSED CONTINUUM OF SELF-DESTRUCTIVE FORCES IN PSYCHOTHERAPY

Within the psychotherapeutic setting, self-destructive forces fall along a continuum from the general or universal to the specific or particular. This continuum actually constitutes a gradient of increasing antitherapeutic influences. At one end is the antitherapeutic factor common to all patient-therapist dyads, namely, resistance. While resistance ordinarily presents formidable obstacles to progress, it can be recognized and used constructively by the therapist and patient.

Toward the other end of the continuum are those rarer, more difficult forms of resistance termed negative therapeutic reactions. These are generally threats to the continuation of psychotherapy and can make extraordinary demands upon the therapist (Gorney, 1979) or even be taken as *a posteriori* indicators of the unsuitability of patients for treatment (Loewald, 1972).

General problems in psychotherapy process and outcome appear to be related to negative therapeutic reactions. Although it has not yet been demonstrated through well-controlled studies, certain types of premature interruption of the psychotherapy process are probably a function of such reactions. Similarly, it is probable that negative therapeutic reactions play a role in some cases of therapeutic deterioration, i.e., cases in which patients get worse as a result of therapy. Such outcomes are a function of the most extreme forces along the proposed continuum of self-destructive influences in psychotherapy.

This review of literature follows the forces from the general to the specific along the continuum of self-destructiveness in psychotherapy. Following a review of the concept of negative therapeutic reaction, attention will be directed toward the process and outcome problems mentioned above; premature interruption and deterioration effects. Finally, classes of variables associated with self-destructive therapeutic forces will be summarized as a prelude to discussion of clinical case material.

FROM RESISTANCE TO NEGATIVE THERAPEUTIC REACTIONS

In the *Introductory Lectures on Psychoanalysis* delivered in 1917, Freud proposed the unlikely proposition that a patient seeking relief from troubling symptoms tenaciously resists the efforts of the therapist throughout treatment (Freud, 1916–1917). The general concepts of resistance included numerous forms such as resistance to the rule of free association, intellectual resistance to psychoanalytic theory, and transference resistance. Freud proposed that resistance was a universal phenomenon in analytic therapy with an essential relationship to progress in the treatment because resistance arose from repressed material central to the neurosis. Indeed, in "Resistance and Repression," he claimed that overcoming resistance is the "essential function of analysis" (Ibid., p. 291).

Nonpsychoanalytic therapists have also recognized the frequency of phenomena included under the analytic umbrella of "resistance." In his synthesis of psychoanalysis and behavior therapy, Wachtel (1977) notes that most practicing behavior therapists acknowledge the frequency of patient behaviors that run counter to the desirable course of therapy. He cites the frequent resistances reported by Rhoads and Feather (1972) in their desensitization studies, but adds that, in general, the behavioral literature has given inadequate attention to such phenomena as patient noncompliance with assignments, missed sessions, etc.

Child and adolescent psychotherapists have also recognized the particular forms of resistance aroused in young patients or their families. Sprince (1971), for example, has discussed at length the problems of maintaining a therapeutic alliance in the face of mother-son collusion against treatment and fear of health. Particular resistances of aggressive children have been addressed by Frankel (1977), and six patterns of resistance found in child and adolescent patients have been analyzed by Marshall (1976) from a learning theory point of view.

Resistance, then, is generally recognized by therapists of varying theoretical persuasions, working both with adult and with child-adolescent patients. While the overcoming or working through of resistances assumes a more central role in psychoanalytic than in other forms of psychotherapy, the existence of high frequency, ostensibly contratherapeutic behavior and the need to deal with such behavior are generally accepted. In contrast, the more specific form of resistance known as the negative therapeutic reaction has been discussed almost exclusively within the framework of adult psychoanalysis. As a potentially self-destructive force within treatment it is both rarer and much more difficult to surmount than other types of resistance.

Leowald (1972) notes that for Freud the negative therapeutic reaction was not primarily a reaction against the therapist or therapeutic technique, but against the improvement of the patient's conditon. Rooted structurally in the superego, the negative therapeutic reaction consists in part of a powerful sense of guilt and a need for punishment that interfere with progress toward improved health. Far from being a well-delineated excess of superego functioning, however, Loewald (1972) states that the reaction in question was, for Freud, often indicative of a more pervasive poorly structured predominance of the death instinct over the life instinct. The more the latter was the case—the less such reactions could be understood simply as harsh superego functioning—the lower the probability of successful treatment.

Horney (1936) pointed out that negative therapeutic reactions occur in those instances when the patient shows worsening of symptoms, discouragement, or desire to terminate following an encouragement or the attainment of real insight. The reaction is thus, paradoxical rather than direct, and follows a good, not a poor, therapeutic interpretation. She described five types of negative therapeutic reactions to good interpretations: those in which the interpretation is perceived as hostile competition, as a narcissist blow, as a movement toward success (which is equated with destruction of others), as an accusation, and as a personal rejection. In the writings of Horney and of Freud, the locus of the negative reaction is within the intrapsychic apparatus of the patient; and, presumably, the reaction would be aroused by successful movement in any type of therapy (Loewald, 1972).

A more contemporary review (Gorney, 1979) locates negative therapeutic reactions within the "bipersonal field" (Langs, 1976) of the psychotherapeutic relationship. While certain intrapsychic and developmental features are hypothesized as likely to characterize patients who develop negative reactions, the view elaborated by Gorney stresses the centrality of the therapist's countertransference negativity in maintaining the stalemate of negative therapeutic reactions and blocking progress toward resolution of the reactions. Gorney's notion of negative reaction is broader than Freud's and Horney's classical view that operationally defines such reactions as negative reactions to interpretations. In the broader, interactional view, the negative therapeutic reaction is a massive attack upon the role and personal qualities of the therapist, giving rise to feelings of frustration, discouragement, and emotional depletion in the countertransference.

The negative therapeutic reaction has not been the focus of writings in child analysis or child psychotherapy, nor has the concept been used by nonpsychoanalytic adult therapists, probably because of its classical operational definition as a paradoxical reaction to interpretation. Although Sprince (1971) organizes her presentation of a case of massive resistance in an adolescent boy around the notion that both the son and mother suffered from an intense fear of successful treatment, and although she describes quite clearly certain treatment phenomena consistent with a negative therapeutic reaction (e.g., increased symptoms following accurate interpretations, the patient's perception of success as an attack on significant others), she does not use the technical term in her article. Nonetheless, this contribution is probably the clearest example of a negative therapeutic reaction in the child literature.

In summary, the major psychoanalytic writings on negative therapeutic reaction cite certain characteristics of the patient, and of the patient-therapist bipolar field, which are likely to contribute to such reactions. The defining characteristic in the patient is a repetitive tendency to become symptomatically worse each time an issue in treatment has apparently been resolved (Freud, 1918), or partially resolved by accurate interpretation (Freud, 1923). A second characteristic is the patient's pattern of aggressive verbal attack upon the therapist (Horney, 1936) including not only the therapist's technique but also the therapist's personal qualities (Gorney, 1979).

With the advent of ego psychology, developmental aspects of negative reaction patients have been emphasized. Olinick (1964) related these therapeutic reactions to negativism arising out of autonomy conflicts in the second year of life. The severity of these conflicts has been stressed by Gorney (1979) in his developmental profile of negative reaction patients. On the basis of clinical case histories, he hypothesizes that such patients have mothers who were depressed and emotionally absent during the separation-individuation process. Consequently, they develop a conflict between the wish for and fear of regressive union with the mother, a conflict accompanied by both rage and longing. Guilt toward the mother, flowing from the equation of movement toward separation with abandonment of the needy mother, then accounts for the need to fail and inability to tolerate therapeutic improvement.

No particular personal characteristics of therapists are posited as leading to negative therapeutic reactions. Rather, any therapist could experience or contribute to the continuation of such reactions. Gorney has developed the countertransference aspects of such reactions at length. In general, the therapist forms a negative countertransference secondary to the feelings of inadequacy and uncertainty regarding technique aroused by the patient's attacks. The negativity within the countertransference blocks the therapist from permitting full expression of the patient's negativism and thus blocks the emergence of developmentally more basic issues. Unless the resulting stalemate is resolved, there is a continuing risk of acting out or of premature interruption of treatment.

Gorney's major contribution has been to delineate the reciprocity of patient and therapist in maintaining a negative therapeutic reaction. Secondarily, he has pointed out certain modifications of technique needed to break therapeutic stalemate, including nonverbal, demonstrative behavioral interventions.

As noted above, no direct applications of the negative therapeutic reaction construct to child psychotherapy have been observed in the literature. From the writings of Sprince (1971) and Gorney (1979), however, certain characteristics of the families of these child patients can be inferred. The primary characteristic would be a parent-child tie in which improvement of the child's psychological functioning would be equated with abandonment of the needy parent. Such a pattern could exist in families where the parent is physically ill, excessively dependent, or depressed. In treatment, Sprince has noted that such a tie would be indicated by behaviors in which the patient accuses the therapist of intrusive attacks and reports on these "attacks" (interpretations) to his parent. In addition, these child patients, like their adult counterparts, are characterized by irrational, guilt-motivated reactions to steps toward improvement, as will be illustrated in our clinical material.

PROBLEMS IN PSYCHOTHERAPY POTENTIALLY RELATED TO SELF-DESTRUCTIVE FORCES

The self-destructive forces mentioned above, ranging from resistance to negative therapeutic reactions can arise in the identified patient or in his family or in the patient-therapist bipolar field. An understanding of these forces is of potential significance in avoiding two major problems in psychotherapy, premature interruption and deterioration effects.

PREMATURE INTERRUPTION

Premature interruption has long been recognized as a major problem in the delivery of psychotherapeutic services. Primarily, it is considered problematic because it creates a waste of service delivery hours; i.e., considerable professional time is given to diagnostic and/or early therapeutic work with patients who then terminate unilaterally or against professional advice (Ross and Lacey, 1961). Moreover, there are conflicting opinions over whether patients who prematurely terminate benefit as much from therapy as patients who continue (Yalom, 1966; Garfield, 1978).

The range of sessions and time involved in the treatment of premature terminators varies widely according to the type of service delivered. In long-term psychoanalytically oriented treatment, patients who remain in therapy for up to eighteen months may still be defined as premature terminators if they stop against therapist advice (Fielding, 1972). Contrasted with this are the data presented by Garfield and Kurz (1952) indicating that the median length of treatment for 560 patients in a V.A. clinic was six interviews. More recent studies (Dodd, 1970; Brown and Kosterlitz, 1964) in university-affiliated clinics yield a similar picture of the short duration of treatment. Reviewing the data on length of stay, Garfield (1978) concludes that most patients stop therapy unilaterally and that such terminations are viewed as problematic by clinicians.

Considerable effort has been expended to determine factors causing premature interruption in adult psychotherapy. In general, the demographic variable of higher socioeconomic status has been found to correlate positively with remaining in therapy in most but not all studies. (McNair, Lorr and Callahan, 1963; Rubinstein and Lorr, 1956; Pope, Geller and Wilkinson, 1975). Other demographic variables such as sex, age, and diagnosis have not yielded significant correlation with remaining in therapy (Garfield, 1978).

In view of the importance of socioeconomic status as a predictor of continuation, several investigators have focused on the differing expectations brought to psychotherapy by lower-class patients. Heine and Trosman (1960) found that patients who expected to be passive and receive directive advice and information from the therapist were more likely to terminate before the sixth week of treatment than were those who expected to be active collaborators with the therapist. To the extent that the therapist failed to fulfill the expectation, patients were less likely to return for treatment. The significance of therapeutic expectancies for continuation, as well as efforts to match expectancies and treatment process have been topics of extensive recent interest which is beyond the scope of this review. The reader is referred to Garfield (1978), Wilkins (1973), Rosen (1976) Levitt (1966) and Goldstein (1962) for detailed reviews.

Another series of studies has investigated dynamic or interactive factors in premature interruption of adult or family psychotherapy. Fielding (1972), in a retrospective interview study, demonstrated that premature interruption occurred in analytic treatment when specific patient behavior aroused specific personality problems in the therapist. Such interactions could represent instances of the negative therapeutic reaction as described by Gorney. Seeman (1974) hypothesized that patients unilaterally terminate dynamic psychotherapy when the interaction between patient and therapist approximates the interaction between patient and parents at the time the patient left home.

In a study of private practice premature terminators, Levinson et al. (1978) found that dynamic reactions to the treatment situation were the most frequent cause of dropping out, followed by intrapsychic factors and countertransference. All of the above studies suffer from major flaws of design (*ex post facto* analysis, lack of "blind" ratings, lack of controls), but they suggest that dynamic factors related to the continuum of self-destructive forces in the therapeutic field can cause premature interruption in individual therapy.

Studies by Shapiro (1974) and Shapiro annd Budman (1973) similarly point to the centrality of the patient-therapist interaction as causing premature interruption in child and family treatment. In either modality, the major reason cited for dropping out was negative perceptions of the therapist's activity level, concern, or empathic capacity. Reciprocally, therapists were found to have had much more positive initial affective reaction to remainers than to terminators, suggesting that termination was partly a function of feeling rejected by the therapist.

Patient or family characteristics have also been shown significant in the decision to remain in child psychotherapy. Holmes and Urie (1975) found that a preparation session which focused on a child's expectations of therapy was effective in reducing premature interruption. Lake and Levinger (1960) found that parents of continuers were more likely than parents of terminators to see the presenting problem as a family problem to which they contributed. Ross and Lacey (1961) found that remainers in child guidance treatment had more developmental difficulties, odd behavior, and somatic complaints than terminators, and that remainer's parents were more likely to be in concurrent treatment and to have endured a waiting list period than the parents of terminators. Levitt (1978) however, found that expert judgment of motivation for treatment, or severity of problem, did not discriminate between remainers and terminators.

DETERIORATION EFFECTS

The growing awareness that the condition of some patients actually deteriorates in psychotherapy is a more recent concern than premature interruption. Bergin and Lambert (1978) present evidence from nine studies of adolescents and adults in individual therapy showing that treated patients show greater variance after treatment than do control groups, i.e., there is more positive and negative movement in the treated group compared to that in the control group. The phenomenon of deterioration does not appear to be confined to a therapeutic school or treatment modality. Bednar and Kaul (1978) review several studies of group therapy yielding evidence of deterioration in up to 8% of treated parents. Likewise, Gurman and Kniskern (1978) report rates of deterioration in marital and family therapies ranging from 0 to 16% in studies reporting such a category. Strupp et al. (1977), while taking issue with the empirical base of the deterioration claims, present personal letters from a wide range of therapists attesting to the existence of deterioration effects across schools, modalities, and types of patients.

Systematic studies of deterioration effects in child psychotherapy have not been carried out. Some research evidence does exist, however, in Rick's (1974) follow-up of adolescents seen in individual therapy by one of two therapists. One therapist, using supportive, adaptive methods for more disturbed patients achieved relative success at follow-up (27% of cases were still psychotic), while the other, using confrontive, uncovering methods had a serious failure rate (84% psychotic).

Bergin (1978) has reviewed factors presently known to influence deterioration. Among patient variables, low ego strength or severity of initial disturbance appears related to deterioration at termination. Strupp et al. (1977) cited many possible therapist factors that could lead to deterioration. Bergin (1978) has taken the position that interactional characteristics of the patient-therapist encounter, rather than demographic or stable trait variables are likely to be of importance in predicting deterioration risk. The Ricks study, cited above, suggests a pathological match between seriously disturbed patients and an inflexible, uncovering, pessimistic therapist causes deterioration. Yalom and Lieberman (1971) found that overly aggressive, intrusive, authoritarian group leaders who tended to demand high disclosure and immediate emotional expression were factors in the deterioration of initially more disturbed patients. Thus, it would appear from the limited data available, that deterioration depends on a mismatch, and that certain patient and therapist factors can be identified as contributing to these negative outcomes.

SUMMARY

Self-destructive forces in psychotherapy are those which lead to the destruction of the therapeutic endeavor or to actual deterioration in the condition of the patient. The existence of such forces is implied by the psychotherapeutic problems of premature interruption and deterioration effects.

Various classes of variable have been examined as contributing toward the destruction of the therapeutic relationship or toward the worsening condition of the patient, both in adult and in child-adolescent psychotherapy. These classes include demographic, personality, and psychodynamic-interactive factors. The demographic variable of socioeconomic status appears related to premature interruption, but it has not been related to deterioration. Essentially cognitive personality variables such as expectancies appear significant in maintaining the therapeutic relationship; but, again, there is little evidence that they otherwise affect outcome.

More global personality variables such as ego strength or degree of disturbance do appear related to outcome and deterioration. Certain types of disturbance in early object relations are also hypothesized as contributing to negative therapeutic reaction within the analytic situation.

Psychodynamic factors, including various forms of mild to severe negative therapeutic reactions probably underlie many clinical instances of premature interruption, lack of improvement, or deterioration. These factors are generally interactive, involving the relationship between patient and therapist.

CLINICAL ILLUSTRATIONS

The following three clinical vignettes illustrate the negative therapeutic reaction in child psychotherapy. Our examples will highlight the effects of guilt, and its self-destructive consequences, as well as the interactive, transference-countertransference aspects of the negative therapeutic reaction.

Case #1.

Betty, age nine, was brought to our clinic by her parents because of increasing unhappiness, difficulties with peers, fears of classroom films, and stomach pains. Teachers observed that Betty frequently put herself into situations in which she came out "looking badly" and feeling "picked on" by others.

In contrast to her more placid, two-year younger sister, Betty was noted by the parents as always having been "headstrong" as a preschool child. This "willfullness" brought considerable punishment upon Betty in the form of frequent verbal scoldings and occasional spankings. Upon entering school, Betty became more docile, somewhat overly polite, and symptomatic by the third grade.

A diagnostic evaluation revealed typical features of a childhood psychoneurosis with strong superego pressures resulting in guilt feelings and inner constrictions. Twice weekly psychotherapy with a female therapist for Betty and weekly parent sessions with a staff social worker were recommended and agreed upon by Betty and her parents.

During the initial four months of therapy, Betty was compliant and cooperative, trying hard to present herself to the therapist as an especially nice little girl.

Unacceptable impulses occasionally broke through such as when she won a game of checkers by cheating—at which point she would suddenly grow tired of board games and move on to other play themes with seeming ease. The therapist detected few overt signs of Betty's mounting inner turbulence which erupted to the therapist's surprise and chagrin during the fifth month of therapy. Betty became teasingly provocative by testing the limits of the usual therapy rules and the therapist's patience. She ran up and down the halls, entering other therapist's offices and conference rooms. She took objects from the therapist's office and left for long periods of time. The therapist was bewildered since there was so little metaphoric play or verbalizations which might give clues as to the precipitants of this increasingly aggravating behavior.

The therapist felt herself drawn into rapidly escalating control struggles with Betty. When the therapist reviewed the "rules" about playing and talking in the office, Betty would accuse her of being mean and not liking her, at which point she stomped out, slamming the office door behind her.

The therapist became aware of countertransference pressures within herself. She questioned the diagnosis of "neurosis" and found herself having punitive thoughts toward Betty. When the therapist interpreted Betty's behavior as due to anger or a wish to "take over," Betty only became worse. Clearly something important was happening, but what was "it"? What was the missing ingredient that was being acted out rather than played and talked out within the therapeutic session? Whatever "it" was, it was confined to the therapist-patient relationship since Betty's behavior, mood, and school performance had become asymptomatic. Her parents reported her to be a happy, relaxed girl at home and at school. Her behavior in the sessions, however, had reached such self-destructive and provocative proportions that therapy itself was in jeopardy.

Clues from Betty's transferences and the therapist's countertransference produced the following formulation. Betty's portrayal of the therapist as mean and not liking her appeared to be an externalization of Betty's own tyrannical superego structures. The therapist's wish to be punitive by "laying down" and enforcing the rules could be viewed as an unwitting assumption by the therapist of Betty's superego externalizations. Thus, when the therapist interpreted the unruly behavior as stemming from anger, Betty's harsh superego only created more guilt which led to more externalization of the "mean" superego onto the therapist which in turn resulted in more running out of the office on Betty's part to avoid the "mean," critical therapist.

We have observed on several occasions that such spiraling, selfdestructive behavior, one form of the negative therapeutic reaction, has led to premature interruption of therapy or an unproductive stalemate. Such results are often rationalized as due to the child's poor motivation, insufficient "ego strength," or parental resistance to therapy.

In the case of Betty, the therapist was able to interpret the externalization of the superego and guilt through the use of simple, concrete metaphors and direct descriptions of how Betty's mind was working. The therapist's direct interpretations could be summarized as follows: "The reason you are running and doing all these upsetting things is not because you are mad or bad, its because you feel you are a bad girl because of some thoughts on your mind. When you feel badly about these thoughts then you think I will feel badly about you and won't like you, so you run to get away from this. When you do naughty things and then think I won't like you, it's really that you don't like yourself for what you are doing."

For many children, such an interpretation must be made in the metaphor. An example would be concretizing the superego or conscience as a mean policeman in the child's head who is always saying "no" or

"You're bad"—then making the therapist into a mean policeman because it's so hard to have the mean policeman in one's own head. The child might then be reminded that policemen can say "yes" and believe that is all right to think and play in the session.

These are nongenetic transference interpretations which may have to be put into words quite early in therapy, as in the case of Betty.

Upon discovering this dynamic of guilt leading to a negative therapeutic reaction, therapists are sometimes tempted to become more accepting and reassuring, telling the child that there should be no need to worry or feel badly about talking or playing out unacceptable, scary, or bad thoughts and feelings in the sessions. This is jumping from the frying pan into the fire, since such reassurance only bypasses the superego structures producing the guilt. Many children view such reassurances as literal temptations "by the devil" which can start up another round of provocative, self-destructive behavior.

Betty responded dramatically to the therapist's interpretation of her guilt and externalizations onto the therapist. Of course, the excessively harsh superego remained but could be externalized into play which the therapist and patient could observe and discuss in the metaphor. For the first time in therapy, the therapist and patient had a sense of working together (therapeutic alliance) and Betty showed evidence of developing observing ego. The negative transference was contained within the play, leaving the therapist free to accept the positive transference which had been swept aside earlier by Betty's externalization of the hostile, tyrannical superego structures onto the therapist.

Betty assigned pretend "play" roles to the therapist thereby revealing in a controlled, secondary process manner, the current state of her hostile or loving superego. For instance, one play theme consisted of Betty and a man running an orphanage for poor, maltreated chldren. The therapist was initially assigned the role of a harsh inspector who made surprise visits and if the slightest error was found, the supervisors of the orphanage (Betty and the man) were dealt with most severely; e.g., one year on bread and water in a dark room. On other occasions, Betty became the harsh supervisor and the therapist, as the orphanage director, was severely punished. Oedipal and sibling rivalry themes were obvious in the play but were not interpreted since the harsh superego structures first had to be modified through interpretation of the play characters and through Betty's gradual identification with the more benign superego of the therapist—who repeatedly sought for mercy in the play.

Much later in therapy, Betty could address in metaphor and sometimes directly the oedipal and sibling rivalry issues; but this was only possible after the extensive work described above on the superego-guilt themes which fueled the negative therapeutic reaction and had come perilously close to destroying treatment.

Illustration #2

Parents are essential to a child's treatment. Their participation, to a greater or lesser degree, is a prerequisite for understanding and working with a child. Parents are, of course, also subject to the powerful forces of the negative therapeutic reaction; and when this dynamic is combined with the narcissistic wounding inherent in looking at their child's emotional disturbance, the therapeutic task is formidable. This is particularly true during the assessment phase. Early in a working relationship with parents, strong regressive fears and longings can be mobilized and powerfully defended against, undermining the therapist's efforts to establish a working alliance. Often, these families are labeled "resistant" or "unmotivated"; but in some cases the negativism and distancing maneuvers of parents may indicate a guilty, self-punitive process which results in premature interruption. The therapist despairs; he feels that his efforts are weak and ineffective and may settle on the "unmotivated parent" label as a way out of feeling inept (Gorney, *op cit*). Often, further therapy and intervention is precluded when parents withdraw the child before treatment can be instituted. Mr. and Mrs. R. were such a couple.

They brought their son for evaluation when he was ten years old because of difficulties in school. Mr. R. said his son had "always been hyperactive," that his handwriting was poor and that he had trouble concentrating. Mrs. R. was puzzled by a decline in their son's standardized test scores, though she pointed out he was doing grade-level work. She also worried about Bobby's fear of amputees, which seemed to be generalizing to include other deformed, retarded, and elderly people. Mrs. R. wondered if this fear was connected to another son's death, four years earlier when Bobby was six. John was their oldest child. When he was sixteen, bone cancer of the right arm was discovered. Following an unsuccessful course of radiation therapy, John's arm was amputated at the shoulder. Six weeks after the operation, metastases were found in John's lungs and he was again treated with radiation. Brain metastases developed and resulted in John's death. The R's mentioned these events only in passing in the initial interview, and Mr. R. discounted his wife's speculation connecting Bobby's symptoms to John's illness.

Mr. and Mrs. R. were both children of "poor but proud" working-class families, with low wages and minimal cultural advantages. They had married young and taken turns putting each other through college. They characterized this period of schooling, combined with beginning their family, as a stressful time (there were four children in rapid succession); but they gave the impression that the shared struggle had solidified their relationship and provided them with material success. Each parent commented on "having it better" than their parents, and Mrs. R. was quick to point out that she hadn't had it "nearly as rough" as her husband. Mr. R's father died of a work-related illness when Mr. R. was fourteen. At sixteen he went into the mill to support his family; and also in that year a favorite older sister was killed in a wreck. He talked about these losses in the same way that he and his wife had told of the early days of their marriage—with a rational, hurried matter-of-factness.

The first clear indication of Mr. R.'s discomfort with the evaluation came as we discussed preparing Bobby for interviews. He suggested telling him that he "had been chosen" to give me the views of a ten-year-old or that he was going to be taking SATs for ten-year-olds. Mr. R. explained that he wouldn't want Bobby to think there was something wrong with him. He seemed to accept the therapist's alternative suggestions, but the therapist decided to delay interviewing the boy based on this evidence of Mr. R's fear. Mr. R. missed the next appointment. His wife explained that he wanted to come but couldn't spare the time from work. In this, as in other things, Mrs. R. was protective of her husband. On this occasion when she came in place of her husband, she spoke with deep feelings about the loss of her first son, of how it had been harder on her husband, who had been unable to help nurse John as he grew weaker. He had been out of town on business when John entered the hospital for the last time, had rushed home when Mrs. R. called him, but couldn't bring himself to see his son before he died. She said her husband didn't like to talk about John because it upset him too much. John was rarely mentioned at home.

An hour before the final parent interview, Mr. R. called to cancel, saying he didn't have time to come in and didn't see how his attendance would help Bobby. He said his wife could tell everything about Bobby that was needed. Mrs. R. continued to bring her son for the remaining interviews and psychological testing. When these were finished, however, difficulties arose over scheduling a time to meet with Mr. and Mrs.R. to go over the results of the evaluation. Finally, an interpretive session was arranged. Mrs. R. was very tense. She came armed with paper and pencils and took notes as the therapist talked. Mr. R. seemed braced for a blow and stared at the floor.

They focused on their child's I.Q. scores, which were well above average. Mrs. R. interrupted several times to be sure she had written down accurately what was said. Which tests had he been given? Were these tests reliable or was Bobby just lazy? Would talking help? She had talked to Bobby repeatedly and there was no improvement in his school work. Mr.

R. suggested that Bobby was spoiled and wondered if stricter discipline was the answer.

A second interpretive interview was suggested and accepted, but Mr. and Mrs. R. didn't come for this hour and didn't call to cancel it. For two months the therapist's phone messages and letters were ignored. Finally, the therapist reached Mrs. R. at work. She was distant and sounded rushed—the call seemed an annoyance. She was not interested in talking further about the evaluation. She said they'd "decided not to begin anything with Bobby" because they had "cracked down on him" and he was doing better school work. Mrs. R. refused to bring Bobby for an interpretive as well, saying that she had told him about the issues raised by the evaluation.

Clearly, the evaluation of Bobby reawakened the grief resulting from their older son's "evaluation" and eventual death; but in addition, one might speculate that it aroused in Mr. R. the guilt from two major losses in early adolescence. The death of his father thrust him into independence prematurely, without benefit of the usual teen-age "refueling" process. He had little opportunity to find out how to be a man. He missed the important phase of adolescent development in which the youth gradually, in increments, tests the waters of adulthood, with parents carefully titrating his ability to assume new freedoms and responsibilities. One day he was a boy, and the next day he was a man—responsible for his mother and siblings. The death of his sister, who had fallen under his protection, must have intensified his guilt and helplessness and deepened his fear of dependence. The therapist's help constituted a threatening invitation to re-experience the painful guilt and depression of an earlier time.

A parental negative therapeutic reaction had emerged early in the evaluation process before a working relationship had developed. The therapist's tentative attempts to verbalize the parental guilt were viewed by the parents as unhelpful criticism and brought attacks upon the therapist and the diagnostic process.

Thus, the parent's initial positive wish for help for their troubled son was swept aside and replaced by the old parental, masochistic position that they must suffer with Bobby's problems since no one will give them any help.

Illustration #3

So far, our vignettes have illustrated how psychotherapy may bring to light and/or become a focus of self-destructive patterns within the child and the parents. Space limitations allow us to touch only briefly on the third member of the "tripolar" field, the therapist. The uncomfortable fact is, however, that latent or overt self-destructive patterns of behavior within the therapist may enter the therapeutic process and if unrecognized and uncorrected may destroy the psychotherapy. If such patterns are lived out in a diffuse manner with all child patients and parents, then, of course, there arises the question of the therapist's suitability for the child field unless personal therapy can be effective in bringing these patterns under conscious control.

It is more common for a child's psychopathology to generate a specific self-destructive response within the therapist.

Tom was an aggressive eight-year-old lad with severe school performance problems. In his therapy sessions, he "motorized" his anxiety by running about the room, jumping on the therapist's furniture and spinning the therapist around in his desk chair. The therapist was annoyed by Tom's behavior but believed that with patience, time, and verbalization of feelings, Tom would eventually settle down.

When the settling down did occur, the therapist began to note increased feelings of passivity as if nothing he could do would alter Tom's behavior. Each session became a trial of endurance with a feeling of guilty relief when it was over.

The therapist mulled over his predicament with Tom while at home to the point that the patient was felt to be an intrusive persecutor who seemed bent on torturing the therapist. Tom's behavior escalated in proportion to the therapist's feelings of helplessness. The patient turned out the lights of the office and threw dangerous objects at the therapist. It was clear by this time that the therapist's rage had led to immobilizing guilt which resulted in self-destructive, therapeutic passivity.

Tom's case was in supervision, so it was no surprise that the therapist's self-destructive pattern was repeated in the supervisor-supervisee relationship. The supervisor found himself becoming critical of the supervisee, wanting to "come down hard" on him for his ineptness and passivity. Conscious discovery of this pattern eventually enabled the therapist to interrupt his masochistic, self-destructive countertransference with Tom. Only then could the therapist directly meet Tom's defensive provocations with therapeutic activity in the form of interpretations and limit setting.

CONCLUSION

In this chapter, we have reviewed "The Concept of the Negative Therapeutic Reaction" and how it is a potential source of self-destructive behavior in child psychotherapy. Case vignettes illustrated negative therapeutic reactions arising primarily from unrecognized guilt within a child, parents and child therapist.

REFERENCES

Bednar, R., and Kaul, T. Experimental group research: Current perspectives. *In* S. Garfield and A. Bergin, (eds.) *Handbook of Psychotherapy and Behavior Change*. New York: Wiley, 1978.

Bergin, A., and Lambert, M. The evaluation of therapeutic outcomes. *In:* S. Garfield and A. Bergin, (eds.) *Handbook of Psychotherapy and Behavior Change*. New York: Wiley, 1978.

Brown, J., and Kosterlitz, N. Selection and treatment of psychiatric outpatients. *Archives of General Psychiatry,* 1964, **11:** 425–438.

Dodd, J. A retrospective analysis of variables related to duration of treatment in a university psychiatric clinic. *Journal of Nervous and Mental Disease,* 1970, **151:** 75–85.

Fielding, B. Aspects affecting premature termination of psychotherapy at a training clinic. *American Journal of Psychotherapy,* 1972, **26:** 268–276.

Frankel, S. The management aspect of psychotherapy with aggressive children. *Child Psychiatry and Human Development,* 1977, **7:** 169–185.

Freud, S. From the history of an infantile neurosis, 1918, *Standard Edition,* **17.**

Freud, S. The ego and the id., 1923. *Standard Edition,* **19.**

Freud, S. *Introductory Lectures on Psychoanalysis* (1916–1917). Translated and edited by James Strachey, New York: W. W. Norton, 1966.

Garfield, S. Research on client variables in psychotherapy. *In:* S. Garfield and A. Bergin, (eds.) *Handbook of Psychotherapy and Behavior Change.* New York: Wiley, 1978.

Garfield, S., and Kurz, M. Evaluation of treatment and related procedures in 1216 cases referred to a mental hygiene clinic. *Psychiatric Quarterly,* 1952, **26:** 414–424.

Goldstein, A. *Therapist-Patient Expectancies in Psychotherapy.* New York: Pergamon Press, 1962.

Gorney, J. The negative therapeutic interaction. *Contemporary Psychoanalysis,* 1979, **15:** 228–337.

Gurman, A., and Kniskern, D. Research on marital and family therapy; Progress, perspective, and prospect. *In:* S. Garfield and A. Bergin, *Handbook of Psychotherapy and Behavior Change.* New York: Wiley, 1978.

Heine, R., and Trosman, H. Initial expectations of the doctor-patient interaction as a factor in continuance in psychotherapy. *Psychiatry,* 1960, **23:** 275–278.

Holmes, D., and Urie, R. Effects of preparing children for psychotherapy. *Journal of Consulting and Clinical Psychology,* 1975, **43:** 311–318.

Horney, K. The problem of the negative therapeutic reaction. *Psychoanalytic Quarterly,* 1936, **5,** 29–44.

Lake, M., and Levinger, G. Continuance beyond application interviews at a child guidance clinic. *Social Casework,* 1960, **91:** 303–309.

Langs, R. *The Bipersonal Field.* New York: Aronson, 1976.

Levinson, P., McMurray, L., Podell, P., and Weiner, H. Causes for the premature interruption of psychotherapy by private practice patients. *The American Journal of Psychiatry,* 1978, **135:** 826–830.

Levitt, E. A comparative judgmental study of "defection" from treatment at a child guidance clinic. *Journal of Clinical Psychology,* 1958, **14:** 429–432.

Levitt, E. Psychotherapy research and the expectation—reality discrepancy. *Psychotherapy: Theory, Research and Practice,* 1966, **3:** 163–166.

Leowald, H. Freud's conception of the negative therapeutic reaction with comments on instinct theory. *Journal of the American Psychoanalytic Association,* 1972, **20:** 235–245.

Marshall, R. "Joining techniques" in the treatment of resistant children and adolescents. *American Journal of Psychotherapy.* 1976, **30:** 73–84.

McNair, D., Lorr, M., and Çallahan, D. Patient and therapist influences on quitting psychotherapy. *Journal of Consulting Psychology.* 1963, **27:** 10–17.

Olinick, S. L. The negative therapeutic reaction. *International Journal of Psychoanalysis.* 1964, **45:** 540–548.

Overall, B., and Aronson, H. Expectations of psychotherapy in lower socioeconomic class patients. *American Journal of Orthopsychiatry,* 1962, **32:** 271–272.

Pope, K., Geller, J., and Wilkinson, L. Fee assessment and outpatient psychotherapy. *Journal of Consulting and Clinical Psychology,* 1975, **43:** 835–841.

Rhoads, J., and Feather, B. Transference and resistance observed in behavior therapy. *British Journal of Medical Psychology,* 1972, **45:** 99–103.

Ricks, D. Supershrink: Methods of a therapist judged successful on the basis of adult outcomes of adolescent patients. *In:* D. F. Ricks, M. Roff, and A. Thomas (eds.) *Life History Research in Psycho-Pathology.* Minneapolis:: University of Minnesota Press, 1974.

Rosen, G. Subject's initial therapeutic expectancies and subjects' awareness of therapeutic goals in systematic desensitization: A review. *Behavior Therapy,* 1976, **7:** 14–27.

Ross, A., and Lacey, H. Characteristics of terminators and remainers in child guidance treatment. *Journal of Consulting Psychology,* 1961, **25:** 420–424.

Rubenstein, E., and Lorr, M. A comparison of terminators and remainers in out-patient psychotherapy. *Journal of Clinical Psychology,* 1956, **12:** 345–349.

Seeman, M. Patients who abandon psychotherapy. *Archives of General Psychiatry,* 1974, **30:** 486–491.

Shapiro, R. Therapist attitudes and premature termination in family and individual therapy. *The Journal of Nervous and Mental Disease,* 1974, **159:** 101–107.

Shapiro, R., and Budman, S. Defection, termination, and continuation in family and individual therapy. *Family Process*, 1973, **12:** 55–66.

Sprince, M. An adolescent boy's battle against recovery. *Pschoanalytic Study of the Child,* 1971, **26:** 453–482.

Strupp, H., Hadley, S., and Gomes-Schwartz, B. *Psychotherapy for Better or for Worse.* New York: Aronson, 1977.

Wachtel, P. *Psychoanalysis and Behavior Therapy.* New York:: Basic Books, 1977.

Wilkins, W. Expectancy of therapeutic gain: An empirical and conceptual critique. *Journal of Consulting and Clinical Psychology,* 1973, **40:** 69–77.

Yalom, I. A study of group therapy dropouts. *Archives of General Psychiatry,* 1966, **14:** 393–414.

Yalom, I., and Liebermann, M. A study of encounter group casualties. *Archives of General Psychiatry,* 1971, **25:** 16–30.

Index

Index

Alcoholism and alcohol abuse, 151, 155
after-care, outpatient treatment, 153-154
case studies of, 156-159
delinquent and non-delinquent, 160-161
detoxification of, 152
literature citations of, 155
treatment evaluation of, 151, 155
treatment modalities of, 159-160

Behavior modification management
applications of, 320-325
basic elements of, 310-311
common problems and approaches to, 311-313
maintenance of, 319-320
matching treatment to problem, 313-316
ongoing evaluation of, 317-319

Child abuse and neglect, 21
Concepts of death by children, 115-116

Drug classification and treatment, 137-145

Family therapy
goals and treatment, 297-307
history of, 292-294
structural family approach to, 294-295
individual development through, 295-297

Learning disabilities
implications for therapy, 40
minimal brain dysfunction in, 35

Pregnancies and abortions
abortion, 217-218
early sexual activity, 210-217
magnitude of problem, 208-210
management of pregnancies, 218-220
Psychogenic hearing loss
audiological considerations, 252-258
incidence of, 261-262
indicators of psychogenic loss, 258-259
Psychotherapy
deterioration effects in, 336-344
negative reactions and resistance, 330-334
premature interruption of therapy in, 334-336

Self-image and sexual role, 32
Severity of pathology, 24
Stressful life experiences
coping with
early childhood in, 180-181, 185-187
external factors in, 184-185
internal factors in, 182-184
adequate, 187
exceptionally good, 187
exceptionally poor, 187-189
management and treatment of, 195-205
resources available for, 190-195

Substance abuse
  definition of terms, 123
  determinants of, 127
  epidemiology of, 124–125
  patterns of, 126–127
  prevention of, 136
  psychobiological factors in, 128–130
  sociological factors in, 130–131
Suicide and self-poisoning
  anti-social symptoms and, 92
  children's concept of death in, 229–231
  ego functioning in, 116–117
  emotional behavior and, 91–92
  environmental determinants in, 94–96
  epidemiology of, 225–227
  family treatment and
    clinical implications and, 278–283
    family crises in, 276–278
    nature of, 274–276
    termination of treatment in, 288–289
    therapy and therapist in, 283–268
  fantasies in, 117–118
  home and family environment and, 93–94
  intelligence and, 91
  intent in, 227–229
  precipitating circumstances, 87–89
  prediction of, 98–99
  prevention of, 96–98; 118–119
  psychiatric symptoms in, 90
  psychological analysis, 236–244
  recidivistic behavior in, 244–248
  taxonomy of, 231–244

Techniques of self-destruction, 108–110
Treatment of drug abusers, 131–135; 139
  depressants, 137–139
  stimulants, 139–144